Advanced Analytics with Power BI and Excel

Learn powerful visualization and data analysis techniques using Microsoft BI tools along with Python and R

Dejan Sarka
Jernej Rihar
Klemen Vončina

Orangeava.com

First published: October 2023

Published by: Orange Education Pvt Ltd, AVA™

Address: 9, Daryaganj, Delhi, 110002

ISBN: 978-93-91246-70-9

www.orangeava.com

Dedicated to

Dejan Sarka: *My son Grega Sarka*

Klemen Vončina: *Zarja, for all the love you have brought into my life. Špela, for all your help, patience and understanding. Mami, for making everything in my life possible. Robi, for always being there for me.*

Jernej Rihar: *Friends and family*

About the Authors

Dejan Sarka, MCT and Data Platform MVP alumni, is an independent trainer and consultant whofocuses on the development of database and business intelligence applications. Besides projects, he spends about half of his time on training and mentoring. He is the founder of the Slovenian SQL Server and .NET Users Group. Dejan Sarka is the main author or co-author of nineteen books about databases and SQL Server prior tothis book. He has also developed many courses and seminars for Radacad, Microsoft, SolidQ, and Pluralsight.

Jernej Rihar is experienced in data analytics, data visualization, data preparation and integrated data systems development, primarily in companies operating in the energy, retail and manufacturing industries. He is currently working in the service industry, serving external client needs by directly developing data-related projects.

Klemen Vončina, MCT, started as a trainer for Microsoft Office, with an emphasis on Microsoft Excel, gradually advancing into Excel BI. He later started focusing more on the various services offered in Microsoft 365, mainly on the Microsoft Power Platform and SharePoint Online. Besides training, he also works on IT projects involving the aforementioned technologies and offers support and consultations to customers.

About the Reviewers

Orrin Edenfield: He has 20+ years of experience with data. Analyzing it, transforming it, curating it, and processing it using a wide range of technology from mainframe systems, and clusters in the public cloud to IoT edge devices. He has wide-ranging experience architecting data solutions for multi-terabyte-sized data sets for healthcare, financial services, manufacturing, and retail organizations.

He cut his teeth on financial services data in the Department of Defense while working as a civilian and then spent 7 years with a global analytics company serving retail and healthcare customers. There,he helped transform the data services organization from an IT cost center to the epicenter of value creation for the company by utilizing automated processing, a global workforce, and modern technology with distributed computing platforms. After that,he spent a year with a large consulting firm helping healthcare, financial services, and manufacturing organizations with distributed computing, cloud, predictive analytics, and other complex data solutions.

At Microsoft, from 2016 to 2018, he was dedicated to helping healthcare organizations be successful with cloud solution deployments as an architect focusing on data warehousing, machine learning, advanced analytics and AI. With a distinct healthcare focus, he helped organizations extract more value from data while spending less by utilizing the cloud.

He now helps global customers in Europe, the Middle East, and Africa to be successful with database, data warehousing, machine learning and advanced analytics services in the cloud. Helping customers maximize the benefits of using the cloud is what hedoes.

Throughout his career, he has created and led global technical teams in a globally distributed environment. He is passionate about what he does and always enjoys learning about the challenges others are facing.

Nicky van Vroenhoven is a BI professional focused on the Microsoft stack and a Data Platform MVP. He mainly works with Power BI, Power Platform and T-SQL. Nicky started working with SQL Server and SSIS in 2005 in the DWH space, and later moved from Power Pivot to Power BI. After working 10 years in BI-consultancy jobs in several industries and companies, he worked for 5 years as a Power BI Administrator at a wealth management bank, and he is currently working as Unit Lead Fabric/Power BI at Powerdobs in the Netherlands.

Nicky has spoken at several User Groups, SQL Saturday Events, the Power BI World Tour and SQLBits. In addition, he enjoys tweeting and blogging about topics like Power BI and PowerPlatform at **https://nickyvv.com**.

In his spare time, Nicky likes to go running, play chess, or try to improve his Rubik's cube record. He is also a husband, father of three and a (former) ballroom dancer.

Acknowledgements

Dejan Sarka: It was my privilege to work in a great team. I had two committed professionals as coauthors. With Jernej and Klemen, there were never any issues with timing or readiness for regular and additional work. In addition, the AVA Orange team that worked on this book was fantastic. Shali, Shubha, Sonali, and others - thank you, along with others from your company, for being so supportive during the process of writing this book. Finally, I must thank my family and friends for their understanding while they lacked my company.

Jernej Rihar: It was an interesting and demanding experience writing this book. Together with a great team, we managed to simplify the complexity and complete the project on schedule. Hopefully, the readers will find the information we have provided useful.

Klemen Vončina: This was my first book, so I really didn't know what to expect. However,the coauthors and the AVA team made the process smooth. Thanks to both coauthors for always going the extra milewith everything regarding this book, and thanks to the AVA team for your support and professionalism. I also want to give special thanks to Dejan for inviting me to join this project and for beinga mentor that anyone could only wish for.

About the AdventureWorksDW Database

In order to show practically the analytical solution we are talking about in the book, we need some demo data. We are using the AdventureWorksDW2019 sample database that is provided by Microsoft. Microsoft provides many versions of the AdventureWorks databases. You can get the complete list of them together with the instruction on how to download and install them at this Microsoft Learn link: **https://learn.microsoft.com/en-us/sql/samples/adventureworks-install-configure?view=sql-server-ver16&tabs=ssms**.

The AdventureWorks databases are pretty old. They were originally published for SQL Server 2008. The databases show the data of a fictitious company Adventure Works that is selling sports articles, especially focusing on bicycles. AdventureWorks is the OLTP sample, and AdventureWorksDW is the data warehouse sample. We decided to use the AdventureWorksDW2019 version. However, we wanted to refresh the dates in the database in order to make it look a bit more modern.

The dates in the database can be found in many columns of many tables. Creating a script to update all of them would be quite long-lasting and tedious work. Fortunately, David Alzamendi, a very distinguished and passionate data enthusiast, already did the biggest part of the work. You can learn more about David through his blogs at **https://davidalzamendi.com/**. You can find the script he published for updating the dates on GitHub at **https://github.com/techtalkcorner/SampleDemoFiles/blob/master/Database/AdventureWorks/Update_AdventureWorksDW_Data.sql**.

Although David did enormous work, there were still a few dates missed. We created an additional script that updates also those dates. The script is provided with this book in the "Preface_Code.sql" file. Therefore, in order to use completely the same data we used when we were writing the book, you have to download and restore the AdventureWorksDW2019 database, execute David's script, and finally execute our script.

Preface

Using Excel and Power BI is practically a key requirementfor a career in analyticsnowadays. The book covers both mentioned building blocks of contemporary business intelligence (BI) in a condensed, although quite complete manner. In addition, readers will gain insightsinto theperformance of the reports and some more advanced topics, such as using data science algorithms in the reports.

The book presents the technologies in a holistic view. Many contemporary BI professionals are pretty narrowly oriented and try to solve all problems with a single tool or language. For example, you can do data enrichment with calculations in many places and with many languages, including source SQL query, Power Query Formula Language or M, Python, R, and DAX. This book discusses the advantages and disadvantages of solutions in different languages.

The book comprises ten chapters that cover the complete development process of a Power BI analytical solution, from data modeling and preparation to creating and publishing reports and deploying dashboards and apps. An overview of security and performance tuning is covered as well.

The book is full of examples and exercises. You can find the accompanying content, all the code and Power BI files, on GitHub at **https://github.com/OrangeAVA/Advanced-Analytics-with-Power-BI-and-Excel**

Chapter 1 will introduce the theoretical background for analytical applications. The two pillars of online analytical processing (OLAP) are the logical design and the physical implementation. With OLAP, we want to enable end users to create different reports and analyze data. The tool must be able to write queries based on the report design, and the queries must be executed atlightning speed. The Star Schema logical model enables tools, like Power BI, to write queries automatically. Columnar storage is the physical storage implementation by Microsoft that provides the appropriate performance. This chapter introduces the two pillars and briefly describes the history of Power BI.

Chapter 2 will cover connecting data sources with Microsoft technology and why that is advisable. We'll take an overview of integrated data systems and introduce Power Query,a tool provided with Microsoft Excel, Power BI Desktop, and some other Microsoft resources that can perform ETL processes with data from data sources. Then we'll overview Power Query Editor, a graphical user interface that offers users the ability to perform transformations in a friendly manner without writing code.

Chapter 3 will start with an exercise to transform a sample of data to a suitable format using Power Query Editor. Then we'll introducethe language behind Power Query – formula language M, which provides good capabilities to perform extract, transform and load (ETL) processes on our data. As using Power Query Editor might not be enough for data processing needs, we will expand on the first exercise by performing optimization using the formula language M.

Chapter 4 will deal with Excel. When it comes to simple analytics and data crunching, Excel is still the go-to tool for most people. This chapter will describe some of the shortcomings of classic Excel and demonstrate how basic knowledge of Excel BI components (Power Query and Power Pivot) can help us in creating an analytical solution that we could never achieve with basic Excel tools.

Chapter 5 will focus on creating a data model in Power BI Desktop and analyzing the data we connected to. We will go through the process of connecting to data from Power BI Desktop, making connections between tables, and enriching the model with calculated columns and measures. We will also get to know some DAX functions and discuss certain theoretical concepts that we must understand to write good DAX.

Chapter 6 will introduce Power BI Desktop as a tool to develop reports for end users. We will overview Power BI Desktop and its screen elements and all the panes and views available for developing and modifying a report, its settings, and its objects. We'll take a look at the most important functionality, such as using filters, visual headers, drill-throughs, and tooltips. We'll take a lookat some of the most common visualizations and their settings, including what are some good color wheel options. We'll also introduce the interface changes in a preview that Microsoft is currently testing.

Chapter 7 will explain how to publish the reports we create. Power BI Desktop is the report creation tool. When the report is created, we will probably want to share it with other people. In that case, the next step is to upload it to Power BI Service. This chapter will describe the various components of Power BI Service and how to use them as well as mention the "on-premises version" of Power BI Service – Power BI Report Server.

Chapter 8 is probably the most advanced of this book. Besides report elements like tables, matrices, and graphs, you can use Power BI also as an advanced data science tool. This chapter introduces advanced analytics capabilities in core Power BI and shows what you can do with the help of external languages, namely R and Python, Azure Machine Learning, and Azure Artificial Intelligence.

Chapter 9 will teach you how to develop optimized data models and reports. Power BI was created for the lightning speed of reports. Nevertheless, it is still good to know how to create efficient datasets. In addition, Power BI can operate in DirectQuery mode, where the data is stored in the source, and Power BI serves as the client tool only. For example, if the data remains in the SQL Server, then you also have to know how to optimize Transact-SQL queries. The chapter provides many useful tips for creating efficient models and reports.

Chapter 10 will cover some Power BI Service capabilities such as various security settings and setting up reports deployed from an on-premises environment using gateways. We will take a look at Power BI row-level security and how everything is set up in both Power BI Desktop and Power BI Service.We'll also take a deeper look at Power BI Service Apps and general tips on keeping a well-maintained data system.

Downloading the code bundles and colored images

Please follow the link to download the
Code Bundles of the book:

https://github.com/OrangeAVA/Advanced-Analytics-with-Power-BI-and-Excel

The code bundles and images of the book are also hosted on
https://rebrand.ly/cde115

In case there's an update to the code, it will be updated on the existing GitHub repository.

Errata

We take immense pride in our work at **Orange Education Pvt Ltd,** and follow best practices to ensure the accuracy of our content to provide an indulging reading experience to our subscribers. Our readers are our mirrors, and we use their inputs to reflect and improve upon human errors, if any, that may have occurred during the publishing processes involved. To let us maintain the quality and help us reach out to any readers who might be having difficulties due to any unforeseen errors, please write to us at :

errata@orangeava.com

Your support, suggestions, and feedback are highly appreciated.

DID YOU KNOW

Did you know that Orange Education Pvt Ltd offers eBook versions of every book published, with PDF and ePub files available? You can upgrade to the eBook version at **www.orangeava.com** and as a print book customer, you are entitled to a discount on the eBook copy. Get in touch with us at: **info@orangeava.com** for more details.

At **www.orangeava.com**, you can also read a collection of free technical articles, sign up for a range of free newsletters, and receive exclusive discounts and offers on AVA™ Books and eBooks.

PIRACY

If you come across any illegal copies of our works in any form on the internet, we would be grateful if you would provide us with the location address or website name. Please contact us at **info@orangeava.com** with a link to the material.

ARE YOU INTERESTED IN AUTHORING WITH US?

If there is a topic that you have expertise in, and you are interested in either writing or contributing to a book, please write to us at **business@orangeava.com**. We are on a journey to help developers and tech professionals to gain insights on the present technological advancements and innovations happening across the globe and build a community that believes Knowledge is best acquired by sharing and learning with others. Please reach out to us to learn what our audience demands and how you can be part of this educational reform. We also welcome ideas from tech experts and help them build learning and development content for their domains.

REVIEWS

Please leave a review. Once you have read and used this book, why not leave a review on the site that you purchased it from? Potential readers can then see and use your unbiased opinion to make purchase decisions. We at Orange Education would love to know what you think about our products, and our authors can learn from your feedback. Thank you!

For more information about Orange Education, please visit **www.orangeava.com**.

Table of Contents

1. **Introducing the Theoretical Background for Democratizing Analytics 1**
    - Introduction 1
    - Structure 1
    - Logical design – star schema 2
    - Dimensions and fact tables 5
    - Columnar storage 14
    - Introducing Power BI and its history 23
    - Conclusion 35
    - Key terms 35
    - Questions 36

2. **Acquiring and Transforming Data From Multiple Sources 37**
    - Introduction 37
    - Structure 38
    - Copying data versus connecting to data sources 38
        - *Classic Excel functionality* 38
        - *Getting into connectivity* 41
        - *Integrated data systems* 43
    - Power Query in relation to Excel and Power BI 46
    - Connecting to data sources 47
        - *Data sources in Power BI Desktop* 49
        - *Data sources in Excel* 52
        - *Data sources in other Microsoft resources* 54
    - Power Query Editor 55
        - *Current view, Queries pane, and Home tab* 55
        - *Other tabs in ribbon: Query Settings and Status bar* 57
    - Conclusion 61
    - Key terms 62
    - Questions 62

3. Power Query Transformations and Formula Language (M) Overview 63

Introduction 63

Structure 64

Data transformation exercise 64

Let's transform the CSV file 64

Power Query Formula Language (M) Overview 69

Elements and Data Structures in M 71

Functions and data types in M 75

Custom functions, Operators and Conditions in M 78

Improvement of M code from the Exercise 81

Let's perform some additional transformations 85

Conclusion 89

4. Building a Simple Analytical Solution with Power Pivot in Excel 91

Introduction 91

Structure 91

Scenario 92

Connecting to data with Power Query 92

Enabling the Power Pivot add-in 94

Power Pivot data view 94

Introduction to calculated columns 96

Introduction to measures 97

Introduction to the diagram view 100

Fact and dimension tables 101

Establishing relationships between tables 102

Primary keys and foreign keys 104

Creating a pivot table based on the data model 105

Calculating averages 108

Exploring functions for counting 110

Editing existing measures 111

Calculating ratios with DIVIDE 112

Understanding the filter flow 114

Introduction to the X functions....116
Key performance indicators (KPIs)....118
Conclusion....121
Key terms....122
Questions....122

5. Enhancing the Model and Business Analysis with DAX....123
Introduction....123
Structure....123
Scenario....124
The first look at the Power BI user interface....124
Importing existing data models....124
Connecting to data....125
Exploring the Power BI Desktop views....127
Delving deeper into the Model view....127
Using the Data view....130
Marking as date table....132
Evaluation contexts revisited....139
Row context....140
Query context....141
Filter context....142
Evaluation context in calculated columns and measures....142
Calculated columns....143
Measures....144
The mighty CALCULATE function....145
Semi-additive measures....148
Creating hierarchies....150
Conclusion....152
Key terms....153
Questions....153

6. Creating Reports in Power BI Desktop....155
Introduction....155

Structure.....156

The Power BI environment overview.....156

Screen elements.....158

Using filters.....160

Filters on this visual.....160

Using slicers instead of the Filters pane.....161

Hiding excessive options from end users.....162

Filters on this page and Filters on all pages.....162

Filters' hierarchy.....163

The Data and Visualizations panes.....164

Drillthrough and Tooltips.....166

Creating visualizations.....170

Header icons/visual headers.....176

Upper ribbon tabs in the Report view.....178

The Bookmarks, Selection, and Sync slicers panes.....185

The Table view on the left ribbon.....187

The Model view on the left ribbon.....187

The ever-changing interfaces: On-object interaction.....190

Conclusion.....191

Questions.....192

7. Using the Power BI Service.....193

Introduction.....193

Structure.....193

The need for the Power BI Service.....194

Power BI Service basic components.....194

Workspaces.....194

Reports.....195

Dashboards.....195

Datasets.....195

Managing workspaces.....196

Working with reports.....199

Publishing reports from Power BI Desktop....................199
Creating reports in Power BI Service.................... 200
Using finished reports....................202
Creating dashboards....................206
Managing dashboards.................... 210
Endorsing content....................211
Organize content into apps 212
Managing data with dataflows 214
Modeling data with datamarts 217
Creating paginated reports.................... 218
On-prem reporting with Power BI Report Server....................222
Conclusion....................223
Key Terms....................224
Questions....................224

8. Data Science in Power BI 225
Introduction....................225
Structure....................225
Analytics in base visualizations.................... 226
Advanced Power BI visuals.................... 230
Adding custom visualizations.................... 233
Using R and Python in Power BI 235
Leveraging Azure AI....................248
Conclusion.................... 260
Key terms.................... 261

9. Optimizing Power BI Models and Reports....................263
Introduction.................... 263
Structure.................... 263
Optimizing the data model.................... 264
Query folding....................271
Performance of reports....................278
Aggregate and dual storage tables 285

Conclusion 293
Key terms 294

10. Deploying, Maintaining and Securing Power BI Assets 295
Introduction 295
Structure 296
Well-maintained BI system 297
Organizing fields into display folders 297
Forming the naming conventions 299
Keeping the Selection pane organized 302
Gateways for on-premises data sources and scheduled refresh 304
Power BI Service security 307
Tenant-level security settings 308
Row-level security 311
Defining the roles in Power BI Desktop 312
Assigning users to roles in Power BI Service 318
Power BI Service Apps for end-user experience 320
Conclusion 323
Key Terms 324
Questions 324

Index 325-329

CHAPTER 1

Introducing the Theoretical Background for Democratizing Analytics

Introduction

The two pillars of **online analytical processing** (**OLAP**) are logical design and physical implementation. With OLAP, we want to enable end users to create different reports and analyze data. The tool must be able to write queries based on the report design, and the queries must be executed at lightning speed. The star schema logical model enables tools, like Power BI, to write queries automatically. Columnar storage is the physical storage implementation by Microsoft that provides the appropriate performance. This chapter introduces the two pillars of OLAP. It also describes the building blocks and the history of Power BI.

Structure

In this chapter, let us discuss the following topics:

- Logical design – star schema
- Dimensions and fact tables
- Columnar storage
- Introducing Power BI and its history

Logical design - star schema

The relational model is the logical model commonly used for modeling the schema of a database for an **online transactional system** (**OLTP**). In an OLTP, or in short, in a transactional system, the data is written to the database in real-time, or online. The data must comply with integrity rules, it must be in accordance with business rules. Therefore, the relational model is ideal for **line of business** (**LOB**) applications, where data integrity is crucial. LOB applications are applications that are important for an enterprise to conduct its day-to-day operations. An example would be an application for an **enterprise resource planning** (**ERP**) system.

The relational model, contrived in 1970 by Edgar F. Codd, enforces data integrity through data types, database schema, declarative constraints, and even programming code through triggers and procedures. When you design a relational database, you go through some predefined processes, like normalization and specialization. In both of these two processes, you are creating more and more tables. Let us not get into the details of relational modeling. The point here is to show that after the model is finished, it is not very suitable for reports and analysis. The big problem is that you might finish with hundreds or even thousands of tables for even a quite small LOB application.

Before continuing, let's do a recap. The relational model is definitely a great model for LOB applications, and for any other applications that need to enforce data integrity. However, querying the model is complex. You need to join multiple tables for even quite simple reports. You must first know where the data you need is stored, which tables and which columns you need to use in the report. *Figure 1.1* shows a small example of a relational model. The figure has been created in **SQL Server Management Studio** (**SSMS**) for the tables in the Sales schema in the AdventureWorks2019 database. AdventureWorks2019 is a demo database by Microsoft, showing how to model a database for LOB applications:

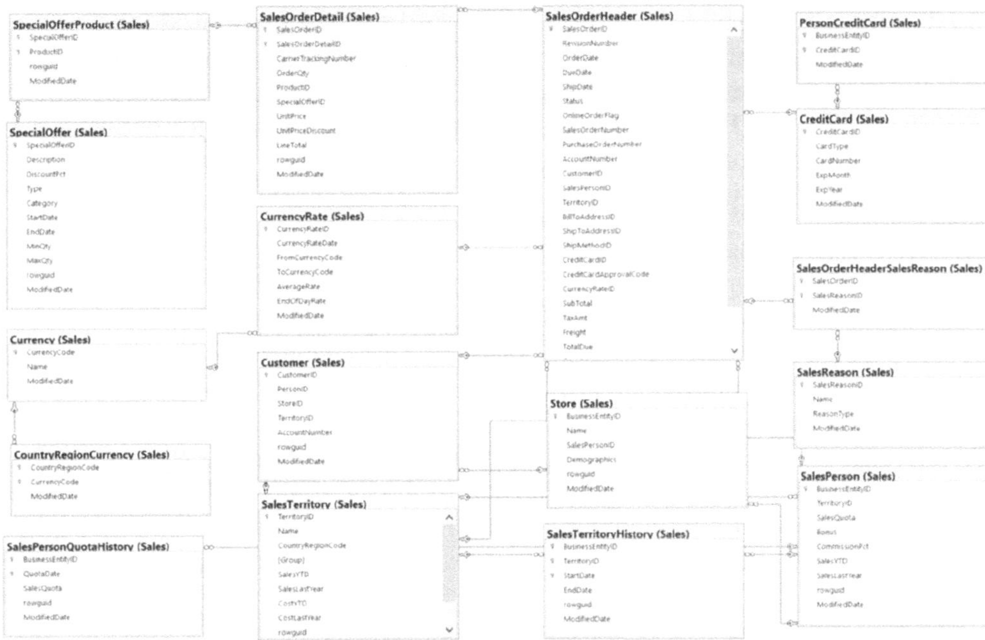

***Figure 1.1**: Sales Part of the AdventureWorks2019 Database Schema*

If you count the tables, you can see that there are already seventeen (17). There is no simple query from this schema. Remember, in a real-world system that supports sales, you could have far larger number of tables. Unfortunately, the number of tables is not the only problem. The relational model does not enforce a naming convention. From the theoretical perspective, it is perfectly OK if you use names like Table001, Table002, Column001, Column002, and so on. Some databases really use similar, from the business perspective, meaningless names. The applications add labels and captions to the user interface, so it turns out that learning a querying language, like **Transact-SQL** (or **T-SQL**) for SQL Server databases, is not the biggest problem. The biggest problem is to learn where, in which columns of which tables, can you find the data you need for your report.

Business always wants to analyze the data over time. Business people want to compare this year's sales with the previous year's sales. They want to follow the behavior of their customers over time. Unfortunately, the databases that support LOB applications frequently store current data only, with no history. This is another problem for creating reports.

Another issue worth mentioning is data quality. A LOB system can live with a small amount of data that must be correct occasionally only. For example, you need to have existent and correct data about a customer only when you are in a contact with this customer, for example, when the customer places an order, when you ship the goods, or when you send an invoice. The data might have been missing a moment before the contact and might be updated incorrectly a moment after the contact. And in a LOB application, you need a few pieces of data only. For example, if the customer is a company, the name of the company, the address, the VAT ID, and probably nothing else. However, for analysis, data like the size of the company, measured by the number of employees, or gross income, would be very welcome.

There are never enough reports. In a modern company, end users must be able to create their own reports. The analytics must not be limited to IT people only; the analytics must be democratized. Of course, you cannot expect end users to learn a query language, and even more to know where to find the data for their analysis in the database. The tool that the end users use to create the reports should be able to create the queries automatically. The users should be able to create reports through the **graphical user interface** (**GUI**), and the tool should create the queries based on this report design. Ideally, the queries should be processed extremely quickly, and return the results instantly. We want to have an analysis in real-time. We want to have an online analytical processing or OLAP system.

We are at a dead end here. IT professionals are not able to create queries from a complex relational model. End users are not able to create the queries even more. So how could a tool be so smart to create the queries needed? Apparently, we need a new data model. Of course, we cannot change the design of the databases that support LOB systems. This means that we need to create new databases with a new model, extract the data from the sources, transform it for the destination schema, and load it into the destination database. The standard acronym for this extract-transform-load process is ETL. But what kind of model do we need?

Without any further hesitation, let's see what a star schema is. The star schema was formally introduced by Ralph Kimball in 1996, although there were some analytical applications that used the same or a similar design already earlier. *Figure* 1.2 shows the star schema for the sales through the reseller channel, created from the `AdventreWorksDW2019` demo database:

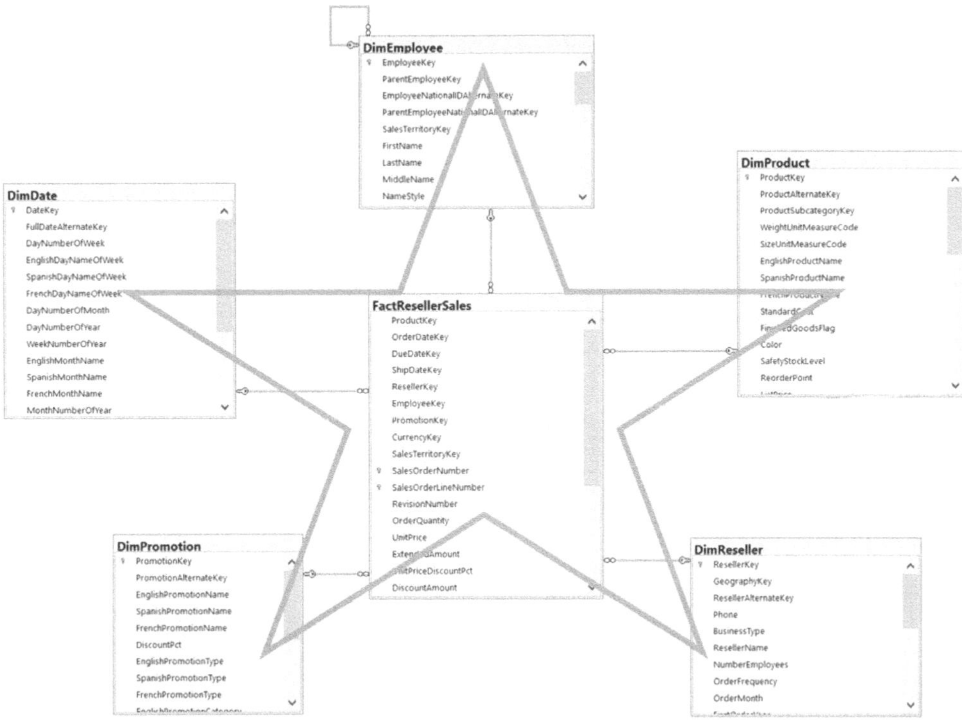

Figure 1.2: *Star Schema for the Reseller Sales*

You can immediately see how the star schema got its name. We have a single central table and multiple surrounding tables. Note that the central table is on the *many side* of every single relationship, meaning that many rows from the fact table are associated with a single row from a dimension table. Now a tool can create queries automatically. The tool must find the central table from the metadata and then join the surrounding tables. Let us see what exactly is included in a star schema.

Dimensions and fact tables

Star schema is an informal standard for designing analytical databases. A star schema consists of two types of tables only: dimensions and fact tables. In addition, the informal standard also defines the column types in these two tables. Let us start the description of these two table types with an example of a fact table. *Figure* 1.3 shows the `dbo.FactResellerSales` table from the AdventureWorksDW2019 demo database:

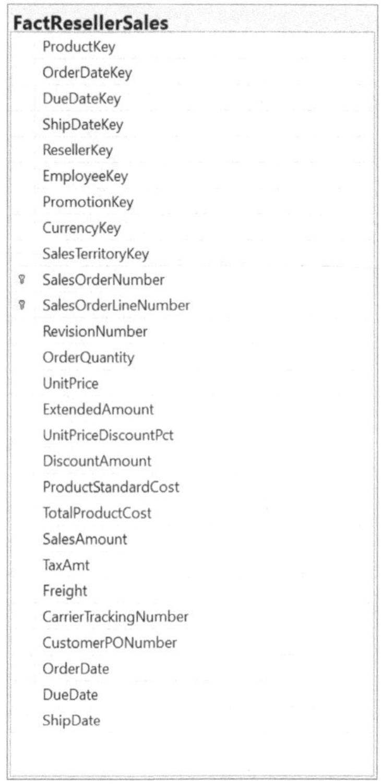

Figure 1.3: *The dbo.FactResellerSales Table*

Let us look at the columns. The first nine columns are foreign keys. The next two columns form the primary key of the table. A primary key in a table uniquely identifies each row. A foreign key is a primary key from another table, called the parent table, imported into a child table to maintain the associations between rows in both tables. For example, `CustomerID` might be the primary key in the `Customers` table and is imported as a foreign key into the Orders table to maintain the relationship between customers and their orders. All of these eleven columns can be grouped into a single group: keys. Keys are the first type of columns in the fact table. The next type of column is the column that is measuring something. They are called measures. Starting with `OrderQuantity` and up to `Freight`, we have ten measures in the table. Measures are the columns you are analyzing, and the columns you are aggregating. Keys and measures are the two main types of columns in a fact table. In the example, you can see some other columns. Columns `RevisionNumber`, `CarrierTrackingNumber` and `CustomerPONumber` help us by connecting the rows to the source system. We can follow immediately why the rows came into our system, for example, some rows came based on a specific customer's purchase order. Such columns are called lineage columns. In the lineage columns, you could also follow who and when transferred the rows from the source system to the analytical database. Finally, the last three columns are just the three dates converted to the datetime data type from the original date key columns, which are integers. These columns are not really needed in the table; they do not bring any additional information, but they can simplify the reports.

There are three types of measures. The most useful measures for analyses are additive measures. Additivity means that you can use the SUM aggregate function for aggregating across any dimension. The `SalesAmount` column from the `dbo.FactResellerSales` table is an example of an additive measure.

Non-additive measures are measures for which the `SUM` function makes no sense across any dimension. The `UnitPrice` column is an example. Summing prices does not make sense either across products, or across resellers, and also not over time.

The third kind of measure is the semi-additive measure. Nearly-additive would probably be a better name because these measures are additive across every single dimension except time. All kinds of levels, like the stock level of a product, are semi-additive measures. In the `dbo.FactResellerSales` table, there is no example of a semi-additive measure. Aggregating semi-additive measures is a bit more complicated because you have to use SUM across all dimensions but time. Over time, you can use the last known state as the aggregate. For example, the aggregate of the stock level of a product for a month would be the level on the last date of that month when the level is known. Let's say that today is March 23rd, 2023. The aggregate for February 2023 would be the state on February 28th, and the aggregate for March would be the state on March 22nd or March 23rd if the last data from March 23rd was already transferred.

Please note that star schema is not a proper relational schema anymore; it is denormalized. The `dbo.FactResellerSales` table does not comply with the second normal form, which states that all non-key columns must be dependent on the full key. A key can be a composite key, consisting of more than one column. The key columns for the composite key of the table are the `SalesOrderNumber` and the `SalesOrderLineNumber` columns. For many foreign key columns, you need to know the `SalesOrderNumber` column value only, to get the value of the column. For example, you do not need `SalesOrderLineNumber` to know the values of the `OrderDateKey`, `DueDateKey` and `ShipDateKey` columns.

Now let us focus on the dimensions. Let me start with the date (or time) dimension. This dimension is present in practically every star schema. It is a somewhat privileged dimension. Because it is always there, Power BI introduces many functions in the **Data Analysis eXpressions** (**DAX**) language, specialized to work with dates. For example, the `PARALLELPERIOD()` DAX function returns the dates from the parallel period of the current context date. The `PARALLELPERIOD(DimDate[DateKey], -1, year)` returns the same date of the previous year for every date of the current year. *Figure 1.4* shows the `dbo.DimDate` table:

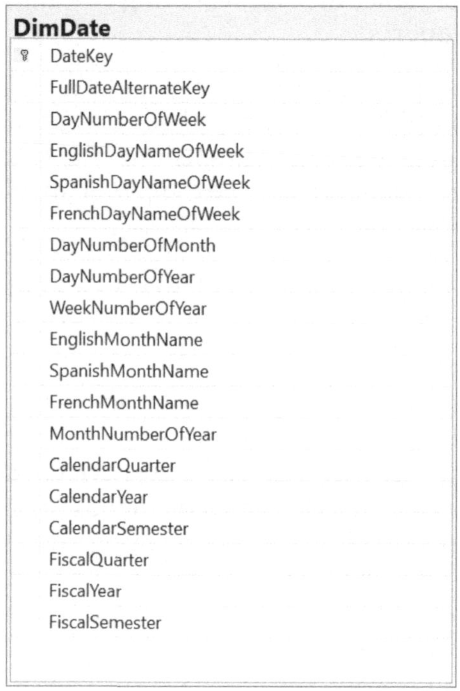

Figure 1.4: *The dbo.DimDate Table*

Because all dates are known, you can populate the date dimension in advance. Like in the `dbo.DimDate`, you can add many calculated columns that create natural hierarchies for aggregates. In the `dbo.DimDate`, you can create two hierarchies from the last six columns:

- CalendarYear - CalendarSemester - CalendarQuarter - month - date and
- FiscalYear – FiscalSemester – FiscalQuarter – month – date.

Natural hierarchies are very useful because they form a natural drill-down path. Users many times analyze data with the divide-and-conquer method. Imagine there is a problem with the total sales amount. You need to find the root of the problem. First, you check sales over years, then you find a year with suspicious numbers. You drill down to semesters, quarters, and months to find the critical months.

Natural hierarchies in the `dbo.DimDate` table breaks the third normal form. Non-key columns should be mutually independent, they should depend on the key only. However, if you know the month, you know the quarter and the semester. But don't worry, everything is fine with star schema denormalization. You are not building a new relational model used in the source systems; you are building a model that is suitable for analyses.

In *Figure 1.5*, you can see the `dbo.DimProduct` table. However, you can also notice two associated tables, namely the `dbo.DimProductSubcategory` and `dbo.DimProductCategory` tables:

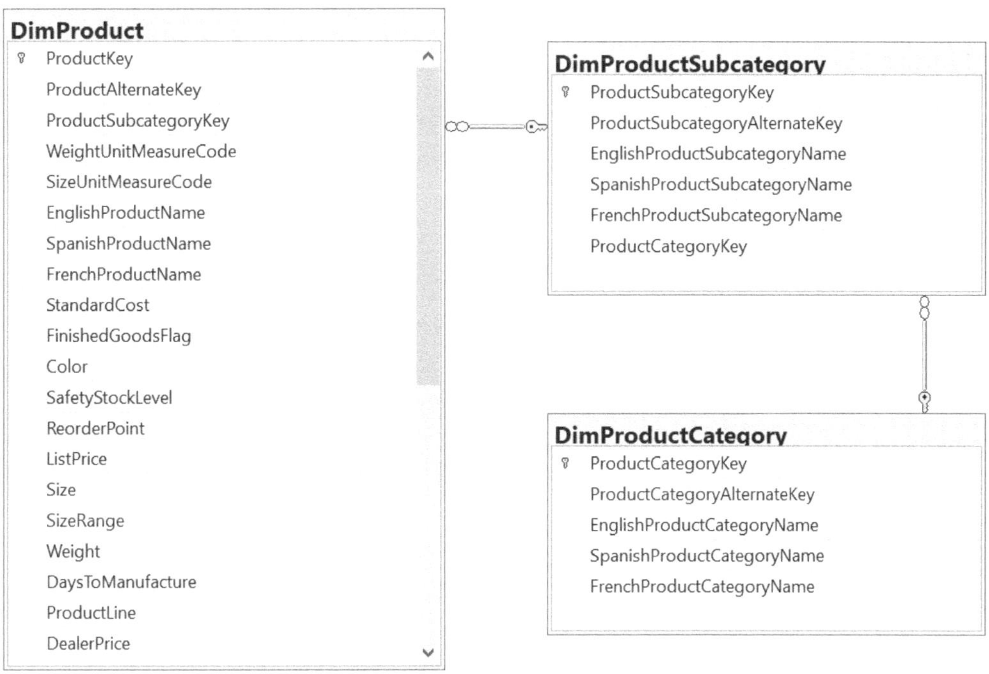

***Figure 1.5**: The dbo.DimProduct Table*

For the products, the natural hierarchy category - subcategory - product is kept in lookup tables. This dimension complies with the third normal form, it is not denormalized. We also say that we have the snowflake schema. For Power BI, you should always try to target star schema. Snowflake schema brings more tables. More tables mean a more complex user interface for creating reports, slower queries, and more work with the ETL process. Therefore, let us repeat: Use star schema always and join the data from the associated tables in source queries or the ETL process.

In a dimension, we also have standard column types. First, we have the key, which is in this example the `ProductKey` column. Then we have column(s) that give the name to a member of the dimension. In the example, we have `EnglishProductName`, but also translations `SpanishProductName` and `FrenchProductName` for the name columns. Then we have columns that are used for analyses, to give the context to aggregated measures. For example, the `Color` column can be used to aggregate sales amounts over colors. These columns are called attributes in the star schema terminology. Some attributes can form natural hierarchies. Finally, we can have columns called member properties. These columns are not used for analyses, they are included only if we need them on the reports. For example, the `SafetyStockLevel` column would probably never be used for aggregations but could be useful as an additional piece of info in a report. Another, maybe even better example, would be a customer's e-mail address.

There is another possible approach – hybrid star and snowflake schema. You can see how the geography data model part is solved in *Figure 1.6*:

Figure 1.6: *Hybrid Schema for Geography*

There are two fact tables, `dbo.FactInternetSales` and `dbo.FactResellerSales`. They are related to appropriate dimensions, the `dbo.DimReseller` and `dbo.`

`DimCustomer` tables. For both customers and resellers, we have the same geography data. There is only one level of the snowflake lookup table, the `dbo.DimGeography` table, which is connected with foreign keys to both aforementioned dimensions. The denormalization starts in this table, with the hierarchy of country – region – city. This model is quite reasonable; however, for the sake of simplicity, we still prefer a complete star schema.

One star schema covers one business area. In the example we used so far, the schema covers reseller sales. What about internet sales? Or product inventory? In the `AdventureWorksDW2019` database, there are more fact tables. A single-star schema has a single fact table. Multiple star schemas are connected through shared dimensions. For example, we could create a product inventory star schema around the `dbo.FactProductInventory` table.

Multiple star schemas are connected through shared dimensions. In our example, reseller sales and product inventory schemas share the product dimension. However, they do not share the reseller dimension. All the star schemas in a single database usually share the date dimension.

A database with multiple star schemas, an explicit date dimension, a good naming convention, and cleansed data in the tables, is called a data warehouse. A data warehouse is stored in a **relational database management system (RDBMS)**, like Microsoft SQL Server. In an enterprise, a data warehouse is typically the source for all kinds of reports and analyses, including Power BI reports. The development of Power BI reports is much faster if a data warehouse is a source. Note also that we mentioned a good naming convention. The names of the tables and the columns are frequently shown on the reports directly. Many times, there is no client application in between that would add descriptive labels. Power BI allows renaming of the columns for clearer reports; however, a good naming convention still helps you developing the reports quickly. In addition, you might use another analytical tool using the same data warehouse data which does not allow renaming. In such a case, a good naming convention in a DW also helps keeping the same name for a single column in different tools.

However, developing and maintaining a data warehouse is quite exhaustive and expensive. Many times, you need ad-hoc reports for the transactional data. Developing a data warehouse, although highly recommended in longer terms, might not be feasible for quick reporting. This is no problem for Power BI; you can query the transactional data directly, and create the star schema model in Power BI, as you will see in the next chapters of this book. However, the process of building the Power BI dataset might be much longer and tiring compared to building it from a data warehouse.

Even if you start with a data warehouse, most of the time you will have to do some additional data modeling in Power BI. An RDBMS-like SQL Server does not have enough metadata needed for analyses. For example, we see the columns that create natural hierarchies in the `dbo.DimDate` table. However, the SQL Server knows nothing about hierarchies. Look at the tabular report in *Figure 1.7*:

EnglishProductSubcategoryName	EnglishProductCategoryName	Sum of ResellerKey
Bib-Shorts	Clothing	234783
Bike Racks	Accessories	157878
Bottles and Cages	Accessories	152262
Bottom Brackets	Components	124399
Brakes	Components	128289
Caps	Clothing	398418
Chains	Components	82761
Cleaners	Accessories	144034
Cranksets	Components	146470
Derailleurs	Components	134703
Forks	Components	70573
Gloves	Clothing	746120
Handlebars	Components	549349
Headsets	Components	95502
Helmets	Accessories	933299
Hydration Packs	Accessories	117391
Jerseys	Clothing	1296962
Locks	Accessories	78358
Mountain Bikes	Bikes	2675230
Mountain Frames	Components	[illegible]
Total		**20678674**

Figure 1.7: *An Example of a Problematic Report*

You can immediately notice multiple problems in this report. For the measure, the reseller key is used, and it is summarized over product categories and then subcategories. What does the sum of reseller keys mean? Nothing, of course. And note that the aggregation order is incorrect, it does not follow the natural hierarchy category -> subcategory. The order is turned around to subcategory -> category.

The report was created in Power BI Desktop; the data is imported from the `AdventureWorksDW2019` database. Here, we have imported the following tables: `dbo.FactResellerSales`, `dbo.DimDate`, `dbo.DimProduct`, `dbo.DimProductSubcategory` and `dbo.DimProductCategory`. Star (or better snowflake) schema was inherited, as you can see in *Figure 1.8*:

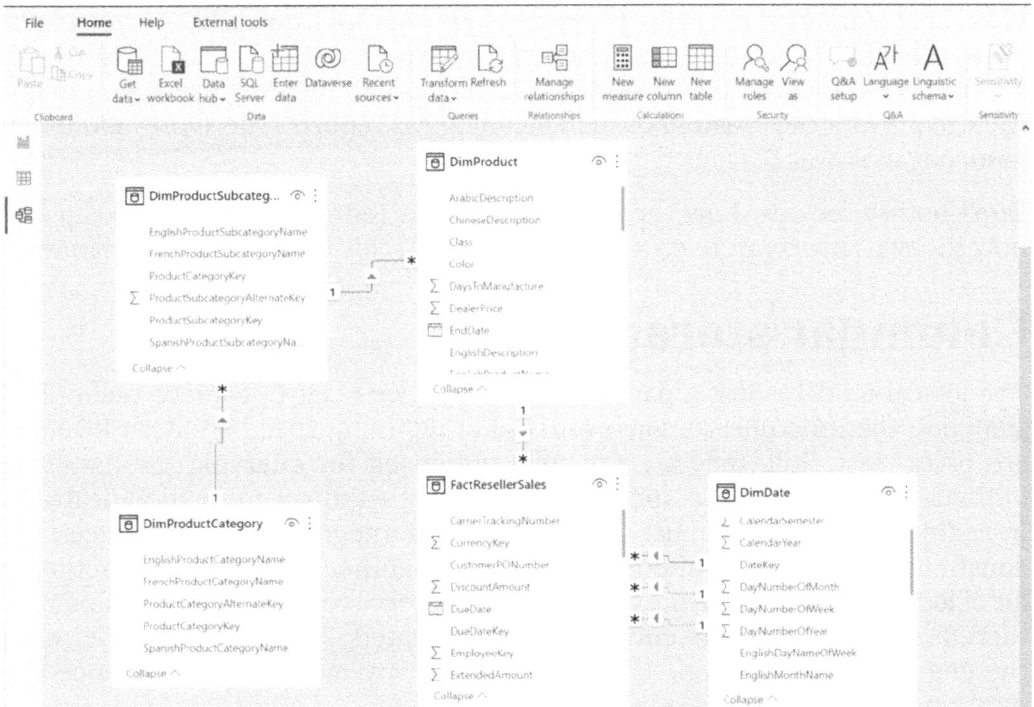

Figure 1.8: *The Data Model in Power BI Desktop*

Of course, it would be possible to create a meaningful report as well, as *Figure 1.9* shows:

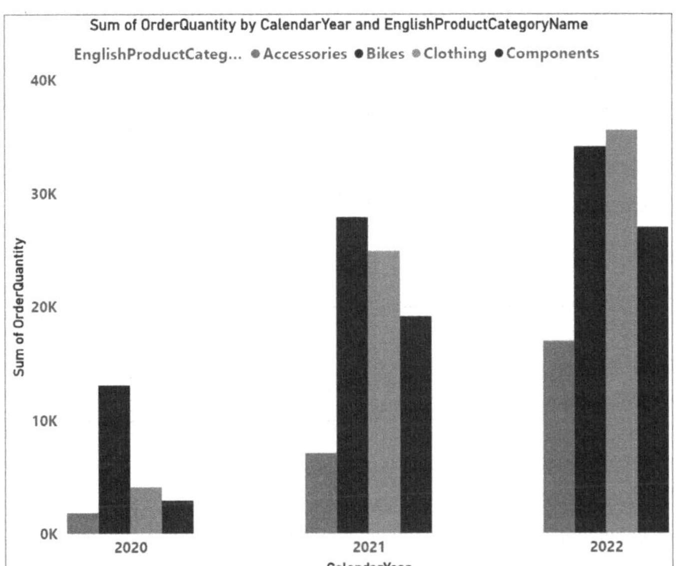

Figure 1.9: A Meaningful Report

If you are creating a dataset for personal usage only, for a quick report, you might be satisfied by inheriting the star schema from your data warehouse. However, if you share the dataset you create in Power BI with multiple users, you might want to prevent the creation of such meaningless reports. Therefore, additional modeling in Power BI is needed.

Don't bother for now how the data was transferred to Power BI Desktop and how the two reports were created. You will learn this in the following chapters.

Columnar storage

The logical model is just a part of the story. If we want to achieve real online analytics, then the queries must execute at lightning speed. Modern RDBMSs are pretty fast. Still, they are not fully optimized for querying the data; the optimization balances the speed of queries with the speed of modifications. In addition, the systems must take care of data integrity, they must check the constraints and maintain multiple commands together as a single transaction. A lot of locking is involved. For example, the SQL Server cannot allow lost updates; therefore, any row that is currently being updated is exclusively locked until the end of the transaction. These facts and many more things influence the performance of queries.

Data compression helps to lower disk input and output (disk IO). Disk IO is read-and-write operations or transfers of data between a **random-access memory (RAM)** and a disk. Compression speeds up reading the data. Nevertheless, there is no free lunch. Compression slows down updates and raises the load on the processors because data must be decompressed before the update and recompressed after the update. SQL Server supports two levels of compression: Row compression and page compression. We will test both of them in order to compare them with columnar storage (columnstore) compression used in Power BI, which Microsoft labels as tabular model technology, to get a feeling of how good the latter is.

Row compression means that every column is stored in variable length format, using only the minimal number of bytes possible. For example, the integer data type has a fixed length of four bytes. Not all integers need four bytes. Smaller numbers can occupy a single, two, or three bytes only. For Unicode character data, we calculate that one character on an average occupies two bytes; yet, many characters can take a single byte only. Row compression uses variable length storage for all columns, including those defined with fixed-length data types, and does the Unicode compression of strings as well. You can immediately imagine that the actual ratio of compression depends on the data. If you are already using variable-length data types and non-Unicode strings only, then row compression cannot help much.

Page compression is built on top of row compression. It adds dictionary and prefix compressions. For the dictionary compression, SQL Server creates a mini dictionary in every single 8kB page, where it stores common substrings from multiple columns in multiple rows on the same page, and stores just the pointers to these substrings in the original data values. Prefix compression is somehow similar. For character data, prefixes are just substrings at the beginning of the strings. However, prefix compression work on numbers and dates as well. For example, you might have numbers 1000, 1001, 1002, 1010, and 1020 in your data. You can store the prefix 1000 in the dictionary, and values 0, 1, 2, 10, and 20 in the original cells.

While row compression might be viable for systems with many updates, page compression is already not recommended for such systems. Let us now test both compressions. We are starting by creating four tables in the AdventureWorksDW2019 demo database:

```
USE AdventureWorksDW2019;
GO
SET NOCOUNT ON;
GO
-- Tables for the compression test
CREATE TABLE dbo.UniqueIntegers
(col1 INT NOT NULL);
CREATE TABLE dbo.UniqueGUIDs
(col1 UNIQUEIDENTIFIER NOT NULL);
CREATE TABLE dbo.BigCardinalityIntegers
(col1 INT NOT NULL);
CREATE TABLE dbo.SmallCardinalityStrings
(col1 NVARCHAR(10) NOT NULL);
GO
```

You can see that there is one column only in every single table. Take a closer look at the data types. We will store unique integers in the first table, **globally unique identifiers (GUIDs)** in the second table, integers with high cardinality (many distinct values, but not unique) in the third table, and strings with low cardinality in the fourth table. The following code inserts the data:

```
-- Insert the data
-- Unique integers
INSERT INTO dbo.UniqueIntegers(col1)
SELECT ROW_NUMBER() OVER(ORDER BY (SELECT NULL)) AS rn
FROM
 (SELECT TOP 1000 CustomerKey
```

```
  FROM dbo.DimCustomer) AS c1(col1)
 CROSS JOIN
 (SELECT TOP 1000 CustomerKey
  FROM dbo.DimCustomer) AS c2(col2);
-- GUIDs
INSERT INTO dbo.UniqueGUIDs(col1)
SELECT NEWID()
FROM dbo.UniqueIntegers;
-- High cardinality integers
INSERT INTO dbo.BigCardinalityIntegers(col1)
SELECT (col1 - 1) / 50 +1 AS col1
FROM dbo.UniqueIntegers;
-- Low cardinality strings
INSERT INTO dbo.SmallCardinalityStrings(col1)
SELECT CAST(col1 % 5 AS NCHAR(1)) + N'AAAA' AS col1
FROM dbo.UniqueIntegers;
GO
```

The previous code inserts one million rows in every table. Before checking the data, let us also create the clustered indices for the four tables. Clustered indices reorganize the data in a table in a logically sorted structure called a balanced tree, or a B-tree:

```
-- Creating clustered indices
CREATE CLUSTERED INDEX cix_UniqueIntegers
 ON dbo.UniqueIntegers(col1);
CREATE CLUSTERED INDEX cix_UniqueGUIDs
 ON dbo.UniqueGUIDs(col1);
CREATE CLUSTERED INDEX cix_BigCardinalityIntegers
 ON dbo.BigCardinalityIntegers(col1);
CREATE CLUSTERED INDEX cix_SmallCardinalityStrings
 ON dbo.SmallCardinalityStrings(col1);
GO
```

To get the impression of cardinality, let us count the number of distinct values in the only column of every single table:

```
-- Check the cardinality
SELECT '1. unInt' AS testData, COUNT(DISTINCT col1) AS cntDist
FROM dbo.UniqueIntegers
UNION
SELECT '2. GUIDs' AS testData, COUNT(DISTINCT col1) AS cntDist
```

```
FROM dbo.UniqueGUIDs
UNION ALL
SELECT '3. bcInt' AS testData, COUNT(DISTINCT col1) AS cntDist
FROM dbo.BigCardinalityIntegers
UNION ALL
SELECT '4. lcStr' AS testData, COUNT(DISTINCT col1) AS cntDist
FROM dbo.SmallCardinalityStrings
ORDER BY testData;
GO
```

Here are the results:

```
testData cntDist
-------- -----------
1. unInt 1000000
2. GUIDs 1000000
3. bcInt 20000
4. lcStr 5
```

You can see that there are only five distinct strings in the fourth table. Now it is time to test row and page compressions. Instead of doing the actual compression, we are just estimating the compression savings with the **sys.sp_estimate_data_compression_savings** system stored procedure:

```
-- Estimating row and page compression savings
EXEC sys.sp_estimate_data_compression_savings
 N'dbo', N'UniqueIntegers', NULL, NULL, N'ROW';
EXEC sys.sp_estimate_data_compression_savings
 N'dbo', N'UniqueIntegers', NULL, NULL, N'PAGE';
EXEC sys.sp_estimate_data_compression_savings
 N'dbo', N'UniqueGUIDs', NULL, NULL, N'ROW';
EXEC sys.sp_estimate_data_compression_savings
 N'dbo', N'UniqueGUIDs', NULL, NULL, N'PAGE';
EXEC sys.sp_estimate_data_compression_savings
 N'dbo', N'BigCardinalityIntegers', NULL, NULL, N'ROW';
EXEC sys.sp_estimate_data_compression_savings
 N'dbo', N'BigCardinalityIntegers', NULL, NULL, N'PAGE';
EXEC sys.sp_estimate_data_compression_savings
 N'dbo', N'SmallCardinalityStrings', NULL, NULL, N'ROW';
EXEC sys.sp_estimate_data_compression_savings
 N'dbo', N'SmallCardinalityStrings', NULL, NULL, N'PAGE';
GO
```

The results are combined in *Table 1.1*:

Table	Original Size KB	Compression	Compressed Size KB
UniqueIntegers	12,960	ROW	10,976
UniqueIntegers	12,960	PAGE	10,976
UniqueGUIDs	24,920	ROW	25,912
UniqueGUIDs	24,920	PAGE	25,912
BigCardinalityIntegers	20,752	ROW	10,968
BigCardinalityIntegers	20,752	PAGE	10,960
SmallCardinalityStrings	28,912	ROW	12,840
SmallCardinalityStrings	28,912	PAGE	11,032

***Table 1.1**: Estimating Row and Page Compression*

Note that these are estimated numbers only and that the data is made up. However, you can notice a few things. The estimated size for GUIDs after the compression is even bigger than the size of the data before the compression. Therefore, GUIDs are very unsuitable for compression. Unique integers did not gain much from the compression as well. However, integers with big cardinality have already gained a lot. The space needed after the compression is reduced by nearly half. But there is a small difference between row and page compression. This is due to the fact that dictionaries are created on the page level, and we still have mostly distinct values inside a single page. If cardinality was lower, or if the dictionaries would be created on bigger data chunks than 8KB pages, then row compression would be more useful. For the strings with low cardinality, you can immediately notice that the compression gain is the biggest. Also, there is an important additional space saving you get with the page compression, compared to the row compression. Still, page compression could be much better if the dictionaries would be created on bigger data chunks than 8KB pages.

Note that SQL Server supports also nonclustered indices, which are efficient for selective queries, when we need to seek for a small subset of rows only. Nonclustered indices are not important in the context of this chapter, where we compare row and columnar storage compression. However, we need to introduce another term: covering indices. A clustered index is a table itself; a table is organized as a book, with table of contents and pages logically ordered. Nonclustered indices are comparable to other indexes in a book, like word index, figure index formula index and similar. Nonclustered index can cover a query if all data needed for a query can be found inside the index. Imagine that you have a nonclustered index on a table with employees' data with two columns only, namely last name and first name. A query that would want to retrieve first and last names only could find all of the data in this nonclustered index. SQL Server would not need to read the data from the actual table. The query would become covered query, and the nonclustered index would be a covering index.

So far, we have used regular row storage inside the SQL Server. SQL Server supports columnar storage as well. This is the same storage as Power BI and SQL Server Analysis Services Tabular (SSAS TAB) use. Therefore, we will be able to check the compression savings with columnstore inside the SQL Server.

Columnar storage means exactly what the name says: storing data column by column, not row by row. Rows represent entities from real life; for example, one row in the customer dimension represents a single customer. We operate with rows, not with columns. Therefore, the information on how to recreate rows from columns must be maintained internally in the database engine. Any update might mean that the engine has to fully recalculate this information. This is why columnar storage is read-only. Don't be confused with SQL Server's ability to update columnar storage. It is not updated directly; SQL Server stores new data in additional row storage and marks old data with a flag, so it is skipped for reading. The new row data is occasionally converted to columnar storage with a background process.

What do we then gain with columnar storage? A lot less disk IO for queries. Since data is stored column by column, the engine fetches only the columns that the query needs. In a way, columnstore indices in the SQL Server are always covering indices, because the engine does not fetch the full rows, unless requested by a query, of course. And we get a lot better compression than with row storage.

Every column is at least partially sorted. This enables the use of run-length encoding compression. For example, if the value ABCDE repeats ten times, you can store it only once, together with the frequency. You can immediately conclude that a column with low cardinality could be compressed better than a column with a high cardinality of data values.

Columns are partially sorted because full sorting would be too expensive when creating columnar storage. Rows are split into row groups of approximately one million rows. Then Microsoft uses its own row-rearrangement algorithm, which with a single pass through the data rearranges the rows in such a way as to get the optimal sort over all columns. Again, optimal does not mean full sort. After the sorting, rows are split into columns.

Now the compression can start. Besides run-length encoding, bit-packing is used. This is similar to row compression. Remember, row compression stores the data with the minimal number of bytes needed; bit-packing goes one level further and stores the data with the minimal number of bits needed.

Columnar storage also uses compression similar to page compression, with dictionary and prefix compression. However, dictionaries are built for row groups of approximately one million rows, which means that this compression in columnstore is much more efficient than page compression. In addition, for the most frequent substrings, a global dictionary is created as well.

Finally, the LZ77 compression is used. This compression was published by Abraham Lempel and Jacob Ziv in the year 1977. The name comes from the first letter of their last names and the last two digits of the year. This compression is also called sliding window dictionary encoding. It treats all data as a stream of bytes and searches for substrings of bytes that repeat in a sliding window. When a substring repeats, the algorithm stores only the info of how many bytes earlier it appeared and how long the substring is. Microsoft's columnar storage uses a 64KB sliding window. Let me show you this in a very brief example. Imagine the following stream of bytes: ABCXYXYXYDEFXYXYXY. You can see that the substring XYXYXY is repeating. Therefore, you can store the stream like this: ABDXYXYXYDEF(9,6), meaning that for the second time, you go back nine bytes and read six bytes.

SQL Server allows you to compress the data in two steps. First, you build a columnstore index without LZ77 compression. Then you can rebuild it and add LZ77 compression. Of course, you can build the columnar storage immediately with full compression. We will show the process in two steps, so we can see the impact of LZ77 compression separately. The following code builds clustered columnstore indices on our four test tables without LZ77 compression:

```
-- Checking the space used and creating the columnar storage
-- First time without LZ77 compression
EXEC sys.sp_spaceused N'dbo.UniqueIntegers', @updateusage = N'TRUE';
CREATE CLUSTERED COLUMNSTORE INDEX cix_UniqueIntegers
  ON dbo.UniqueIntegers
  WITH (DROP_EXISTING = ON);
EXEC sys.sp_spaceused N'dbo.UniqueIntegers', @updateusage = N'TRUE';
GO
EXEC sys.sp_spaceused N'dbo.UniqueGUIDs', @updateusage = N'TRUE';
CREATE CLUSTERED COLUMNSTORE INDEX cix_UniqueGUIDs
  ON dbo.UniqueGUIDs
  WITH (DROP_EXISTING = ON);
EXEC sys.sp_spaceused N'dbo.UniqueGUIDs', @updateusage = N'TRUE';
GO
EXEC sys.sp_spaceused N'dbo.BigCardinalityIntegers', @updateusage =
N'TRUE';
CREATE CLUSTERED COLUMNSTORE INDEX cix_BigCardinalityIntegers
```

```
  ON dbo.BigCardinalityIntegers
  WITH (DROP_EXISTING = ON);
EXEC sys.sp_spaceused N'dbo.BigCardinalityIntegers', @updateusage =
N'TRUE';
GO
EXEC sys.sp_spaceused N'dbo.SmallCardinalityStrings', @updateusage =
N'TRUE';
CREATE CLUSTERED COLUMNSTORE INDEX cix_SmallCardinalityStrings
  ON dbo.SmallCardinalityStrings
  WITH (DROP_EXISTING = ON);
EXEC sys.sp_spaceused N'dbo.SmallCardinalityStrings', @updateusage =
N'TRUE';
GO
```

We are showing the eight results of the **sys.sp_spaceused** system procedure grouped in a single table, namely *Table 1.2*. The procedure returns the data size only, without higher levels of an index. This is why the Original Size KB column values slightly differ from the values in the previous table:

Table	Original Size KB	Compression	Compressed Size KB
UniqueIntegers	12,880	Columnstore	2,680
UniqueGUIDs	24,784	Columnstore	15,696
BigCardinalityIntegers	20,640	Columnstore	2,104
SmallCardinalityStrings	28,680	Columnstore	32

***Table 1.2**: Columnstore Compression without LZ77*

Now this is impressive. Look at the value for the small cardinality strings. The size of the data went from 28,680 KB down to 32KB! This is very impressive. There is some compression gain even with GUIDs. Please note the huge difference between compression rates of high and low cardinality data values. We are not done yet. The following code adds the LZ77 compression and checks the data size again:

```
-- Checking the space used and creating the columnar storage
-- Second time with LZ77 compression
EXEC sys.sp_spaceused N'dbo.UniqueIntegers', @updateusage = N'TRUE';
ALTER INDEX cix_UniqueIntegers
  ON dbo.UniqueIntegers
  REBUILD WITH (DATA_COMPRESSION = COLUMNSTORE_ARCHIVE);
EXEC sys.sp_spaceused N'dbo.UniqueIntegers', @updateusage = N'TRUE';
```

```
GO
EXEC sys.sp_spaceused N'dbo.UniqueGUIDs', @updateusage = N'TRUE';
ALTER INDEX cix_UniqueGUIDs
  ON dbo.UniqueGUIDs
  REBUILD WITH (DATA_COMPRESSION = COLUMNSTORE_ARCHIVE);
EXEC sys.sp_spaceused N'dbo.UniqueGUIDs', @updateusage = N'TRUE';
GO
EXEC sys.sp_spaceused N'dbo.BigCardinalityIntegers', @updateusage =
N'TRUE';
ALTER INDEX cix_BigCardinalityIntegers
  ON dbo.BigCardinalityIntegers
  REBUILD WITH (DATA_COMPRESSION = COLUMNSTORE_ARCHIVE);
EXEC sys.sp_spaceused N'dbo.BigCardinalityIntegers', @updateusage =
N'TRUE';
GO
EXEC sys.sp_spaceused N'dbo.SmallCardinalityStrings', @updateusage =
N'TRUE';
ALTER INDEX cix_SmallCardinalityStrings
  ON dbo.SmallCardinalityStrings
  REBUILD WITH (DATA_COMPRESSION = COLUMNSTORE_ARCHIVE);
EXEC sys.sp_spaceused N'dbo.SmallCardinalityStrings', @updateusage =
N'TRUE';
GO
```

You can see the results in *Table 1.3*:

Table	Original Size KB	Compression	Compressed Size KB
UniqueIntegers	2,680	LZ77	2,440
UniqueGUIDs	15,696	LZ77	15,696
BigCardinalityIntegers	2,104	LZ77	168
SmallCardinalityStrings	32	LZ77	32

Table 1.3: *Columnstore Compression with LZ77*

This time, the biggest gain was on the integers with a big cardinality of data values. We can make a few conclusions here. We can see immediately that GUIDs are not very good candidates for compression. Lower cardinality of data, meaning less distinct values, means better compression. The compression rate for strings with small cardinality is really impressive. The size of the data went down from 28,680 KB to 32 KB only. This is nearly nine hundred times (900) less.

We can also see that the actual compression rate depends highly on the data. Microsoft claims that we can count on approximately ten times compression, which sounds quite reasonable according to our tests.

Since we do not need the test tables anymore, let's clean up the demo database with the following code:

```
-- Clean up
DROP TABLE IF EXISTS dbo.UniqueIntegers;
DROP TABLE IF EXISTS dbo.UniqueGUIDs;
DROP TABLE IF EXISTS dbo.BigCardinalityIntegers;
DROP TABLE IF EXISTS dbo.SmallCardinalityStrings;
GO
```

Columnar storage is only a part of the technologies used in Power BI to speed up queries. Unlike the SQL Server, where we used tables stored on a disk, Power BI stores all data in memory. Of course, memory is much faster than disks, even if you use **solid-state drives (SSDs)**. You can also help speed up the queries by creating aggregate tables. Aggregates are calculated when you create the table, or when you refresh the data. With aggregates, you can get specific queries that use them magnitudes faster. Imagine that you need to compare the total sales amount for this year with the total from the previous year, and you have one million values per year. With precalculated aggregates, you only need to read two values instead of two million values, which are one million times faster. You will learn about aggregates and other important techniques for performance in later chapters of this book. Let us now briefly describe how Power BI evolved over time.

Introducing Power BI and its history

At the beginning of this millennium, **enterprise data warehouses** (**EDW**) became unpopular among managers. The process of building an EDW on an RDBMS took many years and a lot of resources and money. To many managers, it looked like it was a never-ending process. In addition, building a data warehouse is just part of the solution; companies also needed to prepare the ETL application and processes and analytical databases on analytical database systems.

We want to repeat that having a data warehouse is still extremely useful and is the appropriate approach for most analytical projects, but probably not appropriate for ad-hoc and simple projects. However, the data warehouse must be developed in smaller chunks, star schema by star schema, in order to get to the final results, to the reports and analyses, fairly quickly.

With SQL Server 2005, Microsoft offered a full enterprise-grade analytical environment. SQL Server was and still is the RDBMS for data warehouses. **SQL**

Server Analysis Services Multidimensional (**SSAS MD**) was the analytical database management tool for OLAP analyses. SQL Server Integration Services was and still is the tool for the rapid development of ETL applications. Excel was and still is the client application for the SSAS MD. SQL Server Reporting Services was and still is the tool for classical paginated reports. However, with Power BI, you can also use Power BI Report Builder to build paginated reports in the SSRS format, you do not need SSRS for this task. However, in the market, there was an emerging need for simpler tools that could be used by more users, not just IT professionals, for building analytical databases and reports. For a successful analytical solution, the following parts are needed:

- Storage, some kind of database management system
- An ETL tool
- A tool for building reports
- A platform for publishing and sharing reports

Microsoft started to develop a columnar storage database in the year 2006 under the code name Gemini. In the project, SSAS and SSRS teams collaborated. The first product that was released was the Power Pivot add-in for Excel 2010. Power Pivot was considered a part of the SQL Server 2008R2 product line. It did not ship with Office; it was a free download. Power Pivot is the columnar database. Power Pivot introduced a new language, suitable for analytical processing, the **Data Analysis Expressions** (**DAX**) language. Power Pivot is still available in Excel. In *Figure* 1.10, you can see the model view of a simple Power Pivot model:

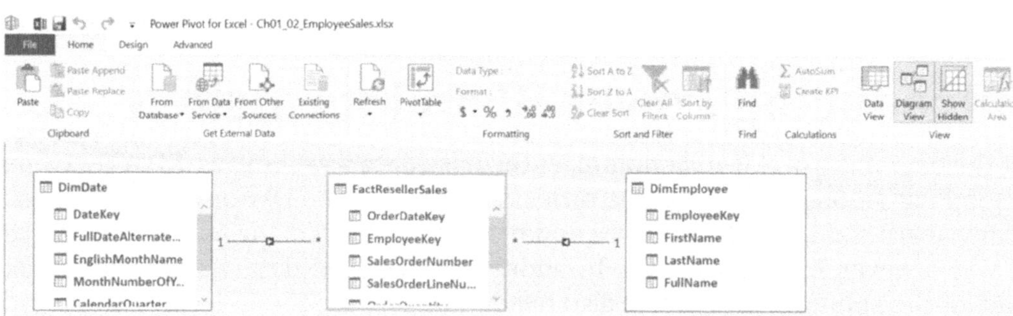

Figure 1.10: *Power Pivot for Excel*

As you can see, the modeling window looks extremely similar to the one in the Power BI Desktop tool, as shown in *Figure* 1.8 earlier in this chapter. The main difference is the color theme - in Power BI Desktop, the main color is grey, and in Excel it is green. After you create the data model in Excel, you can start to analyze it immediately with pivot tables and graphs. With Power Pivot, you can analyze quite huge amounts of data inside Excel, completely bypassing Excel's default limitations of around 1,000,000 rows per worksheet. Power Pivot storage is highly compressed; you are limited to computer memory only. If you count on approximately ten times compression, you can use more than 600 GB of source data in a Power Pivot database inside Excel on a computer with 64 GB memory.

With SQL Server 2012, columnar storage became available on the server side as well. SSAS TAB was introduced side by side with SSAS MD. SSAS MD is not being developed anymore. SSAS TAB is slowly replacing it. SSAS TAB uses the same columnar storage as Power Pivot. You can prepare a server-side database and then use Excel or Power BI Desktop as client tools only. Not every end user is capable of creating a data model. You develop an SSAS TAB database with Visual Studio using the Analysis Services Tabular Project Template. *Figure 1.11* shows a model in the Visual Studio 2022 development environment. You can see the familiar interface again, just that this time the main color is blue:

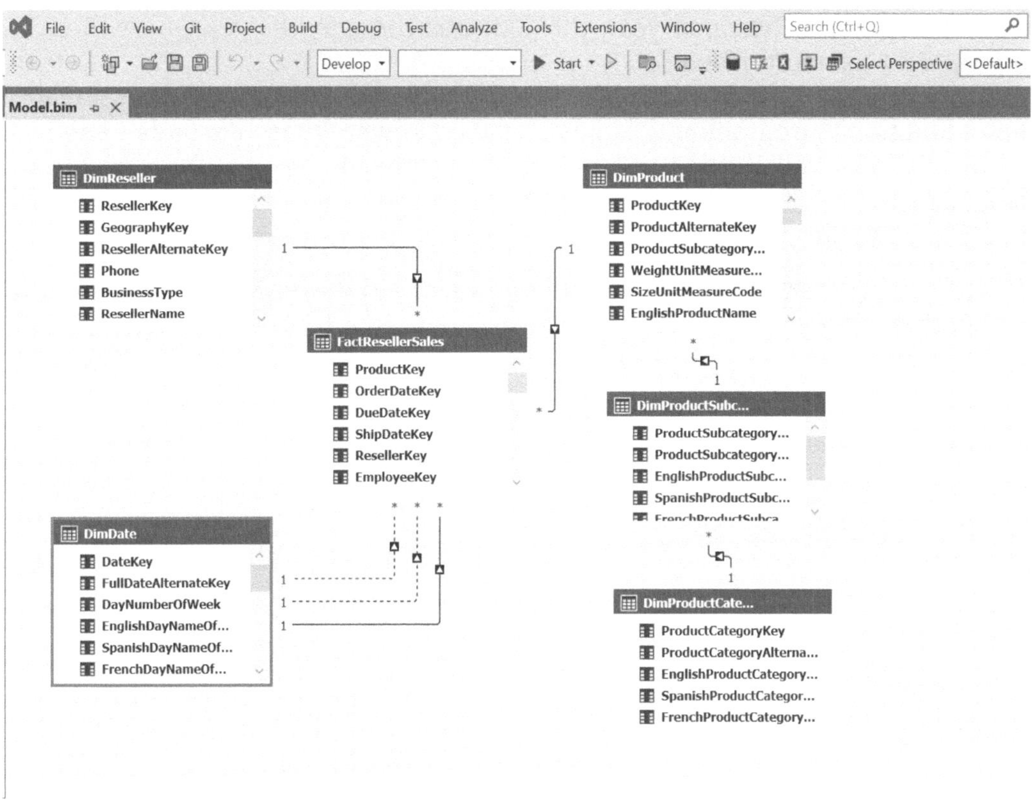

Figure 1.11: *Visual Studio SSAS TAB Model*

Columnstore indices were introduced for SQL Server 2012 RDBMS as well. The first version of the columnar storage was available with nonclustered indices. Nonclustered indices refer to a structure separate from data rows, containing a key value with a pointer to a data row with this key value. Later versions of SQL Server support clustered columnstore indices as well, meaning that you can have data stored in columnar storage only, without row storage. While SSAS TAB still holds the database in memory, you can get an unlimited size of the data inside a SQL Server database.

In the SQL Server 2012 product line, the first publishing and sharing platform was introduced. It was called Power Pivot for **SharePoint Server (SPS)**. This was actually SSAS TAB installed in SPS integrated mode. SSAS TAB provided the database engine for the published reports. Finally, another reporting tool came in the same line. This was Power View, a very simple reporting tool inside SPS for creating reports on the published Power Pivot models. Power View used the Silverlight technology and is nowadays already history.

In the year 2013, the ETL tool, called **Data Explorer**, was introduced as another add-in for Excel. The same year, the tool was renamed Power Query. Besides a **graphical user interface (GUI)** for creating queries to extract the data from multiple sources, transform it and load it to the Power Pivot model, Power Query has a functional programming language called **Power Query Formula Language** or shortly M as well. With the GUI, you can create quite powerful queries in this language, but to get the full power of the language, you might need to write the queries manually.

In the same year 2013, another reporting tool called Power Map was introduced as another add-in for Excel. Like Power View, this tool is nowadays already deprecated as well.

The year 2015 was a very important milestone in Power BI development. Cloud service for publishing and sharing reports was introduced. This is the Power BI Service. This is now the default tool for publishing reports, sharing them through links or creating apps, creating dashboards for desktop and mobile layouts, maintaining security settings and more. *Figure* 1.12 shows a simple dashboard with two tiles that come from different reports:

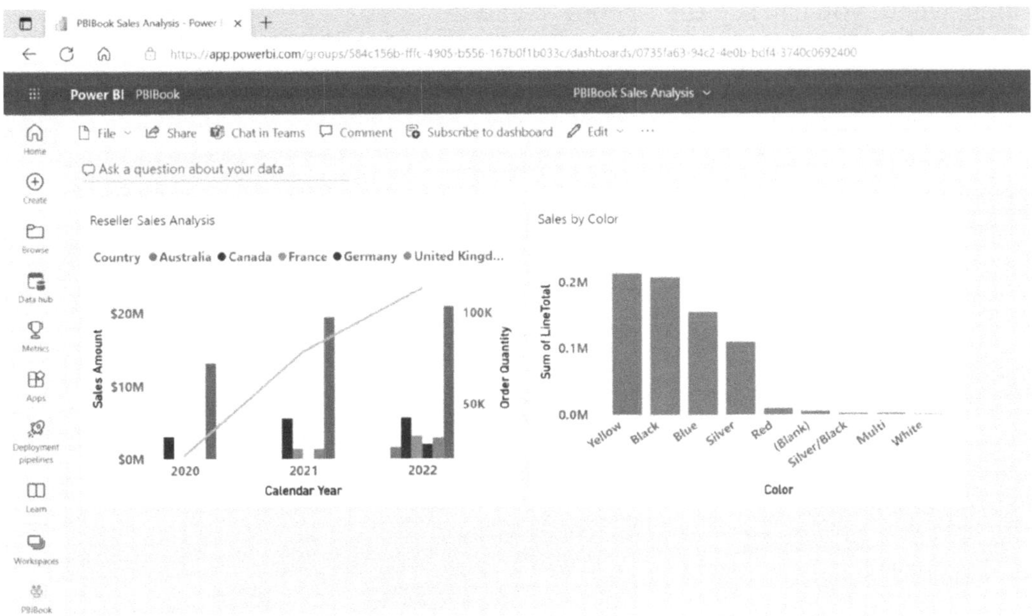

Figure 1.12: *Power BI Dashboard*

Besides Power BI Service, the tool for developing data models, queries, and reports in a single product, called **Power BI Designer** was introduced. The tool was renamed the same year as Power BI Desktop. This is currently the main tool for the development of Power BI elements. It can also serve as a client tool for SSAS TAB. *Figure* 1.13 shows the Power Query window inside Power BI Desktop with the GUI for creating queries, but also with the Advanced Editor window open, where you can see the M code created:

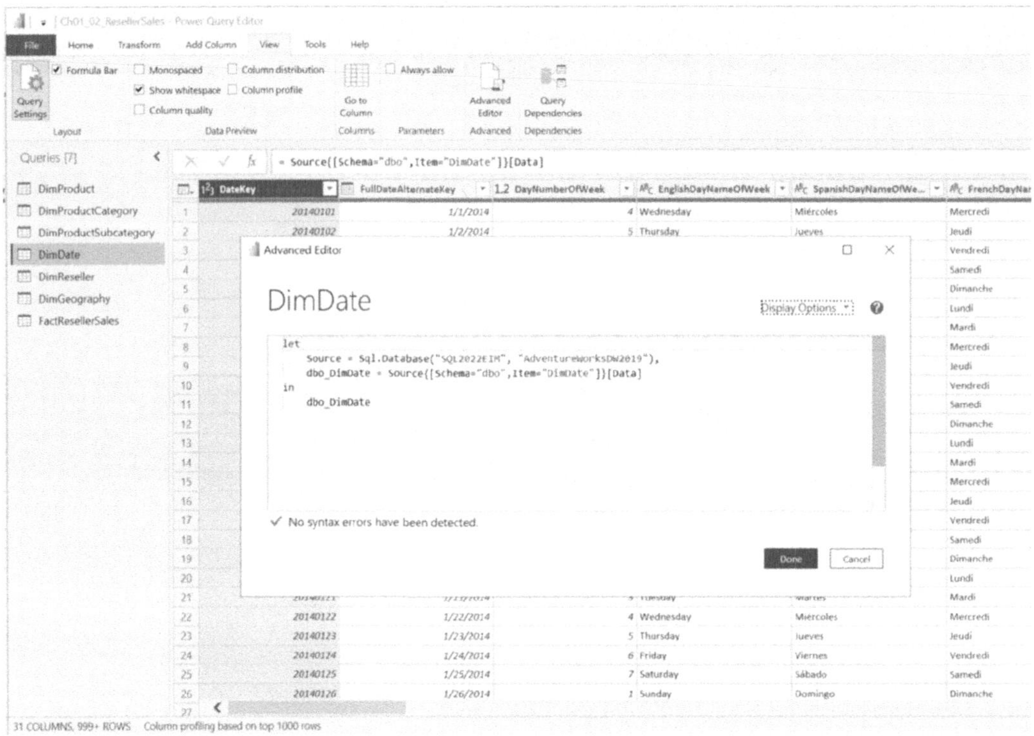

Figure 1.13: *Power Query inside Power BI Desktop*

Many companies like to use classical, paginated SSRS reports. They are very simple to use, include in the application, and even develop them. However, they have limited graphical and OLAP capabilities. The default publishing and sharing of SSRS reports on-premises portal is a part of SSRS and is called Report Manager. You can develop paginated reports with Visual Studio, or with a simpler tool called **Report Builder**. *Figure* 1.14 shows the Report Builder development environment:

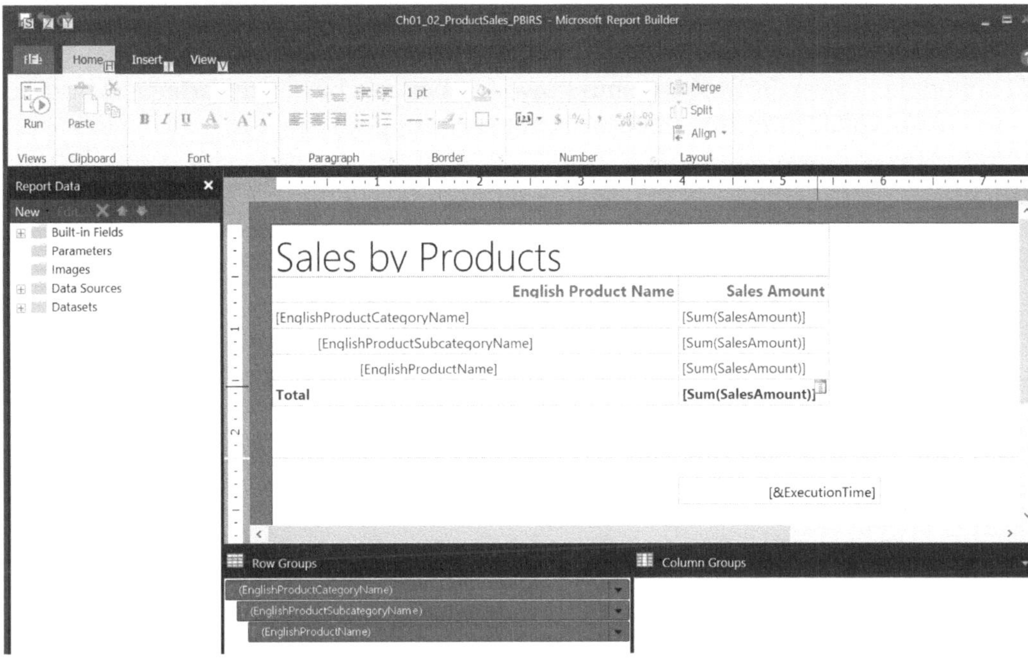

Figure 1.14: *Developing a Report in Report Builder*

Customers wanted to combine paginated and Power BI reports together, they did not want to have two portals, one locally (Report Manager) and one in the cloud (Power BI Service). Microsoft developed an enhanced Report Manager that can host Power BI reports as well as a separate download, but bundled with SQL Server 2017, called **Power BI Report Server** (**PBIRS**). You can see the PBIRS portal with two published reports, one paginated, created with Report Builder, and one created with Power BI Desktop in the same folder in *Figure 1.15*:

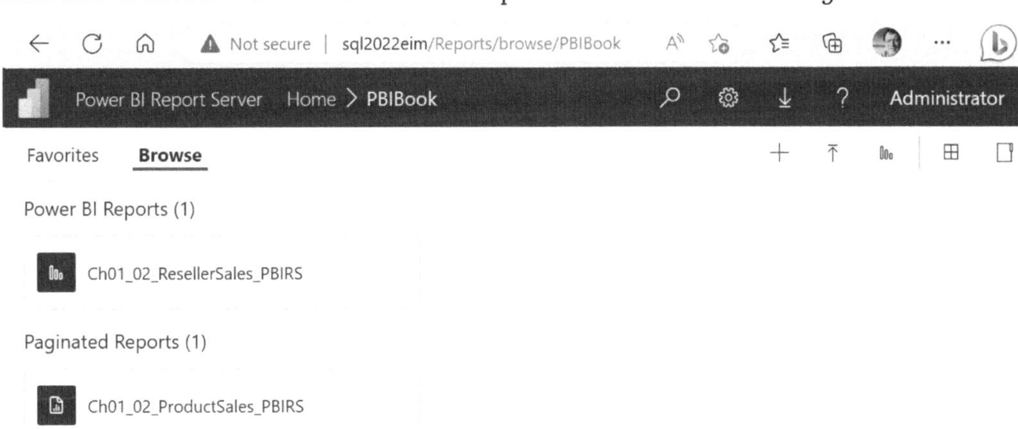

Figure 1.15: PBIRS Portal

With PBIRS, we have a new problem. SQL Server has its own updating schedule with new versions and cumulative updates that are less frequent than the Power BI schedule. Power BI Desktop and Power BI Service have synchronized update schedules. Apparently, we need another development tool synchronized with PBIRS. This is Power BI Desktop for PBIRS. While Power BI Desktop and Service get updated approximately every two months or even more frequently, PBIRS and Power BI Desktop for PBIRS are updated once or maximally twice per year. *Figure 1.16* shows the Power BI Desktop for PBIRS with a report that is just about to be saved (or published) to the PBIRS:

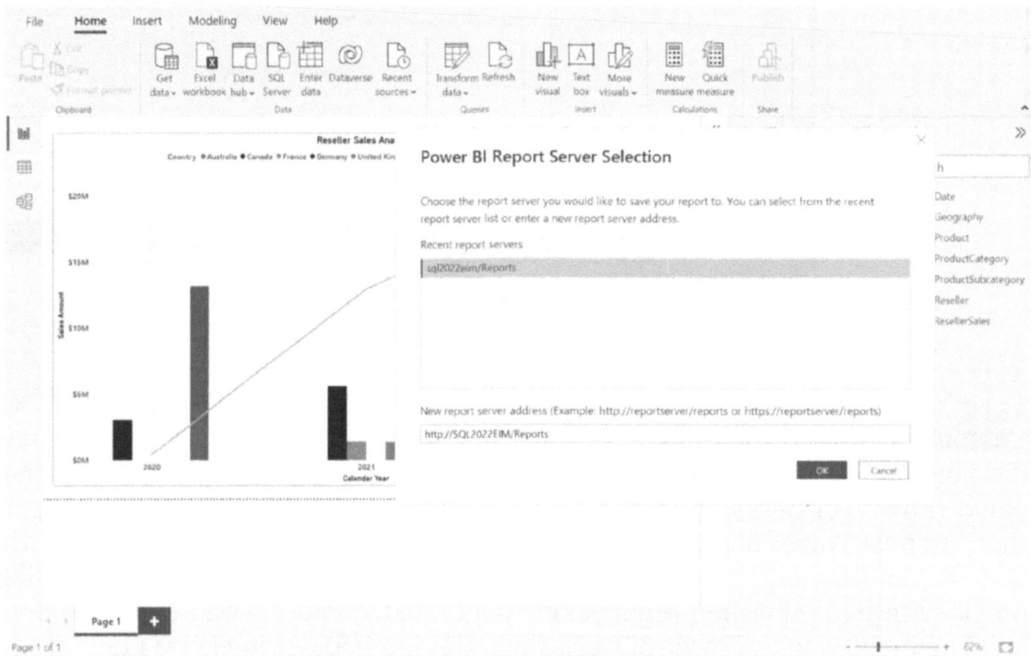

Figure 1.16: *Power BI Desktop for PBIRS*

When you publish a Power BI Desktop file to the Power BI Service, all reports and data are published. You can create additional reports on the published dataset inside the Power BI Service, without using a rich client tool. Can you also create a Power Query without Power BI Desktop? From the year 2018, this is possible as well. Power BI Dataflow is the cloud version of Power Query, inside Power BI Service. *Figure 1.17* shows an example of the Power BI Dataflow. You can see the familiar Power Query environment hosted in Azure:

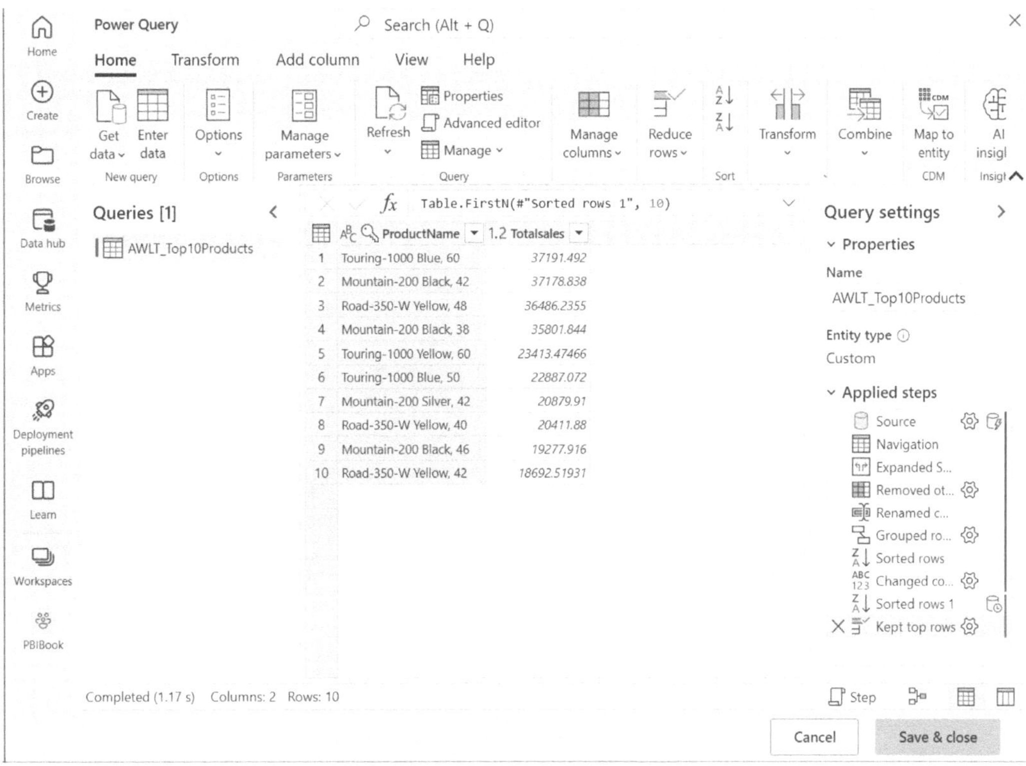

Figure 1.17: *Power BI Dataflow*

In the PBIRS portal, you can combine paginated and Power BI reports. In Power BI Service, you could only see Power BI reports so far. From the year 2019, you can create paginated reports for the Power BI Service as well. The Power BI Paginated Report Builder, built on top of the classical Report Builder, was introduced. You can see a paginated report published in Power BI Service in *Figure 1.18*:

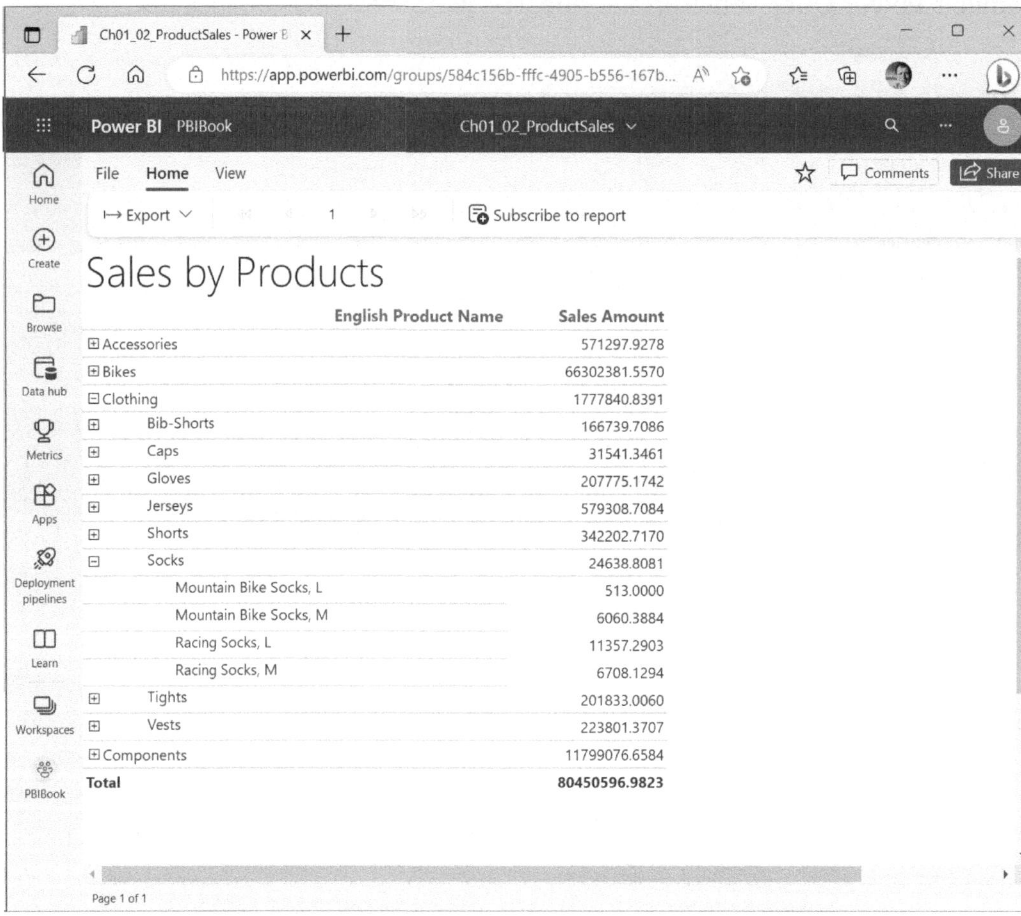

Figure 1.18: *A Paginated Report Published to Power BI Service*

In the year 2021, we got Power BI Datamarts. A Power BI Datamart is a simple Azure SQL Database. You can also call it the citizen data warehouse. You create and manage it from Power BI Service. You do not need to use classical SQL Server tools, like **SQL Server Management Studio (SSMS)**, **Azure Data Studio (ADS)** or **Visual Studio (VS)**. Of course, you cannot do everything with Power BI Datamarts as you can do with the aforementioned tools. Therefore, the optimization options are also limited. Therefore, for any larger project, you should still build a classical data warehouse by yourself. *Figure 1.19* shows an example of a Power BI Datamart:

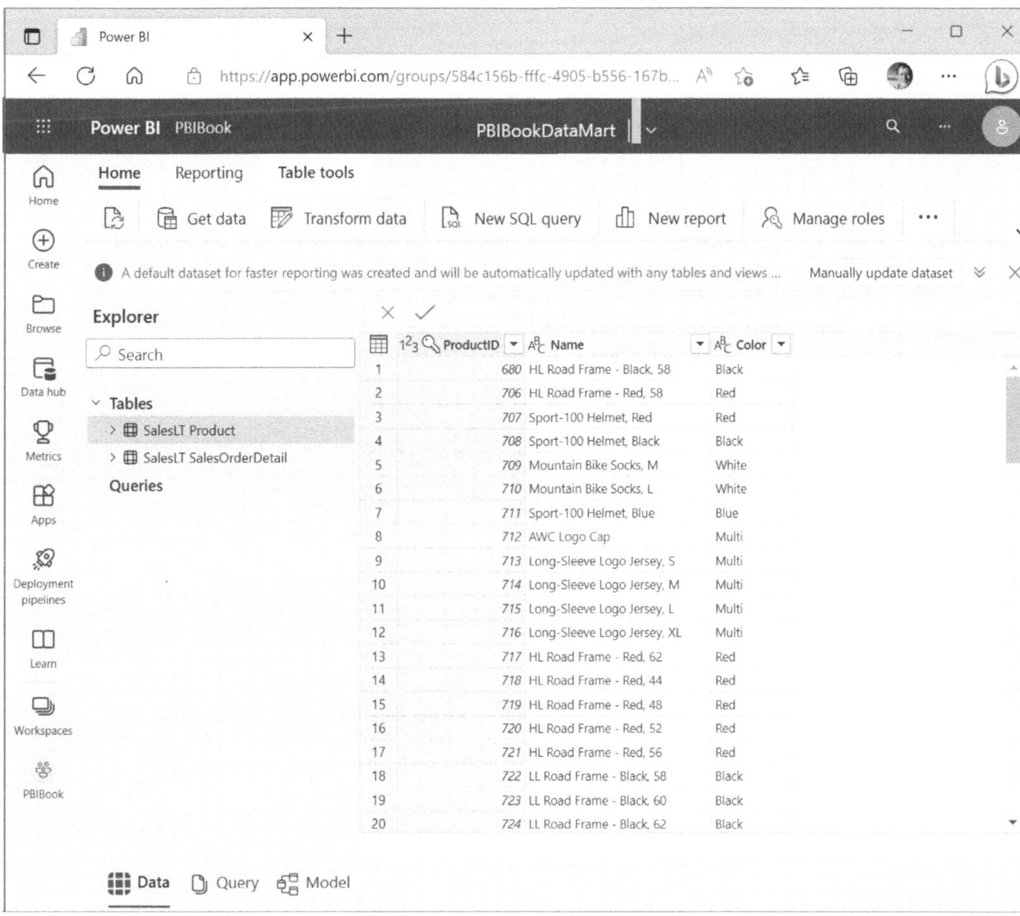

Figure 1.19: *Power BI Datamart*

Finally, there is also a mobile version of Power BI. Power BI Mobile was introduced in 2017 and is regularly refreshed. Initially, it was created for Android, iOS, and Windows 10 Mobile operating systems. The Windows Phone version is dead since March 2021. *Figure 1.20* shows a Power BI service dashboard opened in the Power BI Mobile app:

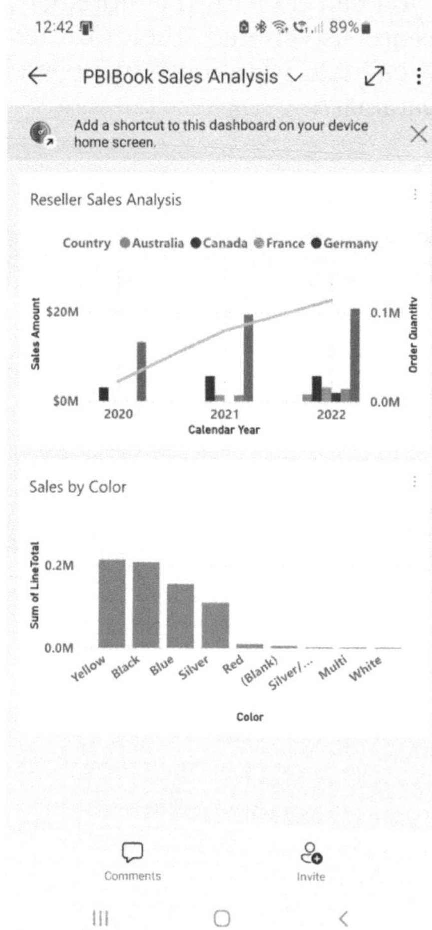

***Figure 1.20**: Power BI Mobile*

Before finishing this chapter, we need to introduce three concepts more. They do not pertain to Power BI directly. However, they are frequently used in a modern analytical environment. A data lake is a repository for storing data in native or raw format, usually physically in blob files. You can use a data lake for staging data, for quickly loading raw data from different semi-structured and unstructured sources. For example, you could use Azure Blob Storage for your data lake. A data lakehouse is a combination of data warehouse and data lake. Azure Synapse Analytics is a cloud service that can serve as your data lakehouse.

The third concept we need to introduce is Microsoft Fabric. Of course, you noticed the plethora of products and services introduced so far. Microsoft Fabric is a new concept that helps simplifying analytical solutions. It is an umbrella for cloud services that deal with data storage, ETL processes, analytical solutions and data science. Microsoft Fabric covers Power BI, Azure Synapse Analytics, TL services like Azure Data Factory, Azure machine Learning and more. With Fabric, you also get an explicit data lake called OneLake.

Wow, that was quite a journey. You might be a bit confused with all the tools and services mentioned. Fortunately, very few companies use all of them. Most companies use either cloud or on-premises versions, rarely both of them. In this book, we will focus on the cloud version, and work mostly with Power BI Desktop and Power BI Service.

Conclusion

Power BI is a big thing. It democratizes analytical processing; it enables citizen analytics for the masses. The two pillars for online analytical processing are the logical pillar or the star schema, and the physical pillar or the database management system optimized for queries with lightning performance. In the whole Power BI suite, there are many products and services. Fortunately, the tools for the same purpose share a common interface. For example, you could see that we have the same interface for data modeling and ETL in Excel, Power BI Desktop, Power BI Service and Visual Studio. Of course, most companies do not use all the tools and services.

In the next chapter, we are going to start importing data into a Power BI dataset with the Power BI Desktop tool.

Key terms

- **Star schema**: This is the logical schema for databases that support online analytical processing.
- **Fact table**: It is the central table in a star schema, where we store values that we want to analyze in columns called measures.
- **Dimension**: It is a table on one side of the relationship with a fact table. Columns that give context to measures are attributes of a dimension.
- **Columnar storage**: This is the physical implementation of data storage, optimized for online analytical processing.
- **Data warehouse**: A database in an RDBMS with multiple star schemas, explicit date dimension, good naming convention, and with cleansed data.

Questions

1. What is the difference between Power BI and paginated reports?
2. What is a Power BI Dataset?
3. What is a Power BI Dataflow?
4. What is a Power BI Datamart?
5. Which tools can you use to create paginated reports that you would deploy on-premises?

CHAPTER 2

Acquiring and Transforming Data From Multiple Sources

Introduction

To gather insights from data it needs to be visualized in a way that it is intuitive for users to understand. To visualize data, we can use objects in Business Intelligence (BI) tools. These objects may be referred to as visualizations. They could be tiles showing a meaningful value called cards, or tables showing several columns with multiple rows of data. They could be charts of different types, such as bar, column, or line charts. To display meaningful values, we need to create measures that perform calculations on our data. An example of a measure is the average value of a set of numbers. But before we can perform any of that, we need to have access to data. We need to bring data to a BI tool. Data need to be formatted in a way that is suitable for its usage by the BI tool. Only then can we perform calculations on data and interpret its patterns and meaning.

Data also need to be cleaned, ensuring there are no unnecessary values and that all values are of the correct data type. We might need to eliminate NULLs or totals at the end of the time series. We don't want a text value saying *null* or *no sales* in a column showing numbered sales. Getting data cleaned and putting it in the right format is called transforming data. It's part of the process called data processing.

Structure

In this chapter, we will discuss the following topics:

- Copying data versus connecting to data sources
- Power Query and its relation to Excel and Power BI
- Connecting to data sources
- Overview of Power Query Editor

Copying data versus connecting to data sources

Users have been copying and pasting data to Excel documents for decades. They use classic Excel formulas to interpret data. We're going to overview how to use classic Excel functionality to create BI reports.

Classic Excel functionality

We might have a comma-separated value file (CSV file) with dates and sales of an item for those dates. A CSV file is a type of flat file, similar to a text document, where values are separated by a delimiter. In *Figure 2.1* we can see an example of a very simple CSV file showing dates and sales quantity of our company's main product type - online educational courses. We have two columns and one row for every date in the year 2022:

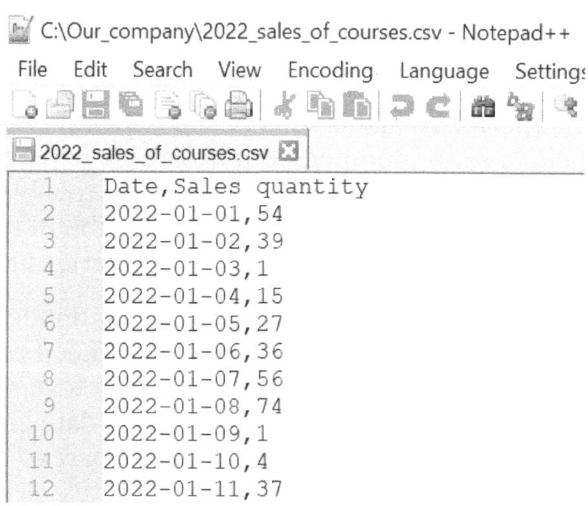

Figure 2.1: *A simple CSV file showing daily sales of courses opened in Notepad++*

Note

CSV files can be opened by Microsoft Excel, or by an application called Notepad++, which is a text and code editor. It offers a richer set of capabilities than the original Notepad that comes as a part of the native Windows experience. Notepad++ is a good tool for any business analyst or developer. It offers advanced text search and replaces capabilities, autosaving, syntax highlighting for different programming languages, multiple tabs, access to plugins, and best of all, it's freely available to download from: **https://notepad-plus-plus.org/downloads/**.

Some CSV files might be too large for Excel to open, but this one is rather short. Depending on localization settings, it might open Excel in a suitable format. The correct format is two columns, one for date and the other for sales quantity. Our CSV file uses delimiter “,”. This is considered a standard delimiter in US English and some other language variants, while some European language variants may use “;”. Differences can arise with date formats, let's say `mm/dd/yyyy` versus `dd.mm.yyyy`. Or they can arise with number formats, where “,” can represent a thousand separators and “.” a decimal separator, or vice-versa. Even in Excel classic functions or in DAX, parameters can be separated by “,” or “;”.

If the CSV file doesn't open in a suitable format, we could split columns by `Text to Columns` in Excel upper ribbon under the `Data` tab. The upper ribbon is common to many Microsoft products. It allows access to the most common options, settings, and functionalities. It is divided into tabs, such as `Home`, `Insert`, `View`, and `Help` and further subdivided into sections, such as `Clipboard`, `Font Alignment`, and `Number`. *Figure* 2.2 shows us Excel's upper ribbon with selected `Data` tab (in the figure labeled as 1) and visible `Text to Columns` option (labeled as 2) under `Data Tools`. Please note that the ribbon was cropped to ensure better visibility:

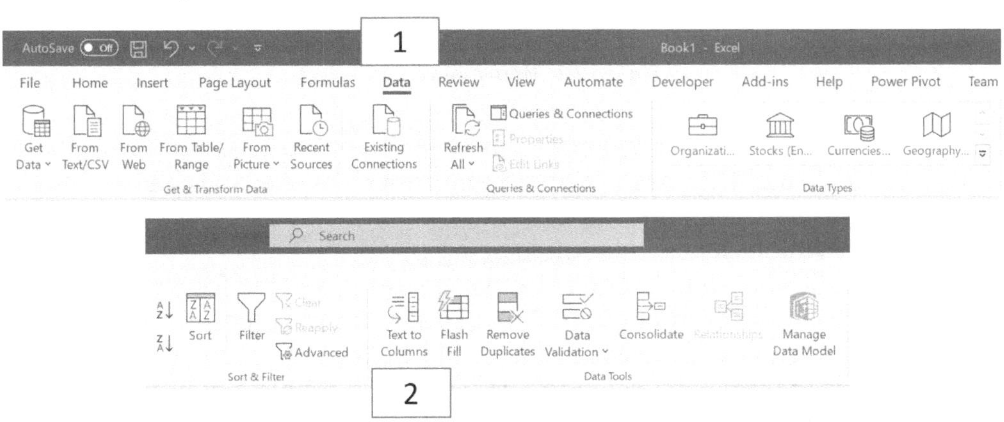

Figure 2.2: *A simple CSV file showing daily sales of courses*

Note

The upper ribbon is key navigation display in both Excel and Power BI. We can access many of the functionalities and options from the ribbon. If it isn't visible in Excel, look for Ribbon Display Options in the upper-right corner of the screen and select option Show Tabs and Commands. Look for the following icon:

`Text to Columns` option brings up an interface window, where we can select `Delimited split` and then a comma in an option for selecting delimiters. Finish will split data into two columns allowing us to create our BI report. We could do a simple data transformation and add a month column to column C with the function `=MONTH(A2)`. Then we could add a couple of calculations to our report, to show some statistical values with the following classic Excel functions:

`=AVERAGE(B:B)`	`=MAX(B:B)`	`=MEDIAN(B:B)`
`=SUM(B:B)`	`=MIN(B:B)`	`=MODE.SNGL(B:B)`
`=STDEV.P(B:B)`	`=MAX(B:B) - MIN(B:B)`	

Table 2.1: *Classic Excel functions for calculating statistics*

Giving us a simple BI report as seen in *Figure 2.3*:

	A	B	C	D	E	F
1	Date	Sales quantity	Month		AVERAGE	42,63561644
2	2022-01-01	54	1		SUM	15562
3	2022-01-02	39	1		STDEV.P	24,62344005
4	2022-01-03	1	1		MAX	85
5	2022-01-04	15	1		MIN	0
6	2022-01-05	27	1		VAR	85
7	2022-01-06	36	1		MEDIAN	42
8	2022-01-07	56	1		MODE	1
9	2022-01-08	74	1			

Figure 2.3: *Simple BI report*

This already tells us something about our data. We could also further expand the analysis on a monthly basis. Conditional functions are suitable, we might use `=SUMIFS(B:B,C:C,I2)` and `=AVERAGEIFS(B:B,C:C,I2)`. The first parameter is the range on which the calculation is being performed and the second is the range with conditional values. The third parameter is a value for the condition. In our report, we've written numbers 1-12 in column I to reference months. We can also add a chart, first by selecting `Date and Sales quantity columns`, then by going to the `Insert tab`, selecting `Recommended Charts`, and pressing `OK`. Our BI report is visible in *Figure 2.4*:

Month	SUM	AVERAGE
1	1198	38,64516
2	1074	38,35714
3	1126	36,32258
4	1411	47,03333
5	1273	41,06452
6	1703	56,76667
7	1356	43,74194
8	1290	41,6129
9	1272	42,4
10	1254	40,45161
11	1373	45,76667
12	1232	39,74194

Figure 2.4: *Simple BI report with monthly analysis and a chart*

Getting into connectivity

So why should we connect to data sources when we can create reports with classic Excel functionality? Can we avoid using complex advanced tools or the necessity of learning a new formula language? There is a short learning curve to getting to know Excel enough to do what we've done. Many business managers, financial sector experts, and traders are creating such reports, and this is why Excel is still so prevalent.

The CSV that we used to create a BI report was very simple. Imagine that it is much more complex. Our company could have a portfolio of fifteen courses, which would require additional columns. Such as columns with product names or identity codes. This could expand our time series length by up to fifteen times. We could have multiple markets, for example, we could sell our courses from a website, from social media accounts, or from platforms specializing in selling courses of multiple authors.

We could have a column with sales data for each product name and a separate CSV file for each market. There is a possibility that courses are available in multiple languages, and we might want to include that in our analysis. We could have customers from several countries. We might want to see other customer information, such as age, education, and so on. The time column in our CSV is showing every date for the year 2022 only, but it could be more complex. It could show hourly data for periods longer or shorter than a year. Another problem is the frequency that these CSV files are being given to us. Imagine that a new CSV file is created with weekly data for each of the fifteen courses in the portfolio. That's fifteen files we'd have to copy and paste every week to our Excel to keep our reports up to date.

Considering the entire data system means viewing things from a systematic perspective. Copying and pasting is not a suitable approach. We are creating data islands or stores of data that aren't externally connected and synchronized with data sources. If we forget to manually update our data, it would quickly become obsolete. We would need to copy data in regular intervals to keep our visualization and measures up to date. This approach is time-consuming and can be buried under everyday tasks.

Now imagine that we're in an enterprise environment, such as in a multinational retail company. We have a legacy database system pushing CSV files to a virtual disk space that is connected to a network. There are better ways to share data between systems, but companies still resort to pushing files with a lack of a better alternative. In real life, CSV files might be complex, with redundant data and requiring the removal of first rows or totals in the last rows. Columns can be separated by more than just a delimiter. Data could contain symbols such as "" or <>. An example of a complex CSV file can be seen in *Figure* 2.5:

```
Export for analysis
Organization ID selected id from 100 to 155
Period from 01.6.2023 to 31.6.2023
Item id is 102301, 114212, 121191, 130165, 130250
Market is NL, DE, PL, CZ, AT, CH
ORGANIZATION/MARKET/ITEM/QUANTITY/PRICE
=<Organization ID>;=<Market name>;=<Item id>;=<Item name>;=<Item type>;=<Color>;=<Purchase quantity>;=<Sold quantity>;=
=<100>;=<NL>;=<102301>;=<GeForce RTX 4090>;=<Graphics card>;=<Black>;=<2>;=<1>;=<4>;=<1107,22 €>;=<1318,53 €>;=<1124,48
=<101>;=<NL>;=<102301>;=<GeForce RTX 4090>;=<Graphics card>;=<Black>;=<9>;=<10>;=<2>;=<832,45 €>;=<1356,55 €>;=<825,58 €
=<102>;=<NL>;=<102301>;=<GeForce RTX 4090>;=<Graphics card>;=<Black>;=<8>;=<10>;=<4>;=<912,63 €>;=<1315,01 €>;=<937,02 €
=<103>;=<NL>;=<102301>;=<GeForce RTX 4090>;=<Graphics card>;=<Black>;=<3>;=<4>;=<1>;=<948,11 €>;=<1507,07 €>;=<951,08 €
=<104>;=<NL>;=<102301>;=<GeForce RTX 4090>;=<Graphics card>;=<Black>;=<11>;=<17>;=<7>;=<946,92 €>;=<1320,62 €>;=<966,97
=<105>;=<NL>;=<102301>;=<GeForce RTX 4090>;=<Graphics card>;=<Black>;=<11>;=<4>;=<6>;=<950,83 €>;=<1400,64 €>;=<961,94 €
=<106>;=<NL>;=<102301>;=<GeForce RTX 4090>;=<Graphics card>;=<Black>;=<7>;=<5>;=<10>;=<959,58 €>;=<1330,75 €>;=<978,52 €
=<107>;=<NL>;=<102301>;=<GeForce RTX 4090>;=<Graphics card>;=<Black>;=<9>;=<1>;=<9>;=<984,15 €>;=<1382,02 €>;=<1029,06 €
=<108>;=<NL>;=<102301>;=<GeForce RTX 4090>;=<Graphics card>;=<Black>;=<11>;=<17>;=<8>;=<995,97 €>;=<1438,98 €>;=<956,73
=<109>;=<NL>;=<102301>;=<GeForce RTX 4090>;=<Graphics card>;=<Black>;=<4>;=<11>;=<8>;=<880,46 €>;=<1503,55 €>;=<906,97 €
=<110>;=<NL>;=<102301>;=<GeForce RTX 4090>;=<Graphics card>;=<Black>;=<4>;=<5>;=<2>;=<949,74 €>;=<1551,98 €>;=<997,58 €
```

Figure 2.5: *Example of complex CSV file*

Complex CSVs become much more troublesome to deal with classic Excel functionality. There are Excel internal limits on how much data can fit into a single sheet. Considering the possibility of daily flat file pushes containing millions of rows of data, we need a better alternative to process data in these files. Files used to pass data between systems can also be referred to as data interchange formats. Another data interchange formats often used are JSON - JavaScript Object Notation, which uses name-value pairs to present data in a way that is readable by humans. XML or Extensible Markup Language is also used and contains name-value pairs enclosed in tags. Internal settings and application's commands can be used to push such files to a location in storage by data source systems.

These files might also be requested by using an **Application Programming Interface (API)**. APIs are a way for different computer software programs to communicate with each other. They can be used to request information from applications and services that are data sources. Python programming language is sufficient technology to work with APIs – to send requests for data interchange formats. This functionality can be achieved with built-in libraries or modules - `requests`, and `urllib`, that need to be imported to be used. There are some third-party options like module `httplib2`.

As mentioned in the previous chapter, another common data source unsuited for direct reporting is transactional systems (OLTP). We should avoid copying data from relational databases behind LOB applications. It would be hard to structure data to a suitable format from the relational database and we wouldn't want users freely connecting to the OLTP. That would risk slowing it down and also present the risk in data privacy. We would prefer a controlled process of extracting data into a staging area or data warehouse during times of least burden, such as night times. Controlled and structured extractions should be automated, lessening the possibility of human-induced error.

Integrated data systems

Microsoft and other providers of BI tools have been trying hard to increase the average knowledge and capacity of performing BI for inexperienced users. This is the idea behind concepts such as democratizing analytics and self-service BI. The general trend is that each user should be capable of performing their own analysis. Reality shows slow progress toward that goal. Market demand was created for specialized BI analysts and firms specializing in delivering professional, highly automatized, and connected data systems.

These are called integrated data systems and can consist of staging areas, data warehouses, semantic models, and end reports showing data visualizations. For a BI system to be called integrated, it has to be connected from data sources to end visualizations and it has to be automated to a high degree. After such systems are created, there shouldn't generally be a need to spend additional time dealing with data, unless changes in business requirements or additional data sources are being introduced. Only integrated systems with formed semantic models and even pre-prepared reports can offer suitable democratization of analytics for users that aren't experienced in these technologies. *Figure* 2.6 shows a schema of an integrated data system, with several data sources and several end reports pre-prepared:

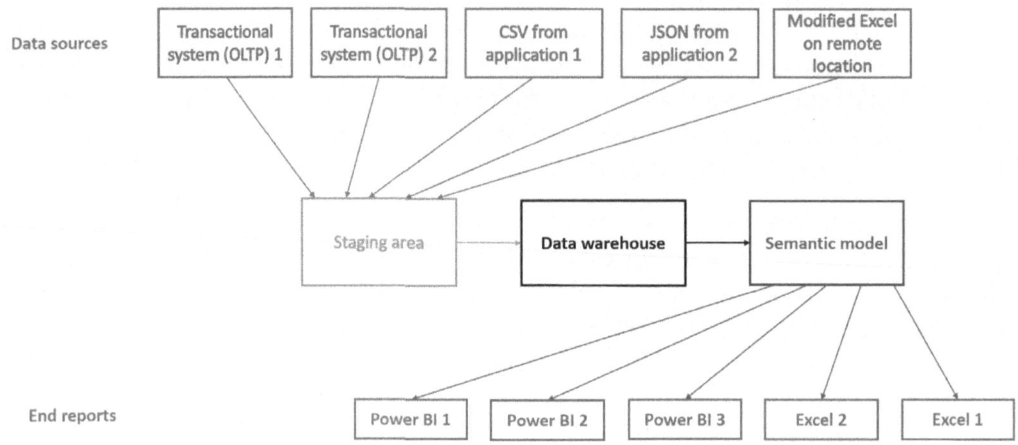

Figure 2.6: *Schema of integrated data system*

In data sources, we might have an ERP system and **Customer Relationship Management (CRM)** system that take care of most day-to-day business and planning needs. There might be two applications that are industry specific tracking systems. These systems are often developed by smaller teams and offer limited connectivity to their transactional systems. Application developers may offer to push their data interchange formats to a remote location or may offer API information to request information. There will often be files that are modified by employees with data that is not found in other data sources.

A staging area is intended to host unstructured or semi-structured data, depending on the complexity of data coming from data sources. From OLTP, it's usually a direct copy of data to avoid burdening the transactional system. From complex data interchange formats, it might make sense to perform partial transformation before reaching the staging area. Between staging area and data warehouse, we can create procedures to transform data to its final or near final form. Data warehouses are used to store historical data or snapshots of data from certain periods while staging area might contain data for shorter periods.

If our data system consists of staging area and data warehouse, it might be a good idea to avoid performing additional data transformations past this point. Although we can transform data in semantic models, we might want to avoid confusion. Semantic models are technologies suitable for analytics and reporting. They offer a view of data that is sensible to business users. They offer a common vocabulary and relationship between data tables and are suitable for filtering. They are either based on **online analytical processing (OLAP)**, also known as multidimensional cube technology, or on columnar storage, known in Microsoft environment as tabular models. These semantic models have embedded calculations in **Multidimensional Data Expressions (MDX)** for multidimensional cubes or **Data Analysis Expressions (DAX)** for tabular models. Tabular model technology is now considered the norm in Microsoft environment.

The tabular model can be created locally in Power BI Desktop or in Excel with Power Pivot technology. In Power BI Service, where they are referred to as datasets. We can also design tabular models in Visual Studio, which is a Microsoft **integrated development environment (IDE)** or a set of tools for developing software solutions. During the Visual Studio installation process, we need to install the extension **SQL Server Data Tools (SSDT)** and later from Visual Studio Marketplace an extension Analysis Services Projects. We can then create data model projects and deploy these projects to SQL Server Analysis Services. We can choose during the installation of SQL Server Analysis Services whether we want to use multidimensional or tabular technology.

As a general rule of thumb, simple ad hoc reports in Excel should only be used when we want to resolve a single issue fast. We might have a simple data source that we could copy and paste for a quick personal analysis using classic Excel functionality for decision support. But when we move towards a professional and enterprise environment, we should always be creating integrated data systems. In order to create integrated data systems, we need a suitable tool to perform data processing or ETL process. Meaning we have to extract data, transform it into a suitable format and load it to the next stage of our system until we reach a BI tool for visualization. As it is visible in the schema of *Figure 2.6*, transformation can be performed in several steps.

We have multiple choices for data processing. An on-premises environment means that infrastructure, hardware, and software are hosted on-site for private use, most often by the company itself. If we have an on-premises SQL Server environment, we can use SQL Server Integration Services, together with SQL Server Agent Job to automatically run these processes. A lot of transformation can be done with T-SQL stored procedures. Procedures offer a good overview of what is going on if we use good procedure names, and schemas and take a careful approach to organizing our code.

Cloud environments are hosted by the public cloud provider, offering computer, memory, and storage as a service, most often to more than one organization. Microsoft's cloud solution is called Azure. If we host our data system on the cloud, we can use cloud services, labeled in the Microsoft environment as cloud resources, that allow automation of data movements and data transformations. Such a resource is Azure Data Factory.

Power BI and Excel reports can be shared to multiple users on a specialized cloud service called Power BI Service. It offers increasing capabilities, including data processing capabilities, as users increase their licensing options ranging from free to premium. Furthermore, we can make use of free third-party programming languages such as Python with usage modules to create ETL flows. Some of the modules for these workflows are Apache Airflow, PySpark, Dask, Petl, and Pandas.

Given that this book is focused on performing BI with Microsoft Excel and Power BI, we will focus on tools that are available with these platforms. Microsoft Excel and Power BI come with a powerful tool for ETL workflows that is called Power Query. It can perform ETL from a range of data sources and it is excellent for working with data interchange formats.

Power Query in relation to Excel and Power BI

Power Query has the ability to connect to data sources, extract data, perform transformations and load data to an environment. It was introduced by Microsoft, first as an Excel add-in to help develop data models in Power Pivot, which will be expanded on in *Chapter 4, Building a Simple Analytical Solution with Power Pivot in Excel*. It offers a consistent experience with a range of different data sources as well as repeatability of transformation processes. It can work with large sets of data and gives us the ability to effectively filter them, allowing us to work only with subsets. Power Query became native to Excel in 2016 and was introduced as a native part of Power BI from the very beginning, ensuring its connectivity to data sources. Power BI was designed with the idea of creating integrated data systems.

Power BI storage is a database, in fact, it is based on columnar storage or tabular model technology. It has constraints, such as enforced data types in a single column. If we designate a column as a decimal or whole number, any text in a row will generate an error. Power BI doesn't have a concept of cells, so it is more focused on using formula and expression languages from the get-go. We are much more likely to use Power Query in Power BI than in Excel. Excel was used for data analysis before Power Query was developed and users can still use this classic Excel functionality without resorting to Power Query.

In Power BI we're likely to avoid copying and pasting data from flat files, although we can. If we want to avoid interaction with Power Query's deeper functionalities, we can do that as well. It can run in the background, while we only use interface windows to connect to data sources. This approach would work only if our data is in a suitable format – in tables consisting of columns and rows, cleaned up, without any unnecessary values, and generally ready to use. This would often only be the case if data was previously transformed, such as if it came from an on-premises SQL Server running a data warehouse.

If data is not in suitable format, we should use Power Query Editor, which is a graphical user interface. It allows interaction with Power Query functionalities by pressing commands in the ribbon and drop-down lists. The upper ribbon is similar to any Microsoft application, it is divided by tabs and split into sections. Power Query Editor can be used to perform step-by-step data transformation until it is suitable for usage.

There is a programming language behind most Power Query transformations. It is called Power Query Formula Language or M for short. Working in Editor will create an M code in the background, which can be viewed and modified. We will discuss this language in the next chapter. However, we can perform many transformations in Editor and according to Microsoft, it in itself should be enough for all our transformation needs. It is probable to assume that a BI professional would need to obtain a working knowledge of M formula language.

We should structure our experience with Power Query logically:

- Firstly, we need to understand how to connect to data sources quickly, when our data is in a suitable format, by using interface windows in both Excel and Power BI.
- Secondly, we need to understand how to access Power Query Editor and how to maneuver around it, and understand what functions are available.
- Thirdly, we need to perform some exercises in order to develop a more intuitive knowledge of how step-by-step transformations work in Power Query.
- Fourthly, we should get an overview of the M formula language so we can understand what is happening in the background.
- Fifthly, we'll look at some ways to improve the automatically generated code by Power Query Editor, as well as perform some additional transformations using M formula language.

Connecting to data sources

Power query offers connection capabilities to many data sources. The exact number of connectors depends on versions of applications or services we are using. New connectors are being added by updates, may differ between services, and some are removed. An overview of common connectors can be seen in *Table* 2.2 and *Table* 2.3:

Microsoft Services	Microsoft Azure	Dynamics 365 and SharePoint
Access Database	Blob storage	Business Central
Active Directory	Cosmos DB	Customer Insights
Excel	Databricks	Dataverse
Dataverse	PostgreSQL	Exchange
Dataflows	Data Lake Storage	SharePoint List
Folder	DevOps	SharePoint Folder
Power BI datasets	HDInsight	SharePoint Online list
SQL Server database	Synapse Analytics	
Analysis Services database	SQL Database	
Teams Personal analytics	Table Storage	

Table 2.2: *Overview of available connectors part one*

Database management systems	Amazon and Google	General and files
Oracle database	Amazon Athena	OLE DB
IBM DB2	OpenSearch Service	ODBC
IBM Informix	Amazon Redshift	Text/CSV
IBM Netezza	Google Analytics	XML
MySQL	Google BigQuery	JSON
MariaDB	Google Sheets	PDF
PostgreSQL		Web connector
Sybase		
Terradata		

Table 2.3: *Overview of available connectors part two*

Besides those, there are quite a few connectors that haven't been listed. We can connect to ERP and CRM systems, cloud solutions, business applications, and services offering analytics. It's usually best to check available Power Query connectors when we have a concrete resource in our hands which we want to analyze or transform data from. Even if we cannot find a suitable data connector, there are options available to create custom connectors by using Power Query

SDK, a toolset that offers a variety of APIs and can be integrated with Visual Studio.

Note

There is a page in the documentation available that lists available Power Query connectors by services: ***https://learn.microsoft.com/en-us/power-query/connectors/****.*

Data sources in Power BI Desktop

When we open a blank Power BI report by launching a desktop application, there could be pop-up windows informing us of update details, giving us some links to learning material, and might even offer us options to connect to data sources. If we close those windows, we are greeted with a welcome screen informing us to add data to our report. One exclusive option worth mentioning in the welcome screen is to Try a sample dataset, which offers a link to tutorials on learn.microsoft.com or gives the ability to load sample data. This will open a connection to Excel document and an interface window as we can expect when connecting to any Excel document.

In an interface window when loading Excel document with sample data, multiple items can be selected, selecting either Excel sheets or tables in our workbook. They may hold the same data in a sample dataset. Pressing Load will launch Power Query's query in the background and load data into a tabular model, while selecting Transform Data will open the Power Query Editor, giving the option to process data. *Figure* 2.7 shows an interface window as it is seen with any Excel documents:

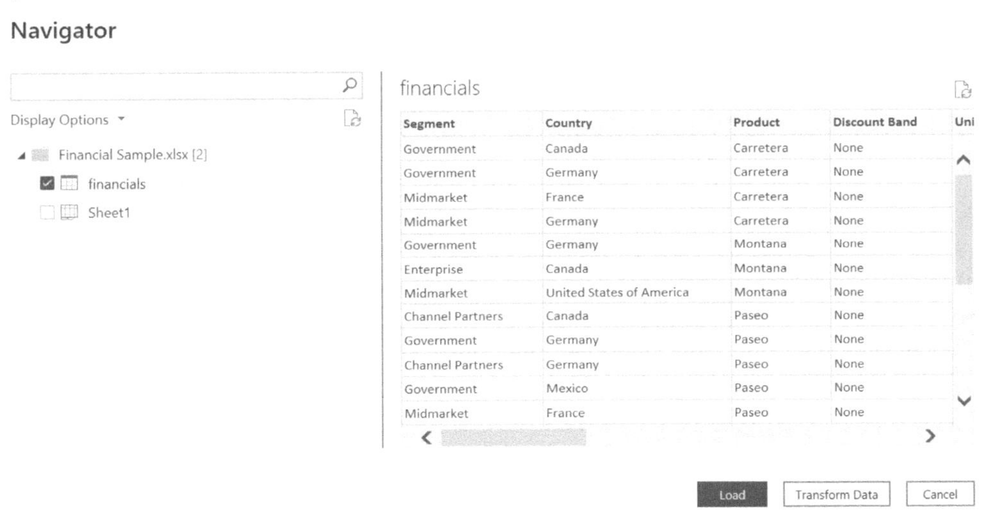

Figure **2.7**: *Interface window when connecting to Excel workbook*

Most of the options in the welcome screen are also available from the upper ribbon in Power BI desktop. As soon as a single table is loaded into Power BI, the welcome screen will change with a message informing us that we should build visuals with our data. The upper ribbon in Power BI Desktop should be similar to that of many other Microsoft applications like Excel or Word. There are options to select tabs such as `File`, `Home`, `Insert`, `Modeling`, `View`, and `Help`. We can see the upper ribbon in *Figure* 2.8. In order to connect to data sources, select the `Home` tab and look for options under the `Data` section (in the figure labeled as 1), or under the `Queries` section (labeled as 2):

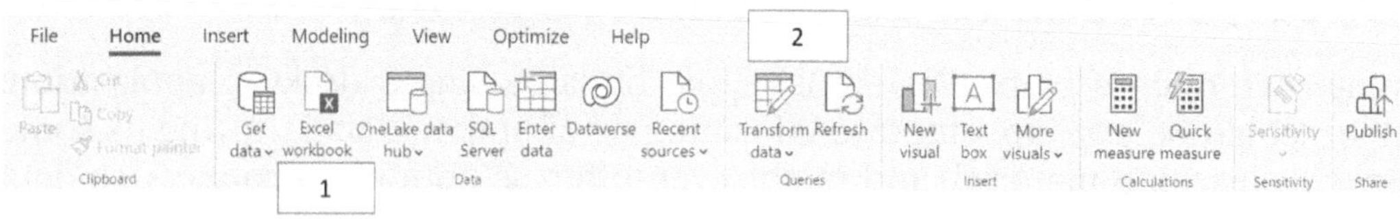

***Figure 2.8**: Upper ribbon in Power BI with tabs and sections*

Under the `Home` tab and `Data` section in the upper ribbon, Excel workbook loads data from an Excel file by opening an interface window and allowing the selection of Excel files. This connector offers the same experience as it was described when connecting to a sample dataset. OneLake data hub allows connectivity to datasets available in Power BI Service cloud environment. Datasets are tabular models in cloud environment. By selecting the option `All`, we can find a list of every available organizational dataset to which we have access. Selecting the option `My data` shows personal datasets and selecting the option `Endorsed by your org` shows datasets that are promoted within the organization. Promoted datasets will often be designed by data engineers in larger organizations and will help you identify data models that are best suited for organizational analysis. Datasets are often formed in Power BI Desktop and are lifted and shifted to the cloud environment when we upload or publish a report. OneLake data hub also allows connectivity to Fabric data items. These are Datamarts, Lakehouses, and Warehouses, all relatively new features. Please note that at the time of writing in July 2023, Microsoft Fabric and its data items are still in preview.

SQL Server connector allows connecting on-premises SQL Server or SQL Server running on a cloud Virtual Machine. A cloud version alternative would be an Azure SQL database connector, which can connect to Azure SQL Database, a cloud resource that is distinct from SQL Server on Virtual Machine. We can define a server name, port number, and database name. Connectivity mode can be chosen, either Import or DirectQuery mode. We will discuss connectivity modes in later chapters. With Advanced options, we can define a timeout period which is the maximum wait time for a response in minutes. We can also specify a T-SQL query to run, and we can choose to Include relationship columns. This will allow us to add columns from connected tables and widen our table with data from connected tables. It could be useful if our analysis is limited in scope, and we don't want to create a star schema. Enabling failover support gives disaster recovery options by switching to a secondary server when the first one is not available. When connecting to any data source requiring credentials, we have to specify them.

Enter data option will allow a copy and paste experience. We can select either column or the first row and simply paste data. We can name our table. Selecting Load will load data into the tabular model. Selecting `Edit` will open Power Query Editor. Dataverse is a data storage consisting of tables and relationships and is used to store data of business applications. It has a common set of tables, metadata, and schemas, following the blueprint of the Common Data Model. Common Data Model was made by Microsoft and its partners to lessen the problems of integrating data between applications and systems. Recent sources will show us a list of sources we have last connected to.

Selecting the arrowed text Get data will show a list of data sources Microsoft considers common. There is an option to connect to Analysis Services by writing server and database names and choosing an import mode. Depending on whether we are connecting to a multidimensional cube or tabular model, we can specify MDX or DAX query. There are options to connect to Text/CSV, Web, and OData feeds. OData or Open Data Protocol is made to solve the problem of integration between services by using APIs. It allows access to web browsers, mobile devices, and desktop application data.

We can select an option Blank query if we are sufficiently knowledgeable in the M formula language and want to write a query. Selecting `More...` or pressing the icon above Get data will open an interface window allowing the selection of all data sources available in Power BI. We can filter data sources by categories File, Database, Power Platform, Azure, Online Services and Other. Under `Queries` section, we can access Power Query Editor by clicking `Transform data` option, in the menu seen in *Figure 2.9*:

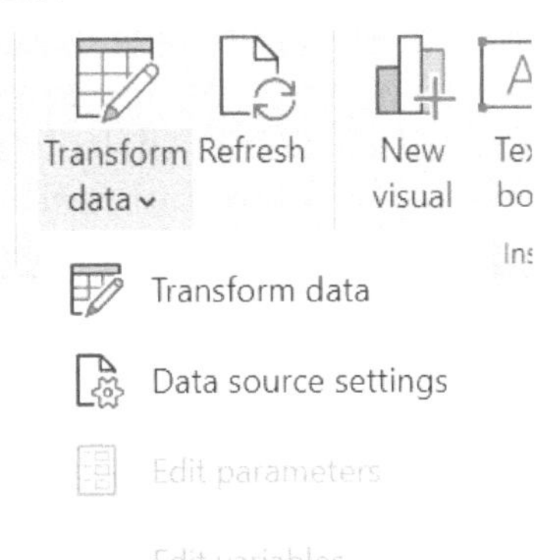

***Figure 2.9**: Query section of upper ribbon in Power BI desktop Home tab*

Power Query Editor can be accessed by clicking the icon above the text Transform data or by clicking the arrowed text and selecting `Transform data`. The drop-down list visible in *Figure* 2.9 offers some interesting options. Data source settings allow us to quickly change data source parameters, without having to go through each individual Power Query's query. Changing connection strings quickly is another advantage of using connectors.

Let's say that the hardware system hosting SQL Server is upgraded. Direct copy of objects was created by database administrators, but the SQL Server name did change. Updating Power BI reports is as simple as rewriting the server's name under `Data source` settings. Reports will immediately switch to the new server, ensuring that fresh data is being delivered. To change the server's name, we can select Data source settings, select an SQL Server data source from a list of sources, press on the `Change Source...` option on the bottom left of the interface window, and change the server's name.

The `Edit parameters` option only becomes available when we create parameters inside Power Query Editor. Parameters can store a value that can be referred to inside Power Query's query. Edit parameters allow us to quickly edit the values of created parameters. The `Refresh` option under the Queries section updates data for all connections made to data sources. We can automate refreshes when the report is published to Power BI Service.

Data sources in Excel

Excel offers an option to use Power Query. Power Query was first introduced as an add-in for Excel 2010 and Excel 2013. It was introduced as a native part of Excel in 2016. Power Query allows working with large datasets. We can avoid limitations present in an Excel sheet, where a limit of little more than a million rows of data exist. Nearing this limit and performing complex calculations can slow down Excel's performance.

Power Query can connect to millions of rows of data and load it directly into a data model to be used with Power Pivot. It allows us to quickly update data from connected data sources with a simple click of refresh button. Before Power Query was introduced, users were limited in their options to perform BI with Excel. They could bring data by copying and pasting it to Excel sheets. Excel formulas such as VLOOKUP might had had to be used to bring connected data with usage of keys. There was perhaps a need to aggregate data to avoid size limits in sheets. Connecting to data sources and loading data into Excel might have to be done with Visual Basic for Applications macros, which are automated procedures running a block of code. The process was complex, and Excel wasn't well suited for the creation of integrated data systems. Users could also have to rely on external systems' capabilities to export data or push data.

In Excel, we can access connectors and Power Query capabilities from the `Data` tab in the ribbon. There are connection options under `Get & Transform Data` categories and under `Queries & Connections`. The upper ribbon can be seen in *Figure 2.2*.

Interface window will appear when selecting an option under `Get & Transform Data`. Excel offers similar experience when connecting to data sources as Power BI. Selecting From Web can connect to web data sources such as website by providing URLs. Option From Table/Range allows loading of what's written in an Excel sheet as a data source to a data model. Selecting From Text/CSV will allow us to load a TXT or a CSV file. When selecting and opening a CSV file, we can choose encoding under File Origin. Encoding is a set of characters in a computer language that represents a symbol or a graphical character. Different types of encoding can be used depending on the geographical location of where the file was created. We can also select a delimiter, which is the symbol a file uses to separate columns. Data Type Detection refers to a number of columns that Power Query will analyze and assume data type for. Transform data option in Text/CSV connector will open Power Query Editor and Load will place data to newly created Excel sheet. Pressing the downward arrow next to Load gives the option of selecting Load To. This opens another interface allowing the selection of a few options, as seen in *Figure 2.10*:

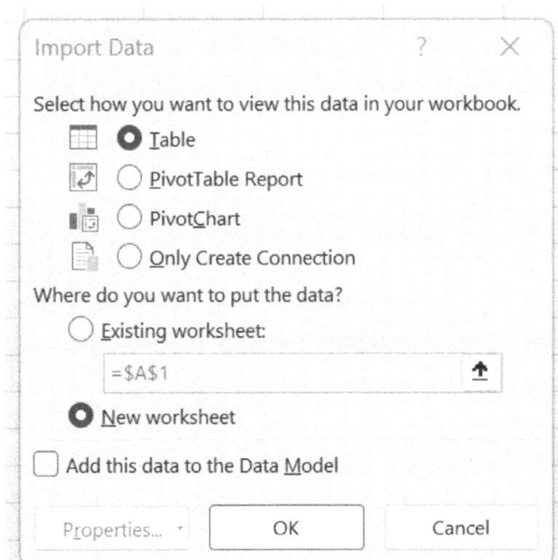

Figure 2.10: *Load To or Import Data options in Excel*

We have a couple of choices with data we're loading into Excel. We can view data as a Table, which will create a table in Excel sheet. PivotTable Report will load our data into Pivot Table format, allowing an input of columns, rows, or values to create Pivot Table. PivotChart is a graphical representation of the Pivot Table. We can choose a new or existing Excel sheet as an output for an object that's being created. An option **Only Create Connection** will not create any object, but it will create a connection and allow the user to select sequent action later. Add this data to the Data Model is a useful option when creating reports with Power Pivot.

In the Excel ribbon under the Data tab and Get & Transform Data section, an option Existing connections opens an interface window with a list of connections and tables. Double-clicking the connection will open Load To or Import Data interface as seen in *Figure 2.10*. From Picture connector is a new feature that loads a picture and analyses it using AI to extract text from selected pictures. We can then insert extracted text into an Excel sheet. Get Data opens a drop-down list, allowing the selection of several categories of connectors. These are `From File`, `From Database`, `From Azure`, `From Power Platform`, `From Online Services`, and `From Other Sources`. Each category has a list of several connectors. From the drop-down list, we can launch Power Query Editor, edit Data source settings (data connector's permissions, paths, or connection strings), and edit `Query Options`. Under the `Queries & Connections` section, we can refresh data from data sources and open the `Queries & Connections` side pane, presenting a list of created queries in a workbook. We can open Power Pivot Editor by double-clicking a query, while single clicking will locate the object in a workbook. Properties option becomes available with some objects such as table and Pivot Table allowing the editing of settings such as refresh control or data formatting and layout. The Edit link option becomes available with some objects such as a table based on SQL Server data source. The table is being updated with fresh data from the database, but we might unlink it as well if we preferred it to be static.

Data sources in other Microsoft resources

We can use Power Query in other Microsoft services. Power Query is divided in two major versions, first being an online version. Online version can be used with Microsoft Azure Data Lake Storage. It is intended to store and perform big data analytics and used for creating enterprise-sized data lakes. We can use Power Query with Microsoft Dataverse to load data to tables from a variety of data sources. Power Query can be used with Power Apps to create custom data models and applications based on data. Power Apps are a Microsoft development environment to create applications and workflows that help with everyday tasks. Microsoft labels ETL processes in a cloud environment as dataflows. Dataflows are stored in the cloud and offer more general data processing as opposed to application-specific experience within Power Query of Power BI or Excel. Services and resources can connect to these cloud-based dataflows. Dataflows offer a centralized experience regardless of the application and give us enterprise- or organizational-scale solutions when using cloud services. These dataflows can be used by data processing resources on the cloud like Azure Data Factory. We can create dataflow activity for ETL processes to bring and integrate data from data sources to the storage system.

Another version is Power Query offline, which is part of Excel and Power BI experience. We can also use Power Query in SQL Server Integration Services as a source. We can create a Power Query connection manager with information regarding the path of let's say an Excel document. We could use Power Query Editor in Power BI Desktop and perform transformations step-by-step and then copy the M formula language code that was created by Editor to Power Query Source. We have to be careful to avoid referencing any external custom functions as this will not work in the Power Query source. This will allow the usage of Formula Language M code to load data to the SQL Server database, which is very useful when transforming flat files, Excel documents, and data interchange formats. Power Query can be used within Visual Studio when creating tabular models for SQL Server Analysis Services. Under the `Tabular Model Explorer` view, we can find the Data Sources folder. Right-clicking the folder and `New Data Source` opens a similar interface window as the `Get Data` option in Power BI. We can choose the connector most suited for our usage.

Power Query Editor

Power Query Editor is a graphical user interface that offers an easier transformation experience compared to writing M formula language code. It should be well suited for most transformation needs. Many actions can be performed in Editor alone and it may be enough to finish data transformation without any code whatsoever. We will analyze the Power BI Desktop version of Power Query Editor. Different services may offer different experiences in some capacities. Updates can change options in ribbon and views, but nevertheless, general functionality should be similar to what's written in this overview.

Current view, Queries pane, and Home tab

Power Query is designed with step-by-step logic. Most transformations or actions result in the creation of a new step following the current one. This means that reversing changes is as simple as deleting the newly created step. *Figure 2.11* shows Power Query Editor with selected `Home` tab after we load the data from an on-premises SQL Server:

Figure 2.11: Power Query Editor

Ribbon offers similar experience as that of Power BI Desktop or other Microsoft applications. We can see several tabs, as well as Formula bar, showing only part of M formula language code related to the selected step in Power Query's query. On the left below the upper ribbon, we can see Queries pane. It shows created queries, parameters, and functions. Groups can be added by right-clicking in an empty space in the Queries pane and selecting `New Group...`. They act as folders and serve organizational purposes. When we right-click a query, we can see several options, including `Delete`, `Rename`, `Duplicate`, and `Advanced Editor`. The Advanced Editor shows the entire M formula language code related to the query and gives the option to modify it. Syntax highlighting and code completion are available. There are options to disable a load of the query to the tabular model by deselecting Enable load or to disable refresh of the query by deselecting `Include in report refresh`.

To the right of the Queries pane and below the upper ribbon, we can see the Current view. It shows a preview of rows and columns of data as it is transformed according to the currently selected step. Below the column names and above the rows, we can see the display of statistics for each column. To the left of the column name, there is a symbol for the data type. Clicking the symbol will open a drop-down list that offers a selection of the following data types:

Power Query data types		
Decimal number	date/time	duration
Fixed decimal number	date	text
whole number	time	true/false
percentage	date/time/timezone	binary

Table 2.4: *Power Query data types*

Option Using Locale in drop-down list is useful for dates that come in different localization formats. Downward arrow to the right of the column name offers filtering and sorting options, similar to those in Excel table. Right-clicking the column name brings up a drop-down list allowing many options. Removal and duplication of columns, removing errors, removing duplicates in rows, or replacing values and errors. Furthermore, there are mathematical transformations, such as Round, Square root, and Power. We can Group By column and Unpivot columns. Renaming of the column can be done by double-clicking the column name. Drag and drop can reorder the columns in a table. Clicking the table icon on the top right of the Current view above row numbering brings a drop-down list. We can add custom columns, keep, or remove rows, copy the entire table, and merge or append queries.

In the ribbon under the `Home` tab, there are options for working with data. Many options can be accessed from multiple places, either from tabs or from drop-down lists by right-clicking elements. `Close & Apply` option in `Home` tab allows different ways of exiting Power Query Editor, with or without applying changes. The `New Query` section in the `Home` tab offers connectivity to data sources or entry of data. Under the `Query` section, we can refresh the preview of either a single query or all queries. We can modify query Properties or view Advanced Editor. The `Manage` option allows deletion, duplication of query, and its usage as a reference. This will create another query with the first query as a source.

We can operate with columns under the `Manage Columns` section and with rows under the `Reduce Rows` section. Sorting is pretty clear by itself, while the `Transform` section offers some interesting options. Use First Row as Headers or Use Headers as First Row is useful when dealing with flat files. Replace values offers to replace any value in rows with another. Group by opens interface window to perform aggregations, for example, count of rows or sum of values in a column by values of another specified column. Split Columns can split by delimiter, position, number of characters when lowercase goes to upper and vice-versa, or when digit goes to non-digit and vice versa.

Under the `Combine` section, `Merge Queries` opens an interface that will allow the joining of two tables side-by-side with a key column common between tables. It works as SQL clause JOIN. Append Queries offers to join two or more tables with one below the other. It works as SQL operator UNION ALL. To successfully append columns, they should have the same names in both tables. If they have the same name but use different data types, columns will not be given a data type and will be introduced as any, meaning that they can hold all of the data types. Appending a different number of columns will create NULLs in rows of extra columns.

AI Insights requires signing in to an Organizational account. This offers **artificial intelligence (AI)** and machine learning capabilities, which may require premium Microsoft licenses. Machine learning is the new trend in data analysis where an automated process learns from a sample of data, analyzes variables, and then tries to predict patterns or future outcomes.

Other tabs in ribbon: Query Settings and Status bar

Steps created by transformations can be viewed in Query Settings on the right side of Power Query Editor. Query Settings allows selection of the named step, which updates the preview in Current view to the level of transformation it was done in the selected step. M formula language code for the selected step can be viewed from Formula bar. Query Settings appears as seen in *Figure 2.12*:

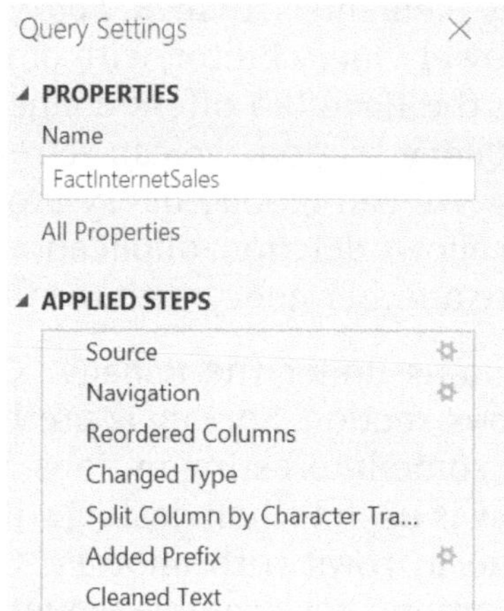

***Figure 2.12**: Query Settings view*

Connecting to SQL Server's database creates `Source` and `Navigation` steps. **Source** displays objects in SQL Server database and **Navigation** displays preview of data of the selected object. Right click an applied step will open some options, such as `Rename, Delete, Delete Until End,` and `Insert Step After`. We can drag and drop steps to change their order, but we have to be careful not to break the query's functionality.

Selecting the gear icon to the left of the step name allows editing of the step's settings. In the Source step of SQL Server connector, we can edit the Server name string and database name. Selecting the gear icon in Navigation gives the option of choosing an object in the SQL Server database. Gear icons in some other steps allow editing of transformation properties. If the query connects to a CSV file, we can change the file path with the gear icon. Connecting to some data sources such as SQL Server allows users to view queries in a native language such as T-SQL. This is done by right-clicking and selecting View Native Query.

On the bottom right of Power Query Editor, we can see the Status bar. We can see the number of columns. By selecting Column profiling based on the top 1000 rows, we can change it to the entire data set, which affects the number of rows Power Query will perform statistics on.

Other tabs are `Transform`, `Add Column`, `View`, `Tools`, and `Help`. In the `Tools` tab, the option `Query Diagnostics` can be accessed. It offers a way to find issues with our queries or data sources, allowing us to fix these problems. The Help section offers access to documentation, training videos, support, and other resources we might find useful. `Transform`, `Add Column`, and `View` tabs can be seen in *Figure 2.13*:

***Figure 2.13**: Transform, Add Column, and View tab in Power Query Editor's upper ribbon*

Transform tab offers the Transpose option which switches rows and columns in a table, so rows become columns and columns become rows. Reverse Rows switches order so the first row becomes last. Count Rows displays the row count result in a query. Under Any Column section, some of the options should be known to us. Fill will replace NULLs, Up option from the cell below and Down option from the cell above. Pivot and unpivot columns are operations with rows and columns. Selecting two columns and unpivoting them brings all the values together in one column called Value. Names of both columns are available in another column called Attribute, which is a description column. Unpivoting increases the number or rows and unpivoting more than two columns will flatten the table.

Pivoting is the opposite process and can be done with two columns. We can select a column and choose a value column in an interface window, while selecting an Aggregate Value Function such as sum or count. This splits the distinct values in rows of the selected column with each distinct value now representing a separate column. The rows are filled with aggregates from the value column depending on the chosen Aggregate Value Function. If the table consists of two columns, we'd end up with a single row with aggregate value. If the table consists of an additional column, aggregate values will be grouped by additional columns. Generally, we should expect fewer rows.

The Move option offers a few preset options to change the sequence of columns but drag and drop is probably more effective. Convert to List makes an M formula language data structure called list out of values from a single column. Format option gives ability to change values inside of a column either to uppercase, lowercase or to capitalize each word. We can add a prefix and a suffix before or after values in rows. We can trim text, which removes leading and trailing spaces, and clean text, which removes characters and symbols that aren't expected in descriptive texts, such as “"\t\#/LF”.

Merge Columns become available when multiple columns are selected, allowing us to merge them into a single column with an option to select delimiter between values. Extract option allows extracting first or last few characters or a range of characters. When extracting the range, we can define the length of extraction and the starting position (first character starts with number zero). With the Length option, the length of values will be written in every row. Extract also gives the option to extract text before, after or between delimiters.

Parse XML and parse JSON allows working with text strings and name-value pairs in these files. When we load a file to Power Query, several name-value pairs may be loaded to a single column. We can split these text strings to several columns and remove unnecessary symbols with these options.

Statistics can be used to show standard calculations of column values such as sum or average in Current view. Standard will perform mathematical operations with a single column, such as adding and multiplying values in rows. Scientific offers options like power and absolute value. There are Trigonometry and Rounding options, as well as Information options, that will show `TRUE` and `FALSE` in every row if the value of the row is even or if it is odd. Date & Time Column section is intended to extract parts of Date/Time data types and perform datetime related operations. Run R and Python script allows us to integrate these programming languages with Power Query capabilities. An example would be running a Python script that fills NULLs based on averages by some other values, for example an average of values from only from the related time period.

Add Columns tab offers many of the familiar options. General section has an option to add calculated columns to our table. Columns From Examples allows the creation of a new column by typing values in every row. AI will try to figure the pattern and create a column based on the pattern. We can use either all or selected columns as reference based on which AI performs pattern recognition. Custom Column opens an interface window which allows selection of columns and preformation of calculations with column values. An Example is addition, by writing the expression: `=[Column1] + [Column2]`.

Invoke Custom Function offers the option to call a function and apply it for each row. Functions in Power Query are used for similar purposes as in other programming languages. We can re-use and re-apply a piece of written code in multiple scripts or queries. Conditional column opens an interface window for writing conditions, starting with an if. Column name, operator, value, and output can all be written. An example of a statement written could be: If UnitPrice (Column Name) is greater than (Operator) 2000 (Value we specify) Then "Expensive item" (Output we specify). Text can be written without any quotations. We can specify the column name of the newly calculated conditional column, add another if clause and specify Else. Instead of values, columns can be selected when supplying Value and Output parameters. Adding an index column adds a numbered columns starting with either 0 or 1. We can customize it by supplying starting index and increment.

View tab allows showing or hiding Power Query Editor panes and views. Query Settings options opens the view on the right side of Power Query Editor where applied steps can be seen. Formula bar shows area above Current view where a M formula language code is visible for the selected step. We can edit the code in Formula bar. Under Data preview section, we can add statistics that appear below column names or under Current view, depending on the option selected. Column quality and distribution give us statistical information about data in our columns below column names, based either on 1000 rows or an entire data set. Scale of statistics option can be modified at the bottom left of the Power Query Editor in Status bar.

Distinct values represent a number of different values appearing in our column, while unique values are those that appear only once. More detailed statistical view of a single column can be viewed by selecting Column profile and choosing a column. Monospaced option changes font in data, while Show whitespace will display characters such as spaces, tabs, and line breaks in data. Query dependencies option allows us to view a diagram of what data sources we are using and what queries run from these data sources. If a query is based on another query, such dependency should be displayed as well. Parameters and information on query's loading into a model are also visible.

Conclusion

If we want to increase our capacity for performing data analysis, we should learn how to use tools such as Power Query Editor to perform data processing or ETL process. Power Query Editor allows users to perform data transformation and data cleaning. It is integrated in both Power BI and Excel. We can also use it to create a data warehouse together with tools such as SQL Server Integration Services or to create tabular models with Visual Studio and SQL Server Analysis Services. In an enterprise environment, we should be striving towards creating integrated data systems with as much automatization as possible – ideally a completely automated system. Any manual labor in data analytics can lead to outdated information and is prone to human error. Connecting to data sources and using Power Query to perform data processing is not as hard as it once was by using legacy technology. Increasing simplicity is in line with trends in democratizing analytics and making analytics available as a self-service tool. It does require some learning, discipline and trial before one can become efficient in using new technologies. When a problem arises while using these technologies, we can resort to Google searching and using AI such as ChatGPT to help us solve it.

In the next chapter, we are going to expand further into the topic of Power Query and perform some data transformation examples. We are going to look into M formula language and perform some transformations by using its functions. This should provide enough information to start using technology in real life scenarios and to understand how we get to the state where we can perform calculations on our data and create visualizations.

Key terms

- **Data interchange format**: Files such as XML, JSON and CSV that offer a way to exchange data between systems. They are standardized in a sense of syntax and structure.
- **Integrated data system**: Data systems that are connected from data sources to end reports. They are referred to as integrated because they format data to the same standard. The number of elements they consist of may vary and they could be highly automated.
- **Tabular model**: Microsoft branding of columnar storage, a highly compressed database that offers good filtering for analysis and offers embedded calculations.
- **Data processing**: Holds a similar meaning to extracting, transforming, and loading of data. It doesn't define the sequence of these processes and it's a broader term. It might also include operations with data and analysis of data. In this chapter, data processing and ETL generally refer to the same thing.
- **Power Query**: A tool provided with Microsoft Excel, Power BI Desktop and some other Microsoft resources that can perform ETL process with data from data sources. It is based on M formula language.
- **Power Query Editor**: A graphical user interface that offers users ability to perform transformations in a friendly manner without writing code. Transformations are performed step-by-step, allowing users to modify any of the subsequent steps.

Questions

1. Why is classic Excel functionality limited with data analysis?
2. Why should we connect to data sources?
3. What are data interchange formats and when can we expect such files?
4. What are key characteristics of integrated data systems?
5. What are some key elements of Power Query?
6. Why should we use Power Query Editor?

CHAPTER 3

Power Query Transformations and Formula Language (M) Overview

Introduction

We've gotten to know the basic data connectivity in Excel and Power BI using Power Query. Power Query allows us to integrate BI tools with data sources – a step in building an integrated data system. In this chapter, we will expand further on the topics regarding Power Query and we'll look at some additional features to cement our understanding. We'll start with a data transformation exercise where we'll imagine that we received a data interchange format that we need to transform for analyzing. Throughout the chapter, we'll return to the transformation example to showcase what can be done with Power Query. We've already seen what the Power Query Editor looks like and made an overview of its functionality. Transformations done in exercises shouldn't be too much of a novelty, but rather a way to reinforce our comprehension of the subject with some practical examples. After our transformation process is completed, we'll take a look into the M Formula Language in the Advanced Editor. We'll overview the rules, the functions, the data structures, and the general syntax of M language. We'll try to optimize the code, not so much in the sense of increasing the speed, but rather in the sense of increasing its organization. We want our code to be well-organized and readable to our teammates. Throughout the chapter, we'll focus on obtaining a deeper understanding of Power Query's functionality and features by expanding on what we've learned in the previous chapter.

Structure

In this chapter, we will discuss the following topics:

- Data transformation exercise
- Power Query Formula Language (M) Overview
- Improvement of M code from the Exercise

Data transformation exercise

We've received a complex CSV file on a remote location, and we want to analyze it with Power BI. The CSV we'll be analyzing has the same structure as to what we could expect in a real-life scenario, but it's lesser in size and number of rows. These CSV files could contain several million rows of data and could reach gigabytes in size. The data represents monthly sales of five items of a multinational electronics retailer. The CSV contains six markets, and these six markets have 56 organizations. We would prefer connecting directly to an OLTP behind the retailer sales system, but there could be several reasons preventing us: It might be a legacy system, for which engineers haven't designed an API, there might be data privacy issues so we're not given direct access, or these are daily pushes and latest data only becomes available so late in the morning, that administrators don't allow connecting to a system which would risk burdening it. In any case, we have a CSV file that we want to transform.

Let's transform the CSV file

If you want to follow along with the exercise, Complex CSV.csv is provided with this book. We can open the file to check its contents. In a real-life environment, it might be advisable to open any CSV files with Notepad++ instead of Excel. There are a couple of reasons for this: Firstly, to avoid Excel internal limitations of a little more than a million rows, secondly Excel might attempt unusual data type conversions depending on the regional settings, and thirdly Excel tends to lock the file for all other users. The file may be accessed by various users, both human users and system-based entities, and they might be locked-out or prevented from modifying the file. Notepad++ generally doesn't lock the file. If changes are made to a file while it is opened in Notepad++, the user who opened the file is informed that changes were made to the file and prompted if he wants to reload it. If a file's dataset includes many rows and is large, Notepad++ might freeze if our computer has a relatively limited size of RAM. This can usually be resolved by closing and re-opening the file. Excel is much quicker in slowing down a computer's performance while opening a large flat file.

We can see how Complex CSV's data looks in *Figure* 2.5 of the previous chapter, when opened in Notepad++. The overview of data when loaded into Power Query will be visible in *Figure* 3.1. By opening a data interchange format in Notepad++, some insights regarding data structure and format can be immediately spotted. We should already have an idea about how to connect to a CSV file from Power BI Desktop:

1. Under the **`Home`** tab's Data section, we can select the text of Get data with an arrow and then Text/CSV. In the interface window, we should navigate to the folder containing `Complex CSV.csv`, select it and click **`Open`** on the bottom right of the interface window.

   Our data is delimited by semicolon ";", which is standard in some European language variants. Text/CSV connector should select the right encoding and delimiter - under File Origin, selected encoding is Unicode (UTF-8) and Delimiter is Semicolon. Unicode is an encoding standard that is supposed to encode characters from almost every writing system, with the number of characters currently around 150 thousand. We can see that our data is not in suitable format – it contains redundant data. We can spot some characters and symbols that we don't need, as well as extra descriptive rows at the beginning.

2. We should select **`Transform Data`** at the bottom right of the interface window to open Power Query Editor. A preview of the first six columns is visible in *Figure* 3.1 in a view that should be known to us:

	Column1	Column2	Column3	Column4	Column5	Column6
1	Export for analysis					
2	Organization ID selected id from 100 to 155					
3	Period from 01.6.2023 to 31.6.2023					
4	Item id is 102301, 114212, 121191, 130165, 130250					
5	Market is NL, DE, PL, CZ, AT, CH					
6	ORGANIZATION/MARKET/ITEM/QUANTITY/PRICE					
7	=<Organization ID>	=<Market name>	=<Item id>	=<Item name>	=<Item type>	=<Color>
8	=<100>	=<NL>	=<102301>	=<GeForce RTX 4090>	=<Graphics card>	=<Black>
9	=<101>	=<NL>	=<102301>	=<GeForce RTX 4090>	=<Graphics card>	=<Black>
10	=<102>	=<NL>	=<102301>	=<GeForce RTX 4090>	=<Graphics card>	=<Black>
11	=<103>	=<NL>	=<102301>	=<GeForce RTX 4090>	=<Graphics card>	=<Black>
12	=<104>	=<NL>	=<102301>	=<GeForce RTX 4090>	=<Graphics card>	=<Black>
13	=<105>	=<NL>	=<102301>	=<GeForce RTX 4090>	=<Graphics card>	=<Black>
14	=<106>	=<NL>	=<102301>	=<GeForce RTX 4090>	=<Graphics card>	=<Black>
15	=<107>	=<NL>	=<102301>	=<GeForce RTX 4090>	=<Graphics card>	=<Black>
16	=<108>	=<NL>	=<102301>	=<GeForce RTX 4090>	=<Graphics card>	=<Black>
17	=<109>	=<NL>	=<102301>	=<GeForce RTX 4090>	=<Graphics card>	=<Black>
18	=<110>	=<NL>	=<102301>	=<GeForce RTX 4090>	=<Graphics card>	=<Black>

***Figure* 3.1**: *Complex CSV loaded into Power Query*

3. Under **`Query Settings`** on the right side of Power Query, two steps can be spotted: **`Source`** and **`Changed Type`**. The latter step is Power Query assuming data types of columns, but in case of Complex CSV's format, it assumes Text data type for all columns. We can delete this step.

If we wanted, we could prevent Power Query from automatically assuming data types, by selecting the File tab in Power Query Editor's ribbon, then Options and settings under the drop-down list and lastly Options. These options should be the same as those accessed from Power BI Desktop's ribbon under **`File`** tab. Options are divided between GLOBAL, which are general settings and CURRENT FILE, which are settings for the report we're working on. Under the **`Data Load`** tab of GLOBAL, we can select an option **`Never detect column types and headers for unstructured sources`** and under the **`Data Load`** tab of CURRENT FILE, we can deselect Detect column types and headers for unstructured sources. Excel offers similar settings.

4. We can remove the first six rows of descriptions to get to tabular format. To do this, we should click the option **`Remove Rows`** under the **`Home`** tab and **`select Remove Top Rows`**. Under **`Number of rows`**, type **`6`** and click **`OK`**.

   At this point we could perform additional data profiling within Power Query Editor. Data profiling means analyzing data to see how it looks, how it is formatted, what topics it contains, and getting any other information regarding data we might need. If we opened a CSV file in Notepad++, some data profiling could've been done there, by moving through the file and checking it. In an integrated data system, data profiling might include checking on data sources, what tables and columns they contain, how data might be retrieved from data sources and in what formats, what are columns' data types, what are existing or possible relationships between tables, etc. Furthermore, data profiling might include assessing metadata, statistics, and quality. If data is of poor quality, it might be a good idea to find a way of improving it in the data source system instead of risking bad results or trying to fix it later in the transformation process. Data profiling can be a very important step when preparing integrated data systems, because it allows understanding of what we're dealing with. Without correct information regarding data, we might set the wrong completion schedules, there is a possibility of incurring additional costs, and worst of all, clients might not be happy with the results of our work.

   Remember, data profiling in Power Query Editor can be performed by going to the **`View`** tab and selecting **`Column distribution`**, **`Column profile`** and **`Column quality`** under the Data preview section. If we're dealing with a large dataset, we can change to **`Column profiling based on entire data set`** in the Status bar at the bottom-left of Power Query Editor. But before we can get the most accurate information from data preview options, we should clean up data first. We want to get rid of excess symbols, such as "=, < and >" and we want to promote the first row to headers.

5. To do that, find **`Replace Values`** under **Home** tab in Power Query Editor. But first remember to select all the columns, as **`Replace Values`** will only perform its operation on selected columns. We can select all the columns with *Ctrl* + A shortcut. In the interface window of **`Replace Values`**, write **`=<`** under **`Value to Find`** and leave **`Replace With`** as a blank. Press **OK** when you're done. Do the same with the symbol ">".

   If we're dealing with an unknown data interchange format, we might want to search the file for any symbols we're replacing with the help of Notepad++, to ensure that we're not unwittingly distorting or altering data. We can bring up the Find window in Notepad++ with a *Ctrl* + F shortcut.

6. In the next step, we want to promote headers by selecting the **Home** tab and clicking **`Use First Row as Headers`**.

   These transformations will provide a much cleaner dataset, although it isn't perfect yet. We still need to define the data types and there are decimal commas and € signs to deal with in the columns with prices. We can select Column distribution, Column profile and Column quality in the View tab. *Figure* 3.2 shows the current stage of the transformation for the last six columns:

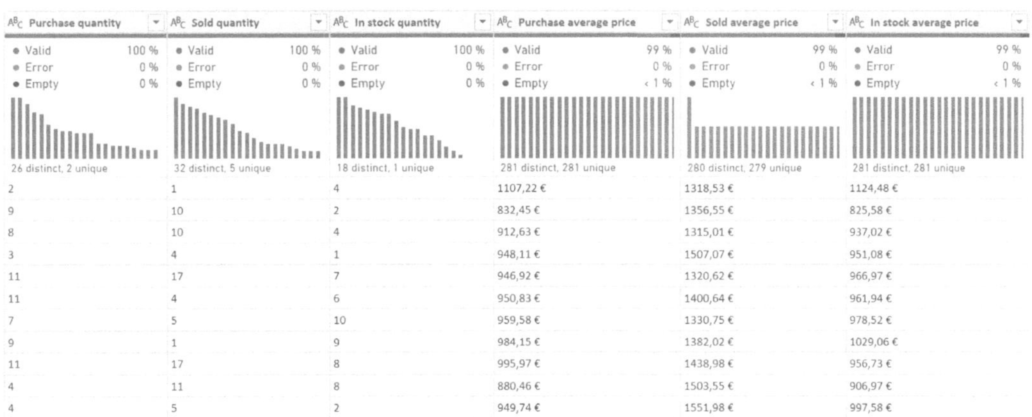

Purchase quantity	Sold quantity	In stock quantity	Purchase average price	Sold average price	In stock average price
• Valid 100 % • Error 0 % • Empty 0 %	• Valid 100 % • Error 0 % • Empty 0 %	• Valid 100 % • Error 0 % • Empty 0 %	• Valid 99 % • Error 0 % • Empty < 1 %	• Valid 99 % • Error 0 % • Empty < 1 %	• Valid 99 % • Error 0 % • Empty < 1 %
26 distinct, 2 unique	32 distinct, 5 unique	18 distinct, 1 unique	281 distinct, 281 unique	280 distinct, 279 unique	281 distinct, 281 unique
2	1	4	1107,22 €	1318,53 €	1124,48 €
9	10	2	832,45 €	1356,55 €	825,58 €
8	10	4	912,63 €	1315,01 €	937,02 €
3	4	1	948,11 €	1507,07 €	951,08 €
11	17	7	946,92 €	1320,62 €	966,97 €
11	4	6	950,83 €	1400,64 €	961,94 €
7	5	10	959,58 €	1330,75 €	978,52 €
9	1	9	984,15 €	1382,02 €	1029,06 €
11	17	8	995,97 €	1438,98 €	956,73 €
4	11	8	880,46 €	1503,55 €	906,97 €
4	5	2	949,74 €	1551,98 €	997,58 €

Figure 3.2: *The current stage of the transformation of Complex CSV file*

   We can notice there are some empty rows in several columns. We can analyze that a little further by checking distinct values. We can click the downward arrow next to the column name, which offers a similar filtering experience as you would expect of the Excel table.

7. If we select the downward arrow next to the **Organization ID** column and scroll down, we can see there is a **`TOTAL`** value at the bottom of the list. System that extracted the data interchange format included totals,

which will not be needed in our dataset. We can deselect **TOTAL** and press **OK**.

In real-life scenarios, we should carefully analyze the files already when opening them in Notepad++. For example, searching for the keywords *total* or *sum* in the **Find** window. Check the find options carefully, such as to deselect Match whole word only, Match case, and to select Wrap around. This way Find will search for partial words, will not be case sensitive and will search wrapped lines in case that Word wrap is applied. Word wrap option will fit a single line to the size of the application window.

Now onto our final data cleaning task - dealing with prices which use comma decimal separators and show the € (Euro currency) symbol. In some European language variants, we could simply change the data type to Decimal Number, and Power Query will automatically remove the "€" symbol. But if our language variant uses decimal points, changing these columns to Decimal Number will generate an error in each row. Power BI Desktop uses the formats for dates and numbers according to Windows Region settings. We can, however, edit localization for each report or file, by going to the Options in File tab, either in Power Query or Power BI Desktop. Under CURRENT FILE, select Regional Settings to change Locale for import. That's a pretty good option if we're creating reports for several regions with different localizations.

1. Assuming that our Locale for import is English (United States) and we don't want to change it, we can simply select the three columns with prices (Purchase average price, Sold average price, and In stock average price) and select an option **Replace Values**. Under **Value To Find**, type "," and under **Replace With** type ".". This language variant doesn't know how to deal with € signs, so we should replace those as well. Again with all three columns selected, write "**€**" in **Value to Find** (notice the space) and leave **Replace With** as blank.

2. We can now select all the columns and select the option **Detect Data Type** under **Transform** tab. This will now create a **Changed Type** step that we've deleted at the very beginning of our transformations. All the columns should be of the correct data type and there shouldn't be a need to change each one individually.

If we check the statistics under **Column Quality** view below column names, we'll notice there are still some empty values left. Selecting the downward arrow next to the Color column shows all available values. Deselecting the (**Select All**) option, selecting the (blank) option, and pressing **OK** shows us the NULLs. Remember, this filtration created a new step under **APPLIED STEPS** of Query Settings. In the Item name column, we can see there are a couple of processors without color. Probably, a color attribute or variable wasn't provided for products that ship with a single color only. We could leave that as it is, but it might not look good in visualizations. If we followed along, we should delete the last step Filtered Rows1 as it is no longer needed.

1. With only the **Color** column selected, open **Replace Values** and leave **Value** to Find as blank, while typing **Not available** in **Replace With**.

This should be the end of basic transformations of Complex CSV file - data should now be in a suitable format to perform further analysis on. In the next part of this chapter, we'll take a look into the M formula language behind our transformation and try to understand its structure and syntax. We'll see if there is any way to better organize our query.

Power Query Formula Language (M) Overview

According to Microsoft, the idea behind Power Query is to combine data from multiple sources and to filter data into its subset. This functionality could be described with the word "mashup", so that is to mashup data from several data sources. We've also seen that the language is effective for connecting to various data sources, transforming and cleaning data, and loading data to a data model. Actions in Power Query Editor and interface windows when connecting to data sources generate M formula language code. The building blocks of M language are variables and expressions performing single or several actions. The results of the expressions are assigned to variables. Entire code that is written is encompassed in the let/in statement. After the let statement, all the variables connected with expressions are written. After the in statement, the variable that is the result of the query is defined. The in statement evaluates the expression of the variable defined, which in turn evaluates all the other expressions needed to get to the defined variable. This is an example of M language code:

```
let
   variable = "expression with function taking a parameter"
,  variable2 = "expression with a function taking variable as a parameter"
,  variable3 = "expression with a function taking variable2 as a parameter"
in
  variable3 // a final result of the code
```

Although variables can be written in any order in the let statement and any variable might be chosen to be the final result of a code, writing it in this orderly fashion benefits both a developer and Power Query tool. A developer can easily see what is going on when code is presented in orderly fashion, while Query Settings in Power Query Editor will display steps correctly under **APPLIED STEPS**.

However, M formula language doesn't care about the order, as code is being evaluated from bottom-up or from an end to beginning. M formula language will first evaluate whatever is written after the in statement, in our example that is **`variable3`**. To evaluate **`variable3`**, it will need to evaluate **`variable2`** and to evaluate **`variable2`**, it will need to evaluate **`variable`**.

Steps start with a variable and end with a comma ("**`,`**"), except for the last step before the in statement. We've written commas before sequent steps 2 and 3, because this seemed to be a more practical and efficient way to organize the code. Commas could've been written at the end of step 1 and 2 as well, but not at the end of step 3 before the in statement, as this would generate an error. Equal sign ("**`=`**") is an assignment operator, which assigns expression to a variable that stores its result. It is most commonly expected that every subsequent step takes a variable from a step before as a parameter, although this isn't a necessity. Besides a variable, functions in expressions might take other parameters, such as text values, functions, or data structures. From our example, we can clearly see how data progresses through a series of expressions until it reaches the final stage. Comments in a code can be included by "**`//`**" for single-line comments or "**`/*`**" and "**`*/`**" for multi-line comments.

Selecting any step in Query Settings of Power Query Editor will provide an overview of that step in the Current view. If we display Formula Bar by going to the View tab and selecting it, Formula Bar will show only an expression beginning with the assignment operator, but not the variable name itself. The step name represents the variable name. A query's whole code can be viewed in Advanced Editor. In newer versions of Excel and Power BI, Advanced Editor shows IntelliSense, which is a drop-down window predicting code as it is being written, and syntax highlighting. At the time of writing (May 2023), the newest version of Power BI offers IntelliSense and syntax highlighting in Formula Bar as well. Office 365 Excel has them as well, but Excel 2019 from MS Office Professional Plus 2019 doesn't offer IntelliSense or syntax highlighting in either Advanced Editor or Formula Bar. Writing M formula language without those might be a problem. We could write it in Power BI's Advanced Editor and then copy the query to older MS products, or we could use code editors such as Visual Studio Code coupled with extensions.

> **Note**
>
> *Visual Studio Code is a lightweight code editor by Microsoft that supports development with a range of programming languages. Installer can be downloaded from* ***https://code.visualstudio.com/download****. We can select either User or System installer, difference being the default installation path, either* **C:\Users*username*** *or* **C:\Program Files***. We can download extensions inside Visual Studio Code by selecting the extensions symbol at the right ribbon. Look for the following icon:* 
>
> *Search for Power Query/M Language and press Install. At the time of writing, this extension offers proper IntelliSense, including parameter info, and syntax highlighting. Additional language support can be added from extensions as well, such as for Python.*
>
> *Notepad++ also offers custom language definitions for syntax highlighting, although adding custom languages is a little harder. There is a detailed description available on how to add it here:* ***https://community.powerbi.com/t5/Community-Blog/Get-your-own-Power-Query-Editor-using-Notepad/ba-p/146347***

M language is case sensitive, as opposed to two other languages by Microsoft commonly used for data analysis: T-SQL and DAX. Because of case-sensitivity, we need to take extra caution when writing code: Meaning that **`Text.Proper`** does not equal **`text.proper`** or **`TEXT.PROPER`**. We have to be careful about case-sensitivity not only with functions, but with variables and filter conditions as well. The variable **`ReplaceValue`** does not equal the variable **`replacevalue`**.

Elements and Data Structures in M

Single values in M formula language are called primitive values. There are several types of them: A number consists of both whole numbers (**`100`**) and decimal number (**`100.5`**), a logical consist of true and false and a text is a string of characters (**"`Hello world`"**). There are also dates consisting of year, month, and day and times consisting of hours, minutes, and seconds. Datetime brings all of these periods together. We could further expand datetimes with zones, by adding hours and minutes offset. As for datetime-related values, there is also duration, consisting of days, hours, minutes, and seconds. There are NULLs written as **`null`**, and binaries, or sequence of bytes. Binaries can be opened in Power Query Editor in several ways, either by Excel Workbook, as a Text File, CSV Document, Html Page, or JSON.

There are three main data structures in M formula language, the first one is a list. A list is a sequence of elements, starting and ending with the symbols "**{**" and "**}**". A list is ordered and can contain varying lengths. Second, data structure is a record, which is described as a set of fields. We could also imagine a record as a table with a single row, although not technically correct, or as dictionaries in some programming languages like Python. Records are enclosed in symbols "**[**" and "**]**". They consist of name-value pairs, meaning that we can define a field name, such as "**Color**" and assign it a field value, such as ""**Black**"". Last, there are tables, which consist of named columns and rows. Tables are created with a function #table, with the first parameter taking a list of column names, and the second parameter taking a list containing several lists. The inner lists hold values for each column and a multitude of them represent all the rows.

It is possible to contain or nest data structures within other data structures, such as records within records, records within lists, lists within lists, lists within a table's column etc. We can index lists by adding a position number enclosed in "**{}**". The index count starts with 0 for the first element. Adding several of those will index a list within a list, for example **{0}{0}** showing the first element of the first list. A record can be indexed by writing a field name in square brackets "**[]**". Similarly, as with lists, a record within a record can be indexed by referring to the field name in the outer record and then to the field name in the inner record, as it can be seen in the following example: "**[TotalSales][January]**". Indexing a table is a combination of both, columns are being indexed similarly as names in records, while rows are being indexed in a similar fashion as elements within a list. An example being "**[Organization ID]{0}**". We can see the following example of M code for several of the elements and data structures we've described:

```
let
// Primitive values
    Number = 15
,   Number2 = 15.5
,   Text = "Hello world"
,   Date = #date(2023, 5, 18)
,   Time = #time(15, 45, 30)
,   DateTime = #datetime(2023, 5, 18, 15, 45, 30)
,   DateTime2 = Date & Time
,   DateTimeZone = #datetimezone(2023, 5, 18, 15, 45, 30, +1, 0)
,   Duration = #duration(0, 22, 30, 30)
,   Logical = false
,   NULLs = null
// Data structures
,   List = {1, "hello", true}
```

```
,    Record = [First = 500, Second = 200, Third = 300]
,    Table = #table({"Organization ID", "Item name", "Sold quantity"},
         { {100, "CPU", 83}, {101, "GPU", 67}, {102, "RAM", 143} })
,    List_within_List = { {1, 2}, {3, 4}, {5, 6}, {7, 8} }
,    Record_within_Record = [ First = [ a = 4, b = 5, c = a + b], Second
= 14, Third = 23]
in
     Record_within_Record
```

We could display each of these in the Current view of Power Query Editor, by selecting the step under APPLIED STEPS, if we wanted. Evaluating a variable holding primitive values will display that value. A list will be shown similarly as a single-column table. The range of options when dealing with a list is much smaller compared to when dealing with a table. For example, we can't change the data type of a list as we could change the table's column data type. A record is shown in the Current view as a set of rows split into two parts, with the left part showing field names and the right part showing field values. Both of these might be converted to a table. A list can be converted by right clicking the word List, which appears in the same area where columns would in a table, and then selecting To Table. A record can be converted by right-clicking in a part where values are displayed and selecting Into Table. Right-clicking values in both a list and a record will allow selection of Drill Down, which functions in the same fashion as indexing.

List within a list would display the phrase **List** for each element in the Current view instead of a value. Selecting the cell with a list will display the preview of the inner list at the bottom of the Current view. Clicking the phrase **List** will drill down to the inner list. Records within records work in a similar fashion. The phrase **Record** would be displayed, selecting a cell would display the preview and selecting the phrase would drill down. In *Figure* 3.3 we can see the example of a table, containing lists in the first column, records in the second column and tables in the third column. We can also see the preview as it would appear at the bottom of the Current view when a cell with a table is selected:

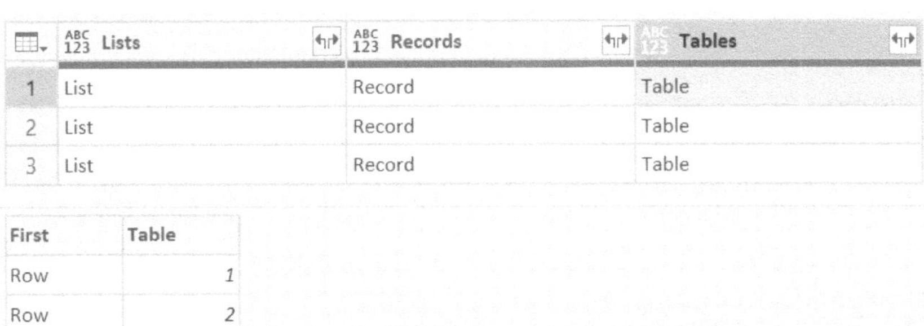

***Figure* 3.3**: *Table with other data structures within as seen in the Current view*

The following code is used to generate table with data structures from *Figure* 3.3:

```
let
    Table_with_data_structures = #table
    (
        {"Lists", "Records", "Tables"},
        {
            { {"a", "first", "list"}, [First = 1, Record1 = 101],
                #table({"First", "Table"}, { {"Row", 1}, {"Row", 2} } )
            },
            { {"a", "second", "list"}, [Second = 2, Record2 = 202],
                #table({"Second", "Table"}, { {"Row", 3}, {"Row", 4} } )
            },
            { {"a", "third", "list"}, [Third = 3, Record3 = 303],
                #table({"Third", "Table"}, { {"Row", 5}, {"Row", 6} } )
            }
        }
    )
in
    Table_with_data_structures
```

At the right of each column name in *Figure* 3.3, we can see the expand symbol that might be important in some cases. This expansion is similar in functionality as when combining multiple files using Folder connector. Folder connector allows connecting of several files with a similar structure together to a single dataset. In our example, expanding the lists by selecting the expand symbol on the left of the column and selecting Expand to New Rows, will create a row for each distinct element of each list. After expansion, the tables and records in the same row as the list will repeat as many times as there are elements in the list we've expanded. In our case, there are three elements in each list, an expansion will generate nine rows with each of the records and tables repeating three times.

Expanding records and tables will generate additional columns. Selecting the expand symbol in Records and Tables columns displays a pop-up window allowing us the selection of all the field names or columns we want to expand. There may be a warning informing us that the List may be incomplete. Selecting Load more will identify all the columns. The option Use original column name as prefix is pretty clear, it will repeat the original column name before the name of all the expanded columns or the field names. With each record containing two names and two values and each of the names being distinct, expanding the Records column will delete the original column and add six new columns. The situation with tables is slightly different. Each of the three tables in the Tables column have only the first column name as distinct, while the second column name is the same in all three tables. Each table contains two rows. Expanding the Tables columns results in four new columns, three for each of the distinctly named first columns and 1 with combined data of all the second columns. This expands the number of rows to 6.

We can also convert a table's column to a list, by right-clicking a column header and selecting Drill Down. In our example table with data structures, converting the Lists column creates lists within a list data structure.

Functions and data types in M

Functions are at the center of Power Query and M formula language. Expressions mainly consist of one or more functions performing a specific action or a task with input parameters. The output is stored in a variable. It is through the use of functions that we perform changes to an input, which is very often a data structure. Input is usually put through several expressions until it reaches the final stage of the transformation and we get the desired result.

Variables hold the results of expressions or the outputs. They identify the step containing all transformations up to that point. In a sense, these variables are fixed and once a variable with a certain name is used, it can't be reused. There is a possibility to connect a record data structure to an outer variable. A record data structure being an expression, it can contain sub-expressions. Within a record containing sub-expressions, we might reuse the variables with the same name as the variable on the outside of the record structure. The innermost variable of the two variables with the same name is evaluated first.

Power Query is a functional language. This refers to programming paradigms, which are styles of programming or ways to structure one's code. From a high-level perspective, functional programming is paradigmatically opposed to imperative programming. Functional and imperative programming paradigms could be further divided into subsets. Different programming paradigms might include different thought processes a programmer would have to go through to shape his code accordingly in order to achieve the desired result. In technical terms, the programming paradigm affects how calculations resulting from functions are being performed. An example being a sum of a set of numbers. Functional language calculates without changing the state of underlying data. In an example of a sum function, a set of numbers could be split into individual numbers and then their addition would be performed. In imperative programming, the state of data could change, a sum of a set of numbers could be performed using iterators with a variable saving each partial addition and thus changing with each iteration.

Note

There are over 700 pre-built functions. These are split into categories depending on their functionality, such as accessing data, combiner, date, list, number, record, table, text, and value functions. We'll take a look at some of these functions in Table 3.1. All of these categories can be viewed and expanded in Microsoft documentation accessed from the following link: ***https://learn.microsoft.com/en-us/powerquery-m/power-query-m-function-reference****. Each category contains a multitude of functions that can be selected and viewed in the documentation. Pages in the documentation for each of the functions explain what a function does and what arguments or parameters it takes.*

It's possible to view the list of all functions inside Power Query Editor while inside a query. We first need to make sure that the Formula Bar is visible by going to View tab and selecting Formula Bar. After that, we might add a new step by selecting the icon on the left side of Formula Bar that adds a new step:

After that, we may write the following command:

```
= #shared
```

After the command has been typed, we can press the *Enter* key or a checkmark next to Add Step. In the Current view, a record structure appears, with field names being function names on the left part of the screen, and field values being function types that can be further drilled down. Selecting a cell with a function shows the preview at the bottom of Current view. We may see a function's signature with a parameter list and a description.

Drilling down into a function by clicking **`Function`** phrase in field values will display a function's information window, with description, parameter list and examples. There is also an interface window where we may enter parameters and even invoke some of the functions, which creates a new query. It might be useful to look around "**`= #shared`**" command next time we're in Power Query Editor to see what are the functions available. Below we can see the example of the function with parameter list:

```
Table.RemoveColumns(table as table, columns as any, optional
missingField as nullable number) as table
```

This function's action is pretty clear by itself, it removes columns from a table. Functions in M formula language are pretty clearly named, with the first part of the name before the dot usually being an object that the function is affecting, and the second part of the name being an action that's being performed. We can see the parameter list, with this function taking three parameters: A table that it is affecting, of table data structure. This parameter will often be a variable from the previous step. The second parameter is columns we're trying to remove. It is described as any, which isn't actually a data type, but rather it shows that it can hold any data type. We would usually supply either a text value or a list of text values as column names. The third parameter is optional, and it tells the function how to behave when the column specified for the second parameter does not exist. For a data type, we can see that it takes a nullable number. **`MissingField.Type`** is the function this parameter refers to. Leaving it blank, writing a NULL or a zero produces an error when specifying the wrong column name, while 1 and 2 allows the operation without errors.

We've already read about data types available in Power Query in the previous chapter. We'll expand it a little further here. In M formula language, any of the distinct primitive values is considered its own data type, for example date, datetime, number, text and binary. We also have data types with data structures, namely record, list and table. As we might have noticed in an example with #shared command, functions are considered a type as well. There is also a logical type, meaning **`true`** and **`false`**, and a nullable type. There is also an abstract type any, which classifies all the values, but it can't be attributed to them.

Some of the functions for constructing values of certain types might differ from the usual **`object.action`** functions, as you might have spotted in some of the code provided in this chapter. Such examples are a table constructor **`#table`**, and datetime constructor **`#datetime`**. There are functions that return a type, such as Value.Type. Some operators might be used with data types, such as **`"hello" is text`**, which returns true. There are other functions that deal with types and type conversions, such as **`Date.From`**, which calculates date from a value, **`Number.FromText`**, which generates a number from text value, **`Table.FromRecords`**, which generates a table from a list of records, and **`Text.From`**, which creates text from value such as datetime or from NULL.

Table 3.1 offers an overview of some of the most common functions by category – it should provide an insight to what the M language can do. Many of these functions should be clear by themselves or we could analyze them in the Microsoft documentation or "**`= #shared`**" command:

Accessing data functions – generally connect to data source and return a table.		
`Access.Database`	`AnalysisServices.Database`	`AzureStorage.DataLake`
`Csv.Document`	`DB2.Database`	`Excel.Workbook`
`Folder.Contents`	`Json.Document`	`Oracle.Database`
Date, **Datetime**, **Datetimezone**, and **Duration functions**		
`Date.AddDays`	`Date.DayOfYear`	`Date.ToText`

DateTime.Date	DateTimeZone.FromText	Duration.TotalMinutes
List functions – used for working with lists		
List.Count	List.FindText	List.Combine
List.Split	List.Contains	List.Sum
Number functions		
Number.IsEven	Currency.From	Number.FromText
Number.Round	Number.Power	Number.RandomBetween
Record functions		
Record.FieldCount	Record.AddField	Record.RenameFields
Table functions		
Table.ColumnCount	Table.IsEmpty	Table.FirstN
Table.AddIndex- Column	Table.Join	Table.RenameColumns
Text functions		
Text.Length	Text.ToList	Value.FromText
Text.Range	Text.Insert	Text.Contains
Text.BetweenDe- limiters	Text.Proper	Text.Trim
Value functions		
Value.Equals	Value.Divide	Value.ReplaceType
Combiner, **Comparer**, and **Splitter** functions		
Combiner.Combine- TextBy_* Delimiter	Comparer.Equals	Splitter.SplitTextBy_* Positions
Expression functions, **Function values**, and **Error handling**		
Expression.Eval- uate	Function.InvokeAfter	Error.Record

_: Function is split due to lack of space in a cell*

***Table 3.1**: Overview of common M formula language functions by category*

Custom functions, Operators and Conditions in M

Operators are very similar to what you would expect in programming languages. There are computational operators, comparison operators, logical operators, etc. With calculations, there is a precedence order to follow, meaning that multiplication "*" has higher precedence than addition "+" or subtraction "-". Precedence can be changed with the use of parentheses "(" and ")". The examples of comparison operators are greater than ">", greater than or equal ">=", equal "=" and not equal "<>". Below we can see the example of some comparison operators in code:

```
let
    Compare1 = 5 = 5   // returns true
,   Compare2 = 6 <> 6  // returns false
,   Compare3 = 6 > 6   // returns false
,   Compare4 = 6 >= 6  // returns true
in
    Compare4
```

Logical and, or, and not are written in lowercase. With two conditions, "**or**" is true when one condition is true, while "**and**" is true when both are true. Not takes precedence over "**and**" and "**or**" operators. It is a unary operator, meaning it takes one element, similar as negation "**-x**" and identity "**+x**". Selection or data access operators were described where we discussed indexing of data structures. Question mark symbols can be used with an item or a field access operator to return NULL instead of an error when index is out of range. This is an example of how it can be written: "**{5}?**" or "**[Record5]?**". The combination operator "**&**" will concatenate text values, lists, tables and merge date with time, as well as merge records.

The keyword "**each**" is used when filtering or transforming values so that a function affects each of the elements in a data structure. The underscore "_" is often used together with each and is a placeholder for an element. For example, the phrase "**each _**" would mean each of the elements. This is an example of using both of these to filter a list structure:

```
let
    List = {1, 2, 3, 4, 5, 6, 7, 8}
,   Number = 3
,   ListFiltered = List.Select(List, each _ > Number)
in
    ListFiltered /* The result is:
        {4, 5, 6, 7, 8} */
```

It's possible to implement conditions to M formula language with the use of the if expression, consisting of if, then and else components. This is an example of using an if statement in M code:

```
let
    a = 6, b = 4, c = 8
```

```
,   IF =
        if a > b and a > c then "a is the largest" else
        if b > a and b > c then "b is the largest" else
        if c > a and c > b then "c is the largest" else
        "two or more numbers are equal"
in
    IF
```

We can create custom functions in the M formula language. In parentheses, we can describe the arguments or parameters that serve as an input to the formula. We could define arguments' data types with "**as**" operator, which also makes it a required argument. Adding a key word optional, as we can see in an example "**(a as number, b, optional c)**", turns an argument back to optional. Behind the closing parenthesis, we might add an "**as**" to define the type of the output. There is an operator with a symbol "**=>**" that can be described as go to, indicating a start of a function's body.

We can place a custom function inside of the base Power Query's query, for example, the one that's processing data from a source. If a function is placed inside of a base query, it is invoked by simply referring to a variable name and providing the necessary arguments in parentheses. In the following example, we can see a list as a source, followed by a function that adds a number to each element of the list.

```
let
    Source = {1, 2, 3, 4, 5, 6, 7, 8},
    CustomFunction = (List as list, Addition as number) =>
        List.Transform(List, each _ + Addition),
    Result = CustomFunction(Source, 0.5)
in
    Result // is {1.5, 2.5, 3.5, 4.5, 5.5, 6.5, 7.5, 8.5}
```

Or we can place the function in its own query, where it can be invoked by several other queries. If we create a query only as a function, this query will be of a function data type and will act as any other function. The problem with this approach is that base queries will no longer be simply copyable to another Power Query environment, as they are now referencing external objects. One of the benefits of Power Query is the ability to copy the code and repeat the data processing we've already coded in other resources. M language query in Power BI can be copied to Excel and we might later see that query is effective and use it with **SQL Server Integration Services** (**SSIS**) to have it load data to our data warehouse. Power Query Source in SSIS cannot reference any external functions, all the functionality has to be written within one query. This simplicity is an advantage and we should only throw it away for a very good reason only.

In *Figure* 3.4 we can see Power Query's queries of different types. Notice the icons on the left of the screen that are different for each query depending on its type. Selecting a query with a function opens an interface window that allows us to test its functionality. We can see that the function takes three parameters, all necessary, a table and two numbers. It returns a list. We'll explain and invoke the function later in the chapter.

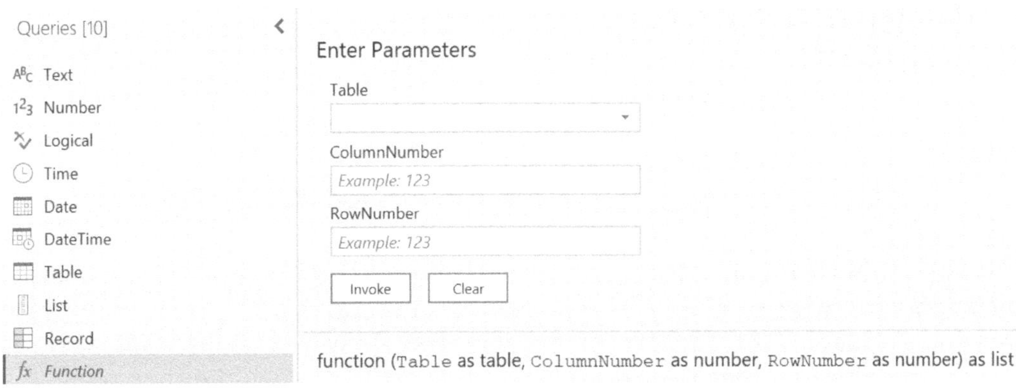

Figure 3.4: *Queries of different types and the custom function interface window*

Improvement of M code from the Exercise

There might be a way to optimize our query in the sense to provide better organization and overview of its functionality. Step-by-step transformations in Power Query Editor are a good way to approach data processing, but M language queries produced might be messy. You can follow along with the exercise, but the results will also be visible from figures. By selecting Complex CSV query and either right-clicking it and selecting Advanced Editor or by going to View tab and selecting it, we can see the query that was created when we performed transformations. The query is pictured in *Figure* 3.5. Please note that in Advanced Editor at the upper-right corner of the editor, under **`Display Options`**, we selected Display line numbers and Enable word wrap:

Advanced Editor

Complex CSV

Display Options

```
let
    Source = Csv.Document(File.Contents("C:\Book\Ch 3\Complex CSV.csv"),[Delimiter=";", Columns=12, Encoding=65001,
        QuoteStyle=QuoteStyle.None]),
    #"Removed Top Rows" = Table.Skip(Source,6),
    #"Replaced Value" = Table.ReplaceValue(#"Removed Top Rows","=<","",Replacer.ReplaceText,{"Column1", "Column2", "Column3",
        "Column4", "Column5", "Column6", "Column7", "Column8", "Column9", "Column10", "Column11", "Column12"}),
    #"Replaced Value1" = Table.ReplaceValue(#"Replaced Value",">","",Replacer.ReplaceText,{"Column1", "Column2", "Column3",
        "Column4", "Column5", "Column6", "Column7", "Column8", "Column9", "Column10", "Column11", "Column12"}),
    #"Promoted Headers" = Table.PromoteHeaders(#"Replaced Value1", [PromoteAllScalars=true]),
    #"Filtered Rows" = Table.SelectRows(#"Promoted Headers", each ([Organization ID] <> "TOTAL")),
    #"Replaced Value2" = Table.ReplaceValue(#"Filtered Rows",",",".",Replacer.ReplaceText,{"Purchase average price", "Sold average
        price", "In stock average price"}),
    #"Replaced Value3" = Table.ReplaceValue(#"Replaced Value2"," €","",Replacer.ReplaceText,{"Purchase average price", "Sold average
        price", "In stock average price"}),
    #"Changed Type" = Table.TransformColumnTypes(#"Replaced Value3",{{"Organization ID", Int64.Type}, {"Market name", type text},
        {"Item id", Int64.Type}, {"Item name", type text}, {"Item type", type text}, {"Color", type text}, {"Purchase quantity",
        Int64.Type}, {"Sold quantity", Int64.Type}, {"In stock quantity", Int64.Type}, {"Purchase average price", type number},
        {"Sold average price", type number}, {"In stock average price", type number}}),
    #"Replaced Value4" = Table.ReplaceValue(#"Changed Type","","Not available",Replacer.ReplaceValue,{"Color"})
in
    #"Replaced Value4"
```

***Figure* 3.5**: *M formula language code from Complex CSV file transformation*

The first thing we can notice is that variable names are more complicated, they can start with a "**#**" and be enclosed in quotations (""""). This is because there is a space in the variable name. The first thing we might want to do is change variables so that they don't contain spaces. We could either replace a space with an underscore ("_") or delete spaces altogether. It's best to do that in Power Query Editor under **`APPLIED STEPS`** of Query Settings because variables are being referenced in expressions' functions. Changing variable names in Advanced Editor requires changes in multiple areas of the code. Instead, we should rather right-click a step and select Rename in Query Settings:

1. In our example, we may simply delete the spaces. The query will look much cleaner.

   It's probably a good idea to delete or replace spaces in any query we're creating. But before making any additional changes, it might be a good idea to duplicate the query we're changing.

2. Right-clicking a query in Power Query Editor and selecting Duplicate will do it. We've named the duplicated query Complex CSV Edited.

3. We might also exclude the backup query from loading to a data model and from refreshing by right-clicking it and deselecting Enable load. This should automatically deselect Include in the report refresh as well.

We could use Microsoft documentation or **= #shared** command to check the functions appearing in our M code. That way we'll get a better understanding of their syntax and parameters. Luckily, in updated versions of Microsoft products, that's even easier. We can click an area with a function and hover over it with a mouse cursor to see its signature. There are several steps for replacing values in our query, that generally only differ in a number of columns that these replacements are affecting. Unfortunately, at the time of writing, there isn't a function like Table. ReplaceValues (notice the s) that would take a list of replacements as an argument, so there currently isn't any very efficient and clean way to join these steps into one.

Yet at steps **ReplacedValue** and **ReplacedValue1**, we can notice that the last argument of **Table.ReplaceValue** function takes a list of all the column names. There's a more efficient way to provide that argument rather than hard-coding all the column names into a list.

4. We might use a **Table.ColumnNames** function, that takes one argument – a table, and returns the names of the columns as a list. Perfect! Replace the following part of the code after the comma "," and before the closing parenthesis ")":

```
{"Column1", "Column2", "Column3", "Column4", "Column5",
"Column6", "Column7", "Column8", "Column9", "Column10",
"Column11", "Column12"}
```

With the following code in **ReplacedValue** expression:

```
Table.ColumnNames(RemovedTopRows)
```

Make sure to apply the changes in both **ReplaceValue** and **ReplacedValue1** steps. We can change the parameter when applying the code to the **ReplacedValue1** step, but in our case it isn't necessary.

In **ReplacedValue2** and **ReplacedValue3**, we can see that prices columns repeat in each line. We might want to replace them with a variable. This could improve the code's readability as well as in the case of additional price columns appearing in our data source, that we wanted to transform as well, we'd have to change the query in only one part.

1. In Advanced Editor, create a variable **PriceColumnsList** before **ReplacedValue2** and assign the list of column names to it by copying the list from **ReplacedValue2** and pasting it after the assignment operator. Change the hard-coded list to a variable in **ReplacedValue2** and **ReplacedValue3** steps. Make sure not to forget the commas.

In the **ChangedType** step, we can see that the **Detect Data Type** option lists all the columns and changes in data types, even those of type text. If we check the Source step, all the columns are of Text data type to begin with, so listing those that remain text isn't necessary. The function Table. TransformColumnTypes in our query took two arguments, the first being a table and the second is a list of type transformations. We can see that the second argument is lists within a list data structure.

2. Delete the entire inner list for the columns: **Market name**, **Item name**, Item type as well, and **Color**. Notice that inner lists are separated by commas, so delete those as well. This is the example of the code block we'll be deleting: "`{"Market name", type text},` ".

   We can further improve the code readability by assigning the lists within a list data structure to a variable.

3. Create a variable **`TypeChangesList`** just before the **ChangedType** step and assign the data structure to it. We could use enter and tab keyboard keys to align the code in a way that we find readable. After that, replace the hard-coded lists within a list inside the function **`Table.TransformColumnTypes`** with the variable we've just created.

   Lastly, we can see that the first expression in the Source variable is made out of two functions. First function File.Contents is used to create a binary data type out of a data interchange format. This binary is then passed into **`Csv.Document`** as an input argument. We might break these two functions into two steps.

4. Create a **`FileContents`** variable before the Source step and assign the line of the code related to the **`File.Contents`** function. Next, insert the newly created variable to the Source step to replace **`File.Contents`** function.

Figure 3.6 shows all the changes we've made to the code to improve its readability and organization. We have also moved the commas separating the steps from the end of the lines to the beginning of the subsequent lines:

Complex CSV edited

Display Options ▾

```
let
    FileContents = File.Contents("C:\Book\Ch 3\Complex CSV.csv")
,   Source = Csv.Document(FileContents, [Delimiter=";", Columns=12, Encoding=65001, QuoteStyle=QuoteStyle.None])
,   RemovedTopRows = Table.Skip(Source,6)
,   ReplacedValue = Table.ReplaceValue(RemovedTopRows,"=<","",Replacer.ReplaceText, Table.ColumnNames(RemovedTopRows))
,   ReplacedValue1 = Table.ReplaceValue(ReplacedValue,">","",Replacer.ReplaceText, Table.ColumnNames(RemovedTopRows))
,   PromotedHeaders = Table.PromoteHeaders(ReplacedValue1, [PromoteAllScalars=true])
,   FilteredRows = Table.SelectRows(PromotedHeaders, each ([Organization ID] <> "TOTAL"))
,   PriceColumnsList = {"Purchase average price", "Sold average price", "In stock average price"}
,   ReplacedValue2 = Table.ReplaceValue(FilteredRows,",",".",Replacer.ReplaceText, PriceColumnsList)
,   ReplacedValue3 = Table.ReplaceValue(ReplacedValue2," €","",Replacer.ReplaceText, PriceColumnsList)
,   TypeChangesList = {
        {"Organization ID", Int64.Type}, {"Item id", Int64.Type}, {"Purchase quantity", Int64.Type},
        {"Sold quantity", Int64.Type}, {"In stock quantity", Int64.Type}, {"Purchase average price", type number},
        {"Sold average price", type number}, {"In stock average price", type number}}
,   ChangedType = Table.TransformColumnTypes(ReplacedValue3, TypeChangesList)
,   ReplacedValue4 = Table.ReplaceValue(ChangedType,"","Not available",Replacer.ReplaceValue,{"Color"})
in
    ReplacedValue4
```

Figure 3.6: *Complex CSV's query edited to improve the code's organization*

Let's perform some additional transformations

As the first exercise in this subchapter, we'll create a parameter to use as a path instead of a hard-coded path. As with custom functions, calling outside parameters makes it so that copying M code to other resources is more complex. But there are certain cases where they might be useful, such as when we have a Power BI report connected to data interchange formats that might change their path or name often. In such a case, a user can quickly modify the parameter, making the report work again.

Inside Power Query Editor, we've duplicated Complex CSV Edited query to ensure a backup. We've also disabled the option Enable load for the backup query. Notice that when we disable the option Enable load, the query name is written in Italic font. Because we've now got two backup queries, we could use groups to better organize our queries. Right-clicking below the last query in an empty area of Queries pane and selecting **New Group...** opens an interface window allowing us to type in the name of the group. We can write **Backup** as a name, and description in a box below if we wish to. Other queries are automatically moved to Other Queries, an automatic group that can't be renamed. For organizational purposes, we can create another group Active Queries and by simply dragging-and-dropping, move the queries between these two groups.

We can rename the **`Complex CSV Edited (2)`** to **`Complex CSV Exercises`**. Under the **Home** tab, find the option **`Manage Parameters`**. Clicking the text allows selection of New parameter. In the interface window, name the parameter **`CSV path`** and keep it as **`Required`**. Under **`Type`**, change to **`Text`** and under **`Current Value`**, write **`test`** for now. This will create the CSV path parameter in **`Other Queries`**. If we were to use more parameters, we might create a group for those as well.

Inside of Complex CSV Exercises, under **`FileContents`** variable's expression, change the hard-coded path to the parameter we created by simply starting to type its name. An IntelliSense pop-up display should present it as an option. We can move through options with the up and down arrow keyboard keys and select the tab keyboard key to accept the option. The parameter will be written as **#"CSV Path"** because it contains a space. This is how we'd have to reference it without IntelliSense. If we wanted, we could replace the space with an underscore.

Selecting **Done** in Advanced Editor will generate an error, understandably, as our current path is "test" instead of a real path. We can still select the **`Close & Apply`** option and close the error window appearing in Power BI. We'll apply the correct parameter in the next step. Under the **Home** tab, select the text of the option **`Transform data`**. Select **`Edit parameters`**. Under CSV Path, write the path to the file. In the Windows environment, we can find the file in the directory and right-click it while holding the shift keyboard key. Select **`Copy as path`** and paste it to Edit Parameters interface window. Delete the quotation marks, as those will be applied by the text data type of the parameter. Once we are done, we can select **`OK`**. We might see the yellow bar below the upper ribbon with the word Apply changes. We can click that, which should load the CSV file without errors.

As for the next exercise, we might have noticed that the CSV file we're transforming doesn't really have a date column. As it was written in *Chapter 1, Introducing the Theoretical Background for Democratizing Analytics*, any star schema model usually includes date dimension. But if we check our data, previews of which can be seen on *Figures* 3.1, 3.2, and *Figure* 2.5 in the previous chapter, we can see that there is information about dates in the third row. This is the row that's written in the CSV file: **`Period from 01.6.2023 to 31.6.2023`**. We can notice immediately that the format is pretty problematic. Not only is it in some European language variants, we can also see that month is currently written with only one character, but we can expect that in the last three months of the year, it'll be written with two. That's a slight complication, but nothing we can't handle.

As for what date we should use, it really depends on the circumstances. If such a file is dropped daily, we might need the period to, which would change each day, while the period from would remain stable for the whole month. But let's say this is a monthly drop, in such a case, the period from would be useful to define the month of data. We'll define two functions. The first one we'll name **`GetDataFromTable`**. Its action will be to filter the table to only the column and the row of our choosing and return the value in that cell, then split the value by the delimiter space and return a list of all the split elements. So, we'll end up with the list data structure of every word in the chosen cell or record.

We can create the function by selecting the text of the option **`New Source`** in the **`Home`** tab of Power Query Editor and then the option **`Blank Query`**. Right-clicking the **`Blank Query`**, we can rename the query to **`GetDataFromTable`**, open the Advanced Editor, and copy the following M code:

```
let
    Function = (Table as table, ColumnNumber as number, RowNumber as
number)
    as list =>
    let
        ListOfColumnNames = Table.ColumnNames(Table)
    ,   SelectColumnName = ListOfColumnNames{ColumnNumber-1}
    ,   SelectColumn = Table.Column(Table, SelectColumnName)
```

```
    ,   SelectRow = SelectColumn{RowNumber - 1}
    ,   ToText = Text.From(SelectRow)
    ,   RowToList = Text.Split(ToText, " ")
    in
        RowToList
in
    Function
```

We'll repeat the process and create another Blank Query naming it **GetDateFromData**. This function will take the list outputted by the first function and split the word that is date into an actual date type. We can provide the function a parameter that is sequential number for the word in the list that represents a date. The following is the M code for **GetDateFromData** function:

```
let
    Function = (ListOfData as list, WhichWordIsDate as number)
    as date =>
    let
        FilterList = ListOfData{WhichWordIsDate - 1}
    ,   SplitDate = Text.Split(FilterList, ".")
    ,   TransformMe = List.Transform(SplitDate, each Number.FromText(_))
    ,   CreateDate = #date(TransformMe{2}, TransformMe{1}, 
TransformMe{0})
    in
        CreateDate
in
    Function
```

Now we'll apply these custom functions to our Complex CSV Exercises Query. If we wanted to avoid invoking custom functions, we could easily as well break these functions down and apply their steps in the base query. We could also modify these functions, that is, modify the delimiter by which **Text.Split** function splits the value. Selecting the Complex CSV Exercises query, we can see that the **RemovedTopRows** step, which is the third step, already removes the information we need. We'll operate before this step, then. We might be tempted to select the Source step in Query Settings, right-click it and select **Insert Step After**, but that is not suitable for what we're trying to achieve. Using **Insert Step After** will modify the M formula language code in a way that the following step takes the newly inserted step as a parameter. That is not good in our case, because we'll be creating a list and a date value that will not be used until later in the query.

We'll open Advanced Editor and between **Source** and **RemovedTopRows** add two lines of code – we'll be invoking the custom functions we just created. At the time of writing, there is no IntelliSense available for custom functions, so we'll have to remember the parameters. First function **GetDataFromTable** takes three parameters, first the table we'll be filtering, second the column number and third the row number. M formula language counts starting with 0 being the first element, but the functions we've created use 1 as the first element, because it is more intuitive for the user. We can check the **Source** step to see that the value containing date is in the first column and third row. We'll write this line after **Source** step:

```
,   RowContainingDate = GetDataFromTable(Source, 1, 3)
```

If we select Done, we can check what we've created by selecting the **RowContainingDate** step under APPLIED STEPS. We can see the list with several elements. The date we're interested in is in the third position, so we'll apply this line as the next step:

```
,   GetTheDate = GetDateFromData(RowContainingDate, 3)
```

Now we have everything we need. We'll simply add the new Start of month column containing date information and our data will look closer to a proper fact table. Add this line at the bottom of the code, below **ReplacedValue4**:

```
,   AddDateColumn = Table.AddColumn(ReplacedValue4, "Start of month",
each GetTheDate, type date)
```

Make sure to change the variable after the in statement to **AddDateColumn** instead of **ReplacedValue4**, otherwise the query will not display APPLIED STEPS properly. Unfortunately, at the time of writing there is no function such as **Table.InsertColumn** in which we could specify the position of the inserted column, so the column gets inserted to the very end of the table.

Simply dragging the column to the beginning in Power Query Editor will create a new step. Power Query named it Reordered Columns and we should rename it to not contain the spaces. The step uses **Table.ReorderColumns** function, which in our case requires the listing of every column name for it to work properly.

We can again put the list of column names outside the **ReorderedColumns** step. Before this step, we'll create the **ColumnOrderList** variable. We can simply cut the list from **ReorderedColumns** and paste it to **ColumnOrderList**. Notice that automatic steps in Power Query create the comma after the expression, so we could move the comma to the beginning of the next line. Make sure to reference the newly created list step in **Table.ReorderColumns** function and make sure to modify the variable after the in statement. We can see the code we've created in *Figure 3.7*:

Complex CSV exercises

Display Options ▾

```
let
    FileContents = File.Contents(#"CSV Path")
,   Source = Csv.Document(FileContents, [Delimiter=";", Columns=12, Encoding=65001, QuoteStyle=QuoteStyle.None])
,   RowContainingDate = GetDataFromTable(Source, 1, 3)
,   GetTheDate = GetDateFromData(RowContainingDate, 3)
,   RemovedTopRows = Table.Skip(Source,6)
,   ReplacedValue = Table.ReplaceValue(RemovedTopRows,"=<","",Replacer.ReplaceText, Table.ColumnNames(RemovedTopRows))
,   ReplacedValue1 = Table.ReplaceValue(ReplacedValue,">","",Replacer.ReplaceText, Table.ColumnNames(RemovedTopRows))
,   PromotedHeaders = Table.PromoteHeaders(ReplacedValue1, [PromoteAllScalars=true])
,   FilteredRows = Table.SelectRows(PromotedHeaders, each ([Organization ID] <> "TOTAL"))
,   PriceColumnsList = {"Purchase average price", "Sold average price", "In stock average price"}
,   ReplacedValue2 = Table.ReplaceValue(FilteredRows,",",".",Replacer.ReplaceText, PriceColumnsList)
,   ReplacedValue3 = Table.ReplaceValue(ReplacedValue2," €","",Replacer.ReplaceText, PriceColumnsList)
,   TypeChangesList = {
        {"Organization ID", Int64.Type}, {"Item id", Int64.Type}, {"Purchase quantity", Int64.Type},
        {"Sold quantity", Int64.Type}, {"In stock quantity", Int64.Type}, {"Purchase average price", type number},
        {"Sold average price", type number}, {"In stock average price", type number}}
,   ChangedType = Table.TransformColumnTypes(ReplacedValue3, TypeChangesList)
,   ReplacedValue4 = Table.ReplaceValue(ChangedType,"","Not available",Replacer.ReplaceValue,{"Color"})
,   AddDateColumn = Table.AddColumn(ReplacedValue4, "Start of month", each GetTheDate, type date)
,   ColumnOrderList = {
        "Start of month", "Organization ID", "Market name", "Item id", "Item name",
        "Item type", "Color", "Purchase quantity", "Sold quantity", "In stock quantity",
        "Purchase average price",  "Sold average price", "In stock average price"}
,   ReorderedColumns = Table.ReorderColumns(AddDateColumn, ColumnOrderList)
in
    ReorderedColumns
```

Figure 3.7: *Complex CSV exercises final M formula language code*

Conclusion

This chapter and the previous one gave us an insight to what is going on behind the scenes of data connectivity in many of the Microsoft resources using Power Query. Power Query and M formula language seem to be a powerful tools to handle data processing tasks. As with any technology, we should answer the questions: Is it here to stay, is it worth learning and using it to get as much experience? While it is impossible to say for sure, we have now seen that Power Query is becoming integrated with some of the cloud Microsoft solutions. That means users are paying operational costs, that is, paying monthly for using Power Query and its functionalities.

Power Query now plays an important role in ETL transformations on Microsoft Cloud and that means an increasing chance that it's here to stay. An IT and data veteran once said: *I don't think the IT industry is yet at the level of the timber industry*, meaning that there are still changes to be expected. Probably, the era of massive IT paradigm revolutions that defined early decades of the IT industry are slowly waning. That could just mean that the tools we're now seeing are here to stay, being incrementally updated, rather than being completely revolutionized. The operational costs model is surely playing a role in that stability. In the next chapter, we're going to take a look into what to do with data once we have it loaded and transformed. We're going to take a look into Excel Power Pivot - a tool that, together with Power Query, in a way revolutionized the approach and capacity of analyzing data within Excel.

CHAPTER 4

Building a Simple Analytical Solution with Power Pivot in Excel

Introduction

When it comes to simple analytics and data crunching, Excel is still the go-to tool for most people. This chapter will describe some of the shortcomings of classic Excel and demonstrate how basic knowledge of Excel BI tools (Power Query and Power Pivot) can help us in creating an analytical solution that we could never achieve with basic Excel tools. Thus far, you have already learned about Power Query and the power that it gives you when connecting to data sources. But connecting to data and bringing it into Excel is only the beginning of building an analytical solution. Since this chapter is meant to be a complete walkthrough of building a solution from scratch, we will briefly cover this topic, anyway.

Structure

In this chapter, we will cover the following topics:

- Connecting to data with Power Query
- Enabling the Power Pivot add-in
- Power Pivot data view
- Introduction to calculated columns

- Introduction to measures
- Introduction to the diagram view
- Fact and dimension tables
- Establishing relationships between tables
- Primary keys and foreign keys
- Creating a pivot table based on the data model
- Calculating averages
- Exploring functions for counting
- Editing existing measures
- Calculating ratios with DIVIDE
- Understanding the filter flow
- Introduction to the X functions
- Key performance indicators (KPIs)

Scenario

You are working for a company called AdventureWorks. The company mainly sells bikes and cycling equipment. The company has decided that they want to upgrade and centralize its existing disjointed analytical solutions that ingest data from Excel workbooks and analyze it with Excel pivot tables. The problem is that the current development of each solution includes creating a huge data table from many other tables so that it can be analyzed with pivot tables. Also, people currently need to repeatedly develop the same custom calculations in the pivot tables they create to get the results they need. Many people in the company have already created their own analytical solutions and now there is confusion as to which solution contains correct data. The company wants to create a simple analytical solution for its internet sales data using Excel BI tools that will be able to combine data from various workbooks, contain reusable metrics and serve as a single source of truth. To that end, the company has already prepared a workbook with the data they want to analyze and the task of creating an analytical solution was assigned to you. You will find the necessary data in the Excel file provided with this book titled **C04_AdventureWorks_Excel_DB**.

Connecting to data with Power Query

When you open an Excel workbook, you can find the Power Query commands on the left-hand side of the ribbon called **Data**. In business scenarios, the data we would like to analyze is often located in various other Excel workbooks. To connect to data in another Excel workbook, go to the **Data** tab, click **Get Data > From File > From Excel Workbook**. Browse to the location where you saved the **C04_AdventureWorks_Excel_DB** Excel file. Select the file and click **Import**.

In Excel, a new window will pop up, asking you which data you would like to connect to. Based on how the data in the workbook is structured, you will see two different icons:

- A black and white grid indicates that the item is a worksheet
- A blue and white grid indicates that the item is an Excel table

In the upper left corner of this window, under the search box, you will also find a check box called **Select multiple items**, allowing you to select more than one item. In the workbook we have prepared for this scenario, all data is contained in multiple tables in this single Excel file, so let's check this box and after that, select the following tables: **FactInternetSales**, **DimCustomer**, **DimSalesTerritory** and **DimProduct**. We will explain the prefixes *Fact* and *Dim* shortly when we talk about establishing relationships between these tables.

If the data we are connecting to had not been thoroughly prepared beforehand, we would click **Transform Data** in the lower right corner of the window displayed in *Figure 4.1*. This would open the Power Query Editor, allowing us to make the transformations you already learned about in previous chapters. But the data we have is ready for analysis, so click the downward-facing arrow next to **Load** and select **Load To**:

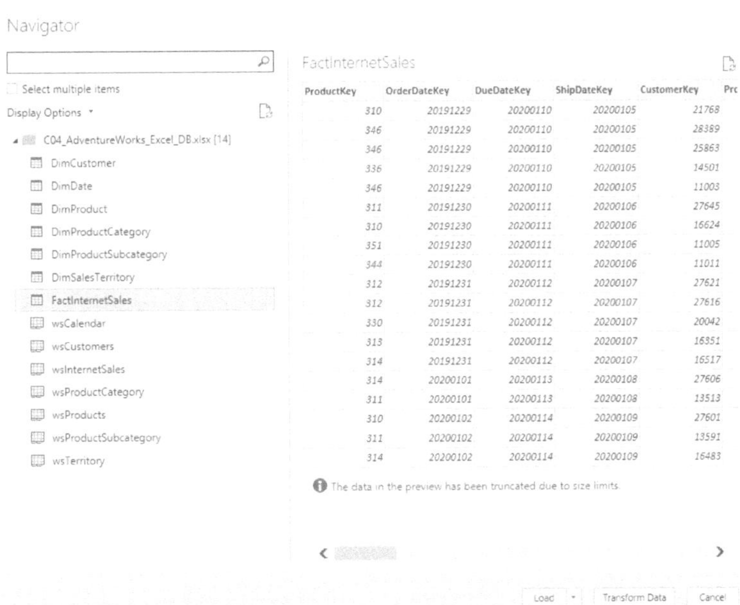

Figure 4.1: *Importing data from Excel*

Since we selected **Load To**, after Excel connects to the data source, it gives us the option to select the method of viewing the data in this workbook. If we wanted to import the tables into the workbook and see all the rows of all the tables we connected to, we would select **Table**. If we wanted to go straight into analysis, we could select **PivotTable Report**. Since we don't need to view the data row by row in the workbook itself, we only want to use the data for our analytical solution, select **Only Create Connection**.

Since our analytical solution will be based on data from multiple tables, before proceeding to click **OK**, we must also be sure that the following check box is checked: **Add this data to the Data Model**. This will allow us to build a relational data source in this workbook with the help of Power Pivot. Without this check box, we would only create queries to the other Excel workbook, but the data would not be imported to Power Pivot. Finally, we can click **OK**. A side pane called **Queries & Connections** should open, showing you the progress of the data loading process.

Enabling the Power Pivot add-in

Now that we have connected to the data we want to analyze, it's time for us to build our data model. For this, we need to open Power Pivot. If you have never opened Power Pivot before, the Power Pivot tab will not be visible in Excel. You must first enable the Power Pivot add-in. You can do this the long way, by clicking **File** in the upper-left corner of Excel to get to Excel's so-called **backstage view**, opening Excel's **Options**, in the left pane of the options window selecting **Add-ins** and then selecting **COM add-ins** from the drop-down menu and clicking **Go**. In the next window, check the box next to **Microsoft Power Pivot for Excel** and click **OK**. This will bring you back into the workbook, where you will see a new ribbon called **Power Pivot**. Click the ribbon and then click **Manage** to open Power Pivot.

A much faster way to enable the add-in is to simply click the **Manage Data Model** command on the **Data** tab. If you haven't yet enabled the Power Pivot add-in, Excel will first open a pop-up window asking you if you would like to enable it now. Click **Enable**. This will enable the add-in and open the Power Pivot window.

Power Pivot data view

When the Power Pivot window opens, you will probably be presented with a grid view of the data you imported. If this is not the case, you can switch between Power Pivot views in two places:

- On the **Home** tab, in the **View** group on the right-hand side, you can choose between **Data View** and **Diagram View**.

- In the bottom-right corner of the Power Pivot window, you can click one of two icons. The first is called **Grid View**, which is the same thing as the aforementioned **Data View** and the second is the **Diagram View**, which we will discuss shortly:

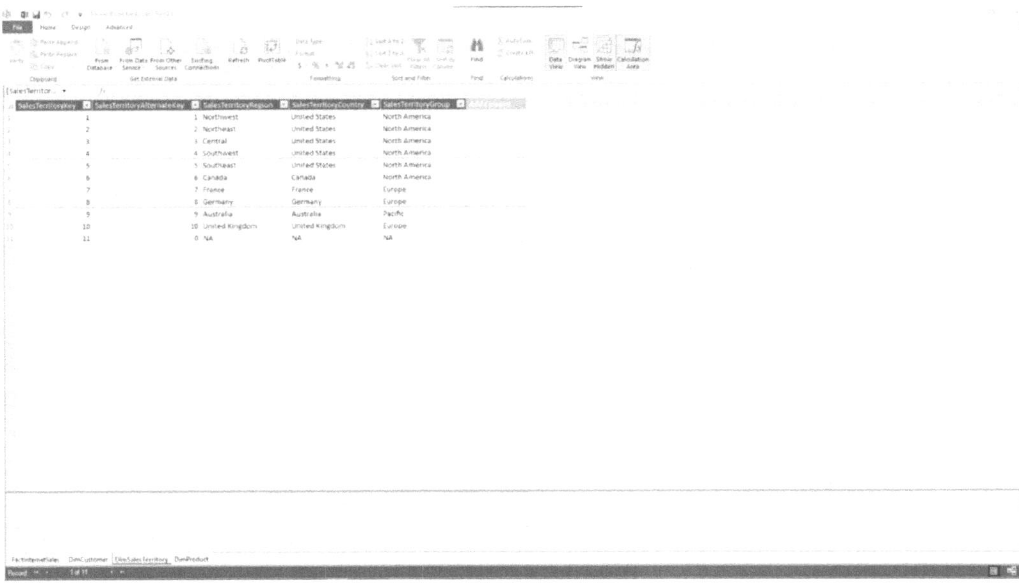

Figure 4.2: *The data view*

Whichever method you prefer, make sure the **Data View**, also visible in *Figure 4.2*, is selected.

Now, in the bottom-left corner of the Power Pivot window, you will see something similar to the list of worksheets in an Excel workbook. These are the tables you imported into the data model through the Power Query connection. You can click the name of any of these tables and Power Pivot will present you with the data of that table in the main window.

For example, if you click the **DimCustomer** table, Power Pivot will present you with the data from that table. You can browse through the data, scroll up and down and left and right. You can click any cell in the data and Power Pivot will output the content of the cell in the formula bar above the data itself. But even though Power Pivot is an Excel add-in with a similar user interface, its intended purpose is quite different and so is the way you use it. For example, if you try to edit a cell, as you would in Excel, you will find out that this is not possible in Power Pivot. Once imported, data values can't be changed in Power Pivot. You can go back to Power Query or straight to the data source and change individual values there.

The data structure is much more rigid in Power Pivot than it is in Excel. You may have already noticed that all the imported data is in tabular format, meaning the first row of data is the header that defines the content of a column, and each row is a complete piece of information. For example, if you switch to the **`DimSalesTerritory`** table, you can see that the row with **`SalesTerritoryKey 7`** contains **`France`** as the **`Region`**, **`France`** as the **`Country`** and **`Europe`** as the **`Group`**.

Data that you want to import into Power Pivot and later analyze with pivot tables must be structured this way, otherwise, you won't get any benefits from Power Pivot as pivot tables won't be able to make any sensible use of the data. If you have worked with Excel tables and pivot tables before, this concept will be familiar to you. In Excel tables, the first row will function as the header. Following the header, each row will present you with a complete piece of information.

Excel pivot tables will take the first row of a table and interpret each cell in that row as a title of the column, and all the other cells in a column as the values of that column. When you create a pivot table, Excel will present you with a list of column names or titles from the table you are using as a source for the pivot table. You would then select the columns you want to use in your analysis and the pivot table will return calculations based on your selection. You will see something similar when you create a pivot table based on the data model you are creating in this chapter.

Introduction to calculated columns

Let's go back to our discussion about the Power Pivot functionalities available in the "Data View". Next to the last column of every imported table, there is a label that says "Add Column". If you click any cell under this label, you can start typing a formula that will be used to create what is known as a calculated column. You can use calculated columns to enrich your data model, adding extra information to it through calculations. Let's look at a simple example.

Due to supply issues, we want to increase the safety stock level of all products by 50%. This is not something you normally do in the data model you are preparing for analysis of current data, but it serves the purpose of demonstration. In the "Data View", navigate to the DimProduct table. In this table, you will find a column called SafetyStockLevel. Now let's use the values from this column and increase them by 1.5.

Navigate to the rightmost edge of the table and click any cell under the "**`Add Column`**" label. Formulas for calculated columns are written in **DAX**, which is an abbreviation for **Data Analysis Expressions**. It is a formula language similar to the Excel formula language, so if you have any experience writing Excel formulas, those skills will come in handy in Power Pivot.

Like in Excel, start the formula with the equals sign **=**. You will notice that the sign appears in the formula bar above the data. After that, click any cell in the **SafetyStockLevel** column. If you look at the formula bar again, you will see a full reference to the column, including the table name in the format **TableName[ColumnName]**. Now, type the asterisk sign *****, which serves as the multiplication operator. Finally, type the multiplier, which in this example is 1.5. Your formula should look like this:

```
= DimProduct[SafetyStockLevel] * 1.5
```

You can notice two things at this stage:

- You can freely add spaces to the formula for better readability without affecting the result of the formula.
- Unlike Excel, it didn't matter which cell was selected when you started typing the formula, and it also didn't matter which cell you selected when clicking the **SafetyStockLevel** column. Power Pivot works with entire columns, it doesn't have the concept of cells. You wrote a formula that applies to the whole column and the formula is applied to the column row by row. Power Pivot knows how to do this because of an evaluation context called the row context, which we will talk about more in the next chapter.

If the formula looks ok, press the *Enter* key. The calculated column currently has a generic name, **Calculated Column 1**. If you want to give the column a more descriptive name, for example, **SafetyStockLevelNew**, you can use one of two methods:

- Right-click the column name and select **Rename Column** from the menu. After that, type in the name you would like to use and press *Enter*.
- Double-click the column name and type in the name you would like to use and press *Enter*.

Your data model now contains a new column called **SafetyStockLevelNew**, which is calculated by multiplying the values from **SafetyStockLevel** by 1.5. You will be able to use this column in any analysis based on this data model. Calculated columns can provide us with much more complicated information than this example, but it was a nice introduction to the topic before we delve into more complex scenarios later in the book.

Introduction to measures

By now, you may have already noticed that there is a thick gray line underneath the data of each table in the **Data View**. Under this line, there are many empty cells. But these empty cells aren't there because there are no more rows in a table. You can try grabbing and dragging this thick gray line upwards and thereby extending the space below the data.

This space is called the **Calculation Area** and is reserved for writing what is known as measures. We already talked about calculated columns, which are new columns in your data model that contain values calculated row by row. Measures on the other hand are calculations that can take data from an entire column or multiple columns, perform complex calculations, and aggregate the data into a single value. We write measures to extract information from the raw data contained in the tables of the data model. Let's look at another simple example.

Our goal is to write a measure that will calculate the sum of money we earned from our sales. All the information regarding orders is stored in the **`FactInternetSales`** table. If you navigate to this table in the **`Data View`**, you will find the SalesAmount column towards the end of the table. This column contains data about the sales amount of each row that we want to add together with a measure. You can select any of the cells under the thick gray line - the *Calculation area* - to store a measure. Some people prefer to store measures under the column that contains the data we are focusing on, while other people prefer to store all measures in a single column at the beginning of a table (this is also what Power Pivot does by default if you create measures through the user interface in Excel, as we will be doing shortly).

You can pick whichever method for storing measures you like; the location of a measure is irrelevant. The measure you will create for this example doesn't even need to be stored in the FactInternetSales table. It just makes sense to do so in terms of organizing content. It will be much easier to find the measure and make corrections to it when it is stored in a logical location. So, click a cell underneath the thick gray line in the FactInternetSales table and let's begin typing the measure.

This time, we won't begin by typing an equal sign, but by typing the name of the measure. Since we want to calculate the sum of the sales amounts, let's name the measure SumOfSalesAmount. Type this name and then add a colon and an equal sign, ":=". This is the combination of characters that lets Power Pivot know we are starting to type a measure.

Like calculated columns, measures are also written in DAX. Since you want to add all the sales amounts together, you can use a function you are probably familiar with from Excel – **`SUM`**. After typing **`SUM`**, add a left parenthesis. Power Pivot will assist you in writing the formula by giving you a drop-down with possible choices to add to the **`SUM`** function. The formula autocompletion is part of a wider functionality called **IntelliSense** that assists you in writing functions. You type **`Fact`** to narrow the selection of choices down to just the columns from the **`FactInternetSales`** table and select **`FactInternetSales[SalesAmount]`** by double-clicking the choice in the drop-down menu. Add a right parenthesis to finish the function and press Enter. Your measure definition should look something like this:

```
SumOfSalesAmount:=SUM( FactInternetSales[SalesAmount] )
```

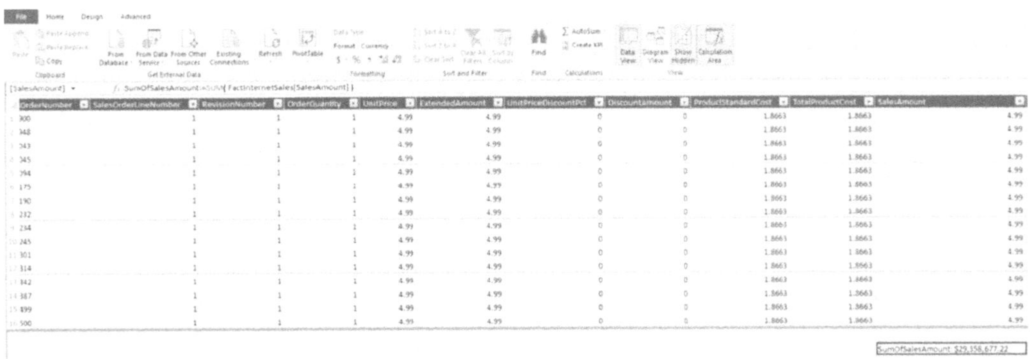

***Figure 4.3**: Writing a measure*

In the cell you selected before you started typing the measure definition, you will now see the name of the measure, followed by the result of the measure, as we can see in *Figure* 4.3. You will probably need to widen the column to see the whole result. It's probably an ugly, unreadable number. It would be better if it was in a readable format relevant to the result, such as currency. To format the result of the measure, first, make sure the cell that contains the measure is selected. After that, you have two options:

- Switch to the **Home** tab of Power Pivot. In the **Formatting** group, click the **Format**: button and select **Currency**. Under the **Format**: button, there are other commands that can help you adjust the number of decimal places and the currency symbol if necessary.
- Right-click the cell containing the measure. From the drop-down menu, select **Format...** and in the window that appears, select **Currency** in the **Category** pane. After you make this selection, you can also select the currency symbol and the number of decimal places. After you make the necessary changes, click **OK**.

The changes to the formatting should be visible immediately. Defining formatting at the measure level is a good practice. This way, when you add the measure to a pivot table, which we will do shortly, all the calculations are already formatted. Since measures can be used repeatedly in as many pivot tables as you like, defining formatting this way instead of defining it in each pivot table individually can be a real-time saver.

You can see that both calculated columns and measures are visible in the Power Pivot window and both are used to make calculations. What is the difference between these two functionalities then? Calculated columns are just like other columns. They are materialized in the data model, loaded into **Random Access Memory (RAM)** when the file is opened and take up space on the disk when the file is saved. Measures on the other hand are only calculated when necessary, for example, when you insert a measure into a pivot table or a visualization and take into account the context in which the measure is displayed, for example, for which country are sales calculated. This is something called the **filter context**, which we will discuss in the next chapter.

It is recommended to use measures whenever you want to do any sort of aggregation, while calculated columns are normally used to flatten the data model or create calculated metadata in a row-by-row manner that you can use to further slice your analysis.

Now that we have made a brief overview of the functionalities in the data view and made an introduction to calculated columns and measures, let's discuss another crucial component of Power Pivot - the **Diagram View**.

Introduction to the diagram view

As discussed, you can switch between Power Pivot views either on the right-hand side of the `Home` tab or in the bottom right corner of the Power Pivot window. Use whichever method you prefer to switch to the `Diagram View`.

In this view, Power Pivot will present you with a more generalized view of the content of your data model. You won't see the row-by-row data of the tables. You will only see the separate tables you added to the data model and the columns they contain. In the next chapter, you will see that the tables can also contain other components, but for now, let's focus on the main functionality of this view - creating relationships between the tables of the data model.

First, let's rearrange the layout of the imported tables. Find the `FactInternetSales` table, grab it by clicking somewhere close to the title, and drag and drop it into the middle of the window. In the same way, arrange all the tables with the prefix *Dim* around the `FactInternetSales` table, as seen in *Figure 4.4*:

***Figure 4.4**: The diagram view*

Why did we arrange the tables this way? Now would be a great time to explain the prefixes *Fact* and *Dim*.

Fact and dimension tables

These are widely used prefixes that describe two types of tables in a data model:

- **Fact**: The table is a fact table. This table contains the data, or facts, that you intend to analyze. In the **`FactInternetSales`** table, each row represents a sold line item and contains relevant data, such as the date the sale was made, the ID of the purchasing customer, the order quantity, the unit price of the ordered product, and so on. You will likely be interested in knowing how many sales you made, how much you earned from those sales, how many unique paying customers you have and so on. You can find out all of this from the data in the fact table. Fact tables typically contain the most rows of all the tables in your data model.
- **Dim**: The table is a dimension table. These types of tables contain attributes and metadata that will give your analysis more meaning and give you more flexibility when creating reports. To give an example, I mentioned that the **`FactInternetSales`** table contains data about customers. But customers are only described in the fact table by their IDs. What if you want to analyze sales by customer age or marital status? This is the sort

of data that dimension tables will contain. Our data model contains a few dimension tables and one of them is **DimCustomer**. It contains not only the unique ID of each customer but a wealth of metadata, such as customer names, email addresses, birth dates, yearly incomes, education levels and more. This allows you to ask yourself questions such as "How many purchases did people with a bachelor's degree born after 1980 make?". Compared to fact tables, dimension tables typically contain a small number of rows.

Rearranging the tables of our data model like this is a nice step in preparation for establishing relationships, as the flow of relationships will be much more visually understandable.

Establishing relationships between tables

The tables are now nicely laid out in the diagram view. But using all the tables in a wholesome analysis that combines data from the entire data model isn't possible yet. Why? The data you would like to analyze is situated in various tables. If you are used to preparing analytical solutions in classic Excel, you would first need to join all the relevant data into one giant table, probably by using a lot of Excel **VLOOKUP** or **XLOOKUP** functions. This is because classic Excel pivot tables can only ingest data from a single range of cells or a single table.

Power Pivot, on the other hand, allows us to use pivot tables to analyze data from various tables. But Power Pivot must know how those tables are related to one another, so we must first establish relationships between them. Let's look at an example of creating a relationship by connecting the **FactInternetSales** and **DimCustomer** tables.

If you look at these two tables, you will notice that both have a column called **CustomerKey**. Let's just note here that having columns with the same name in both tables is not a prerequisite for establishing relationships but it can help you understand the model more quickly. Let's connect the tables by these two columns. To do so, in the **Diagram View**, grab the **CustomerKey** column from either table and drop it on the **CustomerKey** column in the other table.

After you do this, a line will appear between the two tables, displayed in *Figure 4.5*, indicating that a relationship has been established. If you hover your mouse cursor over this line, Power Pivot will highlight the names of the columns that were used to create this relationship. What you have just created is known as a many-to-one relationship (*-1). You can see this for yourself by looking closer at the line between the two tables. You will notice three symbols:

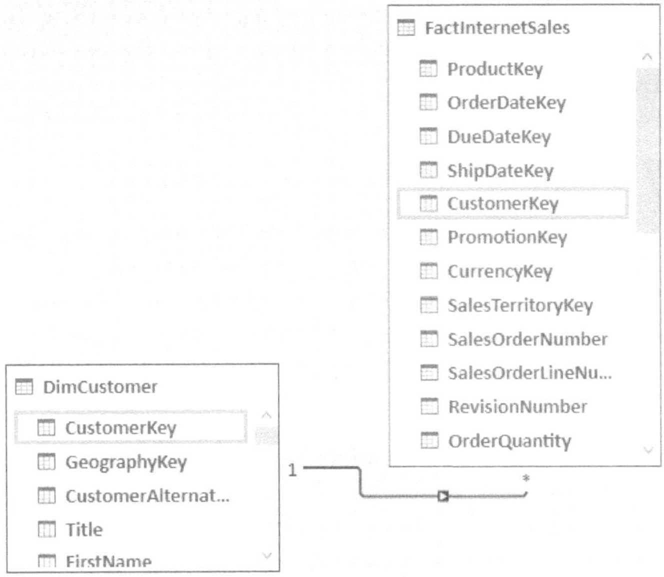

Figure 4.5: *Establishing relationships*

- A * next to the **`FactInternetSales`** table - the asterisk symbolizes, that the **`FactInternetSales`** table is on the *many* side of the relationship. This means that in the **`FactInternetSales`** table, any customer key can appear once or even multiple times if the same customer made more than one purchase in the store.
- A **1** next to the **`DimCustomer`** table - the number 1 indicates that the **`DimCustomer`** table is on the one side of the relationship. This means that every customer key appears only once in the **`DimCustomer`** table. These unique keys are used for matching the customer keys from the **`FactInternetSales`** table to unique customers stored in the **`DimCustomer`** table so that more information about an individual customer can be retrieved, such as their address, name, age, and so on.
- An arrow in the middle of the line – this arrow represents the direction of the filter. As you will see later in this chapter when we create a pivot table, you can use metadata from the **`DimCustomer`** table to filter the sales data from **`FactInternetSales`**. You can, for example, create an analysis of sales by marital status. The marital status data will flow from the **`DimCustomer`** table to the **`FactInternetSales`** data and have a filtering effect on it. You will get separate information about sales to married people and sales to single people.

As you will see in the next chapter when we discuss Power BI Desktop, there are other possible relationship types besides many-to-one (or one-to-many, whatever you prefer) and different settings for the filter flow. But Power Pivot is limited to this one relationship type and the filter always flows from the one side to the many side.

Primary keys and foreign keys

Now that you have established a relationship and seen the most typical relationship type in an analytical data model, let's discuss the concept of primary and foreign keys. The **FactInternetSales** and the **DimCustomer** table are connected through the CustomerKey column that exists in both tables. The columns in both tables contain similar data, for example, 11000, 11001, 11002, and so on.

The difference is that the **CustomerKey** column in the **DimCustomer** table contains each customer key only once, as this table contains each customer only once and the customer key is used to uniquely identify each customer. On the other hand, the **CustomerKey** column in the **FactInternetSales** column can contain each customer key once, multiple times, or not at all. If the business is running well, customers are likely to make recurring purchases in the store, which means their key will appear many times in the **FactInternetSales** table.

The **CustomerKey** column in the **DimCustomer**table is known as the primary key. Primary keys are used to uniquely identify every row in a table. Many rows in the **DimCustomer** table can have the value **Ruben** in the **FirstName** column, but only one row can have the customer key **11002**. Primary key columns reside on the one (1) side of a relationship.

The **CustomerKey** column in the **FactInternetSales** table is known as the foreign key. Foreign keys are used to reference rows in other tables. The uniqueness of values in foreign key columns is not guaranteed, so they reside on the many (*) sides of a relationship. For example, if the **FactInternetSales** contains the customer key **11002**, it means that the purchase was made by Ruben Torres from 5844 Linden Land. Additional information about the customer identified by a specific customer key is obtained from the **DimCustomer** table through the established relationship.

Creating a pivot table based on the data model

You are almost ready to create your first pivot table based on the data model. Before that, let's establish the remaining relationships between the tables. Using the same technique as before - drag and drop - establish the following relationships:

- **`FactInternetSales`** and **`DimSalesTerritory`** through the **`Sales TerritoryKey`** columns in both tables
- **`FactInternetSales`** and **`DimProduct`** through the **`ProductKey`** column in both tables

Now that all the relationships have been established, select the **`Home`** tab, click the button that says **`PivotTable`** and select **`PivotTable`** from the drop-down menu, or click directly on the pivot table icon (a white square containing a blue line with arrows on both ends, as seen in *Figure* 4.6). This will bring you back to the Excel window and open a dialog box called **`Create PivotTable`**, asking you if you want to create the pivot table on a new worksheet or an existing one. For this example, select **`New Worksheet`** and click **`OK`**:

***Figure 4.6**: The Home tab with the PivotTable button*

Excel will create a new worksheet and place an empty pivot table on it. While the pivot table is selected, a side pane called **`PivotTable Fields`** will be visible. If this is not the case, select the **`PivotTable Analyze`** tab and in the **`Show`** group, click the **`Field List`** button.

If this was a classic Excel pivot table, you would see the columns of your single-table data source in this side pane. However, this pivot table is based on the data model and the side pane contains a list of all the tables we added to the data model. Clicking an arrow to the left of the name of any of the tables will expand that table, showing you all the fields of that table, as seen in *Figure 4.7*:

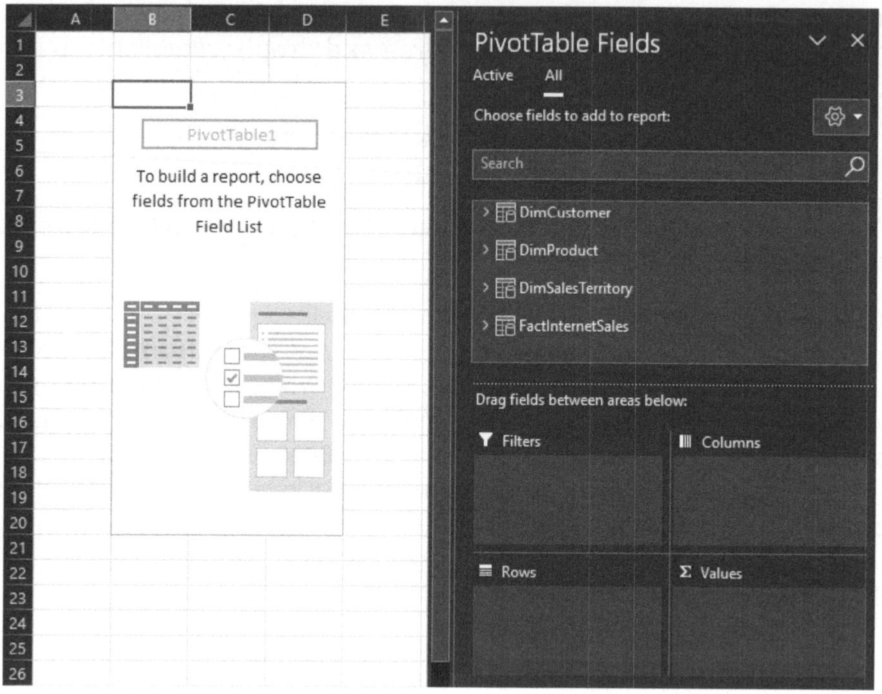

Figure 4.7: *A pivot table with the side pane*

Expand the FactInternetSales table and browse through the available fields. You might remember some of these names from when we were in the **Data View** of the Power Pivot window. Most of these fields are columns of the FactInternetSales table. Now browse to the bottom of the list of fields and you will see an **fx** symbol next to the **SumOfSalesAmount** label. This is the measure we created in Power Pivot. Measures will be listed at the bottom of the fields list when you expand a table, under all the columns of the table, and will be marked with the **fx** symbol before their name.

Let's perform a simple analysis. We want to view the cumulative sales amount by the countries the sales orders originated from. First, check the box next to the **SumOfSalesAmount** measure. This will add the measure to the **Values** area of the pivot table and show you the grand total of sales earnings from the **FactInternetSales** table. We wanted to analyze the sales amount by country, so expand the **DimSalesTerritory** table and check the box next to **SalesTerritoryCountry**. This will add the **SalesTerritoryCountry** column to the **Rows** area of the pivot table. Excel made this default arrangement of fields by the following logic:

- The result of the **SumOfSalesAmount** measure is a numeric value. Numeric fields are added to the **Values** area by default.
- The values in the **SalesTerritoryCountry** column are text. Text fields are added to the **Rows** area by default.

As you will see later, this is only a starting point. We can rearrange the fields in whatever way best suits the readability of the report we are creating. But let's first look at what has changed in the pivot table when we added the **SalesTerritoryCountry** field. Each unique country is now listed in separate rows in the first column of the pivot table, while the second column of the pivot table contains the results of the **SumOfSalesAmount** measure. But the results of these measures are now different in each row. This is because the **SumOfSalesAmount** measure is calculated in each separate cell of the pivot table only in the context of a specific country, while the row with the grand total still contains the sum of the entire **SalesAmount** column of the **FactInternetSales** table.

If you are an experienced Excel pivot table user and this is your first time creating a pivot table based on a data model, you are probably quite excited. The two fields we used come from different tables and can interact with one another. How is this possible?

You will remember that in the **Diagram View** of the Power Pivot window, we established a few relationships. One of them was between the **FactInternetSales** and the **DimSalesTerritory** table through the **SalesTerritoryKey** columns. You will also remember that I mentioned the arrow in the middle of the line visually connecting both tables. In this case, the arrow is pointing towards the **FactInternetSales** table, which means that the **DimSalesTerritory** table can have a filtering effect on the **FactInternetSales** table. How exactly?

Each row of the **DimSalesTerritory** table contains a unique key in the **SalesTerritoryKey** column. Power Pivot can use these keys to identify which sales from the **FactInternetSales** table belong to which territory. For example, in the **DimSalesTerritory** table, **Canada** is listed as the country in the row identified by key number 6. Therefore, when the pivot table we just created wants to calculate the **SumOfSalesAmount** measure for **Canada**, it checks what key the country is listed under, finds out it is 6, and now uses this key to retrieve only the rows that contain 6 in the **SalesTerritoryKey** in the **FactInternetSales** table. After those rows are retrieved, the **SumOfSalesAmount** measure takes the values of the **SalesAmount** column of the remaining rows, sums them, and writes the sum into the appropriate cell of the pivot table.

In the pivot table, we can see that we earned the most from orders coming from the United States. This could be because we have the most customers from the United States. Or it could be that customers from the United States, on average, spend the most per order. Let's write a few more measures to explore this scenario further.

Calculating averages

We wrote our first measure in the Power Pivot window. To write new measures, we don't need to return to that window, we can write them straight from Excel. Notice the **Power Pivot** tab on the Excel ribbon and click it. Notice the **Measures** command in the **Calculations** group and click it. A drop-down menu will appear. Select **New Measure...**. A new window will open with a user-friendly interface that guides you through the process of creating measures.

Let's calculate the average amount of money we earned per sale. As you know, the information is stored in the **SalesAmount** column of the **FactInternetSales** table. Since all the data we will be using comes from this table, in the **Measure** dialog box, select **FactInternetSales** as the **Table name**. This isn't necessary for the functioning of the measure, but it helps with proper measure organization. In the **Measure name** field, type **AverageOfSales**. Typing a description is optional, but it helps when you have complicated measures that reference many other columns and measures. Let's type "This measure calculates the average earnings per sale." Into the **Description** field.

Now click in the **Formula** box after the equals sign **=**. Unlike in the Power Pivot window, you don't use the colon before the equals sign here, it is implicit. Knowledge of Excel functions will come in handy here again. Start typing **AVERAGE** and you will see that DAX also contains this function. You don't have to type the entire function name by hand. Once the user interface suggests the function in the drop-down menu, you can enter it either by double-clicking it or by navigating to it with the arrow keys and entering it with the **Tab** key.

After the function name and the left parenthesis, you can select the name of the column you want to calculate the average of. The user interface will help you again by making recommendations of the columns you can use. But our data model contains many columns, so the menu will be quite long. To narrow down the possible selections, start typing the name of the column you want to use, in our case **SalesAmount**. Monitor the drop-down menu with recommendations while you type. Sooner or later, you will notice that the window will offer you **FactInternetSales[SalesAmount]**, meaning the **SalesAmount** column that resides in the **FactInternetSales** table. Select it either with the double-click method or the **Tab** method. Close the **AVERAGE** function with the right parenthesis. Your function should look like this, as can also be seen in *Figure 4.8*:

```
=AVERAGE(FactInternetSales[SalesAmount])
```

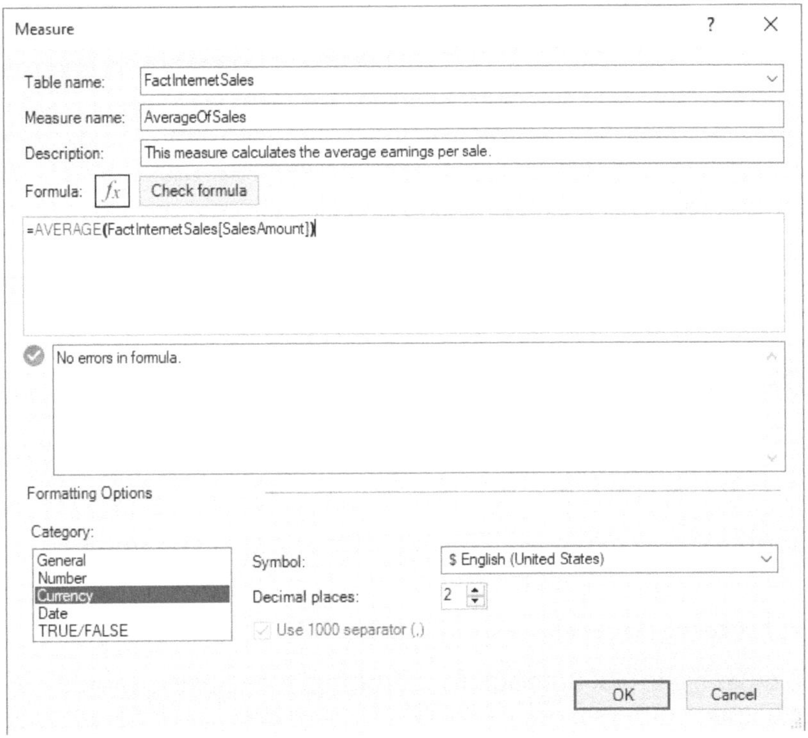

Figure 4.8: *Writing a new measure*

Note that you could also just type the column name without the table name, =AVERAGE([SalesAmount]), but for the purposes of readability and understandability, it is a good practice to type the full path to the column.

A nice functionality of this window is the **`Check formula`** button. It's recommended to always click this button when you finish writing a formula, since the window will immediately tell you, if your formula is OK or if it contains an error. If everything is OK, a green checkmark will appear and a text notifying you that there are **No errors in formula.** If not, you will be notified of possible issues in the formula.

The last step before confirming the measure is defining the format of the result. There are multiple possible categories, such as **`Number`**, **`Date`**, and so on. Since we are calculating the average of sales, select **`Currency`**. After you make this selection, additional options will appear to the right of this menu. You can select additional formatting options, such as the currency symbol and the number of decimal places. For the **`Symbol:`**, let's choose **`$ English (United States)`** and for **`Decimal places:`**, select **`2`**. Finally, click **`OK`**.

If everything is OK with the measure, it will be added to the pivot table automatically. You will notice that the result is different for every country again. In different cells, the averages are calculated for each individual country and for the entire `SalesAmount` column in the `Grand Total` row of the pivot table. Note that this isn't the average amount we earned per sales order. Each row in the `FactInternetSales` table isn't a sales order but a sold line item. Each order can contain multiple items. Therefore, this measure represents the average price of line items we sold. You will find out how to calculate the average earning per sales order shortly.

What about the number of sales we made in each country? The DAX language is also familiar with different **COUNT** functions. Let's talk about those next.

Exploring functions for counting

Again, click the "Measures" command on the "Power Pivot" tab and click "New Measure...". We want to count data in the FactInternetSales table, so select it from the "Table name:" drop-down. Name the measure "CountOfSales". Optionally, add a description, for example, "This measure counts the number of sales". In the formula bar, type the following:

```
=COUNT(FactInternetSales[SalesOrderNumber])
```

This is the most basic **DAX** function for counting. Excel users should recognize it, but the **DAX COUNT** differs from Excel's COUNT in important detail. Excel's **COUNT** function counts only numeric values, whereas the **DAX COUNT** function counts all non-blank and non-Boolean (**TRUE/FALSE**) values. Let's just mention here that like Excel, DAX also contains the **COUNTA** function and their behavior regarding the data they count is basically the same. Both count non-blank values.

Continuing with our measure, click the `Check formula` button to make sure the formula is OK. Select `Number` from the `Category` menu and in the additional options that appear, select `Whole Number` from the `Format:` menu and check the box next to the `Use 1000 separator (,)` label. When you are finished, click **OK**. The measure should automatically be added to our pivot table. But what did we calculate with this measure? As we said, the **COUNT** function counts all non-blank, non-Boolean rows of a column. Since the column we used doesn't contain any blanks, we basically counted the number of rows in the `FactInternetSales` table.

Let's take a closer look at the FactInternetSales table to get a better understanding of how it's structured. In Excel, on the Power Pivot tab, click the `Manage` button. The Power Pivot window will open again. In the `Data View`, switch to the `FactInternetSales` table. If you scroll through the column we just counted, `SalesOrderNumber`, you will notice that some entries in this column repeat multiple times. To browse this column more easily, you can sort it first by clicking the downward-facing arrow next to the column title and selecting **Sort A to Z**. Now find the value **SO51176** in this column. You can also use the filter for this, by clicking the downward-facing arrow next to the column title again, selecting **Text Filters**, **Equals...** and typing the value into the **is equal to** field.

You will see that this is 1 order number that contained two line items. But we counted this order number twice, which is not what we wanted. Our measure can basically be interpreted as a count of line items, but even if this would have been what we wanted, the method for achieving it wouldn't be the best. Let's look at the results in the pivot table, so close the Power Pivot window. You can leave the **FactInternetSales** table filtered and sorted in the Power Pivot window, these settings won't affect your pivot tables.

Looking at the pivot table, we can see that the Grand Total of the **CountOfSales** measure is 60,398, which could, as we said, be interpreted as the number of line items. But we wanted to count the number of individual sales, or we could also say the number of individual sales orders. To do this, we would need to count each value in the **SalesOrderNumber** column only once. Let's write another measure, so click the **New Measure** command.

Let's save the new measure in the FactInternetSales table and call it **CountOfSalesOrders**. Add an optional description like **This measure counts each sales order only once.** The key to the result we want is a function classic Excel doesn't have, but DAX does. Into the formula field, type the following:

```
=DISTINCTCOUNT(FactInternetSales[SalesOrderNumber])
```

As the name suggests, the key characteristic of this function is that it counts each value in a column only once. Click the **Check formula** button to make sure there aren't any errors, format the measure as a whole number with the 1000 separator and click **OK**. When the measure is added to the pivot table, you will see that the results are completely different from the **CountOfSales** measure. This new measure gives us the exact number of sales orders we received from each country listed in the pivot table.

Editing existing measures

As we discussed, the **CountOfSales** measure doesn't make sense. As it currently stands, the most sensible interpretation given the structure of the FactInternetSales table would be that it counts the number of line items. After some thought, we decided that we want to edit this measure and use it to sum the quantity of all items we sold. Let's look at how we can edit the measure to make it reflect this logic.

Like before, click the "Measures" button on the Power Pivot tab, but this time, select "Manage Measures..." from the drop-down menu. In this window, Excel will list all the measures defined in the data model. Click the **`CountOfSales`** measure and click the **`Edit`** button on top of the window. You will be presented with a familiar window. Let's change the name of the measure to **`NumberOfItemsSold`**. We should also change the description to, for example, **This measure calculates the quantity of sold items**.

Let's also change the formula of the measure. Remember that COUNT counts each non-blank, non-boolean row in a selected column once, so it doesn't really make sense when we want to sum up a quantity, as COUNT doesn't differentiate between different numerical values, it just counts them. Change the function to SUM. Now we must also replace the column we are referencing. Change it to FactInternetSales[OrderQuantity]. The formula should look like this:

```
=SUM(FactInternetSales[OrderQuantity])
```

The formatting can stay the same as before. Check the formula. If everything is OK, click OK. Let's note here that currently, every row of the OrderQuantity column contains the value 1, so the result will stay the same. But our measure makes more sense now and will reflect the true number of items sold even if we start writing quantities greater than 1 into the table.

Using the same procedure, edit the name of the "AverageOfSales" measure to "AverageOfSalesPerItem". So open the "Manage Measures" window, select the "AverageOfSales" measure, click "Edit", change the measure name and click "OK".

Calculating ratios with DIVIDE

We now have two measures in our data model that we can combine into an interesting piece of information. We have calculated the number of distinct sales orders (with **`CountOfSalesOrders`**) and the quantity of sold items (with **`NumberOfItemsSold`**). By dividing the results of these two measures, we can get the average quantity of items per order. The reusability of measures to create new measures is one of the great things about measures. Let's create a new measure.

Place the new measure in the **`FactInternetSales`** table and name it **`AverageItemsPerOrder`**. At this point, you can probably start making up your own descriptions, so let's move on to the formula. If you are used to working with classic Excel, you would probably want to write a formula for division with the forward slash / operator. In Excel, you can divide values from 2 cells with a formula such as this:

```
=A1/A2
```

There is no named function for division in classic Excel. What about DAX in Power Pivot? It can also use the forward slash operator for division. But DAX isn't aware of individual cells, so how can we divide two values? Well, we have written two measures that calculate the numerator (**NumberOfItemsSold**) and denominator (**CountOfSalesOrders**) we need to use to get the average of sales. Start typing the name of the first measure, **NumberOfItemsSold**, and the window will soon recommend the name of the measure. You will know that it is measured by the Greek letter sigma in front of the name. Select the measure like you would select a column, with the double-click or the tab method.

After the first measure, type the forward slash and then start typing the name of the second measure, **CountOfSalesOrders**. When the window recommends the measure, enter it. For better readability, you can enter a space before and after the forward slash, DAX won't mind. Also, notice that measure references are not prefixed by table names, even though they are stored within tables. This is why it is a good practice to always prefix references to column names with the table name. This way, you immediately distinguish between references to columns and measures. The measure should look like this:

```
=[NumberOfItemsSold] / [CountOfSalesOrders]
```

Check the formula, format the measure as a decimal number with two decimal places and click **OK**. From the results in our pivot table, we can see that on average, customers from all countries except Australia order more than two items in a single order and that people from the United Kingdom order on average the most products in a single order.

The measure works, but there is a function in DAX that lets us perform what is known as a safe divide. Safe division returns an alternate result when the denominator is 0, so we don't get any errors because of division by 0. The DAX function that can do this is called **DIVIDE**. Let's edit the last measure by clicking the **Measures** button on the Power Pivot tab, selecting **Manage Measures...**, picking the **AverageItemsPerOrder** measure and clicking **Edit**.

Place your mouse cursor directly after the equals sign "=" and enter the **DIVIDE** function. Because division will be performed by the function itself, you don't need the forward slash operator, so delete it. In its place, type a comma ",", which is used in DAX to separate arguments in functions. The first argument is the numerator, in our case this is again the **[NumberOfItemsSold]** measure, the second argument is the denominator, in our case the **[CountOfSalesOrders]** measure and the third argument of the **DIVIDE** function is the alternate result in case of division by 0. Let's use 0 as the alternate result. The formula should look like this:

```
=DIVIDE([NumberOfItemsSold], [CountOfSalesOrders], 0)
```

Check the formula to make sure it's ok, leave the formatting as it was and click **OK**. Since we didn't have any division by zero errors before, the results in the pivot table will stay the same, but the measure is now resistant to such scenarios.

We can use the same method to calculate the average earning per sales order. Create a new measure, name it **AverageOfSalesPerOrder** and type the following formula:

```
=DIVIDE([SumOfSalesAmount], [CountOfSalesOrders], 0)
```

Format the measure as **Currency**, choose **$ English (United States)** as the **Symbol** and click **OK**. The measure will be added to the pivot table. From all the measures in the pivot table, you will see that customers from Australia spent the most per sales order, and also on average spent the most per item bought but purchased the least number of items per order. Customers from Canada, on the other hand spent less per order and per item but purchased more items per order. This can give us an interesting insight into customer behavior.

Understanding the filter flow

Now that we have calculated some information regarding the sales we made and orders we received, let's focus on our customers. The first thing we want to do is find out how many customers from different countries have made purchases from us. Our data model contains the **DimCustomer** table, which contains all our unique customers. We already have a pivot table that filters every calculation we make according to the originating country of the data, so a simple measure that counts data from the customer's table, added to this pivot table should do the trick, right? Let's try.

Create a new measure. Since we will be using data from the **DimCustomer** table, store the measure in that table. Let's call the measure **CountOfCustomers**. Type a description and into the formula field, type the following:

```
=COUNT(DimCustomer[CustomerKey])
```

In this case, counting the **CustomerKey** column is a good idea, because this column serves as the primary key of the **DimCustomer** table and such columns, by definition, cannot contain blank cells that the **COUNT** function would not include in the count. Check if the formula contains errors, format the measure as **Number** and select **Whole Number** in the additional menu. You can also choose to include the 1000 separator. When you are done, click **OK**.

If everything was ok, the measure will be added to the pivot table. However, the results look strange - the result of this measure is identical everywhere in the pivot table. It would be a big coincidence if we had the same number of customers in every county. But we can quickly conclude that this is not what these numbers represent, since the grand total is also the same. Another thing that raises an alarm is a yellow label that appears in the **PivotTable Fields** side pane, saying "Relationships between tables may be needed.". The two buttons that the label contains, **Auto-Detect...** and **CREATE...** won't be of any help here. Let's explore the cause of this issue. Open the Power Pivot window and switch to the "**Diagram View**".

Take a very close look at the relationships between the DimSalesTerritory, FactInternetSales and DimCustomer tables and pay special attention to the arrows in the middle of the lines connecting them, that represent the filter flow. Our pivot table contains the SalesTerritoryCountry column from DimSalesTerritory, and the values of this column flow towards the FactInternetSales table, filtering it. However, there is no arrow pointing from FactInternetSales towards DimCustomer, so the filter cannot transitively flow forward.

This is why the **CountOfCustomers** measure returned the same result everywhere in the pivot table. The **SalesTerritoryCountry** columns sent a filter towards the **DimCustomer** table. The filter got blocked at the **FactInternetSales** table, so the measure always counted an unfiltered **CustomerKey** column from the **DimCustomer** table. As you will see later in the book, Power BI can use two-way filtering, but Power Pivot in Excel doesn't contain this functionality, so we must find a solution with DAX. You can close the Power Pivot window.

Let's edit the formula of the **CountOfCustomers** measure, so find it in the **Manage Measures** window and click **Edit**. The simplest way to get the calculation we want would be the following formula:

```
=DISTINCTCOUNT(FactInternetSales[CustomerKey])
```

This way, we are only counting distinct customer keys located in the **FactInternetSales** table that "survive" the filtering effect of the pivot table. Check the formula to make sure it doesn't contain errors. Since data for the measure is now coming from a different table, store it in the **FactInternetSales** table. Click **OK** and observe the results in the pivot table. The results are the number of distinct customers from every country.

Since we are counting the customer keys in the **FactInternetSales** table, the measure will reflect filtering conditions coming from any table. Remember that the arrows on the lines connecting the tables in the data model are all pointing towards our fact table. Let's demonstrate this by creating a new pivot table.

In Excel, click blank cell outside of the pivot table, open the **Insert** tab, click the arrow below the **PivotTable** button on the far-left side of this tab and select **From Data Model** in the drop-down menu. In the **PivotTable from Data Model** window, select **Existing Worksheet** pick a cell a few rows below the current pivot table and click **OK**. In this new pivot table, first, select the **CountOfCustomers** measure that should be stored in the **FactInternetSales** table. The pivot table will simply show the number of all our customers. Now add the **SalesTerritoryCountry** column from the **DimSalesTerritory** table to the "**Rows**" area of the pivot table. This will slice the result of the measure by country. Finally, add the **Color** column from the **DimProduct** table to the **Columns** area of the pivot table. You can do so by dragging it into this area from the pivot table fields list.

Your "CountOfCustomers" measure should now be sliced by multiple criteria from 2 different tables. We can see that 1875 customers from Australia bought black products, 3577 customers bought blue products and 1780 customers come from Germany. Keep in mind that the calculation performed in every cell is separate from the others. It is based on a subset of data from the source table according to the filters coming from the pivot table. The aforementioned number 1875 is calculated based on the distinct subset of customer keys from the FactInternetSales table, filtered by the sales territory keys representing Australia and the product keys representing black products. If you would sum up all of the numbers in the pivot table, you would get a result much bigger than the actual number of customers in the database.

Before continuing, let's delete the pivot table we created for this example. You can do this by selecting a cell in the pivot table, using the shortcut *Ctrl* + A to select the entire pivot table and then pressing the *Delete* key. After deleting the pivot table, select a cell in the first pivot table again.

Introduction to the X functions

When you were typing functions such as **SUM**, **AVERAGE** and **COUNT**, you might have noticed that you were offered functions like **SUMX**, **AVERAGEX** and **COUNTX**. Nothing like this exists in Excel, these are purely DAX functions. Their role is to take a table, perform a row-by-row calculation on that table, and then aggregate the results of the row-by-row calculations. We previously calculated our total sales by simply summing the values in the **SalesAmount** column of the **FactInternetSales** table. Now we want to add a gross profit calculation.

This will be a bit trickier since our data model doesn't contain a **GrossProfit** column, that we could sum. We could of course create a calculated column, that subtracts the values of the **TotalProductCost** column from the **SalesAmount** column in a row-by-row manner and then aggregate that column, but as we mentioned, to perform numeric operations, measures are a better choice, so let's create a new one.

Store the measure in the **FactInternetSales** table, name it **GrossProfit** and add a description. Now let's try to type a **SUM** function, that would sum the difference between the **SalesAmount** and **TotalProductCost** columns. The attempted function would look like this:

```
=SUM(FactInternetSales[SalesAmount] -
FactInternetSales[TotalProductCost])
```

After you type it, the formula should have a red underline, identifying something that isn't correct. Clicking the **Check formula** button will give you an indication of what's wrong, as we can see in *Figure 4.9*:

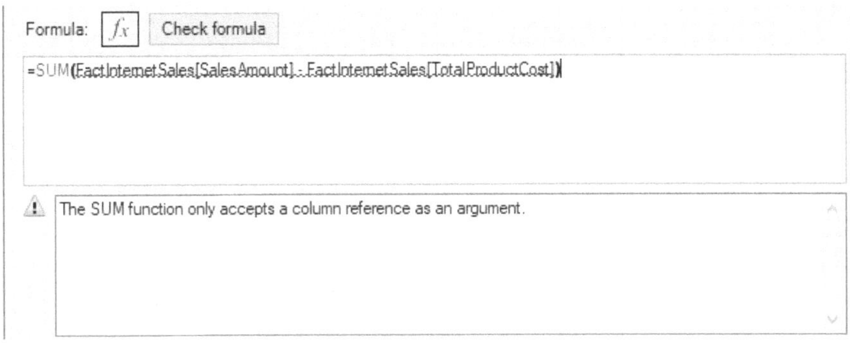

***Figure 4.9**: Checking the formula returns an error*

"The SUM function only accepts a column reference as an argument."

So, the function can only contain 1 argument and it can only be a column whose values we want to add together. To perform the row-by-row subtraction, whose results we want to add together, we need the **SUMX** function. In the formula bar, delete everything except the equals sign **=** and enter the **SUMX** function.

Notice that the function contains two arguments. The first, **Table**, is the table we want to walk through row by row to perform a calculation. In our case, it's the **FactInternetSales** table. The second argument, **Expression**, is the calculation we want to perform in every row of the table. In our case, it's the aforementioned subtraction. **SUMX** will perform the subtraction in a row-by-row manner on the **FactInternetSales** table and sum the results of all subtractions. Here's what the formula should look like:

```
=SUMX(FactInternetSales, FactInternetSales[SalesAmount] -
FactInternetSales[TotalProductCost])
```

Check the formula again, it shouldn't contain any errors. Performing calculations this way is very powerful and can become much more complex as we will see in the next chapter of the book. Each of the X functions performs the defined calculation row by row and then makes the appropriate aggregation (**AVERAGEX** averages, **COUNTX** counts, and so on). Finally, format the measure as US dollars and click **OK**.

Notice that the gross profits are substantially lower than the total sales amounts, which makes sense. But absolute numbers such as these probably won't be enough. We want to find out if we made substantial profits on our sales or barely any. We can use the results of this latest measure to calculate our gross margin. It would also be nice for the report readers to have a visual indication if the margins were good or not.

Key performance indicators (KPIs)

First, let's calculate the gross margin. Create a new measure, place it in the **FactInternetSales** table, name it **GrossMargin** and add a description. In the formula bar, type the following:

```
=DIVIDE([GrossProfit], [SumOfSalesAmount])
```

We will be dividing the gross profit by total sales to calculate our gross margin. When you are done typing, check the formula for errors. The result of the formula will be a ratio, so format the measure results as a percentage, which you will find in the drop-down menu in the bottom right corner of the window if you select **Number** as the category. When you are finished, click **OK**.

You will notice that the gross margins in different countries are almost the same, between 40% and 42%. Let's expand our pivot table a bit by adding the **EnglishProductName** field from the **DimProduct** table to the rows area of the pivot table. Be sure to place it below the **SalesTerritoryCountry** field. You will see that our pivot table now contains a country-by-country analysis of the sales of each individual product. The last column, **GrossMargin**, contains values ranging from around 20% to around 65%. For this example, let's say that our minimum target was a gross margin of 40%. Anything less than that is simply not good enough. A gross margin between 40% and 55% is acceptable and a gross margin of at least 55% or more is great. We have calculated the gross margins and displayed them in the pivot table, but the readability of the report is not good. People usually have a hard time understanding reports that contain large amounts of numbers without any additional visual indicators. In this report, it's hard to quickly figure out which gross margins are hitting our targets, and which aren't. We can create a graphical representation of the goals being achieved or not with Key Performance Indicators or KPIs.

To create a new KPI, display Excel's **Power Pivot** tab and in the **Calculations** group, click the **KPIs** button. In the menu that appears, select **New KPI...**. A new window will open which we can use to define our KPI. First, as the **KPI base field (value):**, select the measure whose results we will take and format according to our criteria. In our case, it's the **GrossMargin** measure. In the **Define target value:** section, we have two options:

- **Measure**: We can use this option to compare the results of the base measure, in our case **GrossMargin**, with the result of another measure. A good example of this option would be if the **GrossMargin** measure calculated the gross margins of the current year and we had another measure that calculated gross margins of the previous year. We could create a graphical indicator showing us if we outperformed or underperformed the previous year in terms of the percentage of the previous year's gross margins.
- **Absolute value**: This is probably the most used option. We can define an absolute value against which we will compare the results of our measure. Select this option and since we defined 55% as a goal, type 0.55 into the field.

When you define the target value, move on to the **Define status thresholds:** section. Here, you will find a red-yellow-green ribbon with two black threshold indicators and a **Target** indicator. The target indicator is always at the value we define, in our case 0.55. The black threshold indicators on the other hand can be moved to reflect our wishes regarding the color of the KPI indicators. When you changed the target value to the absolute value of 0.55, you may have noticed that the numbers above the black threshold indicators changed. They contain a number smaller than the target value. We must now move these indicators to the value where we want a certain coloration to start.

In our case, our target was 0.55 and this is also the point where we want the indicator to become green. So, drag the right threshold indicator to the target line, you will also see the number 0.55 above the indicator. Note that the target value and the point at which we want to color our indicators to become green don't have to be the same. We could have a target value of 100, but if we are already satisfied with 90, we would slide the right threshold indicator to 90. Any value of 90 or more would be colored green.

In our scenario, we also defined 40% as the bare minimum gross margin, so slide the left threshold indicator to 0.4. Anything between 0.4 and 0.55 will have a yellow indicator. Anything below 0.4 will have a red indicator. At this point, we have set up the KPI as our example requires, as we can see in *Figure* 4.10:

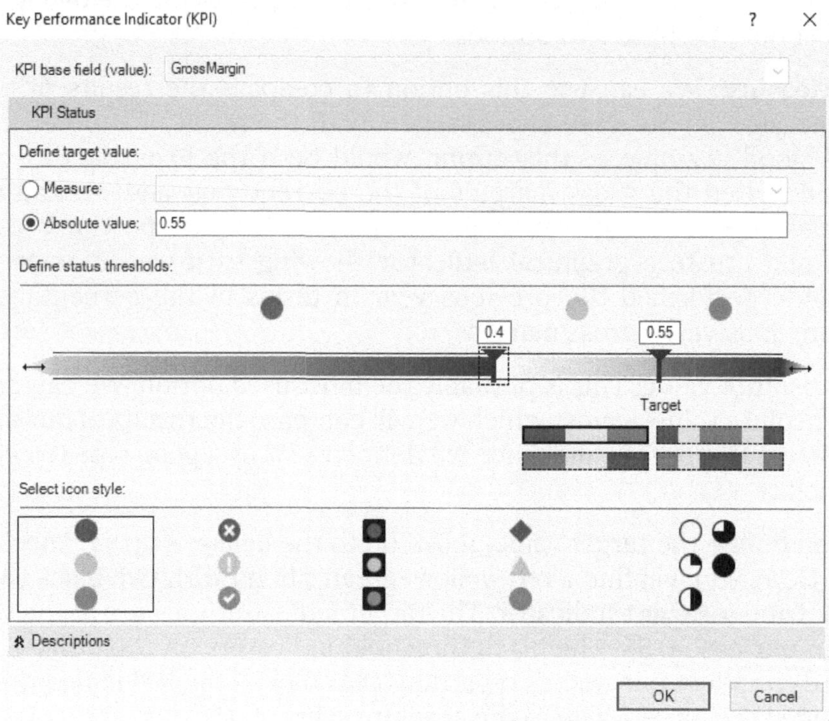

Figure 4.10: *Setting the KPI*

In the bottom-right corner of the **`Define status threshold:`** section, you will see that you can also change the ribbon format. For example, the green-yellow-red ribbon would be appropriate in scenarios where low values are good, and high values are bad (for example, number of complaints).

The last section, **`Select icon style:`**, allows us to select a different format for the indicators we will display in the pivot table. The default traffic lights are good for our example, so click **`OK`**. The pivot table now contains a new column, **`GrossMargin Status`**, but the traffic lights are nowhere to be seen. Rather, the column contains the numbers 1, 0 and -1. This is a bug that Microsoft has never fixed and I'm starting to lose hope that they ever will. These are numeric representations of the traffic lights. For example, -1 represents the red traffic light.

To fix this issue, we must find the KPI in the **`PivotTable Fields`** side pane, remove it and then add it back in. The KPI will be saved in the same table as the base measure, **GrossMargin**, so scroll to the bottom of the **FactInternetSales** table in the **PivotTable Fields** side pane. The KPI will have a traffic light icon next to its name. Expand it and find the **Status** checkbox. Remove the checkmark and add it back. The KPI in the pivot table will now show the traffic light icons. Alternatively, we could also find the KPI in the **Values** section of the PivotTable fields pane and drag it to another position in the Values section. This will also make the indicators appear, after which we can drag the KPI back to the desired position:

Row Labels	SumOfSalesAmount	AverageOfSalesPerItem	NumberOfItemsSold	CountOfSalesOrders	AverageItemsPerOrder	AverageOfSalesPerOrder	CountOfCustomers	GrossProfit	GrossMargin	GrossMargin Status
Australia										
All-Purpose Bike Stand	$10,335.00	$159.00	65	65	1.00	$159.00	62	$6,469.71	62.60%	
AWC Logo Cap	$3,811.76	$8.99	424	424	1.00	$8.99	418	$876.70	23.00%	
Bike Wash - Dissolver	$1,709.25	$7.95	215	215	1.00	$7.95	209	$1,069.99	62.60%	
Classic Vest, L	$2,794.00	$63.50	44	44	1.00	$63.50	44	$1,749.04	62.60%	
Classic Vest, M	$2,476.50	$63.50	39	39	1.00	$63.50	39	$1,550.29	62.60%	
Classic Vest, S	$1,968.50	$63.50	31	31	1.00	$63.50	31	$1,232.28	62.60%	
Fender Set - Mountain	$7,143.50	$21.98	325	325	1.00	$21.98	325	$4,471.84	62.60%	
Half-Finger Gloves, L	$2,179.61	$24.49	89	89	1.00	$24.49	88	$1,364.43	62.60%	
Half-Finger Gloves, M	$2,791.86	$24.49	114	114	1.00	$24.49	111	$1,747.70	62.60%	
Half-Finger Gloves, S	$2,791.86	$24.49	114	114	1.00	$24.49	112	$1,747.70	62.60%	
Hitch Rack - 4-Bike	$6,000.00	$120.00	50	50	1.00	$120.00	50	$3,756.00	62.60%	
HL Mountain Tire	$8,400.00	$35.00	240	240	1.00	$35.00	240	$5,258.40	62.60%	
HL Road Tire	$5,444.20	$32.60	167	167	1.00	$32.60	167	$3,408.07	62.60%	
Hydration Pack - 70 oz.	$10,503.09	$54.99	191	191	1.00	$54.99	189	$6,574.93	62.60%	
LL Mountain Tire	$5,297.88	$24.99	212	212	1.00	$24.99	212	$3,316.46	62.60%	
LL Road Tire	$4,383.96	$21.49	204	204	1.00	$21.49	204	$2,744.35	62.60%	
Long-Sleeve Logo Jersey, L	$2,349.53	$49.99	47	47	1.00	$49.99	47	$540.39	23.00%	
Long-Sleeve Logo Jersey, M	$2,099.58	$49.99	42	42	1.00	$49.99	42	$482.90	23.00%	
Long-Sleeve Logo Jersey, S	$1,999.60	$49.99	40	40	1.00	$49.99	40	$459.91	23.00%	
Long-Sleeve Logo Jersey, XL	$2,599.48	$49.99	52	52	1.00	$49.99	52	$597.88	23.00%	
ML Mountain Tire	$5,938.02	$29.99	198	198	1.00	$29.99	198	$3,717.19	62.60%	
ML Road Tire	$7,122.15	$24.99	285	285	1.00	$24.99	285	$4,458.45	62.60%	
Mountain Bottle Cage	$2,717.28	$9.99	272	272	1.00	$9.99	272	$1,701.01	62.60%	
Mountain Tire Tube	$2,564.86	$4.99	514	514	1.00	$4.99	501	$1,605.58	62.60%	
Mountain-100 Black, 38	$84,374.75	$3,374.99	25	25	1.00	$3,374.99	25	$36,922.39	43.76%	
Mountain-100 Black, 42	$74,249.78	$3,374.99	22	22	1.00	$3,374.99	22	$32,491.70	43.76%	
Mountain-100 Black, 44	$91,124.73	$3,374.99	27	27	1.00	$3,374.99	27	$39,876.18	43.76%	
Mountain-100 Black, 48	$114,749.66	$3,374.99	34	34	1.00	$3,374.99	34	$50,214.45	43.76%	
Mountain-100 Silver, 38	$71,399.79	$3,399.99	21	21	1.00	$3,399.99	21	$31,244.55	43.76%	
Mountain-100 Silver, 42	$67,999.80	$3,399.99	20	20	1.00	$3,399.99	20	$29,756.71	43.76%	
Mountain-100 Silver, 44	$95,199.72	$3,399.99	28	28	1.00	$3,399.99	28	$41,659.40	43.76%	
Mountain-100 Silver, 48	$71,399.79	$3,399.99	21	21	1.00	$3,399.99	21	$31,244.55	43.76%	
Mountain-200 Black, 38	$335,232.47	$2,176.83	154	154	1.00	$2,176.83	144	$153,244.02	45.71%	
Mountain-200 Black, 42	$371,460.52	$2,185.06	170	170	1.00	$2,185.06	163	$169,732.72	45.69%	
Mountain-200 Black, 46	$334,986.58	$2,175.24	154	154	1.00	$2,175.24	141	$153,144.30	45.72%	

Figure 4.11: *The final report*

Our pivot table, displayed in *Figure* 4.11, now contains all our measures sliced by the countries where orders were made from and products that were sold. The report can give us a glimpse into our customer behavior, which products are popular, which products are worth selling, and so on.

Conclusion

This chapter was a brief overview of the capabilities of the Excel BI tools. We started by importing data from Excel using Power Query, connecting the tables together and expanding the capabilities of the model through calculated columns and measures using Power Pivot and then creating reports from the model with pivot tables. This was only a glimpse of what is possible. As you will see in the next chapter, DAX is a powerful language with many built-in functions for various data exploration scenarios.

Key terms

- **Power Pivot**: An Excel add-in that allows you to create a data model within Excel. Use it to establish connections between multiple imported tables, create calculated columns and measures and then create reports based on the model.
- **Data Analysis Expressions (DAX)**: DAX is a formula language you can use to write expressions for calculated columns, measures and tables in Power Pivot for Excel, Power BI and SQL Server Analysis Services.
- **Calculated column**: A calculated column is a new column in a data model created based on a DAX formula. Calculated columns are often used to define extra metadata based on data from other columns, such as price categories based on the product price.
- **Measure**: Measures are used to return an aggregation, such as a sum, an average or a count, based on select data from our data model. Compared to calculated columns, which evaluate a DAX formula row-by-row, measures operate on entire tables or columns, or a subset of that data if so defined by the formula.
- **Pivot Table**: A pivot table is an Excel analytical tool used to aggregate data from a table or multiple tables and slice those aggregations by different criteria coming from our tables (by year, by month, by product category...).
- **Key Performance Indicator (KPI)**: A KPI is a simple Power Pivot visualization, that helps us track the performance of our metrics against a target value.

Questions

1. What is the difference between a calculated column and a measure?
2. Define primary key and foreign key.
3. What are the DAX X functions?
4. Explain some of the advantages of analyzing data with Power Pivot compared to classic Excel functionalities.

CHAPTER 5

Enhancing the Model and Business Analysis with DAX

Introduction

Analytical solutions created in Excel are great for starting your journey into the Microsoft BI ecosystem by using tools you are already familiar with. But to take advantage of all the functionalities that are available to us, we need to use specialized BI tools. In this chapter, we will focus on Power BI Desktop as the go-to tool for creating a data model, delve deeper into DAX and discuss some of the differences between developing a BI solution in Excel and Power BI Desktop.

Structure

In this chapter, the following topics will be covered:

- The first look at the Power BI user interface
- Importing existing data models
- Connecting to data
- Exploring the Power BI Desktop views
- Delving deeper into the Model view
- Using the Data view

- Marking as date table
- Evaluation contexts revisited
- Evaluation context in calculated columns and measures
- The mighty CALCULATE function
- Semi-additive measures
- Creating hierarchies

Scenario

You were impressed by how easily you could combine data from multiple sources into a single data model in Excel and by the pivot tables you prepared from that data. Now you want to go one step further with your BI project by creating a solution with Power BI Desktop that will ingest data that lives in SQL Server. To that end, you have already installed Power BI Desktop on your machine and set up an SQL server with the AdventureWorksDW2019 database and an account with the necessary permissions.

The first look at the Power BI user interface

When you open Power BI Desktop, you will be presented with a pop-up window giving you the options to connect to data, open recent files, presenting links to Power BI sources such as the blog, forums, a list of new functionalities, and so on. Close the pop-up and let's focus on the Power BI Desktop user interface first.

Like Office applications, Power BI Desktop also has a ribbon with different tabs to organize commands. On the left-hand side, you will also see icons allowing you to switch between three different views. The Report view, which Power BI Desktop shows when you open a new file, the Data view and the Model view. Let's first connect to data to see what these different views will show us and allow us to do.

Importing existing data models

As a side note – if you wanted to import a model you already created in Excel into Power BI Desktop, like the one you created in the previous chapter, you could do so by clicking `File` in the upper-left corner of the screen, selecting the Import section and clicking the Power Query, Power Pivot, Power View command. You would then browse to the Excel file containing the data model, select it and click

Open. Power BI Desktop would inform you that it will attempt to extract any data it can from the Excel workbook, as you can see in *Figure* 5.1. Click **Start** and wait for the process to complete. The process imports the entire model, along with the tables, connections, measures and KPIs allowing you to build on the work you already did in Excel with extra functionalities of Power BI Desktop:

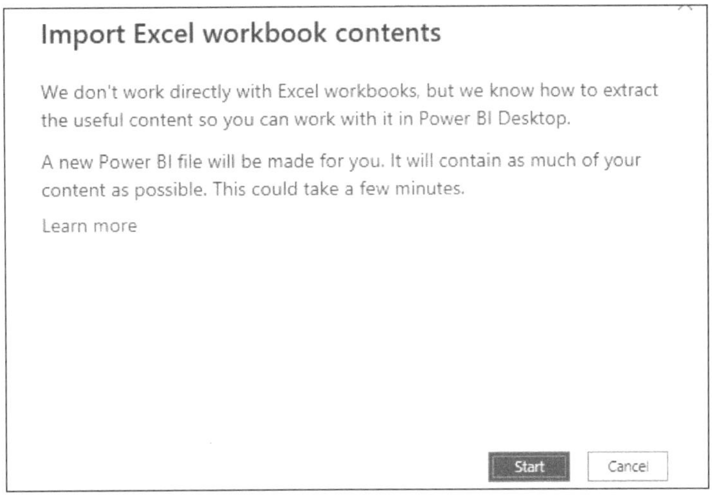

Figure 5.1: *Importing existing data models from Excel*

Connecting to data

However, in this chapter, we will build a new model. If you are still in the Report view, you can click the big Import data from SQL Server tile in the middle of the window, like the one you can see in *Figure* 5.2. Otherwise, no matter which view you are currently displaying, you can click the Home tab and click the SQL Server command in the Data group. Either way, Power BI Desktop will present you with a window for connecting to the server, which is actually the Power Query tool:

Figure 5.2: *Button for connecting to SQL Server*

Into the window seen in *Figure* 5.3, you will type the name of the server you are connecting to into the **Server** field. You can select the database later from a list of databases that the interface will present to you, but if you already know the name of the database, you can type it into the **Database (optional)** field. Below these two fields is a setting that Power Query in Excel does not contain, **Data Connectivity mode**:

Figure 5.3: *User interface when connecting to data from SQL Server*

Power Query in Excel defaults to Import mode, which imports a copy of all the tables you select into the local file. When you work with the data, you are using the local copy. To get the newest data, you need to periodically refresh it. With DirectQuery on the other hand, data stays in the source, no copy is made into Power BI Desktop. Every interaction with the data model triggers a query to the data source.

You might be thinking OK, of course, I want to work with the most recent data, so DirectQuery is the way to go. This isn't such a simple decision. Since DirectQuery needs to make a query to the data source every time you interact with a report, it will be slower than reports built from data in Import mode, where the data is already cached. DirectQuery also doesn't allow all Power Query transformations, DAX time intelligence functions can be problematic, and so on. Import mode is usually the best choice for small to medium-sized datasets and DirectQuery is most often selected when working with huge datasets. The reason is certain limitations to the size of datasets you can upload to the Power BI Service, but more on that in *Chapter* 7, *Using the Power BI Service*.

Leave the default selection, **Import**, and click **OK**. Now on your SQL server, find the **AdventureWorksDW2019** database, expand it and select the following tables: **DimCustomer**, **DimDate**, **DimProduct**, **DimProductCategory**,

DimProductSubcategory, **DimSalesTerritory** and **FactInternetSales**. When you are done selecting tables, click **Load**. Notice that compared to Excel, there is no **Load To** option. Based on your selected connectivity mode, the data will either be imported into the file (Import mode) or just the query definition and data schema will be stored in the file (DirectQuery mode).

Exploring the Power BI Desktop views

Now that we have some data, we can explore what the different views allow us to do. As we already mentioned, you can switch between views in the left side pane of the Power BI Desktop window.

The Report view is where you build all the visuals you want to present to report readers. This view is also very useful during the report development phase since you can instantly test the results of measures you write by adding them to a visualization and checking the results.

The Data view is somewhat similar to its counterpart in Excel Power Pivot. On the right-hand side, you will see a list of tables in the data model. Expanding the table by clicking the arrow next to the table name will present you with the contents of the table, such as the columns, measures and hierarchies. Selecting a table by clickingits name will present you with the content of the selected table. For example, by clicking the **DimProduct** table you will see that it contains columns such as **ProductKey**, **EnglishProductName**, and so on. As you will see later, this is the view we normally use to add calculated columns and do some other things such as change settings on columns.

The Model view is like the **Diagram view** in Excel Power Pivot, but it has more functionalities. Switching to it will reveal the connections between the tables of our data model. You will notice many things we have already talked about, such as the asterisk and 1 character, symbolizing the side of the relationship (many and one). You will also see the arrow indicating the direction of the filter flow. It should flow from the one side of every relationship towards the many sides. Like in the previous chapter, arrange the tables so the fact table, in this case the **FactInternetSales** is in the middle and arrange the dimension tables (with the prefix *Dim*) around the fact table. Pay special attention to the three product tables. Keep them close together since they are related to one another. The fact that the product dimension tables add depth to the model means that this is currently not a proper star schema, but we will sort that out with DAX shortly.

Delving deeper into the Model view

Let's focus on the relationship between the **DimDate** and **FactInternetSales** for a while. You will notice that, unlike other tables in the model, these two tables have three lines, one solid and two dotted, between them. The **DateKey** column of the **DimDate** table connects with three different columns in the **FactInternetSales** table: **DueDateKey**, **ShipDateKey** and **OrderDateKey**. When we imported the tables, Power BI Desktop automatically detected the relationships it could establish, and it detected three between these two tables. But only one relationship can ever be active and that is the relationship symbolized by the solid line. In my case, if I hover over the solid line, I am shown that this is the relationship between the **DateKey** and **DueDateKey** columns.

This means that the default relationship that will be used in our report whenever we slice data from the **FactInternetSales** table by data from the **DimDate** table, for example, by **CalendarYear**, will be the aforementioned one. We will be shown an analysis by years based on the order due dates. But what if that is not the analysis we are most often interested in? It is probably much more likely we will primarily analyze by order dates. Unfortunately, that relationship is currently inactive. Let's look at the effect this has on our calculations.

Switch to the Report view and on the **Home** tab in the **Insert** group, find the Matrix visualization by clicking its icon. The icon looks like a table with the last column and row colored blue. The blank visualization will appear in the central part of the view. Now find the Data pane which is to the far right in the Report view. It should contain the **DimDate** table. Expand it to get the list of the table contents. Find the **CalendarYear** column and click the checkbox next to it.

This will add the column to the matrix visualization, but it will contain the sum of the column contents. As you may have noticed, the column contains a sigma letter next to it in the **Data** pane. This means that it has a default aggregation set that visualizations will use when you add such a column. Power BI Desktop does this for columns that contain a numerical data type. We will look at how these default aggregations can be changed later. For now, simply find the Sum of **CalendarYear** in the **Values** area of the Build a visual pane and drag and drop it into the Rows area. The Matrix visualization should now contain a list of unique calendar years from the column.

Now find the **FactInternetSales** table in the Data pane and expand it. Find the **SalesAmount** column and click the checkbox next to it. The column will also be added to the Values area of the visualization, but in this case, this is what we want. The matrix visualization should now contain the sum of sales amount broken down by calendar years. Remember that in the Model view, the active relationship between **DimDate** and **FactInternetSales** was through the **DueDateKey** column, so the visualization shown in *Figure* 5.4 displays the sales by the years orders were due:

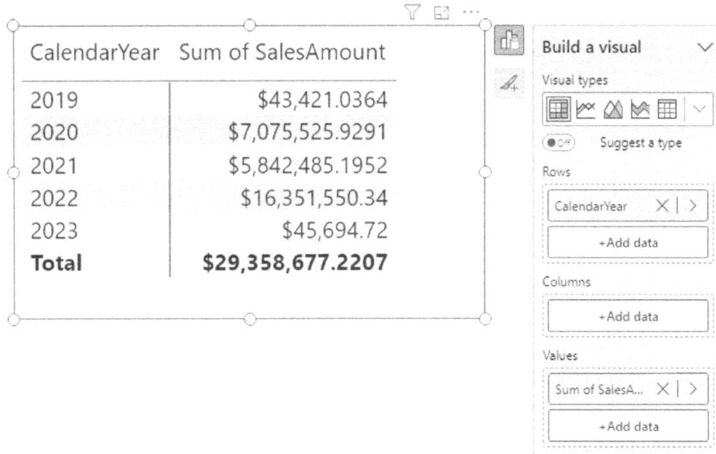

***Figure 5.4**: Matrix visual displaying sales by due date year*

As we said before, it is much more likely that most of our calculations will be based on order dates. To change the default relationship used, we need to change which relationship is active and to do that, we must first switch back to the Model view. We can change the active relationship in two steps. We must first disable the active relationship. Right click the solid line between **`DimDate`** and **`FactInternetSales`**, highlighted in *Figure* 5.5, and click **`Properties`**. Find the checkbox next to Make this relationship active and remove the check mark. Click **`OK`**. Notice that all three lines are now dotted. Next, find the relationship between the **`DateKey`** and **`OrderDateKey`** columns by hovering over the other two dotted lines and paying attention to the column names that get highlighted. Once you have found the relationship, right click the dotted line and click **`Properties`** again. Like before, find the Make this relationship active checkbox and click it, adding a check mark. Click **`OK`**. The line will now be solid.

If you switch back to the Report view and look at the matrix visualization, you will notice that the numbers have changed somewhat. The grand total is still the same, but the year-by-year sums have changed somewhat since the relationship is now using order dates instead of due dates.

This does not mean that we can never analyze our data based on the years orders were placed and the years orders were due at the same time; we would have to switch which relationship is active every time we needed to look at our data from another angle. We simply set the relationship we anticipate will be most used as the active one, and then use a special DAX function, **USERELATIONSHIP**, to force a calculation to use a specific relationship, even if it is inactive:

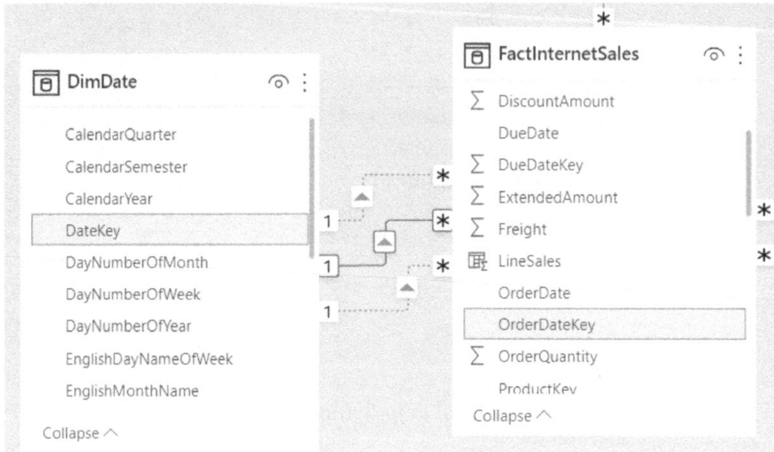

***Figure* 5.5:** *Changing the active relationship*

Using the Data view

As mentioned before, our current model is not a star schema. We need to get rid of the extra layers of depth that the **DimProductSubcategory** and **DimProductCategory** tables give us. We can do this by creating calculated columns in the **DimProduct** table that will calculate values from the related tables. To create calculated columns, switch to the Data view by clicking the table icon in the left pane of Power BI Desktop.

On the right side of the Data view, you will see the Data pane, that contains all the tables of our model. Click the **DimProduct** table to select it. Power BI Desktop will present you with the content of the table. The **DimProduct** table is connected to the **DimProductSubcategory** table through the **ProductSubcategoryKey** column and the **DimProductSubcategory** table is further connected to the **DimProductCategory** table through the **ProductCategoryKey** column. Let's use these relationships to bring in the necessary data.

Either on the Home or on the Table tools tab, find the New column command and click it. The column will be added to the table at the end with a generic name, Column, and you can now type a formula that will be used to calculate the column into the formula bar. DAX contains two functions we can use to grab data from related tables; **RELATED** and **RELATEDTABLE**. Since the **DimProduct** table is on the many sides of the relationship and we want to extract data from a table that is on the one side, we will use the **RELATED** function.

In the formula bar, change the generic column name to something more descriptive, for example, **ProductSubcategory**. After the equals sign, enter the **RELATED** function. You can use the tab or double-click method for formula autocompletion. As the parameter of the **RELATED** function, enter the table name and column name from where you want to extract data, in our case **DimProductSubcategory[EnglishProductSubcategoryName]** and end the function with a right parenthesis. The entire content of the formula bar should look like this:

```
ProductSubcategory =
RELATED ( DimProductSubcategory[EnglishProductSubcategoryName] )
```

As you will see, for each row that has a subcategory key, the appropriate English subcategory name will be imported. Some products in the **DimProduct** table don't have a product subcategory key, which is why the **DimProduct[ProductSubcategory]** column has so many blanks. Let's do the same for categories, so add a new column, give it a meaningful name such as **ProductCategory** and use the **RELATED** function to import relevant data. The formula bar should look like this:

```
ProductCategory =
RELATED ( DimProductCategory[EnglishProductCategoryName] )
```

As you can see, the RELATED function is able to traverse relationships to bring in data from tables that are not directly related to the table we typed the function into. Now that we have all the necessary product metadata in the DimProduct table, we can hide the DimProductSubcategory and DimProductCategory tables. You can do so by right-clicking the table name and selecting Hide in report view.

Note

This chapter will contain some DAX code. To adhere to some standardized code formatting, I will be using the DAX Formatter tool by SQLBI. It is a free tool you can find and use on ***https://www.daxformatter.com/***

Another thing we can do in the Data View is change the default aggregations of columns. A few examples back, we had some additional work when we added the **CalendarYear** column from the **DimDate** table to a visualization - the visualization summed up the years. To stop this from happening, expand the

DimDate table in the Data pane on the right side of the Data View, then select the **CalendarYear** column:

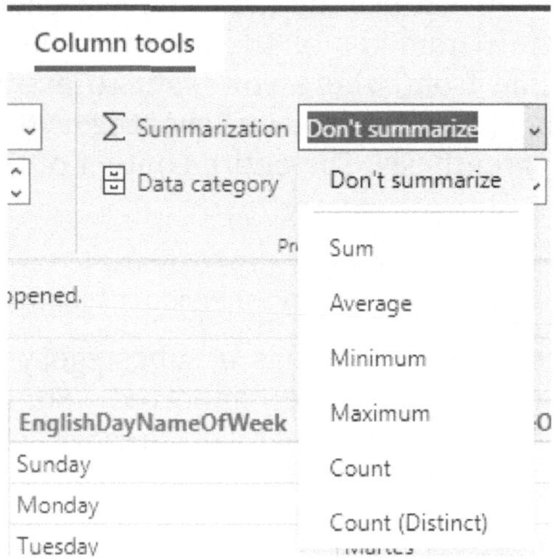

***Figure* 5.6**: *Changing the default summarization*

On the ribbon, you will see a tab called **Column** tools. Click it to get the list of commands. In the **Properties** group, find the **Summarization** drop-down menu, shown in *Figure* 5.6. Currently, Sum is selected. Change it to Don't summarize. When you do this, you will notice that the **CalendarYear** column no longer has the letter sigma next to it. When you add this column to a visualization now, it will no longer be summarized by default, but will be used to break down other data by distinct calendar years from our model.

The Power BI Desktop default behavior can cause issues with other data as well. A typical example is geographical data. Let's say we have sales data for specific countries, but when we want to plot the country data on a map chart, Power BI Desktop incorrectly assumes that the countries are in fact states (for example, Georgia is a country, but also a state in the USA). We can use the Data category command to prevent such issues.

In our case, select the **SalesTerritoryCountry** found in the **DimSalesTerritory** table. This column contains countries, so on the **Column tools** tab, in the **Properties** group, select **Country** from the Data category drop-down menu to help Power BI Desktop correctly plot the data visualizations.

Marking as date table

When we have the Data view displayed, another tab called **Table** tools will be available. This tab contains commands that we will certainly use later, such as **New column**, **New table** and **New measure**. But now let's focus on the command called **Mark as date table**. In data analytics, we often want to measure things through time. How are our sales this year compared to sales five years ago? Have sales gone up year-over-year? Is any month in particular, for example, December, good for our sales?

By default, Power BI Desktop allows us to do such analysis, so-called time intelligence, without any prior setup from our side. But it allows this in a somewhat wasteful manner. Let's look at two settings, that are, by default, turned on in new installations of Power BI Desktop.

Click **File** in the upper left corner of the Power BI Desktop window, click **Options** and settings, then click **Options** to get to the global and current file settings. Under **GLOBAL** - Data Load and under **CURRENT FILE - Data Load**, you will find a Time intelligence setting called Auto date/time. The global setting defines the behavior for all new files while the current file setting of course defines it for the file we are currently working on. So, what does it mean when this setting is turned on?

It means that for each column with a data type of Date, Power BI Desktop will generate a calculated hidden date table. Each of these tables will contain a continuous list of dates, from the first date of the smallest year of the date column for which the date table is calculated, to the last date of the largest year of that column. Additionally, the tables will contain the following calculated columns based on the date: **Day**, **MonthNo**, **Month**, **QuarterNo**, **Quarter** and **Year**.

Since these date tables are hidden from us, how do we know they exist and how can we use them? Close the options dialog box for now and return to the Data view with the **DimDate** table selected. Find and select the **FullDateAlternateKey** column. On the **Column** tools tab, in the Structure group, notice that the Data type is defined as Date. Now take a closer look at the **FullDateAlternateKey** column that is listed in the Data side pane. Notice that it has a calendar icon next to its name. You are also able to expand this column. If you do this, Power BI Desktop will present you with a hierarchy called Date Hierarchy. If you expand it, you will find **Year**, **Quarter**, **Month** and **Day**, which come from the hidden date table for this column.

Notice that the same is true for other columns in our data model. The **DimCustomer** table for example contains two columns that have such hidden date tables working behind the scenes - **BirthDate** and **DateFirstPurchase**.

What this means is that we can go to the Report view, create another matrix visualization and put the **Year** field from the Date Hierarchy of the **BirthDate** column in the rows area of the visualization. This way, we are capable of slicing any data, for example, sum of sales by the year of birth of our customers, without any additional preparation of our data.

Another way of noticing and using these columns is through DAX. Let's first create a basic total sales measure. In the Report view, select the **FactInternetSales** table, go to the Table tools tab and click the New measure command. Write the following piece of DAX:

```
Total Sales =
SUMX (
    FactInternetSales,
    FactInternetSales[OrderQuantity] * FactInternetSales[UnitPrice]
)
```

The measure will calculate the sum of the row-by-row multiplication of the **OrderQuantity** and **UnitPrice** columns from the **FactInternetSales** table. We first selected the **FactInternetSales** table to make sure that the measure was saved into this table, purely for the purpose of proper measure organization.

Note

The FactInternetSales table contains a SalesAmount column that we could use to simply sum the sales. The measure would be:

```
Total Sales =
SUM ( FactInternetSales[SalesAmount] )
```

But for demonstrational purposes, we will be using the SUMX variation since it will give us the opportunity to explain certain DAX concepts in a simple manner.

Now add a card visual to the report page. You will find it in the on the **Home** tab in the **Insert** group, displayed as an icon with 123 written on it. Add the **Total Sales** measure to the card by clicking the checkbox next to the measure name in the Data pane. The displayed result is a little over twenty-nine million. This is the sum of all sales from our model.

Now let's try to measure only the year-to-date sales. We can use the **Total Sales** measure as the base calculation but evaluated in a different context. Check that the **FactInternetSales** table is selected and create a new measure. We will use the **TOTALYTD** function:

```
Sales YTD =
TOTALYTD ( [Total Sales], FactInternetSales[OrderDate].[Date] )
```

Add another card visualization and add this measure to it. The **TOTALYTD** function will evaluate the **Total Sales** measure according to a specific subset of dates. It will only calculate sales based on the order dates up to the current date of the current year. At the time of writing, the date is May 1, 2023, and the result presented on the card visualization is a little over forty-five thousand dollars, as shown in *Figure* 5.7.

Note that the data in our model only goes as far as 2023, so if you are following this chapter later than 2023, the result of this measure will be zero. To adjust the data for learning purposes, use the SQL script provided with this book to push the dates further into the future:

Pay special attention to the **`FactInternetSales[OrderDate].[Date]`** notation. This is the way in which you reference the columns of the automatically created date tables using DAX. When you were typing the function and pressed the dot symbol, you were presented with a list of all the columns that the hidden date table contains, including two that are not visible in the date hierarchy - **`MonthNo`** and **`QuarterNo`**. You can use these columns in DAX functions, but the **`MonthNo`** column plays another role - it is used to properly sort the **`Month`** column:

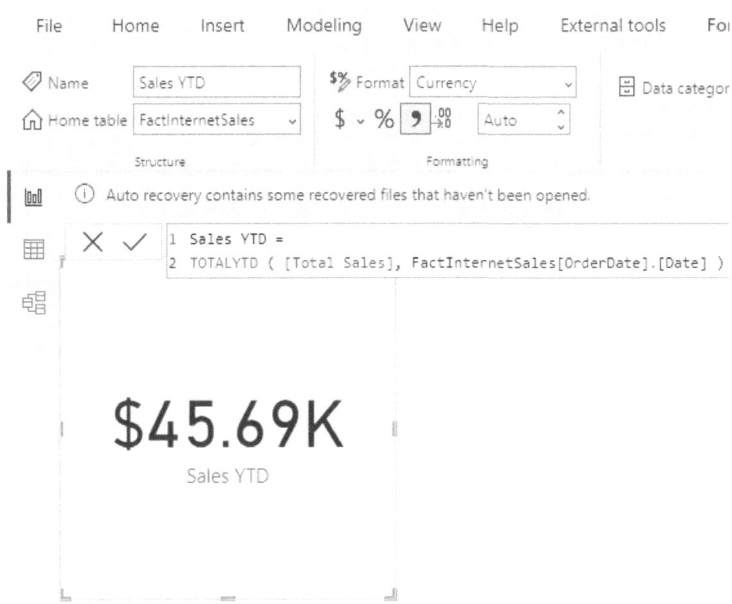

Figure 5.7: *Working with automatically created date tables*

To see the issues with month names, let's create a new matrix visual in the Report view. Expand the **`DimDate`** table and add the **`EnglishMonthName`** column to the visualization. As you will see, the month names are not sorted chronologically, but alphabetically. Therefore, any date table, even an automatically created one, needs to contain a column with month numbers so it can properly sort month names.

To see this in action, we can use the table that we will be using as the date table for our data model. Switch to the Data view, expand the **`DimDate`** table and select the **EnglishMonthName** column. Now find the Sort by column command on the Column tools tab. From the drop-down menu, select the **MonthNumberOfYear** column, which contains months as numbers (January = 1, February = 2, and so on). Now if you switch back to the report view, you will see that the month names in the visualization are sorted chronologically.

So far, we have seen that the hidden date tables give us some additional options when it comes to slicing our data, but I mentioned that this is done in a wasteful manner. This is because Power BI Desktop created one table for every single date column in our data model. These calculated tables will be using up disk space and RAM, even if we never use them in our analysis.

Let's do a simple experiment. Save the file you have created so far and note the size of the file. In my case, as you can see in *Figure* 5.8, it is 2,285 KB. Now let's delete these automatic date tables by switching off the Auto date/time option for the CURRENT FILE in the Power BI Desktop options. Save the file again and note the size of the file. In my case, as shown in *Figure* 5.9, it's 2,100 KB:

***Figure* 5.8**: *Auto date/time turned on*

If you have been following along with the examples, you will notice in the Report view that the card visual with the Sales YTD measure has stopped working. The Sales YTD measure itself has also stopped working. This is because the columns it referenced no longer exist:

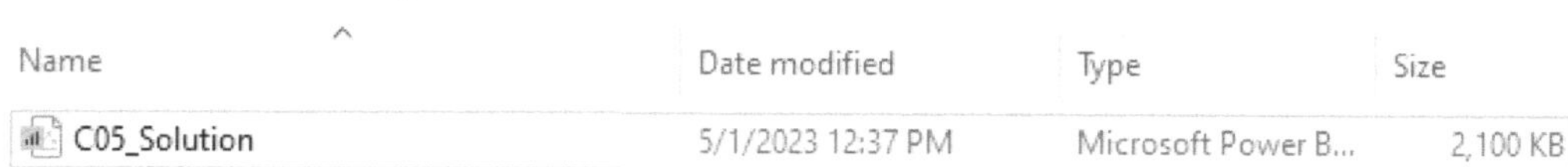

***Figure* 5.9**: *Auto date/time turned off*

Note

Like we said, the automatically generated date tables are hidden from view, they won't appear anywhere in Power BI Desktop (except as a date hierarchy next to each date column or as a special syntax when writing DAX). If you want to explore all the hidden details of your data model, such as hidden tables, query performance etc., I recommend a free tool called DAX Studio. You can find it here: ***https://daxstudio.org/***.

As you can see, this simple model already saves some space by turning off the auto date/time option. There are other drawbacks to the auto date/time functionality. An increased model size also means increased refresh times. You should also note that the auto date/time option only works with tables stored in Import mode. Since we can't see these date tables anywhere in the model, we also can't manage them. This means we can't add additional columns that we might require for time intelligence, such as week numbers, days of the week, and so on .

The fact that each date column creates its own date table also means that we can't have a single source of filtering. This can be especially painful in models containing two or more fact tables that span the same date range. We can't tell all the fact tables to show us results of measures filtered by a specific year with a single setting. We would have to filter each fact table separately, using the Year column of the automatically generated date table connected to each fact table.

As you can see, there are many reasons why we may want to approach working with dates a different way. In our example, if we want to perform time intelligence with data in the **`FactInternetSales`** and **`DimDate`** tables, a different approach is even required. This is because the **`FactInternetSales`** and **`DimDate`** tables are not connected through columns that are of the Date or Date/time type, but rather through key columns of the Whole number type.

The recommended method is to use a purpose-built date table, that we can connect to our fact table (or even multiple fact tables) and mark it as a date table. In our data model, the **`DimDate`** table will serve this purpose. If the need arises, you can mark additional tables as date tables.

Before marking the **`DimDate`** table as a date table, let's make a quick demonstration so we'll see that time intelligence functions really don't work correctly. In the report view, select the Sales YTD measure. Correct it as follows:

```
Sales YTD =
TOTALYTD ( [Total Sales], DimDate[FullDateAlternateKey] )
```

We will be using the **`TOTALYTD`** function again, but this time, we will use the **`FullDateAlternateKey`** from the DimDate table as the source of dates. Now add a matrix visualization to the report page, put **`EnglishMonthName`** from **`DimDate`** into the Rows area, **`CalendarYear`** from **`DimDate`** into the Columns area and Sales YTD that should be in the **`FactInternetSales`** table into the Values area. Expand the matrix visualization if necessary to get a view of all the data.

Immediately, something doesn't look right. The **`TOTALYTD`** function should evaluate the **`Total Sales`** measure as a yearly running total for each year. But we can see that this is not the case. The total of February 2022 is smaller than January 2022. Also, 2023 only contains a value for January. Even if we didn't make a single sale in February, the year-to-date sales should at least be the same value as January. Now let's see what happens when we have a designated date table.

To mark the **DimDate** table as a date table, select it in the Data side pane in either the Report view or Data view. Then, on the **Table tools** tab, click the **Mark as date table** command and select **Mark as date table** from the drop-down menu. Alternatively, right-click the **DimDate** table in the Data pane, you can do this in any view, and select the **Mark as date table** option:

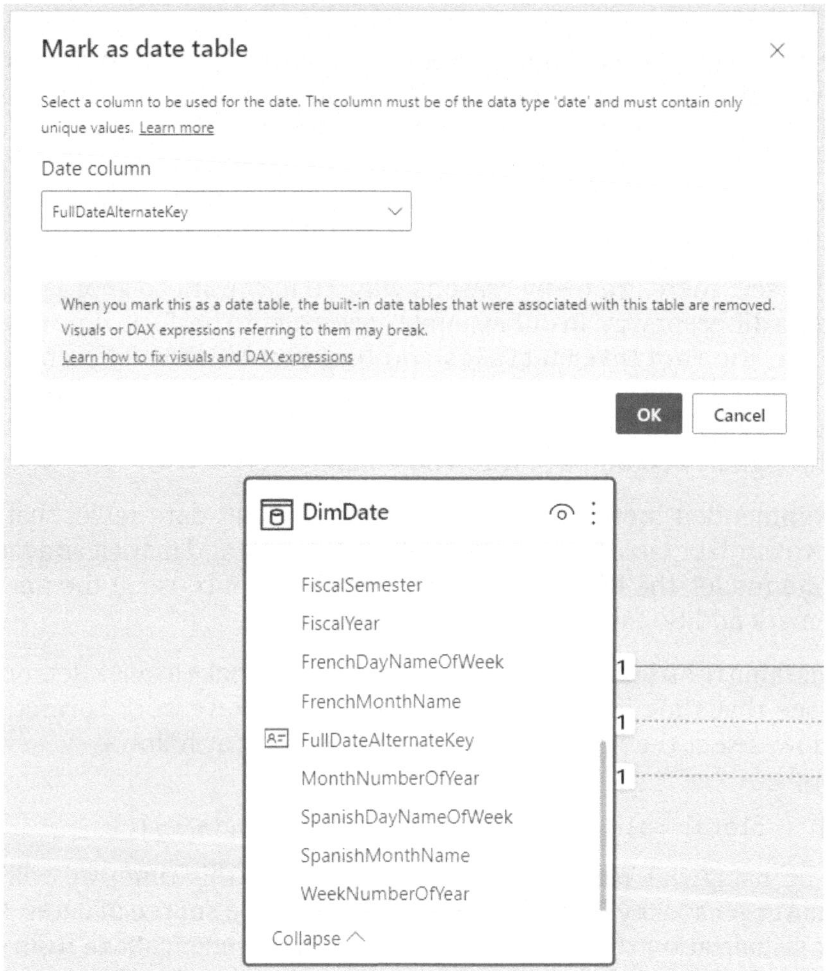

Figure 5.10: *Marking the DimDate table as a date table*

You will be presented with the window shown in *Figure* 5.10 from which you will need to select a column of the Date or Date/time type. The column you will use as the date column must contain contiguous, unique dates that span full years, be it calendar or fiscal years. In our example, this is the **FullDateAlternateKey** column. This column also mustn't contain any blanks. With the **FullDateAlternateKey** column selected, Power BI Desktop will tell you if it passes validation. If the column is validated successfully, press **OK**.

The matrix visualization with the Sales YTD measure should now be showing correct results. Before, the DAX engine didn't know how to use the **`FullDateAlternateKey`** column in a time intelligence context, because the active relationship between **`DimDate`** and **`FactInternetSales`** is established through the **`DateKey`** and **`OrderDateKey`** columns. Now we have told DAX which column to use as the source of all dates in this relationship. DAX now uses this information to rewrite the filter context in which the **`Sales YTD`** measure is evaluated.

For example, the February 2022 value is no longer calculated based on the sales made in February 2022, but based on the sales made up to the last visible date in that context. If this sounds strange, add the **`DayNumberOfMonth`** field from the **`DimDate`** table into the Rows area of the matrix visualization (under the **`EnglishMonthName`** field). Now expand the data for February by clicking the plus sign next to the month label.

You will see that the sales are increasing on a day-by-day basis. The last visible date under the context of February 5, 2022, is that same date, so the value shown are the total sales under 2022 up to that date. The last visible date for February 2022 as a whole is February 28, 2022, so the visualization shows the cumulative sales of 2022 up to that date. You will also notice that 2023 now contains values even for months when no sales were made since it shows total sales for that year up to the last visible date in the current context.

The subtotal for columns may also seem strange. The **`TOTALYTD`** function evaluates the measure based on the largest year visible in the current evaluation context. If we were displaying the **`Total Sales`** measure, the subtotal for columns would evaluate data for all Januarys in our model. But in the **`Sales YTD`** measure, the evaluation context is changed to only consider data for the largest visible year, which is 2023. The data will therefore be the same as in the 2023 column.

To make the visualization less confusing to report readers, we should probably turn the column subtotals off. We can do this by selecting the matrix visualization and clicking the Add or remove visual elements button represented by a brush icon. In the small pane that opens, we can find the checkbox for column subtotals and turn it off.

Evaluation contexts revisited

To write DAX, it is not enough to simply know a lot of DAX functions, which arguments they need and how we can combine them into complex formulas. To fully understand how DAX works, we also need to understand some theoretical concepts, namely the DAX evaluation contexts. DAX has three evaluation contexts: row context, query context and filter context. We briefly discussed the row and filter contexts in *Chapter* 4, now let's take a deeper dive.

Row context

We have been using the row context each time we created a calculated column without paying any attention to it. We have also created our own row context each time we used an iterator, such as **SUMX**. Let's switch to the Data view and select the **DimProduct** table to examine the row context in action.

In the **DimProduct** table, we created two calculated columns: **ProductSubcategory** and **ProductCategory**. Calculated columns automatically create a row context. What this means is that the calculated column checks the required values for each row of the current table and does the calculation we defined in the formula.

For example, the formula for **ProductSubcategory** takes a row-by-row look at the **ProductSubcategoryKey** column, which is used for the relationship with the **DimProductSubcategory**, and retrieves the appropriate value from the **EnglishProductSubcategoryName** column of that table. As you can see, row context can be a powerful ally as it can traverse relationships.

Contrary to calculated columns, measures have no idea of a row context by themselves, we must create it with DAX. That is where iterators come in. Iterators are a class of DAX functions that know how to create a row context on a table. You will recognize most iterators by the X at the end of the function name, such as **SUMX**, **AVERAGEX**, and so on. We have seen that we can use the SUMX function to make a calculation and then perform addition of the results of that calculation:

```
Total Sales =
SUMX (
    FactInternetSales,
    FactInternetSales[OrderQuantity] * FactInternetSales[UnitPrice]
)
```

In the **Total Sales** measure, we used the SUMX function to add the results of multiplication of the **OrderQuantity** and **UnitPrice** columns. We couldn't do this with a simple **SUM** function, as it can only take a single column as an argument. A formula such as this wouldn't even be accepted, as it has too many arguments:

```
Total Sales SUM Invalid =
SUM (
    FactInternetSales,
    FactInternetSales[OrderQuantity] * FactInternetSales[UnitPrice]
)
```

We could also make the following logical error, using the **SUM** function twice, multiplying the sum of two columns:

```
Total Sales SUM Wrong =
SUM ( FactInternetSales[OrderQuantity] ) * SUM (
FactInternetSales[UnitPrice] )
```

The multiplication of two sums is very different from the summation of multiplication of two columns. In the Total Sales measure, the **SUMX** function doesn't add the values of **OrderQuantity**, then add the values of **UnitPrice** and then multiply those two values. It creates a row context over the **FactInternetSales** table and multiplies the **OrderQuantity** and **UnitPrice** columns row-by-row, then performs addition on the results of all those multiplications.

Query context

The query context defines what values from our data model are used in a specific calculation. Let's switch to the Report view and create another matrix visualization. If you are running out of space on the report page, you can delete a visualization by selecting it and pressing the Delete key or you can create a new page by clicking the plus icon in the bottom left corner of the screen.

Add the Total Sales measure to the matrix visualization. The visualization will now contain a single cell, for which the query context is returning the sum of the row-by-row multiplication of all values from the **OrderQuantity** and **UnitPrice** columns from the **FactInternetSales** table. Next, add the **CalendarYear** field from the **DimDate** table to the Rows area of the matrix visualization. Now the results of the Total Sales measure are broken down by the year an order was placed (earlier, we made the relationship between **DimDate[DateKey]** and **FactInternetSales[OrderDateKey]** the active relationship). In the cell showing sales for 2022, the query context is only retrieving the data from the rows of **FactInternetSales** where the year of the order date is 2022.

The query context can also come from other report elements. If we add a slicer to the report page, add **ProductCategory** from **DimProduct** as the field to the slicer and select, for example, Accessories on the slicer, the query context on the matrix visualization for 2022 will now be orders placed in 2022 for products that fall into the Accessories category, as we can see in *Figure* 5.11.

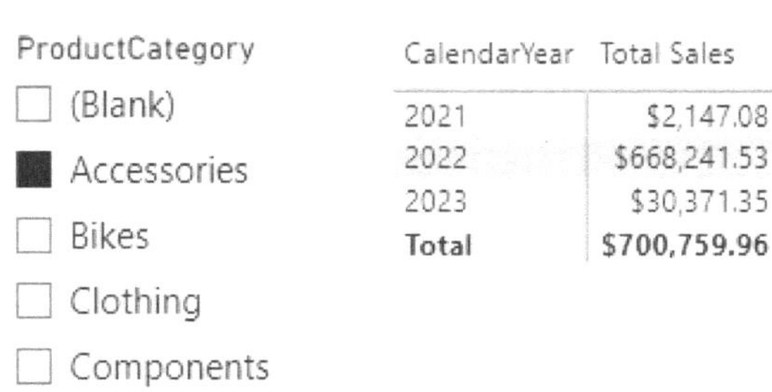

***Figure* 5.11**: *Query context*

Filter context

The filter context has a similar effect to the query context. It is applied over the query context to further define which values are retrieved for a specific calculation. The difference is that the filter context is defined with DAX code. This can be done with a subset of DAX functions called filter functions, the most important of which is probably **CALCULATE**. We will dedicate a separate section to **CALCULATE**, but for now, let's create a single measure for this example:

```
Total Sales College Educated =
CALCULATE (
    [Total Sales],
    DimCustomer[EnglishEducation] = "Bachelors"
        || DimCustomer[EnglishEducation] = "Graduate Degree"
)
```

This measure will change the evaluation of the Total Sales measure to only consider sales made to customers with either a bachelor's or a graduate degree. The double pipe operator, **||**, is a DAX logical operator that makes an OR comparison between two statements. When we add this measure to the matrix visualization, the changed filter context is added on top of the existing query context. If we build on the example we explored in the section on query context, in the 2022 cell for this measure, the visualization will show us just the sales where the order was made in 2022, the items ordered fall into the Accessories category and the customers who made the order have a college education.

Note

Because of very subtle differences, many resources don't differentiate between query context and filter context, mentioning only filter context to describe both concepts. Distinguishing between the two is crucial as the filter context can be used to complement or even overwrite the query context. In such cases, we may not be able to deduce the result of a measure by simply looking at a visual, we may also need to examine the measure shown on the visual. Descriptive measure names also help in making the results of measures easier to understand.

Evaluation context in calculated columns and measures

We have already made a short introduction into evaluation contexts, calculated columns and measures in the previous chapter. Now that we have a better understanding of evaluation contexts, let's look at how they are used in calculated columns and measures.

Calculated columns

As discussed in the previous topic, calculated columns automatically create a row context, meaning that each row of calculated columns has an understanding of the values that other columns contain in the same row. This understanding can also traverse relationships, no matter on what side of a relationship we are writing the calculated column formula. Let's switch to the Data view, select the **`DimProduct`** table and create a new calculated column with the following formula:

```
ProductSales =
SUMX (
    RELATEDTABLE ( FactInternetSales ),
    FactInternetSales[OrderQuantity] * FactInternetSales[UnitPrice]
)
```

In the formula, we are creating a column that calculates the sales of each product in the **`DimProduct`** table. As shown in *Figure* 5.12, the row context reads the product information of a specific row and then uses that information to get the sales of that product from the **`FactInternetSales`** table. This is where the **`RELATEDTABLE`** function comes into play:

Status	ProductSubcategory	ProductCategory	ProductSales
Current	Tires and Tubes	Accessories	$15,444.05
Current	Tires and Tubes	Accessories	$9,480.24
Current	Tires and Tubes	Accessories	$7,425.12
Current	Tires and Tubes	Accessories	$21,541.38
Current	Tires and Tubes	Accessories	$34,818.39
Current	Tires and Tubes	Accessories	$48,860
Current	Tires and Tubes	Accessories	$22,435.56
Current	Tires and Tubes	Accessories	$23,140.74
Current	Tires and Tubes	Accessories	$27,970.8
Current	Tires and Tubes	Accessories	$27,105.65

***Figure* 5.12**: *Calculated columns have an automatic row context*

We already used the **`RELATED`** function, which only returned a related value from a column. Here, we need to retrieve an entire table of values, that is, the table of sales of a particular product. We then use the **`SUMX`** function to iterate over that related table, multiplying order quantity by unit price and then performing addition on the products of multiplication.

You may notice that we are actually using nested row contexts. The first-row context comes from the calculated column. Then we defined another row context with the **SUMX** function. So, we are iterating over every row of the calculated column and inside of that, we are iterating over every row of the related table of product sales.

Understanding that row contexts can be nested is important if we want to write DAX code correctly. Let's look at another example. Switch to the **FactInternetSales** table and make another calculated column with the following formula:

```
LineSales =
SUMX (
    FactInternetSales,
    FactInternetSales[OrderQuantity] * FactInternetSales[UnitPrice]
)
```

The formula is almost the same as in the previous example, except that we don't need to retrieve values from another table, so we didn't need the **RELATEDTABLE** function. But the results don't seem correct. Every row contains the same value, which is completely off – over twenty-nine million dollars.

If we understand the row context, the reason for this result will be obvious. The calculated columns already have a row context, but inside of this row context, we created another one with **SUMX**. So, inside an iteration over **FactInternetSales**, we created another iteration. Each row therefore takes all the values of **FactInternetSales**, multiplies order quantity by unit price and adds up the products, Since calculated columns already have a row context, the correct formula would be such:

```
LineSales =
FactInternetSales[OrderQuantity] * FactInternetSales[UnitPrice]
```

Measures

Unlike calculated columns, measures don't create a row context by themselves. If we don't need to perform a row-by-row calculation in our measure, this isn't a problem. We can use aggregators, such as **AVERAGE**, to compute the result of a measure:

```
Sales Average =
AVERAGE ( FactInternetSales[SalesAmount] )
```

However, if we need to perform an aggregation on a row-by-row calculation, we need to create the row context programmatically. This is why iterators, such as the X functions exist. For example, to calculate the average of sales, you could use AVERAGEX in a measure as such:

```
Average Of Sales =
AVERAGEX (
    FactInternetSales,
    FactInternetSales[OrderQuantity] * FactInternetSales[UnitPrice]
)
```

Let's switch to the Report view, create a line chart, put the **`Average Of Sales`** measure on the Y-axis and **`DimDate[CalendarYear]`** on the X-axis. The calendar years now represent the query context - each year on the *x*-axis is telling the **`Average Of Sales`** measure to only calculate the average of sales for a particular year. Now, let's create a new measure that will contain a filter context:

```
Average Of Sales Bikes =
CALCULATE ( [Average Of Sales], DimProduct[ProductCategory] = "Bikes" )
```

The measure changes the context of the Average Of Sales measure so only sales of bikes are included. The measure is still evaluated in the original query context, that is, for each calendar year separately. Adding this measure to the same line chart will show us the average of sales that only include bikes. We will see that the line closely follows the line of the Average Of Sales measure up until 2022, when we started to sell more clothing and accessories, which are cheaper than bikes, so the average of all sold items went down. We can also see that the Average Of Sales Bikes only extends to 2022, which means that we haven't sold any bikes in 2023 so far.

Now that we have seen how calculated columns and measures work with the evaluation contexts, let's take a closer look at the function that is capable of changing the filter context, **`CALCULATE`**.

The mighty CALCULATE function

So far, we have already used the **`CALCULATE`** function in a few measures. Let's build on the previous example to gain a further understanding. Type the following measure and add it to the line chart:

```
Average Of Sales Married Canadians =
CALCULATE (
  [Average Of Sales],
  DimCustomer[MaritalStatus] = «M»,
  DimSalesTerritory[SalesTerritoryCountry] = «Canada»
)
```

The new measure will take the **`Average Of Sales`** measure, which will now be evaluated in the query context, coming from the line chart visualization and on top of that, the filter context coming from the **CALCULATE** function – marital status equals married, and country equals Canada.

What if we wanted to create a measure that will draw a straight line on the line chart that we could use for comparison or as a baseline? For example, we want to have a straight line based on last year's average of sales so we can see if our customers are, on average, spending more money this year. Let's type the following measure:

```
Average Of Sales Last Year =
CALCULATE (
    [Average Of Sales],
    DimDate[CalendarYear]
        = ( YEAR ( TODAY () ) - 1 )
)
```

The measure will evaluate the **Average Of Sales** measure in a filter context, where calendar year of sales will be the year of today's date minus one. When we add the measure to the line chart, we will get a straight line, representing the average of the sales in the previous year, but the line is also being drawn for years in which we don't have any sales. You can see this issue in *Figure* 5.13. When we modify the filter context based on a column that is also used in the query context, the filter context overwrites the query context. This means that at each datapoint on the line chart, the query context for calendar year is removed and the filter context for calendar year is added:

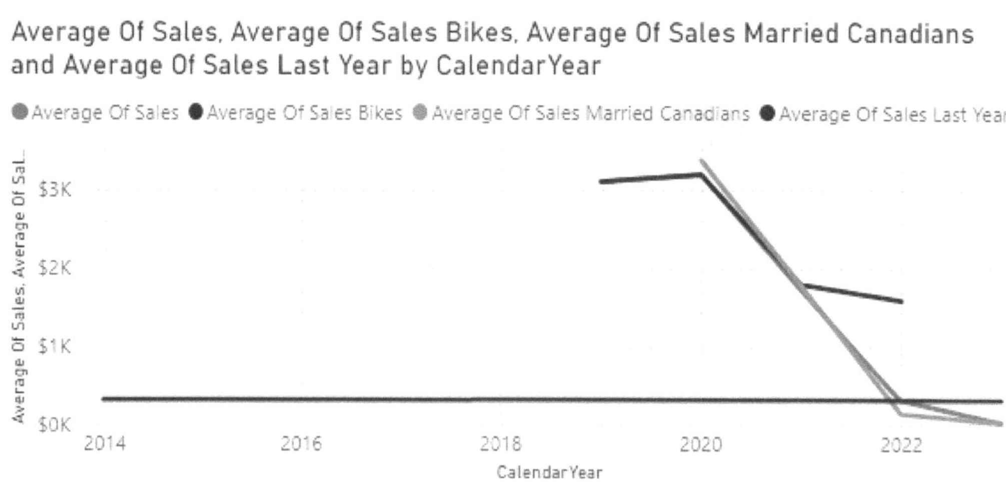

***Figure 5.13**: Line extending back to years with no sales*

So why does the line extend back to 2014? The reason is the same. The dates in **DimDate** go back to 2014. But since we didn't have any sales data before 2019, the line chart, by default, didn't show the items with no data. Now that we have overwritten the query context with the filter context, those items have data. The average for sales of the previous year was the same in 2014.

To solve this issue, we need to change the line chart settings. First, make sure that the line chart is selected, then click the **Add or remove visuals** button and click the **More options** button. A new side pane called Format will appear. Find and expand the X-axis options. In the **Range** section, use the **Minimum** setting to define the smallest value on the X-axis. You can type a fixed value, in our case that would be 2019, or you could first define a measure and then select it by clicking the **fx** button. The user interface and the line chart are displayed in *Figure* 5.14. The measure for determining the smallest sales year would look like this:

```
Min Sales Year =
MINX ( FactInternetSales, YEAR ( FactInternetSales[OrderDate] ) )
```

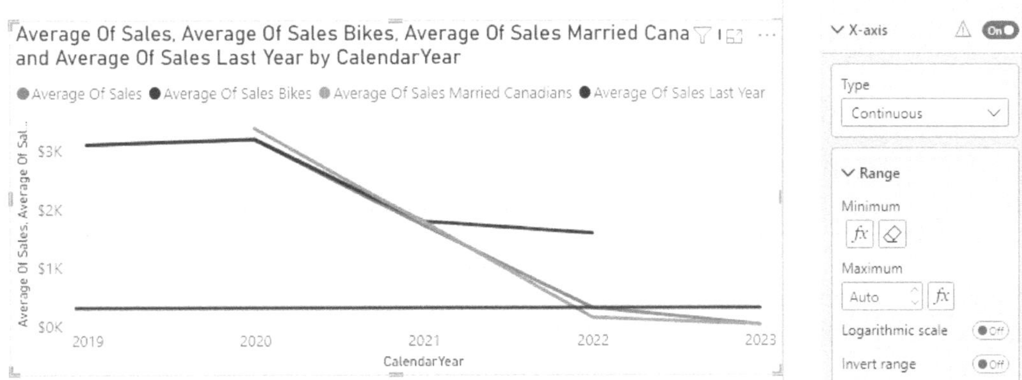

Figure 5.14: *Minimum for X-axis set to the Min Sales Year measure*

Now let's discuss a typical use case for the **CALCULATE** function - using it to determine ratios. Let's say we want to find out what percentage of all our sales we made to each individual country. We have already written the **Total Sales** measure to determine the aggregate sales, so we can create a matrix visualization and add the `Total Sales` measure and the **DimSalesTerritory[SalesTerritoryCountry]** to it.

The visual shows us the total sales to each country. Now to calculate the percentage of all sales made to a specific country, we would need to divide the total sales made to that country by the grand total of sales. This can be done by overwriting the query context with a fresh filter context, that includes all sales, no filters applied:

```
Total Sales ALL =
CALCULATE ( [Total Sales], ALL ( FactInternetSales ) )
```

The measure will evaluate the **`Total Sales`** measure by iterating over all the data in the **`FactInternetSales`** table. We have used the **`ALL`** function to tell DAX to include all data from our fact table, regardless of the query context. You can add the measure to the matrix visualization to get a feeling of what the measure is doing – calculating the grand total of all sales everywhere in the visual, but you probably won't keep it on the visual on a report you intend to publish. The **`Total Sales ALL`** measure will only serve as an intermediate step for the measure we really need on the report:

```
Percent Of All Sales =
DIVIDE ( [Total Sales], [Total Sales ALL], 0 )
```

SalesTerritoryCountry	Total Sales	Percent Of All Sales
Australia	$9,061,000.5844	30.86%
Canada	$1,977,844.8621	6.74%
France	$2,644,017.7143	9.01%
Germany	$2,894,312.3382	9.86%
United Kingdom	$3,391,712.2109	11.55%
United States	$9,389,789.5108	31.98%
Total	**$29,358,677.2207**	**100.00%**

***Figure* 5.15**: *Using CALCULATE as an intermediate step to determine percentages*

Adding this measure to the visualization, as displayed in *Figure* 5.15, will give us the percentage of sales made to each country. At first, the result will be a decimal number, but with the measure selected, we can use the Measure tools tab to format the result as a percentage.

Semi-additive measures

When we are writing measures, most of the time, we are, knowingly or unknowingly, writing additive measures. These are measures that can be summarized over any dimension. The **`Total Sales`** measure we have already written is a prime example. If we display the measure on a matrix visualization and add **`DimProduct[ProductCategory]`** to rows and **`DimDate[CalendarYear]`** to columns of the visual, the **`Total Sales`** measure will correctly display the sales for each year by each category. Also, the row totals, column totals and the grand total will be correct.

Semi-additive measures however can only be summarized over some dimensions, but not by all, typically, the dimension is time. For this example, connect to the

AdventureWorks database again and import the **FactProductInventory** table. This table contains a day-by-day state of the inventory of products. Switch to the model view and make sure the following relationships are established:

- `FactProductInventory[DateKey] - DimDate[DateKey].`
- `FactProductInventory[ProductKey] - DimProduct[ProductKey].`

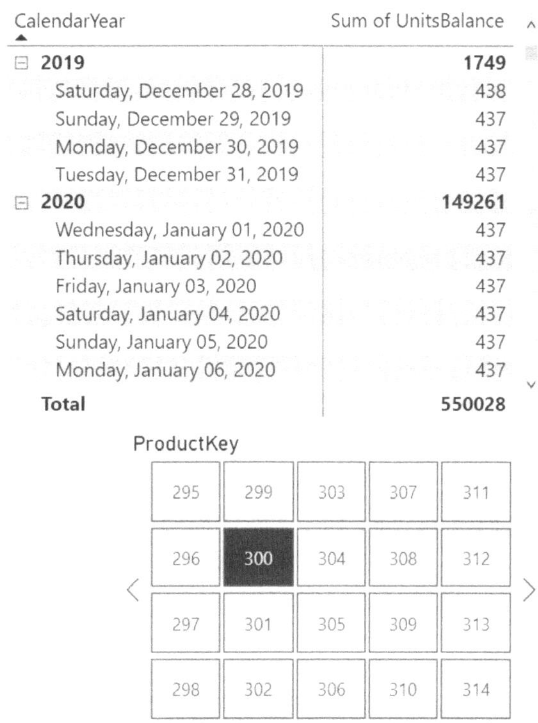

***Figure 5.16**: Typical issue when displaying data that is not additive over time*

Now switch to the report view and add a matrix visualization with **DimDate[CalendarYear]** and **DimDate[FullDateAlternateKey]** in Rows area and **FactProductInventory[UnitsBalance]** in the **Values** area. Additionally, add a slicer to the report page and put **DimProduct[ProductKey]** into the **Field** area. Change the default slicer layout by clicking the **Add or remove visual elements** button, clicking **More options** and in the Format side pane, expand **Slicer** settings and from **Options**, select the **Tile** style.

Select product key three hundred. Now select the matrix visual and click the **Expand all down one level in the hierarchy** button, that is represented by a branching arrow in the upper-right corner of the visual.

You will see a daily breakdown of the unit balance grouped by years. But as you can see in *Figure* 5.16, the matrix visual is showing the sum of daily balances for each calendar year and in the grand total field, which doesn't make sense since a daily balance of product inventory can't be aggregated.

Note

Simply dragging and dropping columns into the values area of a visualization is not a best practice. This creates a so-called implicit measure. Implicit measures can sometimes yield unpredictable results. It is always better to write our own measures, known as explicit measures, in which we define exactly what we need to happen. I simply used an implicit measure here to demonstrate that a sum of the units balance column wouldn't work correctly. It wouldn't work even with an explicit measure such as

```
Sum Of Units Balance =

SUM ( FactProductInventory[UnitsBalance] )
```

In this example, we could solve the problem of the visualization making an aggregation of balances by calendar year by modifying the filter context to only take into account values on the last date visible in the query context:

```
Last Date Balance =
CALCULATE (
    SUM ( FactProductInventory[UnitsBalance] ),
    LASTDATE ( DimDate[FullDateAlternateKey] )
)
```

The measure is making an aggregation on the unit balances, but if you add the measure to the matrix visualization, you will see that the aggregate data for the year 2019 is the same as the data for December 31, 2019. That is because the last date visible for 2019 is December 31. You will see similar results for every other year we have unit balance data for. If this is bothersome, we can disable these yearly *aggregates* by clicking the Add or remove visual elements button and unchecking the Row subtotals checkbox.

Creating hierarchies

To make report creation a bit easier, we can organize our dimensions into groups using hierarchies. For example, if we often analyze our data based on geographical information, we could create a hierarchy that groups the geographical data we most often need in a sensible order.

You can create hierarchies in any of the three views by right-clicking a column name in the Data side pane and clicking **Create hierarchy**. In our example, let's say we want to create a hierarchy based on the sales territory region, country, and group. The top-level dimension of this hierarchy should be **SalesTerritoryGroup**, so right-click this column in the Data side pane and click **Create hierarchy**.

In the Data pane, you will now see a new grouping under the **DimSalesTerritory** table with a default name of **SalesTerritoryGroup** hierarchy. To give it a different name, you can right click the hierarchy and select **Rename**. Let us call the hierarchy **Sales Territory Hierarchy**. Next, right-click **SalesTerritoryCountry** and click **Add to hierarchy** and select the **Sales Territory Hierarchy**. Finally, right-click **SalesTerritoryRegion** and add it to the hierarchy as well.

Next time you need to create a report based on the sales territory data, you won't need to add each individual column to a visualization. Switch to the Report view, create a new report page, add a matrix visualization to a report page and add the **Total Sales** measure to it. Now click the checkbox next to **Sales Territory Hierarchy**. The entire group is added to the visualization with one click and the **Total Sales** measure is now sliced by the top-level dimension in the hierarchy, **SalesTerritoryGroup**.

To analyze the total sales by the data in the hierarchy, you have multiple options in the upper-right corner of the matrix visualization. You can click the downward facing arrow, Click to turn on Drill down, and select a specific **SalesTerritoryGroup** to expand that specific group down one level, into countries. If you do this, you can then click the upward facing arrow to go back up one level.

If you are at the top level, you can click the two downward facing arrows, Go to the next level in the hierarchy, to go down one level, in our case to **SalesTerritoryCountry**. You will be shown all the countries, not just the ones from a specific group.

Another option is the arrow that splits into two points. That command expands the hierarchy one level further, slicing the Total Sales measure by **SalesTerritoryGroup** and by **SalesTerritoryCountry**, and, if you click this command again, by **`SalesTerritoryRegion`** as well. By fully expanding the hierarchy, you get the analysis shown in *Figure 5.17*:

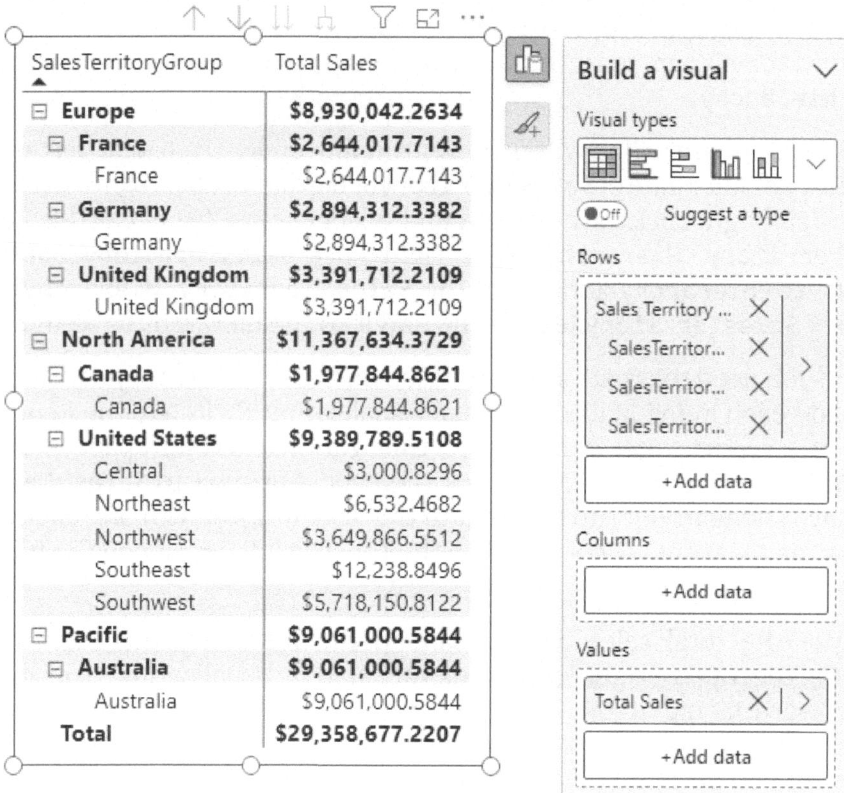

Figure 5.17: *Matrix visualization with all hierarchy levels expanded*

Conclusion

In this chapter, we made an overview of the Power BI Desktop user interface, connected to data and then built up a data model. We demonstrated how to make connections between imported tables, how to set up active relationships, how to set up a date table and explained why it is important for time intelligence functions. We also described the different evaluation contexts and how they are tied to measures and calculated columns. As we have seen, having a theoretical understanding of the DAX language is important if we want to write DAX code that returns correct data. It is also important if we want to use DAX to programmatically change the evaluation contexts.

As you may have noticed, this chapter was not about creating good-looking reports. The visualizations we created were put there purely for testing our measures. In the next chapter, we will focus on how to use Power BI Desktop to create readable and visually appealing reports we can use for business decision making.

Key terms

- **Evaluation context**: DAX distinguishes between three evaluation contexts: query context, row context and filter context. They define what data from the model a DAX function will operate on. The evaluation contexts allow for the reusability of measures, as the same measure can show different results, depending on the evaluation context.
- **Date table**: A dimension table in a data model made specifically to enable time intelligence. By default, Power BI Desktop automatically creates simple date tables for each date column in our model. But for in-depth time intelligence, we create our own date tables. They must contain continuous dates encompassing entire years (January 1 to December 31) for all the years in our data model.
- **Hierarchy**: We create hierarchies by structuring data from our model in a way that makes hierarchical sense, for example, product category, product subcategory and product. We create hierarchies so our report creators have a prepared structure by which to drill through data, not needing to figure out the hierarchical model by themselves.

Questions

1. Which evaluation contexts exist in DAX?
2. What is the primary function for changing the filter context?
3. What do we need to be mindful of when we have multiple relationships between a fact and a dimension table?
4. What is Power BI Desktop's default behavior when we have columns containing dates in our model?
5. Why would we want to have a special date table in our data model?

CHAPTER 6
Creating Reports in Power BI Desktop

Introduction

Up to this point, we have seen what is needed to create data analysis solutions that are useful for a multitude of users. We need as many stakeholders as possible, or as necessary, to execute data-driven decisions, so we want our solution to be nice-looking and easy-to-use. We need a suitable structure of data, both in a logical sense – that is the star schema – and in a technical sense – a technology that is good with querying. We need our data system to be automated and integrated, meaning connected to external data systems in a way that lessens the manual labor. We have seen that this can be done with the help of Power Query and M formula language. As dataflows are bringing data from data systems to a central location, we can place transformations to deliver data in a suitable format. Once data is in a suitable format, we can start creating data models, connecting tables to a diagram and creating calculations to summarize insights. We have seen some of that in the previous chapters, for both Excel, with Power Pivot functionality, and Power BI Desktop. These are two of the most common and strongest BI tools on the market.

In this chapter, we are going further into Power BI Desktop, which is a good development tool for creating insightful BI reports. Together with Power BI Service, we can utilize the reports on an organizational scale. Power BI reports can serve decision makers for a variety of purposes – decision makers may be looking at how sales are going in comparison to last year, or in comparison with goals or plans, or they may be interested in stock levels, in operating finances, or in human resources, and so on. The first step of every analytics project is to see what has been going on in the past. That is described with the term descriptive analytics. We are going to see some of the descriptive capabilities of Power BI in this chapter.

Structure

In this chapter, we will discuss the following topics:

- The Power BI environment overview
- Screen elements
- Using filters
- The Data and Visualizations panes
- Drill through and Tooltips
- Creating visualizations
- Header icons/visual headers
- Upper ribbon tabs in the Report view
- The Bookmarks, Selection, and Sync slicers pane
- The Table view on the left ribbon
- The Model view on the left ribbon
- The Data panes in three views
- The ever-changing interfaces: On-object interaction

The Power BI environment overview

Power BI Desktop is a report development tool. It is generally not intended to be used as a data visualization-only experience, that is rather the job of Power BI Service – a cloud environment intended to host Power BI reports and provide users with a click-to-filter experience for them to gain insight from data. Generally speaking, Power BI Desktop offers many development options that could confuse end users, while the Power BI Service report screen is focused on only the necessary elements for a visualization experience. However, with updates and premium licenses, Power BI Service does offer increasing development capabilities.

Power BI Desktop can be used as a data visualization experience for a single advanced user, as a self-service BI tool, but when we introduce multiple users, things tend to be complicated. The Power BI Desktop report file (.pbix) would have to be saved on a remote location accessible by all the necessary users. Securing access would have to be done on a hosting system rather than being easily managed on Power BI Service. Experience shows that users tend to apply filters to reports and tend to save their customizations, so if we wanted to host the Power BI Desktop files, it would probably be a good idea to automatically re-create the base file on a remote system periodically. For example, every 24 hours the Power BI report file is replaced to ensure that the report has not been tampered with.

Besides Power BI Service, there is an additional option to host Power BI reports on Power BI Report Server, which is an on-premises environment. It is a good option for institutions avoiding cloud solutions, such as some governmental organizations. To build a report that is publishable to Power BI Report Server, we need a version of Power BI Desktop that is usually older than the latest version and it can be downloaded from the following link: **https://powerbi.microsoft.com/en-us/report-server/**. The licensing needed is either Power BI Premium or SQL Server Enterprise Edition with Software Assurance, so we can see that option will be chosen many times by those having SQL Server databases. At the time of writing (June 2023), there needs to be a single Power BI Pro license to publish reports, but no licenses are needed to interact with the reports.

Power BI Desktop can be installed from Microsoft Store and in such a case, we are supposed to receive automatic updates. The installation file can also be downloaded from the following link: **https://powerbi.microsoft.com/en-us/desktop/**. This installs a stable single version of the application, so in the case of major changes, such as a windows interface change, we can monitor the situation more closely. Power BI Desktop is being updated almost every month, which should be in the same periods as Power BI Service. Rolling updates mostly offer a good experience, though they can sometimes provide problems in a production environment. Major changes are usually introduced first as a preview and only later as the default setting for all users, giving us some time to adapt.

By my experience, problems can be expected during development. Minor problems included some visualizations not working as intended, such as Bookmark Navigator not displaying correctly which bookmark is currently selected. Major problems included gray screens for all the reports connected to the tabular models hosted on an on-premises SQL Server Analysis Services. These problems bring frustrations to end users, who have little patience and understanding for problems caused by updates. They can usually be resolved by the developer's diagnostic and corrective actions.

In the case of gray screen, the solution was to update the gateway application. Gateway is a component used for establishing communication between two networks, that of on-premises data sources and that of Power BI Service. Setting it up will be described in the last chapter of this book. After a newer version has been installed, the reports were properly displayed. Usually, the problem with these types of error is that the reason for the problem is not clearly written and developers have to solve them by guessing and trials. A more stable environment is offered for Power BI Report Server, which is updated three times per year, namely in January, May, and September, but it offers less in terms of features.

Screen elements

We have already introduced the views on the left ribbon of Power BI Desktop, which are the **`Report`** view, the **`Table`** view, and the **`Model`** view. Please note that the Table view was known as the Data view up to August 2023:

- In the **`Report`** view, we can create a canvas with objects and visualizations that form our reports.
- In the **`Table`** view, we can view all data in our model in a tabular format, as well as apply some changes to tables and columns.
- In the **`Model`** view, we can create a diagram with our tables and further modify some of the properties regarding our fields, that is columns and measures.

We have also introduced the **`Home`** tab of the upper ribbon which offers capabilities to connect to external systems with Power Query. It can be seen in *Figure* 2.8 in *Chapter* 2, *Acquiring and transforming data from multiple sources*.

The **`Home`** tab offers a similar experience in all the views, but exact options may vary from view to view, and they can change with updates. We will take a look at some of the other tabs later in the chapter.

The **`Report`** view shows a canvas or a report page in the center screen. We can insert visualizations and other objects, such as text boxes, shapes, buttons, images, and so on, to the canvas. Following the canvas is the lower ribbon that is showing the report pages as well as offering some options to interact with report pages, as it can be seen in *Figure* 6.1:

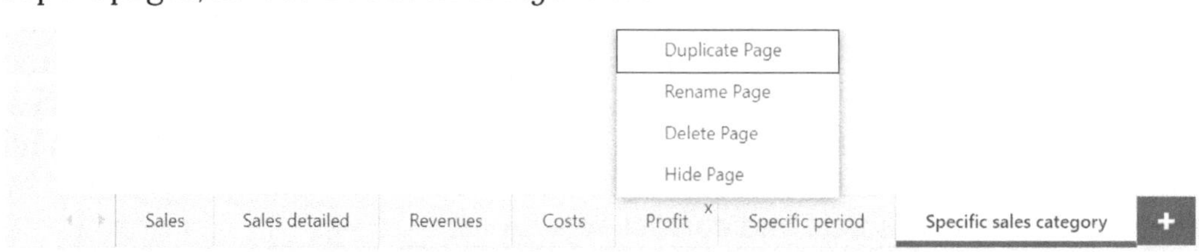

Figure 6.1: *Power BI Desktop's Home tab's lower ribbon*

We can see the seven pages of the report. Selecting the box with the page name will display the report page. We can add a new report page by clicking the green box with the plus symbol. Left-clicking the symbols with left and right arrows will scroll the pages when there is more pages that can be displayed on a screen. Scrolling by using these symbols will not display the page without us clicking the box. Right-clicking the symbols will display a pop-up list with all the pages.

Right-clicking the report page shows the options visible in *Figure* 6.1. Hiding the page makes it invisible to end-users when the report is published to Power BI Service. This can be useful for cases when our page is intended as a support page, rather than the main report page, such as for Power BI's drill-through or custom tooltip capabilities.

Drill-through is Power BI's capability to expand a visualization into a whole new report page. This new report page might be prefiltered depending on what dimensional value is selected in the original visualization. The new report page can contain any number of visualizations to explain the original chart in detail.

Tooltips are pop-up windows displayed on the visualization when we hover over the information it is displaying. Basic tooltips show basic values, such as measures, while custom tooltips show a small window of a report page, which may be fitted with visualizations of our choosing. We will explain the tooltips in more detail later in the chapter.

We can often use **`Duplicate`** page during our development to keep the same canvas structure and only modify the measures that the visualizations are displaying. Reports often display same type of charts from different angles, such as the first page displaying quantity and second value (or amount).

On the right side of the screen in **`Report`** view, there are three panes available from the get-go, that we can expand by clicking them: **`Filters`**, **`Visualizations`**, and **`Data`**. Please note than with the new preview feature called On-object interaction, Visualizations pane is gone, to be replaced by the **`Format`** pane and by the buttons on the right of every selected visualization. We will discuss this feature later in the chapter. Because at the time of writing in June 2023 this is still a preview feature, we have mostly focused on discussing the default interaction experience.

- The Visualizations pane offers options to build and format visuals, or to format a report page, and advanced analytic options for some visualizations.

- Data pane displays the tables in our model, and within those, we can see columns, calculated columns, measures, and hierarchies. We can only see those objects designated as visible in **`Data`** or **`Model`** view.

- Filters pane allows us to add a filter to the selected visual, to the selected report page, or the whole report.

These panes can be seen in *Figure 6.2*. As we have warned, the Power BI environment is ever-changing. On-object interaction or other upcoming updates can bring changes to the interface, including to the upper ribbon. General interaction will most likely remain similar:

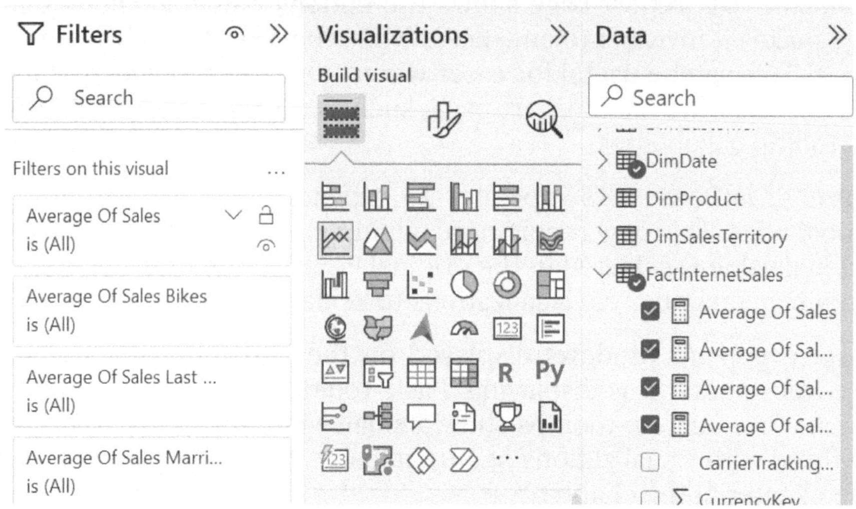

***Figure 6.2**: Three panes on the right side of the Power BI Desktop's report view*

Using filters

Using filters is a key aspect of Power BI experience. In this subchapter we will overview different filters' options and how they work.

Filters on this visual

In *Figure* 6.2, we can see **`Filters on this visual`** under the Filters pane. By default, every measure or column that has been added to the visual is listed under **`Filters on this visual`**. We can filter by the added fields, or we could add additional fields to the list. This option allows visualization's filtering in a specific way that could be different to how other visualizations are filtered. We should generally avoid this functionality unless there is a very good reason to use it.

The point of Power BI is for the end user to select their own filters and to use interactive filtering between visualizations. That means that the first visualization's display can be used to filter another visualization, by left-clicking the first visualization's data point in the display.

If we are using **`Filters on this visual`** to only show a certain **`ProductSubcategory`**, which is a column or an attribute from a dimension table, but the end user filters the report to another **`ProductSubcategory`**, the prefiltered visualization will display **`Blank`**. In only rare cases should **`Filters on this visual`** be used, for example, when we have added a measure to a Table visual, and we only want to display the rows in the table where the measure's value is larger than zero.

Using slicers instead of the Filters pane

As we can see in *Figure 6.2*, the Filters pane can be hidden from end users when a report is published to Power BI Service. We can do that by selecting the eye symbol to the right of the keyword **`Filters`** on the Filters pane. That is not what we would usually be doing unless our users prefer to use slicers. Slicers are a visualization type that is placed on a canvas. They are used for filtering and some users will find their experience more interactive. We can see several slicers in *Figure 6.3*:

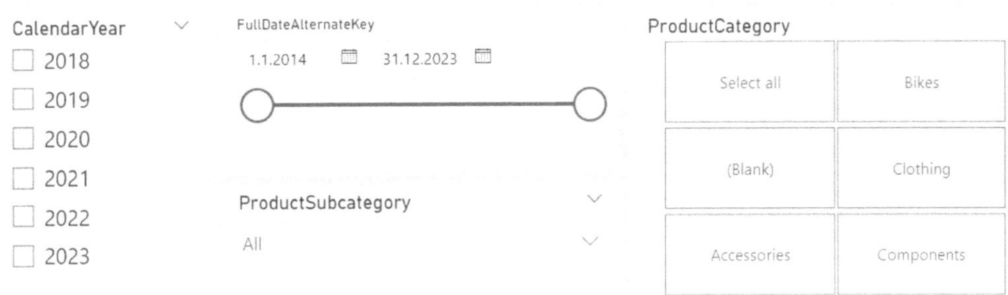

Figure 6.3: *Slicers with different formatting*

All of these are the same visualization type - slicers. They were formatted differently by going to the **`Visual`** > **`Slicer settings`** > **`Options`** > **`Style`**. We will say more on formatting visualizations later in the chapter.

As for using slicers, an end user once explained to me, that the majority of filtering they were making was by using interactive filtering between visualizations. This means that they were left-clicking visualization's data points which in turn filtered other visualizations. By that logic, using the **`Filters`** pane was unintuitive for them. They preferred using slicers.

Slicers can also be modified to affect only selected visualizations, by using the **`Edit`** interactions functionality under the **`Format`** tab in the upper ribbon.

Hiding excessive options from end users

If we are using the **`Filters`** pane, we should consider hiding every filter placed under **`Filters on this visual`**. This is to avoid confusing our end users once a report is published to Power BI Service. When end users select a visual, they might see every filter available under **`Filters on this visual`** and there may be dozens of them in some visualizations. This could be overwhelming. End users might apply filters to the visual thinking that they are applying them for the whole report.

Filters can be hidden by hovering over every individual filter and selecting one of the three symbols that appear on the right side of the filter. This can be seen from the **`Average Of Sales`** filter in *Figure 6.2*. Clicking the eye symbol hides the filter from end users when the report is published to the Power BI Service and is in reading mode.

The lock symbol makes a filter uneditable while in reading mode, yet still visible. If we are applying a prefilter when we are designing a report, we should lock it and keep it visible. This way end users will see the preset filters in the **`Filters`** pane and will more likely understand data they are analyzing. The last symbol, the downward arrow, opens the filtering options. Those depend on a type of data we are dealing with. With measures, we have the options such as is less than, is greater than, is, is not, and so on. With columns or attributes from dimension tables, we can select either basic filtering, which allows the selection of distinct values, or Advanced filtering, with the options such as contains, starts with, and so on.

Filters on this page and Filters on all pages

Other two options available in the Filters pane are more commonly used. They are **`Filters on this page`** and **`Filters on all pages`**. The first one, **`Filters on this page`**, is used when we are creating a multi pages report and we want one page to only show a subset of data. For example, a report is showing Sales since 2016, but the second page is specialized in a way that it only shows current-year sales. The second page could show a more detailed display, which may be achieved by selection of visualization types, drilling down deeper into hierarchies, and by use of filtering.

To apply such a filter to a report page, we can drag the **`CalendarYear`** column and select the current year. That would be a non-dynamic solution. Alternatively, we could create a new column - **`IsCurrentYear`** and drag it to the Filters pane and set it to **`TRUE`** (or 1, depending on how we label it). This column would be calculated during the ETL process.

When using **Filters on this page**, we have to be careful about using **Filters on all pages**. If there is an option to filter by year column under **Filters on all pages**, end users might find that confusing and filter themselves into **Blanks**. They could do so by selecting a year other than the current year prefiltered under **Filters on this page**.

If this can occur, they should not even be given an option to make the mistake. Using **Filters on this page** can fit well when general filtering is done by slicers. When we are using **Filters on this page**, we do not place slicers on a report page for filters we are already prefiltering, such as in our example the slicers for the **CalendarYear** column. There is a hierarchy when it comes to filtering that we will explain in a moment. As in the case with any prefiltering by using the **Filters** pane, we should lock the preset filter but keep it visible.

Filters on all pages will affect a whole report and can be considered an ideal way to filter Power BI reports, that is, if reports are simple and end users are willing to use the Filters pane. If that is the case, we should not be using slicers and instead use a whole canvas for displaying insights with charts, matrices, and so on. Ideally, we should put all the filters we consider using under **Filters on all pages**. End users can apply them as they please. This offers the most theoretically correct experience along with hiding every filter under **Filters on this visual** for each visualization and not using **Filters on this page** at all.

If data was not prefiltered during data processing stage, we can use **Filters on all pages** to pre-filter an entire report for end users. This can be the case when we are using same source of data for multiple reports.

Let us say that we have a general stock transactions table, detailing every company's material transaction. We are creating a Power BI report that is displaying only the incoming and outgoing stock, that is, material being delivered to the company and material leaving the company. But the stock transactions table is also labeling internal movements of stock between warehouses. The internal movement is labeled in the **TransactionType** column with value 3. We can add the **TransactionType** column under **Filters on all pages** and select Filter type as **Basic filtering**. We could select the box next to the Select all option and deselect the box with value 3. That is how we ordered an entire report to ignore every row that has the value of 3 in the **TransactionType** column. Alternatively, we could apply the filter in Power Query or use objects such as views in SQL Server and filter with **WHERE** clause.

Filters' hierarchy

There is a hierarchy when it comes to filters in Power BI Desktop. If a filter is applied in Power Query, filtered data is not going to be loaded into a tabular model at all. The next highest level is row-level security. We will discuss this topic later in the book. The third level is **`Filters on all pages`**. If we apply a filter under it, such as `CalendarYear = 2022`, we are not going to see anything else than 2022 options under **`Filters on this page`**, **`Filters on this visual`** and in a slicer placed on a canvas. This can be seen in *Figure 6.4*:

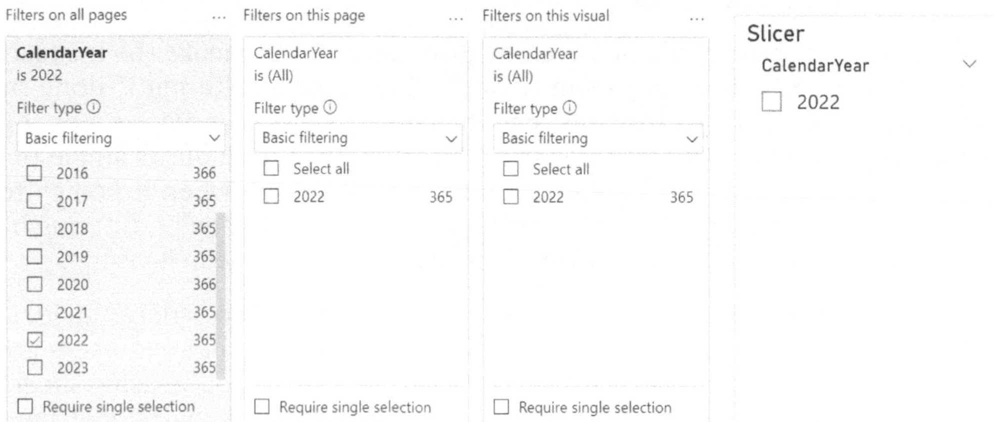

Figure 6.4: *Filters' hierarchy in Power BI*

The logic does not apply backwards. If we apply a filter for **`CalendarYear = 2022`** under **`Filters on this page`**, we will see only the 2022 under **`Filters on this visual`** and in a slicer. However, all options will remain visible on **`Filters on all pages`**, potentially leaving end users the possibility to filter themselves into **`Blank`**s. This can happen if an end user applies a filter for **`CalendarYear = 2023`** under **`Filters on all pages`**, while the **`CalendarYear = 2022`** filter is applied under **`Filters on this page`**, resulting in an empty subset of data.

The Data and Visualizations panes

If we return to *Figure 6.2*, we can see the two right arrows next to the **`Filters`**, **`Visualizations`**, and **`Data`** panes. Those will collapse the panes back to the side of the screen. The two left arrows the right ribbon will reopen them.

The Data pane is the right-most pane in Power BI Desktop. It is simple to understand – we can see all objects that were not hidden, that is tables, columns, measures, and hierarchies. Tables in the Data pane can be expanded. Columns and measures can be added to the canvas by drag-and-drop or by checking the box next to their name. If no object is selected on a canvas, the column or the measure is added to a new visualization of default type. If a visualization is selected, the field will be added to the selected visualization.

The **`Visualizations`** pane works differently depending on whether a visualization is selected or not. If a blank canvas is selected, there are two tabs selectable: **`Build visual`** and **`Format page`**.

The latter offers the Canvas settings option, including preselected possibilities for canvas sizes. The default option 16:9 gives a height of 720 pixels and a width of 1280 pixels. We can define a custom size as well, for example, 1600 × 900, which keeps the most commonly used ratio of 16:9, but will make it slightly easier to calculate visualizations sizes and positions on a canvas grid. Please note that if we change a canvas size, we might have to adjust font sizes on visualizations as well.

We can also apply the **`Canvas`** background option. Selecting a slightly gray background, for example, the first gray option under theme colors (named White, 10% darker, with Hex code of #E6E6E6) looks very nice. We should set an option Transparency = 40% to get a slightly lighter tone. The gray background will make visualizations with white background more visible.

The **`Filter`** pane and **`Filter`** cards options will color the Filter pane and filters placed to the pane. We can format their display colors once a report is published to Power BI Service. We may consider leaving it as default, or we could use company colors.

The Build visual tab will place visualizations to the canvas if no object is selected on the report page. Starting from the top left to bottom right, these are default visualizations available at the time of writing in June 2023:

Default visualizations available in Power BI Desktop		
`Stacked bar chart`	`Stacked column chart`	`Clustered bar chart`
`Clustered column chart`	`100 % Stacked bar chart`	`100 % Stacked column chart`
`Line chart`	`Area chart`	`Stacked area chart`
`Line and stacked column chart`	`Line and clustered column chart`	`Ribbon chart`
`Waterfall chart`	`Funnel`	`Scatter chart`
`Pie chart`	`Donut chart`	`Treemap`
`Map`	`Filled map`	`Azure map`
`Gauge`	`Card`	`Multi-Row card`
`KPI`	`Slicer`	`Table`
`Matrix`	`R script visual`	`Python visual`
`Key influencers`	`Decomposition tree`	`Q&A`
`Smart narrative`	`Metrics`	`Paginated report`
`Card (new)`	`ArcGIS Maps for Power BI`	`Power Apps for Power BI`
`Power Automate for Power BI`		

***Table 6.1**: Default visualizations in Power BI Desktop*

We will take a look at some of these visualizations in this chapter and others in later chapters. By selecting the three dots symbol on the **Visualizations** pane, we can access AppSource, a Microsoft marketplace that provides access to custom visualizations. We can also develop custom visualization and import them in **.pbiviz** format (Power BI visual files).

Drillthrough and Tooltips

There are options to designate a report page as being a drillthrough page. Visualizations on other report pages can be expanded to the drillthrough page. To designate a page as a drillthrough page, we can select a blank canvas and under the **Build visual** tab find the option **Add drill-through field here**.

We can drop any dimension column to this field, for example, **CalendarYear**. Make sure to designate **Allow drill through when** option to **Used as category**. After that, any visualization on other pages that uses the **CalendarYear** column as an axis can drillthrough to the page we designated as a drillthrough page.

A drillthrough can be performed by right-clicking a data point and selecting Drill through and then the name of the page we designated as a drillthrough page. We can see the **Drill through** options in *Figure* 6.5. **Drill through** settings are set on Page 3 (the page designated as drillthrough page) and can be seen on the left side in *Figure* 6.5, while a visualization with **CalendarYear** in an axis, as it is seen on the right side in *Figure* 6.5, can be on any other page:

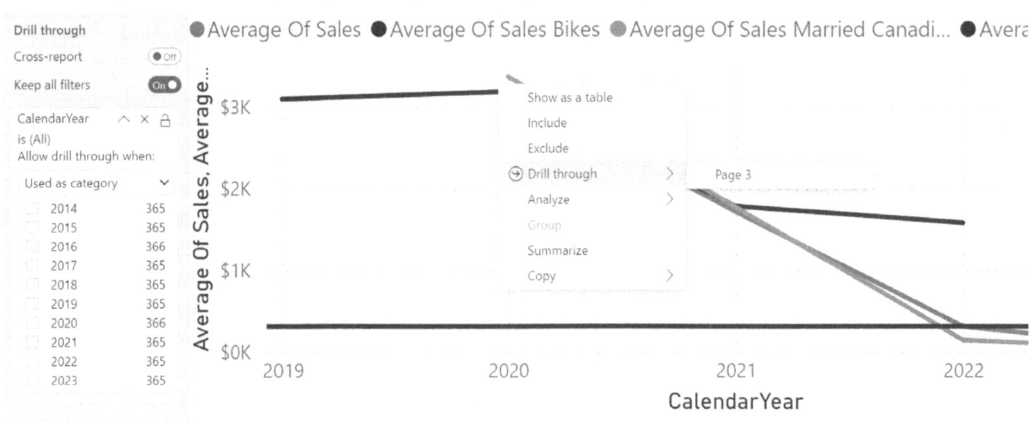

Figure 6.5: *Drill through settings and access from visualization*

The **Keep all filters** options is necessary for passing the filters to the drillthrough page. Let us say that our Line chart with **CalendarYear** in the axis is on the first page of the report. Right-clicking a data point above **CalendarYear = 2020** will pass that filter to Page 3 and all visualizations on Page 3 will only show subset of data for the year 2020.

As soon as a page is designated as the drillthrough page, the back button appears at the top-left corner of the canvas. With a simple mouse click, we can return to the previous page (or *Ctrl* + left-click in Power BI Desktop). The Cross-report option allows jumping to another report and passing the filters along. One must first enable the option to use cross-report by going to **File**, **Options and settings**, **Options**, and under **CURRENT FILE's Report** settings enable the option **Allow visuals in this report to use drill-through targets from other reports**. This option should be enabled for both source and destination report.

Understandably, reports have to use the same tabular model, or different models with the same names of tables and columns that may vary in a schema structure, quantity of tables, or data granularity. Other than that, setting up drillthrough is very similar. We set the **Cross-report** option to on in destination report and add the dimension column to **Add drill-through field here**. A back button does not work when using cross-report drillthrough, only when using single-report drillthrough. Both reports should be published to the same workspace on Power BI Service.

While cross-report drillthrough certainly is fancy, it might cause additional confusion with end users. One possible use case is having aggregated data in a source report to increase the speed of the model. Aggregated data may be part of a larger picture. A destination report uses a model with more detailed data. The level of detail in a table is referred to as data granularity.

Drill through within a single report can be useful when a report creator is presenting a report to stakeholders in real-time. A single main page of the report can be the object of presentation. If any question on more details regarding data that is being presented arises, the presenter may simply dig deeper into any visualization to show new pages of details.

But if a report is published to Power BI Service with multitude of end users using the report to gather their own insights, we might consider avoiding usage of drillthrough. The added complication of functionality may outweigh its benefits. We should prefer to use more report pages - which are clearly visible to users and that they can scroll through to support their data-driven decisions. The simpler the report, the more likely the users will use it, and the more valuable it will be. Also, in earliest stages of data analysis solutions implementation, there is an increase in the value of simplicity. End users are just getting to know new solutions. We want to present them in a way that is easy for them to use and understand. They will likely demand additional options themselves, which will increase complexity. So, starting simple is the key.

Tooltips are the pop-up windows appearing when we hover over a visualization that was placed on a canvas. In the most basic form, they are simple windows showing values of measures and columns placed under axes or value fields. Some visualizations offer the possibility to add fields to **Tooltip** field type when building a visualization – meaning that those values will not be displayed on the visualization, but rather only in a tooltip window. The basic tooltip can be visible on the left side in *Figure 6.6*.

The second possibility is to use the modern visual tooltip, which is a preview feature at the time of writing in June 2023. We can enable it by going to File, **Options and Settings**, **Options** and select **CURRENT FILE's Reports** settings. Check the option **Use modern visual tooltips with drill actions and updated styling**. To have it enabled for every new report, we can go to GLOBAL's Preview features and select **Modern visual tooltips**. We can see the modern tooltip on the right in *Figure 6.6*. We can see that in the modern visual tooltip, we can access **Drill through** and **Drill down** features by simply interacting with the tooltip rather than through other means. Drill up option also appears in the modern tooltip if our visualization is down one level in hierarchy:

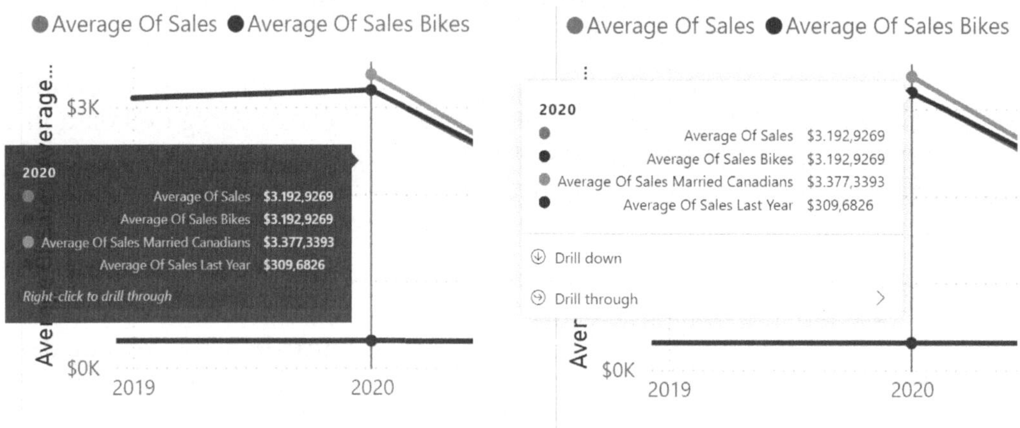

***Figure 6.6**: Basic and modern visual tooltip hovering over a chart*

There is a third option, the ability to create custom tooltips. Custom tooltips are a mixture of tooltips and drillthrough. We can set a report page to serve as a tooltip. It pops-up when we hover over a visualization, and it passes the filters from the visualization to the report page serving as tooltip.

Designating a report page as a tooltip is simple. Without having any objects selected, we can go to Format page under the Visualizations pane, much like we did when we resized the page's canvas or applied the background color. Under Page information, set the option **Allow use as tooltip** to on. This will by default resize canvas size to **Tooltip**, which has a height/width of 240/320 pixels. We can re-set the size by going to Canvas settings and selecting Custom under type. Regardless of the size selected, the pop-up window will automatically scale when using custom tooltips. Nevertheless, enlarging it from 240/320 pixels will make it appear larger.

When a visualization is selected on a canvas, the **Visualizations** pane's **Build visual** tab looks similar as to when no object is selected. Additional places to drop fields from the Data pane might be available. Exact number of these field type boxes depend on the type of a visualization. In a Line chart, following field types are available: **X-axis**, **Y-axis**, **Secondary y-axis**, **Legend**, **Small multiples**, and **Tooltips**. In *Figure* 6.7, we can see the **Build visual** tab along with field types for four visualization types: **Table**, **Matrix**, **Line and stacked column chart**, and **KPI**:

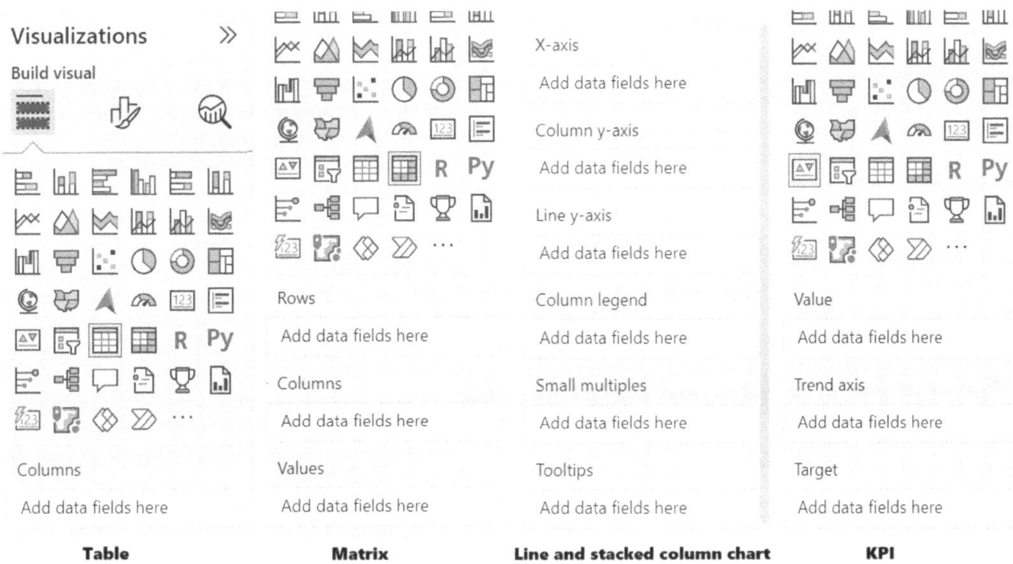

***Figure* 6.7**: *The Build visual tab and field types*

We might have to check the Microsoft documentation to see exactly how different field types affect the structure of a visualization. Other tabs available in the Visualization pane is now Format visual instead of Format page. As the name suggests, the Format visual tab offers options for formatting.

Custom tooltips can be added to any visualization by first selecting the visualization. In the case of a Line chart, we can go to the **Format visual** tab, where we can find two subtabs: **Visual** and **General**. Under **General**, we can find the **Tooltips** category. When expanded, under the option Type, we can change it from **Default** to **Report** page and under Page, we should select the page that we designated as the tooltip. Remember, we can hide the pages that are tooltips or that serve as drill throughs. In *Figure* 6.8, we can see the custom tooltip in action on the **`Line`** chart. We can also notice that the grey background offers enhanced visibility to visualizations with white backgrounds:

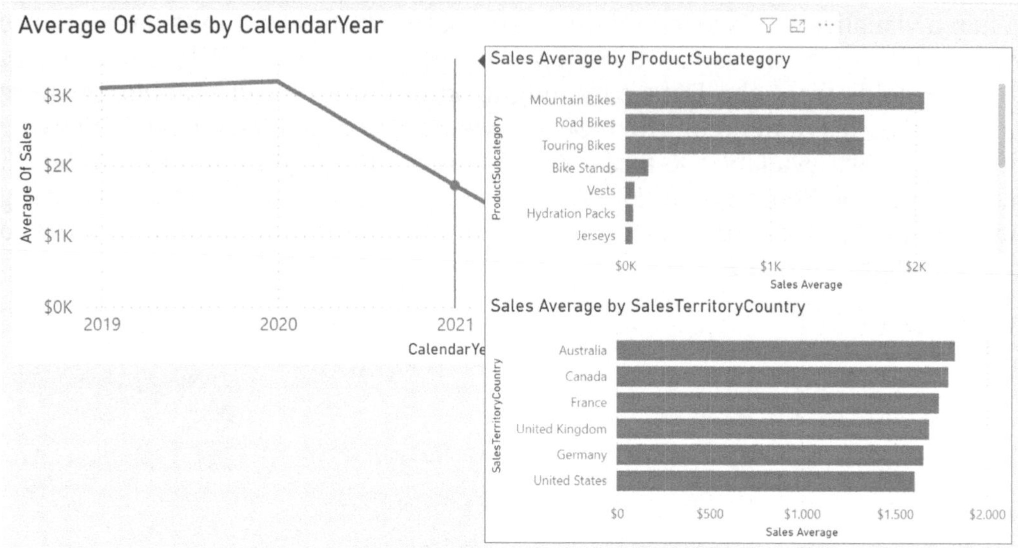

***Figure 6.8**: Custom tooltip on a visualization*

Creating visualizations

Whenever a visualization is selected, we can change the visualization type by selecting another icon representing different visualization types. Visualizations have distinct field types, to which we can add measures or columns. Table only has one field type called Columns. To create a Table, we can simply search for **`CalendarYear`** in the Data pane and select the checkbox. Table seems to be the default visualization Power BI Desktop chooses. Any field containing numbers could be summarized by default. In the case of **`CalendarYear`**, that is not good. We have already seen how to correct this: By going to the Table view, finding the **`CalendarYear`** column, and under Column tools changing the Summarization option from **`Sum`** to **`Don't summarize`**. Alternatively, we can change that in each visualization, under the Build Visual tab, by selecting the arrow next to the field name and changing it from **`Sum`** to **`Don't summarize`**.

We can add measures such as **`Total Sales`** or **`Average of Sales`** to the table. Adding multiple columns and measures can be easily done. When we are adding fields from different tables, we have to be mindful of the relationships in our model. We have to consider the cross-filter directions. In a logical star schema, we can expect fewer problems. When we change the visualization type from Table to Matrix, there is no longer a single type of field. Now we can add fields to **`Rows`**, **`Columns`**, and **`Values`**. If we place **`CalendarYear`** into Rows and **`Total Sales`** into values, we get a Matrix with a very similar structure to the Table. Only the lines in the visualizations indicate that these are not the same visualization type. If we add **`CalendarYear`** to Columns, the visualization now looks very different, as it can be seen in *Figure* 6.9:

Table

CalendarYear	Total Sales
2019	$43.421,0364
2020	$7.075.525,9291
2021	$5.842.485,1952
2022	$16.351.550,34
2023	$45.694,72
Total	**$29.358.677,2207**

Matrix | CY in rows

CalendarYear	Total Sales
2019	$43.421,0364
2020	$7.075.525,9291
2021	$5.842.485,1952
2022	$16.351.550,34
2023	$45.694,72
Total	**$29.358.677,2207**

Matrix | CY in column

2019	2020
$43.421,0364	$7.075.525,9291

***Figure 6.9**: Table and two matrices*

Matrix works very similarly to Excel's Pivot Table. It is very good for displaying aggregated data and it is suitable for working with hierarchies. We may have aggregated data in the primary view, and we may choose to drill down and display increasingly detailed data. Both Matrix and Table can display larger quantities of data for the end users interested in detail. Visualizations such as charts will usually display one or two, or in rare cases three or more measures in combination with a single column from a dimension table. Less often than a single column from a dimension table, we may use a hierarchy, that is, several columns from a dimension table which are inter-connected.

The usage of tables and matrices should serve a similar purpose to the drillthrough in showing detailed data, but like we have said, drillthrough might be too complicated to implement effectively in an organizational scale. We can get the necessary details to end users in a finished report page, containing several charts and a matrix or a table at the bottom-right of a report canvas. A matrix or a table could easily contain dozens of measures and even multitude of columns that bring evaluation context to measures.

Another alternative for end users to get detailed analysis or analysis of data from different angles is to connect to the tabular model themselves by using Power BI Desktop or Excel Power Pivot. They could connect to a tabular model deployed to SQL Server Analysis Services or Azure Analysis Services, or to a dataset hosted on the Power BI Service. Advanced users may create visualizations as they see fit. In this and the later chapters, we are going to analyze some of the visualizations that can be used to create insightful BI reports.

When a visualization is selected, the second tab of the **`Visualization`** pane is Format visual. There are two subtabs under **`Format`** visual: **`Visual`** and **`General`**. **`General`** is very similar in all visualizations. We can change the size and position of visuals, add padding, modify how visual interacts in relation to others, adjust their response when scaled, modify the title and subtitle, change the background color, border, and shadow, modify header icons, and customize tooltips. The **General** subtab should become quickly intuitive to developers. Header icons are the icons appearing either above a visualization, or on the visualization's title if it is enabled. Header icons allow interaction with a visualization and can be seen in *Figure* 6.10:

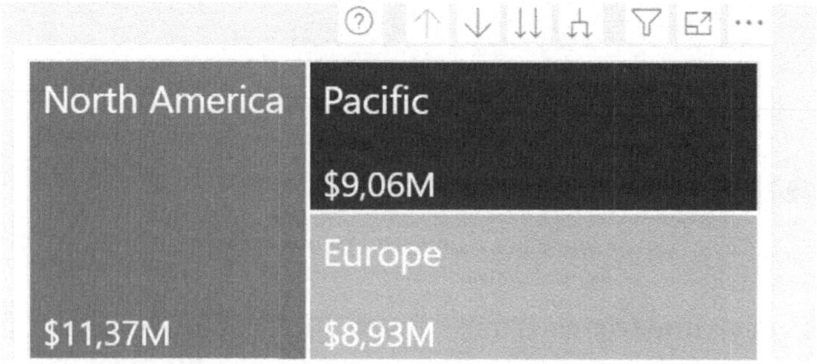

Figure 6.10*: Header icons on a Treemap visualization*

Treemap is a visualization that is particularly suitable for displaying non-continuous attributes, such as categories or hierarchies, rather than time. We can see it in *Figure* 6.10 displaying a few distinct values in a very lovely way. Notice the colors of the distinct values – shades of grey and blue. These are the default colors we suggest using, the shades of grey and blue ranging from light to dark. Only if these are not enough should we introduce other light colors, such as light orange, light pink, or light gold.

Alternatively, we can use shades of company colors. This is a particularly good idea if we want to promote the brand of our organization. We can insert company's logos and other branding material to our reports in the form of images. We may choose whatever approach suits us best. We can modify Treemap colors by going to **Format** visual in the **Visualizations** pane, selecting the **Visual** tab and expanding the category **Colors**. As with most visualizations, we can use a Treemap to filter other visualizations on the canvas. But Treemap might be better suited for this job because of its nice looks. To filter using a Treemap, simply select the square with a distinct value.

If there are many distinct values in an attribute, Treemap might not be the best approach. We should use a clustered bar chart or a clustered column chart. If values of the displayed category are long and there are very many of them, clustered bar chart will be preferred. We can see the clustered bar chart displaying Total Sales by product at the left side in *Figure* 6.11 and it is doing a good job. We can widen the amount of space given to product names by adjusting Max area width on this path: **Format visual** > **Visual** > **Max area width**. We have also turned off the Title for Y-axis and X-axis as those are already clear by the visualization's Title. We have enabled Data labels and adjusted display units to thousands under **`Format visual`** > **`Visual`** > **`Data labels`** > **`Display`** unit. We have also turned value decimal places to zero. Available options slightly differ depending on a visualization type. If multiple measures are displayed, we can also include a legend:

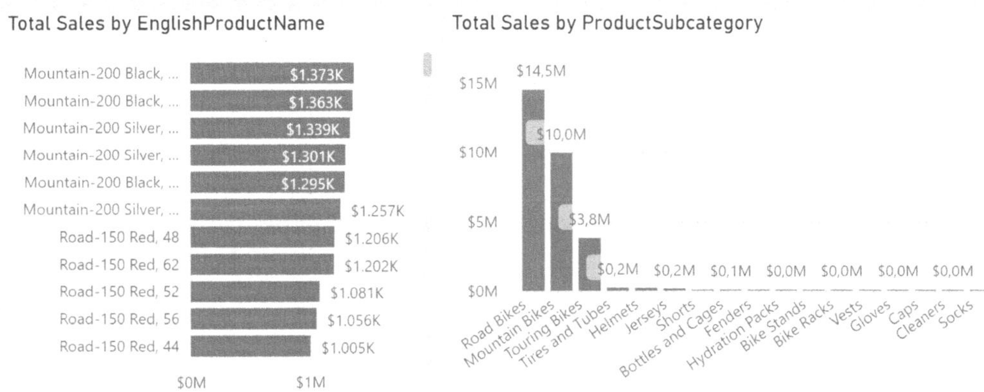

***Figure 6.11**: Clustered bar chart and clustered column chart*

The clustered column chart can be seen on the right in *Figure 6.11*. We can see that it displays **`ProductSubcategory`** and given that there are fewer distinct values and that values are shorter in length, clustered column chart is a suitable option. We have applied white background with 50% transparency for data labels, to make them more visible. You can notice the grey canvas background we have already discussed. Also, notice the gap between the visualizations - this is by design. Small gaps between visualizations are designed for visual appeal. We should also be mindful of the size and position properties of visualizations. Preferably, they should be rounded to 10 or 5, which will make it easier to adjust pixels of all visualizations.

In a professionally created report, pixels of visualizations should be carefully adjusted. Just dragging a visualization will most often result in non-rounded numbers, such as Height = 397 and Width = 343. Those numbers should be rounded and gaps between objects should be adjusted. Remember, we may also modify canvas size if needed. Power BI scales a canvas automatically according to the size of our screen. Even if pixels are perfectly matched, visualizations in the same horizontal or vertical position could be non-perfectly aligned on some resolutions. You would be surprised how often end users notice that. If they do, we can assure them with a clear consciousness that we have done everything we could to ensure perfection.

What is the difference between clustered and stacked charts? When adding more than one measure to the chart, in clustered charts, these measures are placed one next to the other. In stacked charts, these measures are placed one on top of the other. Different colors are used to indicate the portion of a whole that each measure fills. Following that logic, stacked charts are useful when we are observing calculations that are parts of a whole. And what is 100% stacked chart? In normal stacked charts, the size of the bar or the column is relative to an absolute value, that is the sum of all the measures added to the chart. In 100% stacked chart, all columns or bars are of the same size. This means that relative parts each measure represents are more clearly visible.

Line charts are useful for showing the evolution of measure's value over time. Date hierarchies can often be used in X-axis of Line charts, and they may be hierarchically expanded using header icons. We will explain those in the next subchapter. I have not seen much use for Area chart and Stacked area chart. The difference in area and line charts is that in the former, the area between the line and the axis is filled. Stacked area chart places one measure above the other.

Line and clustered column charts are useful when displaying two measures of very different types, such as Total Sales in currency format and Gross margin in percentage. We have already introduced the DAX calculations for these measures in the previous two chapters. Additionally, we have created the **`MonthNameShort`** calculated column with the following expression: **`= LEFT([EnglishMonthName], 3)`**. Short names look better in line chart.

The **`MonthNameShort`** column in could have been created in Power Query or SQL Server. In any case, make sure to use the Table view's Column tools option **`Sort by column`** to sort **`MonthNameShort`** by **`MonthNumberOfYear`**. We have placed the **`CalendarYear`** and **`MonthNameShort`** fields under X-axis. We have placed **`Total Sales`** under Column y-axis and Gross Margin under Line y-axis. We have also used the header icon **`Expand all down one level in the hierarchy`**, which we will explain in more detail in the next subchapter. We can see the result in *Figure 6.12*.

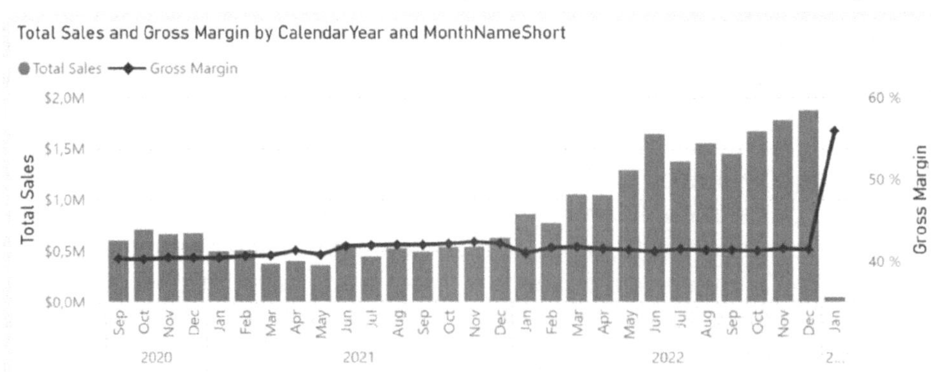

Figure 6.12: *Line and clustered column chart*

The default sort of Total Sales in descending order is unsuitable, so we changed it to **CalendarYear MonthNameShort** in ascending order. We have turned off the Title for x-axis and lessened the font sizes for the legend and the visualization's title. The default colors seem to be shades of blue, so we left that as it is. We've turned on **Visual** > **Markers** and applied the Type symbol by expanding **Markers** > **Shape** category. Under **Legend** > **Options**, we changed the Style to **Line and markers**. This option makes it clearer which symbols in the legend represent lines. Especially useful when there are many measures in a chart.

Power BI offers several options to display very important measures. These are **Card**, **Multi-row card**, **Card (new)**, **KPI** and **Gauge**. They are usually placed at the top or at the top left of the report. Alternatively, they can be placed above or below charts to convey additional information. Several cards can be placed above charts, without gaps to serve as a visualizations group.

When end user filter interactively by clicking data points in visualizations, the cards will be filtered as well. Card contains one measure and multi-row card contains several. **Card (new)** is a new preview feature that offers the most formatting options out of the three mentioned, such as picture backgrounds, defining layout orientation, and distinctly formatting each measure. An increase in performance is also advertised. In *Figure* 6.13, we can see these visualizations:

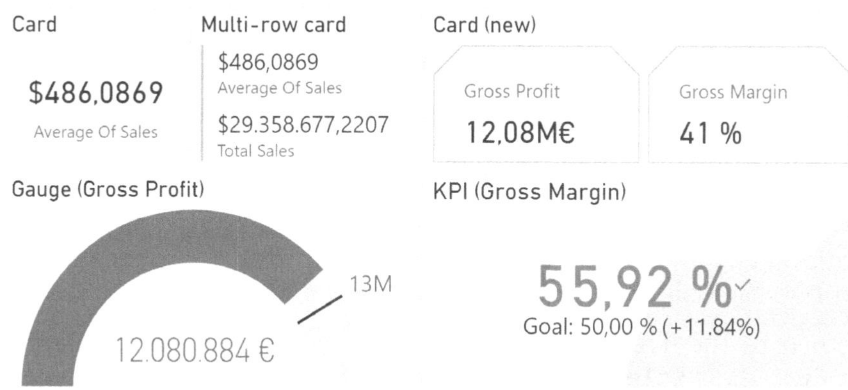

Figure 6.13: *Several visualizations useful for displaying important information*

Gauge takes a numeric measure under the Value field type. We have used Gross Profit. It can take minimum, maximum, and target measure as well. These measures can be relative, such as measure for maximum value is **Gross Profit * 1,3**. They can be an absolute number, such as measure for minimum value is 10.000.000. Or they could be gathered from goals or plans fact tables with DAX.

We have applied some formatting options to the **Gauge**, such as **Visual** > **Data labels = Off**, **Visual** > **Callout value** > **Display units = None** and **Visual** > **Callout value** > **Value decimal places = 0**.

KPI visualization can be confusing. We can create them with the following steps: We can build a line chart first. We can place a date attribute, such as **CalendarYear**, to **X-axis**. **Y-axis** can hold a measure, for example, Gross Margin. We can change the line Chart to KPI. This creates the KPI visualization without a Target. We can then place a measure to the Target field that is created in a way similar to how we have described when discussing Gauges. Once we have converted the Line Chart into a KPI, the X-axis field type became the Trend axis, and the Y-axis became the Value. We can place other attributes to the Trend axis to see how they affect the KPI.

Header icons/visual headers

Header icons or visual headers allow interaction with a visualization. They appear when we hover over visualizations and can be seen above the Treemap in *Figure* 6.10. They appear either above the visualization or in the area of the title and can be turned off if we switch the Format visual > Header icons to off. This does not seem to affect anything in Power BI Desktop, but rather it should disable them when reading the report in Power BI Service. Another possibility is to switch them off in Settings and Options, by going to the **CURRENT FILE's Report settings** option and selecting the option **Hide the visual header in reading view**.

These are the header icons visible in *Figure* 6.10: 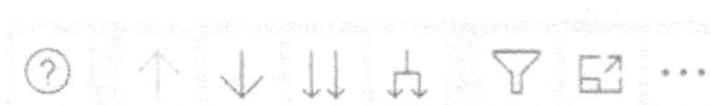

The first one from the left is Help tooltip. When we hover over it, this offers either a text message of our choosing, or we may use the custom tooltip by designating a page as a tooltip in a way that we have discussed before. If that is the case, two tooltips are possible - a regular tooltip when we hover over visualization's display and a custom tooltip when we hover over the Help icon. The next two symbols are Drill up and Drill down.

If we return to the Treemap in *Figure* 6.10, we can the Total Sales measure divided by the **SalesTerritoryGroup** attribute. However, it is the **SalesTerritoryHierarchy** that was added to the **Category** field type of the Treemap. The **SalesTerritoryHierarchy** consists of the **SalesTerritoryGroup**, **SalesTerritoryCountry**, and **SalesTerritoryRegion** attributes.

By selecting the downward arrow symbol, the third option from the left, which is **Drill down**, we can select any of the three distinct Sales territory groups in the Treemap. This expands only the selected group into the lower level of the hierarchy, meaning SalesTerritoryCountry. We can either deselect **Drill down** or select another square to go further down to the last level in the hierarchy - to **SalesTerritoryRegion**. Selecting the upward arrow, which is the second option from the left, or Drill up, will return the visualization display to the one higher level in hierarchy.

The next option is called **`Go to next level in the hierarchy`**. Instead of us having to select the category that will be expanded, this option will simply display the one hierarchy below the one that is being displayed now. If the **`SalesTerritoryGroup`** attribute was displayed in the Treemap, selecting this option would display only the **`SalesTerritoryCountry`** attribute in the Treemap.

The fifth option from the left is **`Expand all down one level in the hierarchy`**. With this option, each value of the first hierarchical category is expanded by all of the corresponding values in the second hierarchical category – with both the first and the second categories displayed. Let us take the value **`North America`** in **`SalesTerritoryGroup`**. Expanding it down one level in the hierarchy to **`SalesTerritoryCountry`** will display the **`North America United States`** and **`North America Canada`** values. So, we will see both the higher and the lower hierarchical categories displayed at once.

The third option from the right is **`Filters on this visual`**. Selecting it will display all the filters affecting this visualization, wherever they may come from; other visualizations, slicers, or the **`Filters`** pane. If a visualization is not showing the desired result, we should check the filters affecting it. Often, we will find unexpected filters being applied. The second symbol from the right is Focus mode, which expands the visualization throughout the whole screen. If our model has many dimensions, we will often cram many different viewpoints into a single report page. This means visualizations of limited sizes, the situation where Focus mode comes in handy.

The first option from the right expands into many options, such as **`Export data`**, **`Show as a table`**, **`Spotlight`**, and **`Sort axis`**. Export data can be done to **`.CSV`** file from Power BI Desktop. However, once a report is published, the option to export to Excel file becomes available as well. Spotlight greys out other visualizations, which is rarely useful, perhaps only in cases where report is being presented and we want to focus audience's attention to a single visualization. The **`Show as a table`** option works in a similar way as Focus mode, it expands the view throughout the whole screen. However, now we can see both the visualization we are expanding, and the visualization adjusted to tabular format. There are more options available once the report is published to Power BI Service. Pin button allows pinning of the selected visual of a report, along with all the filters affecting the visual, to a dashboard. A dashboard is a type of overview in the Power BI Service that can consist of visualizations from multiple reports as well as additional objects. It is intended to provide a more concise overview of insights we are getting from BI.

There are some premium capabilities available in Power BI Service's visual headers, such as Get insights, the feature to automatically explore trends and anomalies using AI. AI will try to provide an explanation as to why the trend is moving the way it does. There are abilities to gain insights from individual visualizations, from dashboard tiles, and from datasets. We can also use pre-trained machine learning models with Azure Cognitive Services. Anomalies show large or small, unexpected values and the Get insights option is effective at warning us about the location of anomalies in data. The location could be a specific date. Trends show a lengthy increase or decrease in time series. AI provides warnings such as how much did a value increase, by what percentage and since when. There is also a KPI analysis, which warns users when a value varies from a target by a large margin. AI will also try to guess as to why this is happening.

With the new Microsoft Fabric, we can expect an increase in AI and machine learning capabilities to gain insights from our data. Microsoft Fabric is a combination of Azure services and Power BI Service resources to deliver one on-cloud Microsoft solution for data analysis and data science. Services such as Data Factory, Synapse Data Engineering, Synapse Data Warehousing, Synapse Data Science, Synapse Real Time Analytics, and Power BI under are provided in a bundle. As with any cloud resource, we should be mindful of costs. The good thing is, that according to Microsoft, there should not be any need to migrate our resources from Power BI Service to Microsoft Fabric, rather its options should become available, mostly to Power BI Service users with premium licenses.

Upper ribbon tabs in the Report view

The objective of this section is to provide exact information on available features, but rather to provide an overview of what can be done. Microsoft is quickly changing the layout of Power BI Desktop's upper ribbon and as we will notice later in the chapter, even turning on some preview features will alter the ribbon by a large margin. Stability in this sense should not be expected, we should rather expect many changes.

We have seen the **Home** tab of Power BI Desktop in *Figure 2.8* in *Chapter 2, Acquiring and Transforming Data from Multiple Sources*. Besides data connectivity options and Power Query Editor, we can also refresh data, add new visuals, a text box, and access AppSource marketplace for custom visualizations. We can add a new measure, but we should be careful to have the right table selected when using this option. As by good practice, measures should be placed to the table they are mostly affecting. If a measure is created from multiple tables by relying on relationships between tables, it should be placed in the table for which it makes the most sense. Preferable way to add new measures is by right-clicking a table in the Data pane and selecting the New measure option.

There is an option to apply sensitivity labels. Sensitivity labels are Microsoft's approach to data privacy by labeling certain data as sensitive or confidential. Sensitivity labels can prevent data exfiltration, that is theft of data. Sensitivity labels must first be enabled on a tenant from the Power BI Admin portal on Power BI Service and can then be applied in either the Power BI Service or Power BI Desktop resources.

Sensitivity labels also require at least a Power BI Pro license. For the sensitivity labels flowing from Purview, we might also need the **Azure Information Protection** license. Microsoft Purview is a family of products associated with governing data, protecting information, and managing risks and compliance.

On the Power BI Service reports and dashboards, sensitivity labels can be found under Settings. In Power BI Desktop, we can use the Sensitivity icon in the **Home** tab. We have to be signed in to an account that meets licensing requirements. There are sensitivity labels available in SQL Server since version 2019, but they do not seem to be connected to the Power BI sensitivity labels. If we are using the SQL Server sensitivity labels, there might be a need to reapply them manually in Power BI environment.

The last option on the **Home** tab is **Publish**, which brings the interface window to choose the Power BI Service Workspace that will host the report. The **Home** tab in the upper ribbon can vary depending on whether the **Report** view, the **Table** view, or the **Model** view is selected. Remember, views are switched on the left ribbon of Power BI Desktop.

Under the **Report** view, there are the **Insert**, **Modeling**, and **View** tabs that we will take a closer look at. They can be seen in *Figure 6.14*. The **Optimize** tab will be presented in *Chapter 9*, *Optimizing Power BI Models and Reports*, while the **Help** tab is pretty clear by itself – it offers some information regarding the Power BI products and some help with building reports:

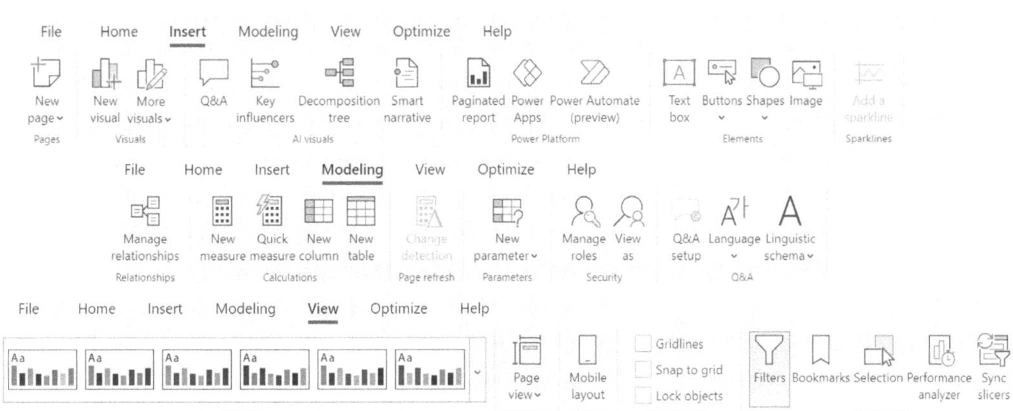

Figure 6.14: *Insert, Modeling, and View tab of Power BI Desktop's Report view*

As in Power Query Editor, many features can be accessed from multiple tabs, views, or right-click menus. The **insert** tab offers a way to add a new page, as it can be done from the lower ribbon, as well as a new visualization, which can be done from the Visualization pane as well. The four visualizations using AI that are promoted are Q&A, Key influences, Decomposition tree and Smart narrative. We will look closer into advanced capabilities of Power BI in *Chapter 8, Data Science in Power BI*.

Q&A is a visualization that allows the asking of natural language questions to return the result, usually a chart. The questions are written as follows: What is the total sales by product category. It is important to stress that as report developers, we should be answering those questions for end users by preparing suitable reports. Many of the viewpoints should be covered by the usage suitable visualizations in multiple report pages. However, if we think that end users will seek answers using the Q&A, we can define the synonyms for fields under the Model view's properties by selecting a field. Synonyms are used for referring to the same field by using several different words, the ones that end users might be using.

Smart narrative is an interesting visualization that writes what can be seen on the Power BI screen. What is written in the Smart narrative is automatically adjusted by filters we select. We can see the text it generates in *Figure* 6.15, with and without the filter applied:

***Figure 6.15**: Smart narrative with or without applied filter*

The **`Paginated report`** option offers a way to print out the report and will be described in more detail in the next chapter.

Power Apps and Power Automate offer a way to connect with the functionalities of Power Platform. Power Apps are easily creatable apps that we design with little code to perform some action. Using this visualization, a Power Apps app can be embedded into a Power BI report. A user can perform an action from within the report. The example would be the action to send some data to the data warehouse the Power BI report is connected to. Power Automate simplifies the experience of creating automated tasks, such as automatically downloading an attachment that was sent to us by e-mail. The Power Automate visualization can help with implementing these automated flows into the Power BI report, that is, with a click of the button from within the report, we can send the e-mail with the data from the report.

Text box is a simple object in which a text value can be written. The Buttons option offers several buttons with different symbols, which can be added to a canvas. Buttons can be formatted in a variety of ways, including by defining different backgrounds and text colors. We can modify the background and text colors when a button is hovered or pressed. Buttons can be provided with actions, such as **`Back`**, **`Bookmark`**, **`Drill through`**, **`Page navigation`**, **`Q&A`**, **`Web URL`**, **`Apply all slicers`**, and **`Clear all slicers`**. Buttons can display a tooltip, either a text value or a single measure of the text type. Additional functionality could be added in future.

Two relatively new objects are the **`Page`** and **`Bookmark`** navigators. They are essentially a couple of buttons working together as one object. **`Page`** navigator is used to move between pages with the selected pages being highlighted. The options under **`Visual`** > **`Pages`** allow us to hide hidden pages or of any page we select. **`Bookmark`** navigator is used to select bookmarks. We will describe how bookmarks work in the next subchapter. Depending on the settings under **`Visual`** > **`Bookmarks`**, we can display either all the bookmarks in the report or one group of bookmarks. With both navigators, we can modify Visual > Grid layout settings to either the horizontal or vertical orientation. This option modifies how the selectable buttons will be stacked, either one next to the other, or one below the other. There is a third option, where we can define Grid orientation and decide the number of rows and columns for the buttons. We can also modify Padding, which are spaces between buttons. Both navigators are dynamic, meaning that they automatically add or delete new pages or bookmarks as they are added to or deleted from the report.

Shapes are pretty clear; we can create objects such as rectangles. They used to serve as a single background to multiple visualizations that a developer wanted to act as a single instance. This is no longer necessary, now that we can group objects in the Selection pane and apply a background for the group. We will take a look at this in the next subchapter. Now they primarily serve the design purposes.

Images offer the ability to add pictures from a computer. They can be useful, as we can insert an image and define its action under **`Image`** > **`Action`**. We can design custom pictures and provide them with Web URL or Bookmark actions.

Sparkline is a preview feature that is used for tables and matrices. It adds a small line chart to a new column in a visualization. When we select **`Add a sparkline`**, we can choose the Y-axis, which is usually the measure that we want to draw, for example, **`Total Sales`**, and the X-axis, that is, the category we want to draw the measure over. In such a small chart, probably only a time dimension would make sense.

Under the **`Modeling`** tab, we can select the **`Manage relationships`** option which brings forth an interface window where all relationships in our model can be seen. Change detection is used for DirectQuery sources, that is when we are directly connected to a database, rather than data being imported first. In the DirectQuery scenarios we can turn on automatic page refresh.

New parameter creates a calculated table with one column and adds a slicer to a canvas. Calculated table can either be based on Numeric range or Fields. In a case of Numeric range, we can define a minimum value, a maximum value, and an Increment. The Fields option allows us to drop columns and measures to create a parameters table. Numeric parameters also create a measure that returns the number we have selected. We may use that measure in a formula. The slicer on the canvas allows us to change the value of the created measure, which can be referenced by other formulas. Fields parameters table's column can be used in conjunction with other visualizations, so the newly created parameter slicer can affect these visualizations.

In *Figure* 6.16, we created **`SelectCalculation`** parameter with three fields, the measures Average of Sales, Gross Profit, and Total Sales. The newly created slicer was modified to allow only a single select under Slicer settings > Options > Selection > Single select = On. Other than that, the Style of the slicer was selected as Tile. We have added the Pie chart visualization and the column **`SalesTerritoryGroup`** under the Legend field type. We have added the **`SelectCalculation`** column to the Values field type. The result is pictured in the figure here:

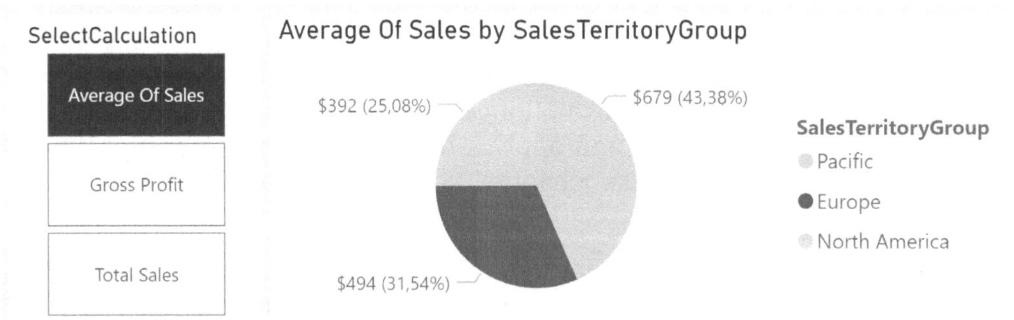

***Figure 6.16**: Fields parameters used with Pie chart*

Selecting any of the calculations on the left slicer, as seen in *Figure* 6.14, will change the display of the Pie chart to the selected measure. Pie and donut charts can be used for the same purpose, that is to display the dimension categories with very few distinct values. Preferably, only two distinct values.

Q&A section under **Modeling** tab help us to modify how the **Q&A** feature works, it offers a centralized options page to deal with questions that might be asked in Q&A visualizations.

Security section refers to something called **Row-level security** (**RLS**). The general idea of RLS is to restrict what data can be viewed by what users. The most common scenario is limiting views by geography dimension, meaning that users can only see data from their country or region. All of the users can use the same report but can see different data. Under **Manage roles** we can create a new role, such as North America. Right clicking **DimSalesTeritory** offers an option to select **SalesTerritoryGroup** column. Clicking it will already prepare the DAX expression. Changing **Value** to **North America** and selecting **Save** will create a new role that can only see North America territory group.

Under the **View** tab, we can select any of the pre-prepared themes that are available. We might find something we like, or we can create our theme by selecting the downward arrow at the left side of the themes window. In the drop-down window, we can select **Customize current theme**. We can modify several options, such as the default colors for visualizations under **Name and colors** > **Name and colors**. We can define the shades of blue and grey here. Under Text, we can define font sizes. I have always considered the default font size for cards to be quite large. We can change that under **Text** > **Cards and KPIs**. We have also got options to modify the visuals, page, and Filters pane formatting. Once we have changed the settings, we can select **Apply**. We are given an option to **Save current theme** in the drop-down window. Selecting this option will allow us to choose the save folder for the JSON file. This theme can be imported to any Power BI Desktop report by selecting the **Browse for themes** option.

Page view is used to change how the current report page is displayed in relation to the screen. With the options **Fit to page**, **Fit to width**, and Actual size, we can choose the one that is best for us. Under Page options, we are given the option to lock visualization objects in place. This can be used when all objects are perfectly aligned at a pixel level, and we want to avoid moving them by accident. The **Snap to grid** option adjusts visualizations' default move to 8 pixels. The Gridlines option will display a grid on a canvas.

Mobile layout is a very important option. It allows us to place report page's visualizations as they would appear when the report is viewed on a mobile phone in a vertical display. We can place visualizations one below the other in an order that we see fit. Rarely, if objects are small, we can place them one besides the other in the mobile view. The objects can be formatted in a different way as opposed to how they are formatted in a non-mobile layout. This can be useful to provide the best possible experience. Under the Show panes section, we can turn on additional panes that appear besides the **Filters**, **Visualizations** and **Data pane**. These are the **Bookmarks**, **Selection**, **Performance analyzer**, and **Sync slicers** panes. Performance analyzer will be introduced later in the book, while the rest will be introduced in the next subchapter.

When selecting an object on a report page, two additional tabs appear. The **Data/Drill** tab offers many of the same functionality as it can be found elsewhere. The **Visual table** option displays the selected visualization and the same data in a tabular format throughout the whole screen. The **Drill** action section offers similar functionality to header icons.

Under the **Format** tab, we can find the Edit interactions option. It allows the modifying of how visualizations interact with each other. By clicking on any visualization with the **Edit** interactions option, including slicers, we can define the way it affects other visualizations. Once we select the visualization, these symbols will be visible over other visualizations: 

The left-most option is Filter, also referred to as cross-filter. Let us say we select the **SalesTerritoryGroup = North America** data point in the first visualization. The second visualization displays **SalesTerritoryCountry** in a bar chart. It is set to Filter in relation to the first visualization. All countries, but those in the **North America SalesTerritoryGroup** will disappear from the bar chart.

The second option is highlight, also referred to as cross-highlight. If this option is selected on the second visualization in relation to the first visualization, selecting North America in the first visualization will dim all values displayed in the second visualization that are not from the countries in **North America**. Only the values related to the countries in the **North America SalesTerritoryGroup** will remain highlighted.

The third option is **None**. Selecting this option on the second visualization means that the first visualization will not filter the second visualization in any way. With the Edit interaction option, we can create slicers that only affect certain visualizations. The default interaction between all the visualizations in cross-highlight. We can change the default interaction to cross-filter by selecting the option under **File** > **Options and settings** > **Options** > **CURRENT FILE's Report settings** > **Change** default visual interaction from cross highlighting to cross filtering.

The Bookmarks, Selection, and Sync slicers panes

These panes can be seen in *Figure* 6.17. The Selection pane offers a similar experience as we may have been used to if we ever prepared presentations in Microsoft PowerPoint. We can select any object in the canvas and order it depending on the priority of display. Objects that are listed above on the Selection pane will cover objects that are displayed below.

As we can see in *Figure* 6.17, visualizations can also be grouped together. We can do this by selecting several of them either by *Ctrl* + left-click or *Shift* + left-click and then selecting the three dots symbol next to any of them. We can then select the option **`Group`** > **`Group`**. When visualizations are grouped together, selecting one of them on the canvas will select the whole group. We can modify General settings of the group by going to **`Visualizations`** pane > **`Format`** visual, including applying background under **`Effects`**:

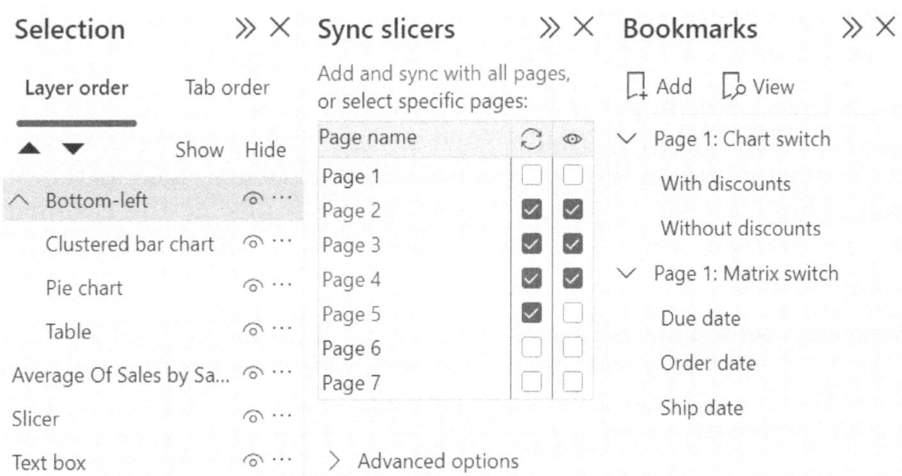

***Figure* 6.17**: *Selection, Sync slicers, and Bookmark pane*

The eye symbol allows the hiding of a visualization or group, which can be useful when used together with bookmarks. Bookmarks provide the ability for a report to remember applied settings in relations to the **`Data`**, **`Display`**, and **`Current page`** options.

`Current page` is the easiest to understand - a bookmark remembers the currently selected page. Display means, that bookmark remembers the current state of visualizations - whether they are hidden or not. And Data means that bookmark remembers all applied filters, whether they are set in the Filters pane or in slicers.

When we hover over a bookmark in **Bookmarks** pane, the three dots symbol appears, similar to the one we can see in the **Selection** pane. Clicking the three dots symbol pops-up a drop-down list. In the drop-down list we can select which of the **Data**, **Display**, and **Current page** options will affect the bookmark.

Related to the **Display** option in bookmarks, we can also modify whether a bookmark affects All visuals or Selected visuals from the drop-down list. If the option for **All visuals** is selected, we do not have to do anything else other than clicking the Update to create a bookmark. Clicking **Update** will take a snapshot of a report depending on what options are selected. If we select the option **Selected visuals**, we have to have the visuals selected in either the report canvas or in the **Selection** pane. Once the visualizations are selected, as well as the option Selected visuals in the drop-down list, we can click the Update to create a snapshot of the display for the selected visuals.

Clicking a bookmark in the **Bookmarks** pane brings forward the snapshot - our display will be as it was during the creation of the bookmark. When selecting multiple bookmarks in the Bookmarks pane, we can group them together. **Bookmarks** can be very useful in a case where we want to present two viewpoints for the visualization in a single report canvas tile.

We might have a Matrix in the bottom-right of a report canvas with a couple of measures sliced by one attribute, such as date. End users might want to see the details for the same measures by a different attribute, such as the region. Bookmarks are ideal for these situations. Instead of placing the two matrices side by side, we can place them one on the top of the other and switch them using bookmarks.

The **Sync slicers** pane is unique for every slicer. Imagine that we create a slicer on a report canvas and add the **CalendarYear** column from the **DimDate** table. The slicer is intended to filter by calendar year and will affect most of the visualizations on the report page by default. Remember, if we want to change that, we can simply use the Edit interactions option under the Format tab. By default, our slicer will filter all of visualizations in the report page, except for other slicers containing columns from the same dimension table. We may set the slicers to filter other visualizations however using the **Edit interaction** option, but that is still available only for the current report page.

If we want the slicer to affect other report pages, we can use the **Sync slicers** pane. Our newly created slicer is now only available on one page. In the Sync slicers pane, we can see the list of all the pages, along with two checkboxes - the left one means synchronicity and the right one means visibility. Selecting any option may check both boxes and that will create a visible slicer on the selected page that is in sync with the slicer on our current page.

Deselecting the left checkbox will keep the newly created slicer on another page, but they will no longer be in sync. Filtering the first slicer will not affect the slicer on another page and vice-versa. Keeping the left checkbox checked and deselecting the right checkbox will hide the filter on another page, making it invisible on the canvas and only visible from the Selection pane, but still in sync with the first slicer. That is how we can define filtering across pages with precision. We have to do this for each individual slicer that filters a certain attribute.

The Table view on the left ribbon

The Table view is the second view on the left ribbon in which we can see all data of the tables that loaded to the data model. We can see all the rows of all the tables, even the hidden tables and columns. If we are creating a tabular model locally, all data will be visible to everyone with access to the Power BI Desktop file. That is not the case if a tabular model is hosted on SQL Server Analysis Services. In such a case, the Table view is not visible at all, increasing the privacy of Power BI Desktop files.

On the right of the screen in the Data pane we may select any object as well as perform a search by entering keywords. If a measure is double-clicked, we can see and modify its formula in the Formula bar below the upper ribbon. When we open a measure in the Table view, we can open another measure in the Report view from the Report view's Data pane. That is useful if we want to quickly check another measure's formula.

The Table tools tab offers some options such as **Mark as date table**, **Manage relationships**, **New measure**, **Quick measure**, **New column**, and **New table**. Selecting any column enables another tab in the upper ribbon, that is the **Column tools** tab. This offers the ability to change column's name, **Data** type, and **Format**. The **Format** option allows presenting of a same datatype in different ways. The Date datatype can be written as Short Date, Long Date, and a variety of different combinations of years, months, and days with different separators (for example, yyyy-mm-dd or mm/dd/yyyy). Once a measure is selected, we can modify similar settings in the **Measure tools** tab.

The Model view on the left ribbon

Model view is the diagram view of our data model. We can see all the tables represented by a square. We can move and adjust their location. We can see a snapshot of the Model view in *Figure 5.5* in *Chapter 5, Enhancing the Model and Business Analysis with DAX* and *Figure 1.8* in *Chapter 1, Introducing the Theoretical Background for Democratizing Analytics*. With a drag and drop, we can establish connections between columns and create a data model. The squares representing the tables can be either in an expended or collapsed form. When expanded, all columns and measures are displayed within the square representing the table. These squares may be resized however we see fit. When table's square is collapsed, we will only see the columns that are part of model's relationships.

Double-clicking a relationship opens an interface window in which we can modify the cardinality, the cross-filter direction, and whether the relationship is active. With the logic of the star schema, the majority of relationships in a data model are going to be one-to-many relationships with one-sided cross filter direction. That is filtering from the one-side to the many-side. On the one-side of the relationship, we have a dimension table and on the many-side, we have a fact table. In tabular models, filtering direction is always coming from the one side. In some products offering older versions of tabular model technology, this might be the only possible relationship to establish. The ability to be able to filter from the many-side towards the one side depends on the version of technology providing tabular models. At the time of writing (June 2023), Power BI offers both-ways filtering for one-to-many relationships, but in logical star schema, these are not common. Bidirectional filtering should be used with caution as it can bring problems to the data model. The model can become ambiguous, meaning that there are multiple paths for transferring a filter between tables, which is not good.

One-to-one relationships, as rare as they may be, apply filter in both directions. One-to-one relationships would only be used in special cases, such as cases concerning privacy, speed optimizations or data partitioning. In a usual star schema application, we are not going to be seeing many of these. However, we might have to deal with many-to-many relationships. The most common filtering direction for these is both-ways. This can introduce problems in modeling schema, such as the circular reference. In Visual Studio's Analysis Services tabular model extension for the 2019 SQL Server version, only the both-ways filtering direction is possible. Newer versions of Power BI Desktop offer one-sided filtering for many-to-many relationships, which can prevent many of the problems in a data model. In older versions of tabular model technologies, we can build bridge tables to re-create one-sided many-to-many relationships.

Right-clicking a square representing the table or selecting the three dots at the top-right corner of the square offers similar options as right-clicking an object in the Data pane. Selecting the eye icon on either a table or a column will hide it from the Report view.

Another pane is available in the Model view, that is the **`Properties`** pane. We can modify name, description and synonyms for objects in the **`Properties`** pane. When selecting a column or measure, we can modify the **`Display folder`** option, which is a good way to organize our objects. In text columns, we can set the **`Sort by column`** option and Data category, in which we can identify a column as the one representing Address, City, Continent, and so on. In any column we can define Summarize by, while in a numeric column we can define Format, set Percentage format, modify Decimal places and add Thousands separator. In numeric measures, we can apply similar options, as well as define the Home table option. For tables, we can define the Storage mode under advanced.

When a blank canvas is selected, the Properties pane offers another option: Pin related fields to top of card. Switching it on will display the columns that are in a relationship on the top of the squares representing tables in the Model view.

Let us explain the topic of storage modes a little further. Import mode is what we are going to use the majority of time. Importing means that data is stored with a Power BI file (.pbix file) and is published to Power BI Service as well. This should provide a fast-filtering experience with the columnar storage technology. We can expect to use importing with any normal-sized dataset. What is considered a normal-sized dataset is relative, much like what is considered big data. With an increase in computing and memory, as well as the technological improvements such as in the field of compression, a normal-sized dataset increases in size as well. As a rule of thumb, if an import to our computer is taking too long, we are dealing with big data.

In such a case, maybe we should consider using DirectQuery, which connects to a source system and retrieves data in real time. Queries are executed directly in the source system, a useful feature for large datasets. There is also a question of data privacy, in a very strict environment it may not be permitted to perform extraction of the data from the source system, which rules out importing. There is also the Dual mode option, which is useful in the case of composite models. Composite models are data models created with data from more than one data source, often of different types. Some of the tables might be imported, others might be directly queried, the tables that are connecting these, often dimension tables, can be selected as being in the Dual mode. According to Microsoft documentation, this allows Power BI to choose the most efficient form of data retrieval.

There is also a special form of Direct Query called Live Connection, which is used for data sources offering semantic model services, such as Azure Analysis Services, Analysis Services on an on-premises environment and a Power BI dataset deployed to the Power BI Service. Semantic models store their calculations, such as DAX for tabular models, while live connection provides a means to use these calculations without importing them into Power BI. This eliminates the necessity of refreshing Power BI since the data is dynamically updated whenever the semantic model is refreshed. In essence, Power BI's tabular model is replaced by the semantic model of another service. In live connection, Power BI gets only the metadata of the model and not the data. We can see the diagram in the Model view, but we cannot modify many settings. The Table view disappears completely, which adds another layer of data privacy. Semantic models are usually created by engineers to offer a centralized data model for end users.

The ever-changing interfaces: On-object interaction

As we have stated before, Microsoft can often introduce interface changes that can drastically change the location of settings. This can introduce some frustration for both students and professional developers. We should remember that most functionalities stay the same, rather only how we access them changes. There was a new interactive option introduced as a preview feature. It is called On-object interaction and it can be turned on from: **`File`** > **`Options and settings`** > **`Options`** > **`GLOBAL's Preview features`** > **`On-object interaction`**.

This feature changes the way we approach building visualizations. The **`Visualization`** pane that offers the ability to select a visualization type, fields that form the visualization, and many of the options regarding visualization's formatting. The **`Visualization`** pane is now removed. Instead, many of these options can be accessed by selecting the icon next to each visualization. There are two icons available, the first one is **`Add data and build your visual`**, which offers ability to select visualization type and to add fields to visualizations. It can be seen in *Figure 6.18*:

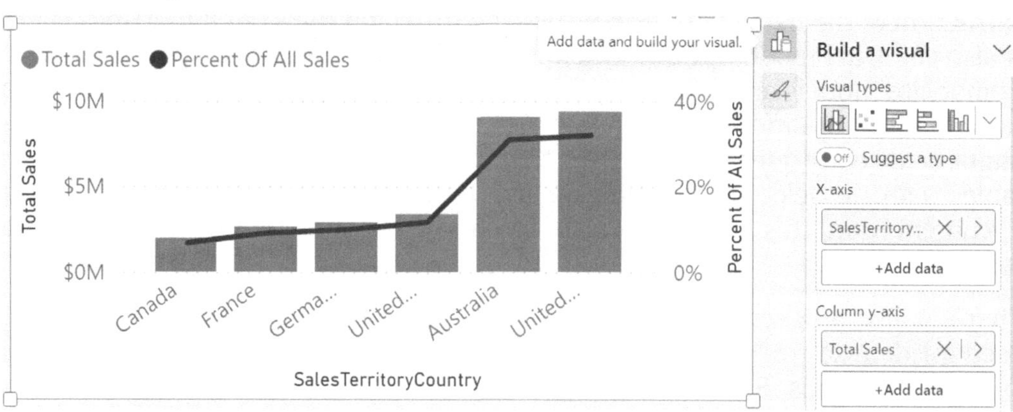

***Figure 6.18**: On-object interaction: Add data and build your visual*

The second icon is **`Add or remove visual elements`**, which offers the option to add or remove common elements of the visualization in a pop-up window. It can be seen in *Figure 6.19*. Selecting **`More option`** opens the Format pane, which is very similar to the Visualizations pane and offers more detailed formatting options. We can closely define chart options such as **`Title`**, **`Legend`**, **`axes`**, **`Columns`**, **`Lines`**, **`Markers`**, **`Data labels`**, and so on. Many objects on a chart are now clickable: Double-clicking the **`Y-axis`** Title (Total Sales) introduces a pop-up window that allows the renaming of the title directly, rather than by going to the pane. Double-clicking many of the chart's objects will display the new Format pane which replaced the **`Visualization`** pane. We can also right-click and select the option to format in the drop-down window, as can be seen in *Figure* 6.19. The option to create and change visualizations is now available in the **`Home`** and **`Insert`** tabs of the upper ribbon:

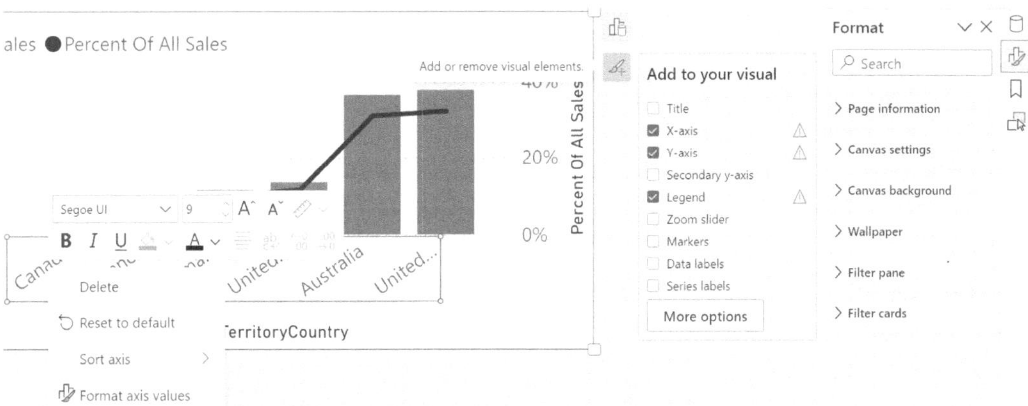

***Figure 6.19**: Add or remove visual elements and right pane*

Another major change is how we can interact with the panes. All of the panes, except for the **`Filters`** pane, are now switched using the newly created right ribbon, which seems to be called Pane switcher. It can be seen at the right side in *Figure* 6.19. Selecting the corresponding icon switches the pane that is appearing on the screen. We can probably expect additional changes for On-object interaction, until the two interaction experiences become a single unified experience. Hopefully, we will not see another complete revision of the interaction experience.

Conclusion

We have overviewed the Power BI Desktop interface and descriptive capabilities of Power BI Reports. We have seen that Power BI Desktop is an important tool for developers to understand, as it offers many capabilities to create insightful reports for end users to employ in their data-driven decisions. We have overviewed the most useful visualizations available, but not all of them. The reader can find some additional visualizations presented in the remaining chapters of this book. And after reading the book, we are encouraging readers to continue researching the world of BI by themselves. Updates are always bringing new capabilities and new tools or bundles of tools into the market for us to explore.

Besides descriptive analytics, there is diagnostic analytics, which focuses on understanding why something happened in the past. It asks questions about t the reasons behind some of the outcomes . We have also got predictive analytics, which tries to predict what is going to happen in the future. Prescriptive analytics goes even further as it tries to provide us with recommended actions that we should perform. All of these are widely considered more advanced forms of analytics that increase the value of our BI solutions. However, we should also warn, that they can come at a cost, either if they are implemented using Microsoft cloud resources or if they are programmed in-house with tools such as Python and R. Data science is the term used to describe these advanced manipulations of data. The Microsoft on-cloud resources dealing with data science usually require expensive licenses or include high operational costs, while in-house analytics using free third-party tools requires lots of knowledge and advanced developers, which again, are expensive investments. We are going to take a look into some advanced capabilities in the coming chapters.

But before any of that, we need to overview Power BI Service, the platform organizations use to share their reports with end users. We will take a look at it in the next chapter.

Questions

1. What is Power BI Desktop used for?
2. What are some graphical user interface options available in Power BI Desktop?
3. Describe the three views in Power BI Desktop.
4. What is the purpose of the panes in Power BI Desktop? Which panes are available?
5. What are some common visualizations and what are they used for?
6. Describe tooltips, drillthrough, and visual headers.

Chapter 7
Using the Power BI Service

Introduction

So far in this book, we have already discussed how to connect to data, how to import it into Power BI Desktop, how to create a data model with all the calculations we need and how to use Power BI Desktop to show those calculations on visualizations, grouped on report pages. So why do we even need something like the Power BI Service?

Structure

In this chapter, the following topics will be covered:

- The need for the Power BI Service
- Power BI Service basic components
- Managing workspaces
- Working with reports
- Creating dashboards
- Endorsing content
- Organize content into apps

- Managing data with dataflows
- Modeling data with datamarts
- Creating paginated reports
- On prem reporting with Power BI Report Server

The need for the Power BI Service

Imagine that we want to share the Power BI report you created with somebody. So far, we have a `.pbix` file with everything we have developed. We could simply send someone the entire `.pbix` file in an email, upload the file to cloud storage like OneDrive or share it to a file the other person has access to.

The problem with this way of sharing is that we lose control of the file and the data it contains. In most cases, if we sent the `.pbix` file as an attachment, we have already sent a separate copy of the file and the person can do whatever they want with it, including making edits to the reports and the measures and forwarding it to other people. If the file was saved to a file share, people might create their own copy of the file, save it to their local disk, make changes to it, share it with other people and present it as the source of truth.

The Power BI Service solves these issues. It is a software as a service offering that allows us to distribute the insights into our data that we got by creating reports in Power BI Desktop in a controllable manner, with options to define finely grained permissions on various components of the service that we will talk about shortly. Newer functionalities of Power BI Service also strive to remove the need for Power BI Desktop altogether, with options to connect to data, make necessary transformations and perform data modeling without leaving the Power BI Service.

Power BI Service basic components

When we log in to the Power BI Service and start exploring the user interface, we may be a bit overwhelmed by the available options. To get started in the service, it is useful to understand a few basic building blocks.

Workspaces

Power BI workspaces are the containers of content we and other people upload and create in the service. They are used for organizing content and collaborating with other people. We can access the different workspaces for which we have permissions to by clicking the **`Workspaces`** button on the left-hand side of the Power BI Service user interface.

Reports

You analyze data so you can present it to users in a meaningful, understandable way. This is what reports are meant for. Reports are a component of a workspace and consist of a single page or multiple pages that contain visuals, such as charts, tables, cards, and so on that display data and ways to interact with that data, such as slicers. They also contain a filter pane you can use to filter selected visuals. Everyone who has access to a workspace can see the reports contained in the workspace, but it is also possible to share individual reports with other users. Since this creates objects with unique permissions, which can make permissions management much harder, it is not a good practice. The data shown in a report can only come from a single dataset. If we need to use data from more than one dataset in a report, we can use Power BI Desktop to connect to multiple datasets and create what is known as a composite model. This creates a new dataset, which is a combination of existing datasets, that we can use to create new reports.

Dashboards

A dashboard is a summary of the most important information about a certain topic. It consists of tiles of various sizes that display information. The tiles come in the form of visualizations that already exist in a Power BI Service report that you pin to the dashboard, but you can also add tiles that contain other types of content such as custom text, images or YouTube videos to a dashboard. Contrary to reports, a single dashboard can contain tiles from a variety of reports that could be created from a variety of datasets, but only reports in the same workspace can be used as the source of tiles. Like reports, it is also possible to share individual dashboards with people who are not members of the workspace that contains the dashboard. Again, since this can make permissions management much harder, it is not a good practice.

Datasets

Power BI Service datasets are the components used as the data source for reports and dashboards. A dataset contains information about the transformations we performed on the data in Power Query, the tables we connected to, the relationships we established between the tables, the measures and calculated columns we created, and so on.

Datasets in the Power BI Service vary greatly based on the way we connected to the data:

- If we used **`Import mode`**, a copy of the data was saved in the dataset when we published the report through Power BI Desktop. This means that even if our data is on premises, users will be able to browse the reports based on a dataset that imported data, even if we do not have a gateway to our on-premises data source. However, in order to display current data in reports and dashboards, the dataset will have to be periodically refreshed, either by republishing the dataset manually, which is not a long-term solution or by implementing an on-premises data gateway.

- If we used **DirectQuery mode** or Live Connect, no actual data is saved in the dataset. For DirectQuery, the data schema is saved and for live connections, only the connection string to an existing model is saved. Therefore, if our data source is on premises, without an on-premises data gateway, the reports will not have any data to show.

A single dataset can be used for many reports and dashboards and can even be used across different workspaces. If a dataset is used for more than one report, it is known as a shared dataset.

Managing workspaces

In the Power BI Service, we access workspaces by clicking the **Workspace** icon in the left side pane of the Power BI Service window. We will be presented with an additional side pane containing a list of all the shared workspaces we have access to and an option to create a new workspace through the **+ New workspace** button located at the bottom of the pane, provided our Fabric administrator has not disabled the creation of workspaces for us. At the top of the workspaces list will be a special workspace called **My workspace**.

Every Power BI Service user gets their own **My workspace**. This is our personal workspace that no one else has access to. We cannot share the entire workspace, but we can give people access to certain content we upload to this workspace or create in it, such as reports and dashboards. As such, My workspaces are generally used when someone has data, they want to work on by themselves, but they might want to share the results of their data analysis in the form of a report. The general type of workspace on the other hand, can be shared with other users or groups in its entirety. It is therefore a better approach to use the general type of workspace when we wish to use the sharing feature.

By clicking the **+ New workspace** button, we will be presented with a new side pane, visible in *Figure 7.1*, giving us the option to name and describe the workspace and upload a workspace image. Under **Advanced options**, we can also list people that can be contacted when users have problems using certain parts of the workspace, for example when a report is not refreshing. We can also assign a type of license required to access this workspace, for example, Pro. When we are done with the settings, we can click **Apply**:

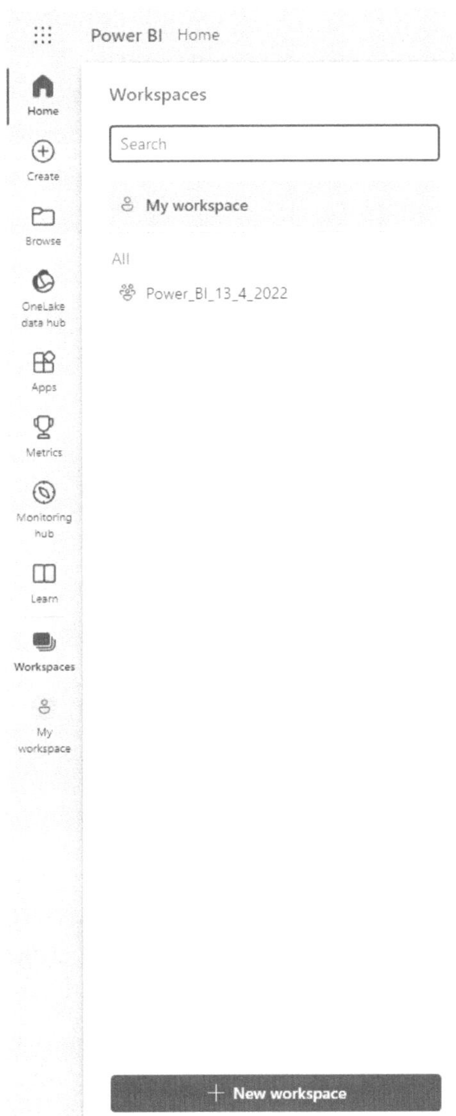

***Figure 7.1**: List of accessible workspaces*

The workspace will be created. For now, we are the only ones who have access to it. If we want, we can immediately share it with other users or groups by clicking the **`Manage Access`** button on the ribbon and then clicking **`+ Add people`** or groups. We will be presented with an input box for searching for users or groups. We can select multiple users or groups and then define their level of access a.k.a.

role to the workspace with the drop-down menu below the input box. We can choose from four different roles, as seen in *Figure 7.2*:

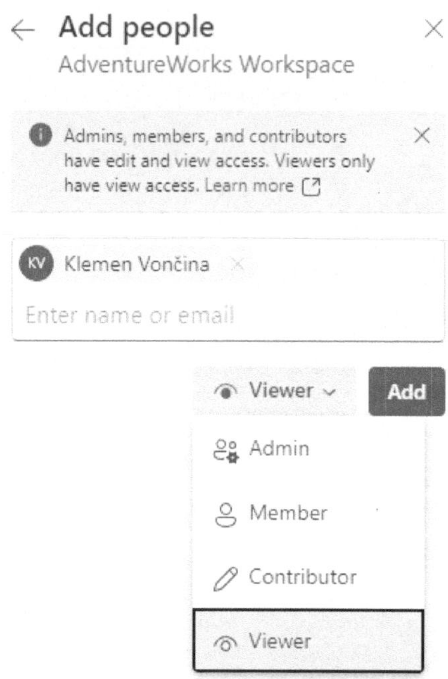

Figure 7.2: *Defining workspace permissions*

- `Admin`: Has full control over the workspace, including the permission to delete the workspace. An admin can also add and remove other admins. Additionally, an admin can allow workspace contributors to update the workspace app. We will talk about apps later in this chapter.
- `Member`: Has lower permissions than an admin but can still add other people to the workspace, giving them a maximum of member-level access. Members can also share individual workspace items and give users with a lower level of access permissions to reshare items. Members can also publish and unpublish the workspace app, update the workspace app, change app permissions, share items in the app and feature the app on other users' home pages.
- `Contributor`: Users with this role can create content in the workspace, modify it and delete it. They can also make changes to the on-premises gateway settings if they also have permissions on the gateway itself. If given reshare permissions, they can also share items with other users. If a workspace admin has allowed it, contributors can update the workspace app.

- **Viewer**: Can view items, such as reports and dashboards, and interact with elements, such as slicers, charts, and so on.

Once we have selected the users or groups, we wish to share the workspace with and selected the role we wish to assign to them, we can click **Add**.

When we have access to a large number of workspaces, it can be hard to quickly find the workspaces we most commonly use. In those cases, the recently used functionality of pinning workspaces can be handy. To pin a workspace, we need to open the Workspaces side pane, hover over the name of the workspace we wish to pin and click the pin icon to the right of the workspace name. The pinned workspaces will be listed under **My Workspace**.

Workspaces are the containers of content in Power BI Service. When we publish a report from Power BI Desktop, we need to select a workspace we wish to publish it. When we publish a report from Power BI Report Builder, we also select a workspace we wish to publish to. But we can also create new content straight from a workspace by clicking the **+ New** button on the ribbon and selecting the type of content we wish to create. We will discuss how to create various types of content in the following sections.

Working with reports

Building reports for ourselves or our users is probably the reason we started using Power BI. To share reports from the Power BI Service with our users, the reports must first exist in a workspace. We can create reports in a workspace in two different ways:

- Publishing from Power BI Desktop. This is the more common way. We connect to data from Power BI Desktop, create measures and reports there and then publish the results to the service. This way, we create a report and a dataset at the same time.
- Straight from the Power BI Service, by clicking the **+ New** button on the ribbon in a workspace and selecting Report. Reports must be created based on data, so here you will be presented with the option of entering data straight into an Excel-like sheet or using a dataset that already exists within the service, thereby creating what is known as a thin report that has a live connection to the existing dataset.

Let us discuss both methods more in-depth.

Publishing reports from Power BI Desktop

Once our report is created, we can click on the Publish button on the **Home** tab, visible in *Figure 7.3*. If we have not signed into Power BI Desktop before, we will be prompted to do so now. We are signing into the Power BI Service through Power BI Desktop, so here we need to sign in with the same account we use for the Power BI Service:

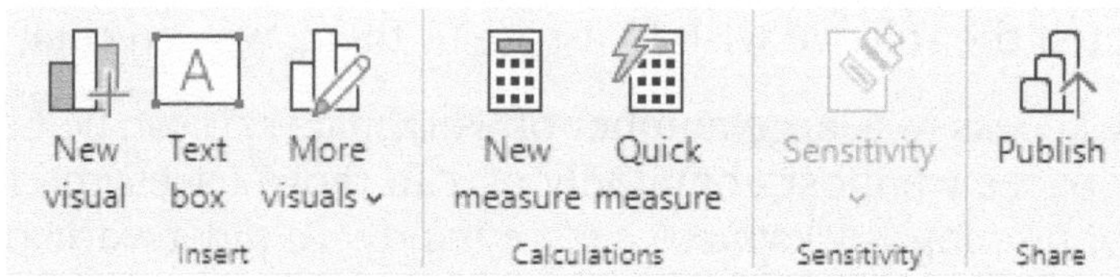

Figure 7.3: *Part of the Home ribbon with the Publish button*

After we are done signing in, we will be presented with a list of workspaces in the Power BI Service that we have access to. We select the workspace we wish to publish the report to and click **`Select`**. We will be presented with a pop-up window named **`Publishing to Power BI`**, which will show us a success message after the report is successfully published to the service. When we see it, we can close this window.

After we publish the report, we can go to the service and open the workspace we published the report to. We can notice that a report and a dataset with the same name have been created.

If we want to make changes to your report after it has been published, we can make the changes in the original **`.pbix`** file and publish it again in the same workspace. When we select the workspace in Power BI Desktop, we will receive a warning that a dataset with this name already exists in the service and that replacing it may replace a certain number of reports and dashboards. Before deciding, we can click **`View impact`**. We will be redirected to the service, where we will see a lineage view of the dataset in question, meaning which reports and dashboards depend on this dataset. Back in Power BI Desktop, if we click **`Replace`**, the updated report will be uploaded and will be available in the service.

Republishing reports from Power BI Desktop can also be an improvised way of refreshing a report. If our data is on premises and we attempt to refresh the dataset from Power BI Service without having first implemented a data gateway, the refresh will fail. Of course, for production environments with on-premises data, a data gateway needs to be implemented. But for testing or learning purposes or if our data gateway is temporarily down, we can refresh our data by opening the same **`.pbix`** file that was the original source of the report, refreshing the data locally and then republishing the report to the same workspace.

Creating reports in Power BI Service

Publishing reports we create in Power BI Desktop is the most common method of creating reports. But it is also possible to create reports directly in the Power

BI Service. When we are in a workspace, we can create a report by clicking the `+ New` on the ribbon and then selecting Report. We will be presented with a new page with two options, as visible in *Figure 7.4*:

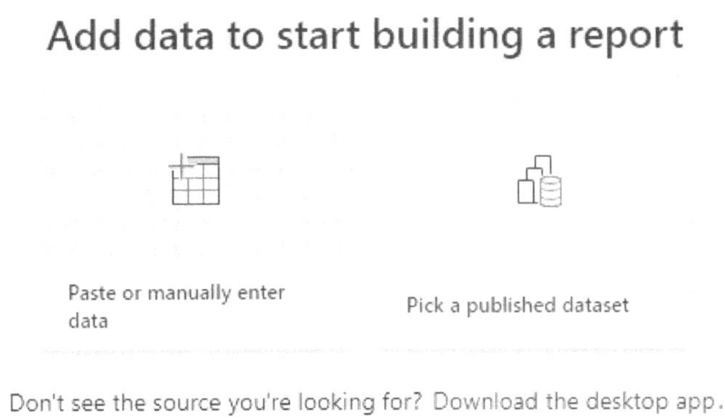

Figure 7.4: *Building reports straight from Power BI Service*

- **`Paste or manually enter data`**: With this option, we first create a dataset in an Excel like interface. This is actually a Power Query window that we can type or paste data into. This probably will not be the go-to choose for most reports, since the window only contains a few functionalities and because the dataset we create will only contain a single table. After we enter the data, we can click the button in the bottom-right corner of the window to either auto-create a report, in which case Power BI Service will try to create a meaningful single-page report from the data we entered, create a blank report and do everything from scratch, or to only create a dataset from the data we entered and create a report at a later time.
- **`Pick a published dataset`**: This option allows us to create another report from a dataset that is already in Power BI Service. When we select this option, we are presented with the OneLake data hub window, that allows us to browse through datasets. At the top, we can switch between All, which shows us the datasets we have access to, My data, which shows us datasets we own and Endorsed in your org, which displays datasets that have been set as endorsed. On the left side of this window, we can expand Explorer, which allows us to further narrow down the displayed datasets by workspaces. After we have selected a dataset, we can use the buttons in the bottom-right corner of this window to either auto-create a report, which will automatically generate a report Power BI Service deems interesting according to the data in the selected dataset, or to create a blank report and build all the pages and visuals from scratch.

Whether we choose to enter data manually or if we pick an existing dataset, if we choose the option to auto-create a report, we must not forget to save the report when satisfied with the results. Unless we save it by clicking the **Save** button on the ribbon, giving the report a name and placing it in a destination workspace, the report will be discarded.

Using finished reports

Once a report is created, users who have access to it, either via permissions to the workspace or via direct permissions to the report, will be able to view it in the Power BI Service. But users can do many other things besides just viewing the reports by using the commands on the ribbon when a report is open.

By clicking on the **File** button on the ribbon, users with view permissions can create a copy of the report in a workspace where they have edit permission. The copy of the report is based on the same dataset as the original report. Users can also print a report page and this functionality can also be used to save a report page to a PDF file. It is also possible for users with view permissions to generate an embed code so they can display the report on a SharePoint page or another type of internal website or portal and even an embed code for Power BI Embedded Analytics (the **Developer Playground** option). Users with view permissions may also generate a QR code that other users that have at least view permissions can scan and access the report directly.

Users that have edit permissions on the report have another option available under Embed report, that is, **Publish to web (public)**. This type of embed code allows users to embed reports into public-facing websites, emails, social media posts, and so on. We need to be careful when using this option since it can expose confidential internal data to the entire world as viewing the report requires no authentication whatsoever. Any data security that would be set up on such reports could therefore not be enforced, which is why publicly sharing reports that have row-level security set up is not possible. Because of the possibility of leaking data to the public, even though users who can edit reports will have the option to generate a public embed code, they will be unable to actually generate it unless the organizational Power BI administrator has allowed the creation of public embed codes for the entire organization or at least for certain security groups in the Fabric admin portal. The creation of public embed codes can be enabled org-wide or only for specific security groups.

Another option users with permissions have is to edit a report under the **File** button in **Settings**. Clicking this option opens a side pane where you can change the report name and description, change the contact person or group for the report and various other settings. We will take a closer look at the settings under the Endorsement group in a dedicated section.

The next button, **Export**, allows users to export a report into various formats. There are options to export to Excel, PowerPoint, and PDF. Let us take a look at what each of the options can do:

- **Analyze in Excel**: This option does not recreate our current report in an Excel file. It creates a new Excel workbook at the root of our OneDrive for Business. If we do not have OneDrive for Business, the Excel workbook is downloaded to our computer. The Excel workbook contains a connection to the dataset that the report we created it from was based on. We can use classic Excel functionalities, such as pivot tables, to analyze that data in a way we might be more familiar with. This option will not be available to users who can only view the report as build permissions on the underlying dataset are required.
- **PowerPoint**: This option expands into two additional commands:
    - Embed an image, which allows us to save the current report page or all the report pages as images in a PowerPoint presentation. Clicking this command will open an Export window giving us the options to export with either Current Values, which means based on the filter settings we may have changed when browsing the report, or Default Values, meaning with the data that is shown on the report when we first open it. Additionally, there is an option to exclude hidden report tabs (pages). Interestingly, users would have to explicitly set that they do not want to export any pages that are hidden. Also, there is currently no way to disable the option to export hidden report tabs. The last setting is called Only export current page. If the checkbox is left empty, all report pages will be exported to PowerPoint, each to its own slide. When you click **Export**, Power BI Service will start generating the PowerPoint file and when it is ready, the download will start. When the file is downloaded, we can open it and we will see that the images that show report pages also serve as hyperlinks back to the report.
    - Embed live data, which allows us to show a live Power BI report page in PowerPoint with the help of the Power BI add-in for PowerPoint. When we click this command, we will be presented with a window that contains the option to preserve filter selections in the embedded live data (Embed report with the data filters you selected) and a link we can copy straight into the Power BI add-in for PowerPoint. Alternatively, we can click **Open in PowerPoint**, in which case Power BI Service will generate a new PowerPoint file for us, containing the page that was open when we clicked this command. We may notice that the report is interactive, for example, if we click on a visual, it will cross-filter other visuals on the report page (if cross-filtering is set up on the visuals). In the

bottom-right corner of the embedded live page, we also have the option to refresh data straight from PowerPoint by clicking the **Data options** button, represented by a bar chart icon and clicking **Refresh**.

- **PDF**: This option is similar to embedding an image in PowerPoint. The options are the same, except that instead of a PowerPoint file, we will get a PDF file with either a single report page or all report pages, depending on our settings.

Next, comes sharing options. The Share button on the ribbon is visible to everybody, but unless we have reshare permissions, we will only be able to send a link to the report to people who already have access. Workspace admins and members can share a report with anybody, even external users, considering any limitations that the Fabric administrator may have set. But workspace contributors and viewers need to be granted reshare permissions if we need them to be able to further share a report.

Giving access to specific items such as reports to individual users is not a good practice, as it makes keeping track of active permissions very hard. It is best to share entire workspaces or content that is bundled into apps. It is also a best practice to share content with security groups.

When we click the **Share** button, if we have reshare permissions on the report, we will be given the options to share with people in our organization, people with existing access (not actually sharing with, just sending another link to people who already have access) and specific people, which can also be external users. Underneath these options, we can select the **Allow recipients to share this report** checkbox if we wish to give the users, we are sharing the report with reshare permissions. The last setting, **Allow recipients to build content with the data associated with this report**, gives users build permissions on the dataset the report is based on. This means that users will be able to use the underlying dataset to further explore the data with functionalities such as Analyze in Excel on the report.

The next button on the ribbon, **Chat in Teams**, is just a shortcut to paste the report link to someone or somewhere in Microsoft Teams. Even though it says Share to Microsoft Teams in the window, you are not giving access to the report to anyone who does not already have it. Users without permission to the report will be denied access.

You can only use the **Get Insights** command if the workspace containing the report is hosted in a Power BI Premium capacity, Fabric capacity or if you have Premium Per User licenses. The command opens a side pane on the right-hand side of the report and shows any interesting trends and anomalies it finds in your data.

The **`Subscribe to report`** button allows us to subscribe ourselves or others to periodical emails that will contain a snapshot of a report page and, depending on settings, a link to it. When we click this button, a side pane will open on the right-hand side, allowing us to add new subscriptions with the **`+ Add new subscription`** button at the top or edit existing ones through the Manage all subscriptions link at the bottom of the side pane.

In a subscription, we can define basic settings, such as enter recipients into the Subscribe field, and configure if we want the report in the email to include any changes to filters, drilldowns, and so on. that we may have made with the Include my changes checkbox and set the frequency and time of the emails being sent. Clicking the **`More options`** link will expand additional settings, where we are also able to, for example, set an end date for the subscription and set the content of the email, for example, the message the email will contain and if the email should include a link to the report in Power BI.

Next to the **`Subscribe to report`** button, users with permission to edit the report will see an **`Edit`** button. Clicking this button will switch the report into edit mode, which allows us to use the data model the report is built on to create new visualizations, edit existing ones, change filter settings, and so on.

The last button on the left side of the ribbon is an icon with three dots, as shown in *Figure* 7.5. Clicking it will show additional options, which vary depending on permissions. Users with view permissions will be able to see related content, which lists dashboards that use visuals from the report and the dataset the report is based on. Interestingly, users with view permissions on the report also see the View dataset button, even though if they do not have build permissions on the dataset, it will only notify them that they cannot access the dataset. Otherwise, it will display the dataset the report is based on:

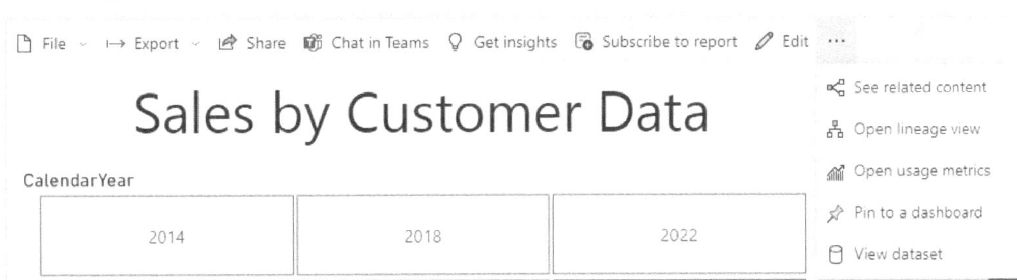

***Figure 7.5**: Various options for managing reports*

Users with at least contribute permissions will have some other commands available. They will be able to switch to a lineage view, which will show how all the workspace content is intertwined. They will be able to create a usage metric report, which is a single-page report about report usage in the last 90 days. The usage metric report is not editable, and it also does not show up in the workspace content. We can however click **`File`** in the upper left corner of the report and use the **`Save a copy command`** to create an editable copy of this report that also shows up in the workspace.

Note

At the time of writing this book, there is an option to turn New usage report on in the upper right corner of the usage metric report. This creates a more detailed usage report, spanning multiple pages. It is probable that this new usage report will be the standard usage report format sometime soon.

Finally, users with at least contribute permissions will also see the Pin to a dashboard command, which will pin the entire page to a dashboard as a live page, meaning changes to the report page will be reflected on the dashboard tile displaying the page.

Creating dashboards

Contrary to reports, we cannot create dashboards in Power BI Desktop, Dashboards are created only in the Power BI Service. We can create a dashboard straight from the main workspace window, as shown in *Figure* 7.6, by clicking the **`+ New`** button and selecting Dashboard. We are presented with a window for entering the desired dashboard name. When we enter a valid name, we can click **`Create`**. We will automatically be redirected to a new empty dashboard we can populate with tiles:

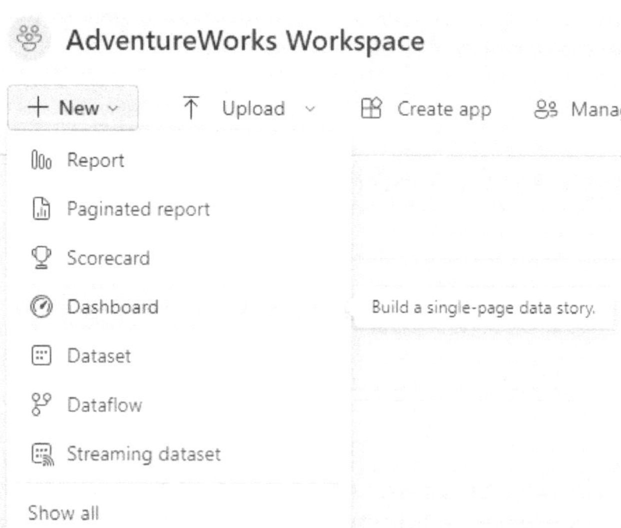

Figure 7.6: *Creating a dashboard from a workspace*

Another way of creating a dashboard is by opening a report that contains a visual we want to display on a new dashboard, hovering over the visual with our mouse cursor and then clicking the pin icon called Pin this visual that appears next to the visualization.

When we do this, a new window will appear, asking us if we want to pin to an existing dashboard or to a new one. By selecting New dashboard, an input box for entering the new dashboard's name appears. When we enter the desired dashboard name, we can click the **Pin** button. After we pin the tile to the new dashboard, a pop-up will appear for a short time in the browser with the option of taking you to your new dashboard. The other way to access the dashboard is to go back to the main workspace window and clicking the name of the dashboard in the list of the workspace contents.

Depending on the way we created your dashboard, it will contain zero or one tile. We can pin more existing report visualizations to the dashboard by going to another report, finding the visualization we would like to pin, hovering over it and selecting the pin icon visible in *Figure* 7.7, but this time selecting the Existing dashboard as the destination for the visual and then selecting the dashboard from the **`Select existing dashboard`** drop-down menu:

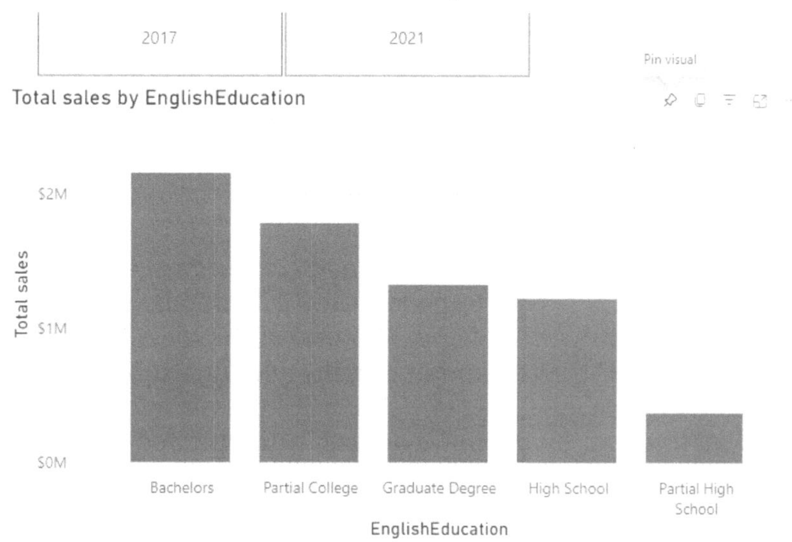

***Figure* 7.7**: *Pinning a visual to a dashboard*

When we have pinned visualizations from reports to a dashboard, clicking the pinned tile in the dashboard will take us to the report the visual originates from. When we hover over a pinned tile, three dots will appear in the upper-right corner of the visual. By clicking them, we will be presented with additional options, visible in *Figure 7.8*:

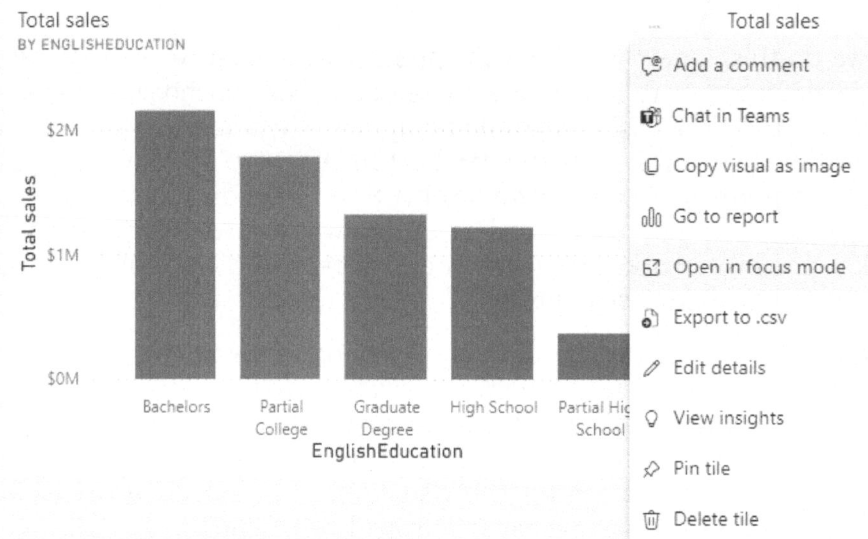

Figure 7.8: *Dashboard tile options, with Open in focus mode highlighted*

An interesting one is **Open in focus mode**, which expands the tile so you can see it in more detail. In this view, we are still able to use visual-level filters via the filter pane. When we are done exploring a tile in focus mode, we can click the **Exit Focus mode** button in the top-left part of the screen.

By clicking the three dots, we can also change certain properties of the tile by clicking **Edit details**. A property pane called Tile details will appear on the right-hand side that allows us to change the title of the tile, that is, the text that is displayed at the top of the tile and optionally adding a subtitle for additional clarity. We can also display the last refresh time of the tile and set a custom link. As we already mentioned, by default, clicking a tile pinned from a report will take us to that report. But we can change this behavior so clicking a tile will take our dashboard readers to a URL of our choice. After we make the desired changes, we can click **Apply**.

As we have already mentioned in the section about reports, it is also possible to pin an entire report page to a dashboard. To do this, we need to open a report and browse to the page we would like to pin. After that, we click the **Edit** button on the ribbon and then click the **Pin to a dashboard** button. We will be presented with a familiar window, where we can choose to pin the page to a new or existing dashboard. As we will see, the button for pinning the report page to a dashboard is called **Pin live**. This way, we pin what is called a live tile, meaning any changes made to the report page will be reflected in the pinned tile. Another reason for this name is that we can click the different visuals on a live tile and the live tile will behave just like the report page would, meaning the cross-filtering and cross-highlighting of visuals works.

Since clicking the live tile is meant for cross-filtering and cross-highlighting visuals, to use a live tile as a shortcut to go to the report page, we need to click the three dots that appear when we hover over the live tile and select **Go to report**.

After we have added a couple of visualizations to the dashboard, we will probably want to rearrange and resize them. To rearrange visuals, we simply drag and drop them to the desired location. The other visualizations on the dashboard will automatically move out of the way. To resize a visualization, we grab it by the bottom-right corner and drag it inward to make it smaller or outward to make it bigger.

When we are already in a dashboard, we can also add custom content to the dashboard by clicking the **Edit** button on the ribbon and selecting **Add a tile**. There are five types of tiles we can add, visible in *Figure 7.9*:

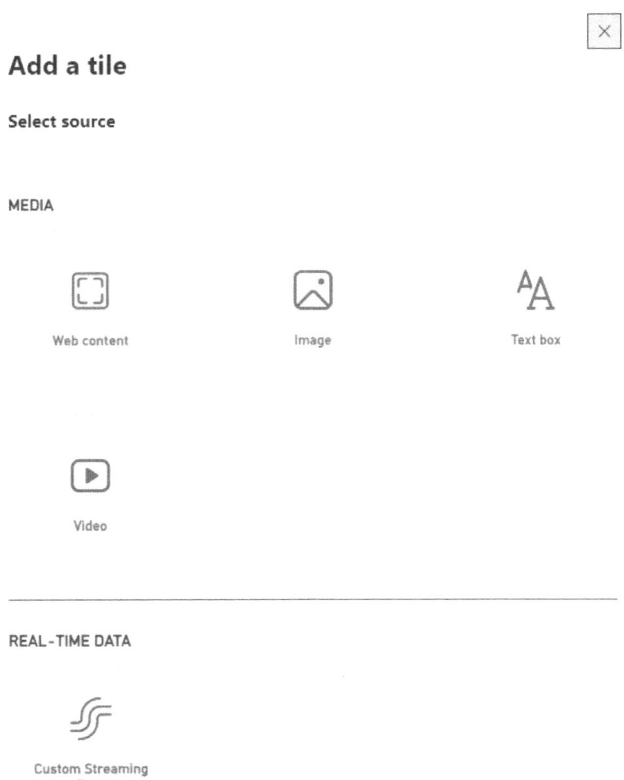

Figure 7.9: *Adding additional tiles*

- **Web content**: This type of tile is used for displaying HTML content. We can enter custom HTML code such as a paragraph to display some custom formatted text or an iframe to display an entire webpage or we can copy and paste an embed code from online sources such as Twitter.
- **Image**: We can use the image tile to display an image, such as a company logo, from an online source.
- **Text box**: Text boxes can be used for adding a heading to the dashboard so the topic of the dashboard is immediately clear to dashboard viewers. We can also add text boxes next to visualizations to make it clearer what a visualization represents.
- **Video**: We can display a video from YouTube or Vimeo to make the content of the dashboard more dynamic and interesting.
- **Custom Streaming Data**: If we have data that is constantly being updated and we wish to display it in real time, we can create a Custom Streaming Data tile.

Managing dashboards

On the ribbon, dashboards mostly have the same commands as a report. We can share a dashboard, post the link to the dashboard to Teams, create a subscription to the dashboard, and so on.

The **Edit** button however contains some commands specific to dashboards. We have already talked about the **Add a tile** command. The drop-down menu also displays the Dashboard theme command. Clicking this command opens a side pane, visible in *Figure* 7.10, which allows us to choose between built-in color variations (**Light**, **Dark**, and **Color-blind friendly**) and create a **Custom** theme for the dashboard. At the top of this side pane, we also have the option to upload a custom JSON theme or download the current JSON theme, that we can use as a starting point for creating our own JSON:

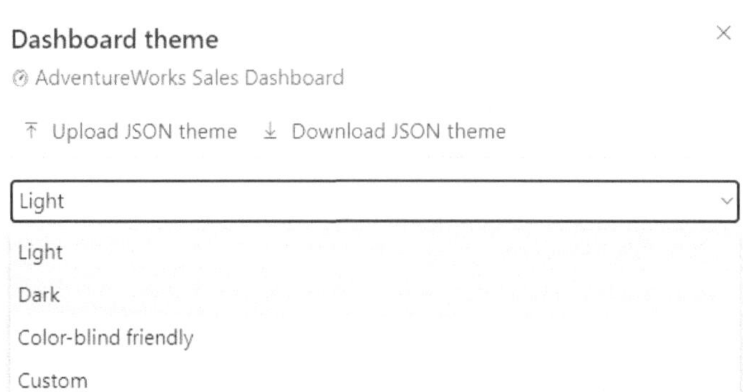

***Figure* 7.10**: *Changing a dashboard's theme*

Another command in the Edit drop-down menu is the Mobile layout, which opens a new window that contains a side pane that allows us to select the tiles you wish to display in the mobile version of the dashboard and the order in which to display them by dragging and dropping them around in the simulated mobile screen in the center of the window.

Endorsing content

Since a lot of people may have permission to create content in the Power BI Service, we may encounter issues with users not knowing which reports are considered trustworthy at an organizational level and which are just clutter. Endorsing content allows us to promote quality content with different statuses. Let us take a closer look at endorsing reports, but you can use a similar approach to endorse datasets, dataflows, and apps.

By default, a report we create does not have any special status. Users that have access to it can find it and view it, but they are not encouraged in any way to interpret such a report as more legitimate than any other that is available to them. By setting a report as Promoted, when users browse the content of a workspace, promoted reports will have a special Promoted tag in the Endorsement column of the workspace.

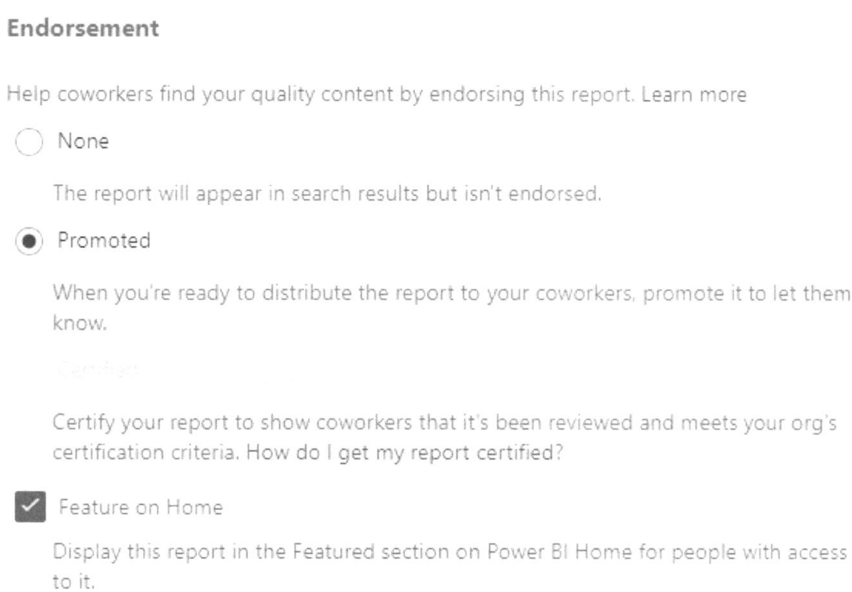

Figure 7.11: *Setting a report as Promoted*

To set a report as promoted, open the report's settings, either from the workspace by clicking the three dots that appear when we hover over the report name and then clicking **Settings** or from the report itself by clicking **File** and then **Settings**. Under the **Endorsement** section, we will have various endorsement statuses available, among them **Promoted**, as seen in *Figure* 7.11. We can select it and click **Save**.

The problem with the **Promoted** status is that anyone who can edit a report can set its status to **Promoted**. If this status is used too many times, it loses its meaning. Luckily, another, more restricted endorsement status called **Certified exists**. Most users, even if they are workspace administrators, will be unable to set a report as certified. This is because first of all, certification must be enabled on the tenant level by a Power BI administrator and second, a user must be authorized by a Power BI administrator to set a report's status as certified (through membership of an authorized security group). We set a report as certified in the settings pane the same way as we set a report as promoted.

Another setting under the **Endorsement** section is Feature on Home. Reports with this setting turned on will be displayed on the home page of the Power BI Service to users who have access to it, making it easier for them to find and access the report.

Organize content into apps

A Power BI app is a component of the Power BI Service that allows Power BI designers to bundle related content into a single package that can then be distributed to end users. Apps make it easier for end users to view content that may come from dispersed sources. Instead of going to a workspace and open many different reports and dashboards, users only need to open a single app.

To create an app, we go to the workspace that contains the content we wish to bundle and click **Create app** on the workspace ribbon. In the first step of the app creation process, we enter an app name, add an App description, select an app logo and theme color, define contact information, which end users can use in case of problems using the app, configure the global app settings, such as if this app should be installed automatically to intended users, and enter a link to a dedicated site we may have with instructions for using the app. When we are done with this step, we can click **Next**: Add content in the bottom-right corner of the screen.

In the next step, we can click the downward-facing arrow next to the **+ Add content** button on the left side of the window which allows us to create a new section in the app. We can use sections to organize custom links we create, which we will discuss shortly. If we wish to add content to the app, we can click directly on the **+ Add content** button. This will open the **Add content** window, where we can switch between two tabs: **Add from workspace** and **Add a link**.

From the **`Add from workspace`** tab, seen in *Figure* 7.12, we can select dashboards, reports, and Excel workbooks we wish to bundle into the app. We do this by marking the checkboxes next to each element we wish to add. When we are done, we can click **`Add`**. This will add each element as a new section in the app, which we can see in the left pane:

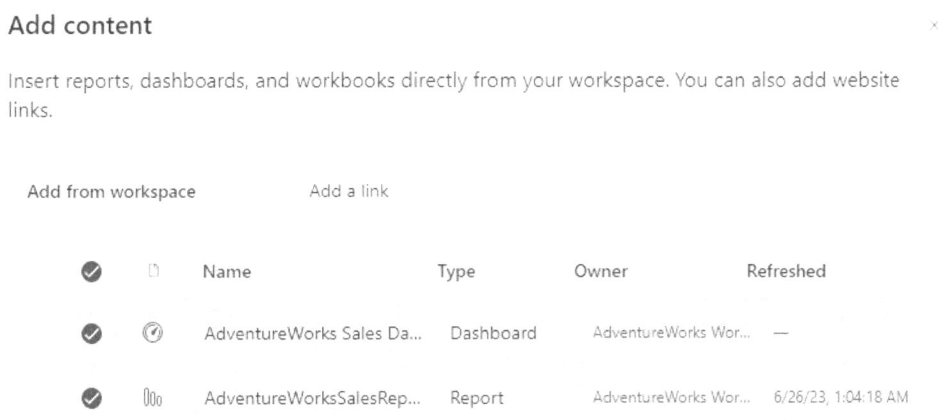

Figure 7.12: *Adding content to an app*

The **`Add a link`** option on the other hand allows us to add a custom hyperlink to the app, which can lead us to an internal or public website with additional information relevant to the app. We define a link name, which is the display name that will be listed in the app, enter the link itself, define whether to open the link in a new tab, the current tab or in the app area and lastly, which section we wish to place the link into. When we are done with adding content, we can click the **`Next: Add audience`** button in the bottom-right corner of the screen.

In this last step, we define the users or groups to which we wish to make the app available. The combination of users and groups along with their permissions to the app is called an audience. By default, a single audience is created, named after the workspace. We can see this audience on the ribbon in the upper-left corner of this window. If we want to rename an audience, we can double-click on the audience's name and change it. In this same ribbon, we can also create more audiences by clicking the **`+ New Audience`** button.

When we select an audience, we can make changes to the content that will be visible in the app by showing or hiding it in the pane on the left-hand side. We can show or hide content by clicking the eye icon next to the name of the item. Also, in the side pane on the right-hand side of this window, we define the members of this audience. An important detail here is that if we decided to install the app automatically to users, we cannot select Entire organization as the app audience in the side pane on the right-hand side.

Under the advanced section, we can also give audiences the permission to share the datasets that reports in the app built upon and build permissions on the datasets, so they can use them to build new reports from the datasets. When we are done configuring audience settings, we can click **Publish app**.

When we decide to publish an app, we are notified that it can take a while before the app becomes available. After the app becomes available, users can go to the apps section by clicking the **Apps** button in the left side pane of the Power BI Service. Clicking this button displays the list of apps a user has installed for themselves or that have been installed automatically for them.

If we wish to add additional apps to our apps list, we can click the **Get apps** button in the upper-right corner of the Apps window. This will open the Power BI apps window which we can use to browse and install available apps. If we are looking for an app our organization has made available, we can switch to the **Organizational apps** tab. After we find the app, we wish to add, we can click **Get it now**. It will be added to our list of apps.

Clicking the app name in the list of apps will open the app and display the content contained in the app. The content that is visible to us depends on the app audience we are part of.

Note that if we change the reports and dashboards that are part of the app, the changes will not be reflected in the app automatically. We must first update the app. To do so, we need to go to the workspace that contains the content of the app and click **Update app** on the ribbon. Here we can also make any other desired changes to the app by changing the options on the three app settings tabs seen in the upper-left corner of the screen. When we are done, we can click the **Update app** button in the bottom-right corner of the screen and clicking **Update** in the window warning us about potentially long app update times.

Managing data with dataflows

The most common procedure for connecting to data is opening Power BI Desktop and selecting the appropriate data connector. We then use the Power Query editor to make the necessary transformations and bring the transformed data into the data model. But if we make numerous reports based on the data from the same source, it can be tedious to go through the same transformation steps each time. Instead of this, we can create a dataflow in the Power BI Service and use it as a data source in Power BI Desktop.

To create a dataflow, we go to a workspace, click **+ New** on the ribbon and select Dataflow. In the next window, visible in *Figure* 7.13, we select what we want to base our dataflow on. For this example, we will select **Add new tables**, which allows us to start from scratch. In the next step, we choose the data source we wish to connect to. If you are familiar with Power Query, these connectors will probably be familiar to you. We can connect to cloud sources as well as on-premises sources. If we look at the upper-left corner of the screen, we will see that we are using Power Query from the Power BI Service. For our example, we will select the SQL Server database connector:

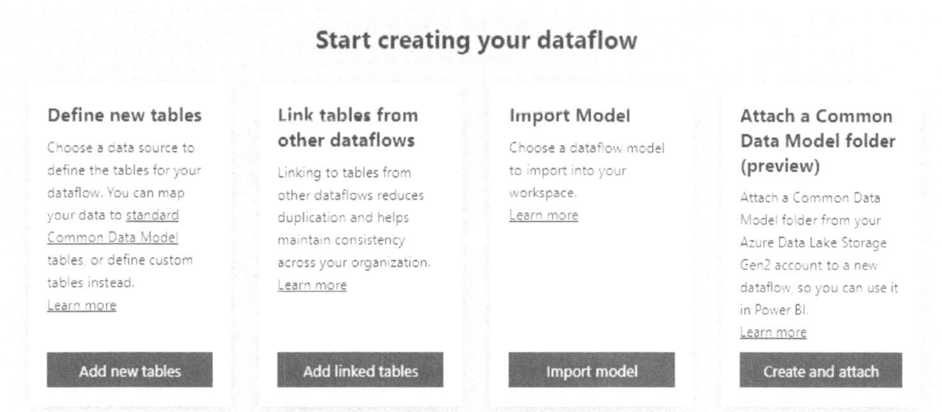

Figure 7.13: *Starting with a dataflow creation*

In the next step, we define the necessary connection settings. For SQL Server, we need to enter the server's name and optionally we can also enter the database name. Under **Advanced options**, we can enter a SQL statement if we have already written the necessary transformations with T-SQL.

Since we are connecting to on premises data from the Power BI Service, we need to have a Power BI data gateway implemented. Under **Connection** credentials, we can select **Create a new connection**, select an existing data gateway, choose the authentication method we wish to use, and enter the credentials with appropriate permissions on the data source. The user interface is shown in *Figure* 7.14 When we are done, we can click **Next**:

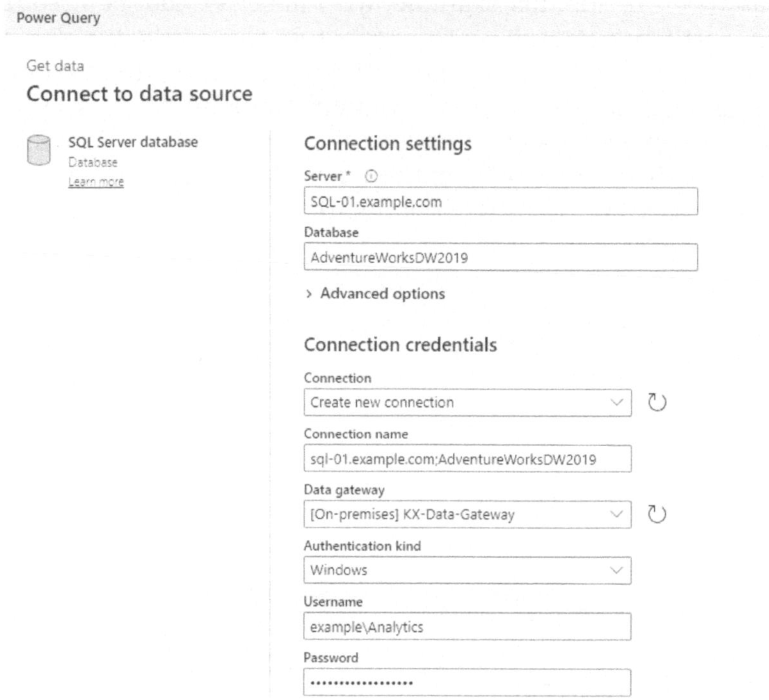

Figure 7.14: *Connecting to on-prem SQL data with dataflows*

In the next step, we need to choose the data we wish to connect to. If we have not defined the database name in the previous step, we can expand a database now and then click the checkboxes next to the tables we wish to use. Once we are done with selections, we can click the Transform data button in the bottom-right corner of the screen.

In the next step, the Power Query editor will be available to us to make the necessary transformations to the data. When we are done with transformations, click the **Save & Close** button in the lower-right corner of the screen.

To use the dataflow, we can open Power BI Desktop and from the **Home** tab, click the **Get data** dropdown and select the **Dataflows connector**. We may need to sign in with our organizational account first. After that, we can expand the Workspaces container in the left pane, expand the workspace that contains the dataflow we wish to connect to, expand the dataflow with the tables we wish to use, select the tables, and then either select Load to use the data from the dataflow directly, or select **Transform Data** to make any additional transformations. After we connect to the data, we can use it to make new reports in Power BI Desktop and publish them to the service.

Modeling data with datamarts

Using dataflows, the Power BI Service connects to various data sources and stores the data in an Azure Data Lake Gen 2. The data is stored as tables without any established relationships. If we wish to create a complete, ready-to-use data model in Power BI Service, we can create datamarts.

Datamarts also leverage dataflows for connecting to data and transforming it. After we connect to data, however, it is stored in an Azure SQL Server where we can model it. When we are finished, it is made available to us in the Power BI Service as a dataset.

To create a datamart, we need to go into a Power BI Premium or **Premium Per User** (**PPU**) workspace. We then click the **`+ New`** button and select **`Datamart (Preview)`**. At the time of writing this book, datamarts are still in preview.

After the datamart is provisioned, we can connect to data by clicking the **`Get data`** button on the ribbon. The underlying technology to connect to a data source is Power Query, so all the skills we have with Power Query will come in handy here. We will be presented with different connectors for connecting to different data sources. For this example, we will use the SQL Server database connector.

In the **`Connect to data source`** window, we need to enter the database server name and set up the connection credentials. To connect to an on-premises data source, we need to have an existing Power BI data gateway. We then select the data gateway, pick an authentication method, and enter the appropriate credentials. When we are done, we can click **`Next`**.

In the next window, we select the tables we wish to use in the datamart. When we are done with selections, we can click **`Transform data`**. We can use the familiar Power Query editor to make the necessary transformations to our data. When we are done, we can click **`Save`**.

When we click **`Save`**, the data will be loaded to the datamart. We can then use the datamart to manage the model by using the commands on the ribbon. We can, for example, create measures with the **`New measure`** command or create row-level security roles with the **`Manage roles`** command. In the bottom-left corner of the screen, we can switch to the **`Model`** tab to manage the relationships between the tables, as seen in *Figure 7.15*:

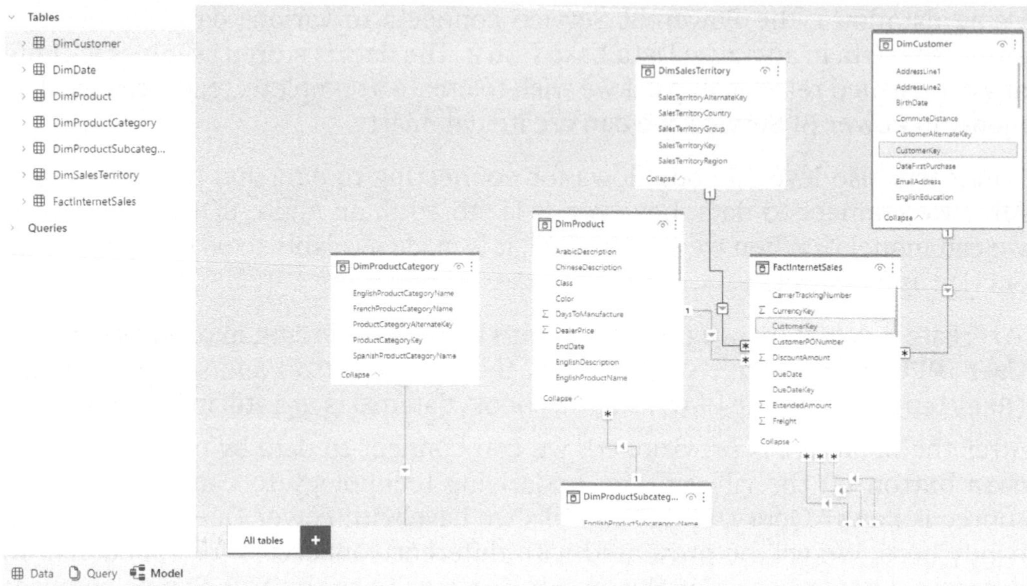

***Figure 7.15**: Managing table relationships in Power BI Service*

As we can see, the commands in a datamart are a basic subset of the data modelling commands from Power BI Desktop. After the datamart is created, a dataset is automatically created in the background. If we select the New report command on the Home tab in the datamart, we will create a new report that will use this new dataset. We can also navigate back to the workspace, click the **`+ New`** button on the ribbon, select Report, click **`Pick a published dataset`** and the dataset named after the datamart will be available for report creation.

We should note that datamarts are still in preview, so functionalities are subject to change. Also, datamarts are a premium feature, so bigger licensing costs are involved if we wish to use them. Even though datamarts bring some data modeling features to the Power BI Service, they might not have a very bright future. In the background, they are an Azure SQL database where you do not have any control. They probably will not replace Power BI Desktop as many modeling features are missing. There are also some Microsoft Fabric features, such as Data Warehouse, which already allow you to model data in a more advanced way.

Creating paginated reports

If we encounter the need to print our reports, we will quickly find out that the standard Power BI reports are not well suited for this requirement. Imagine that we have a table or matrix visual with so much data that we need to scroll up and down to see everything. Using the **Print this page** command under the **File** button in the report, the printed page will only display the data that was currently visible in the report. The table will not automatically split into multiple pages.

This is why we may require paginated reports. We can create paginated reports straight from the Power BI Service by opening the dataset in a workspace and clicking the **Create paginated report** button in the side pane on the right-hand side. This opens a simple interface from which we can select the columns and measures of the dataset we wish to use from the Data side pane on the right-hand side.

Using the Build side pane, we can rearrange the order of the data used in the paginated report and enable or disable totals on numerical columns and measures by clicking the arrow next to the column or measure name and unchecking **Show totals**.

For a more advanced approach to creating paginated reports, we need to use a dedicated tool called **Power BI Report Builder**. Like Power BI Desktop, this is a separate download we must first install on our device. When we run Power BI Report Builder, we will be presented with a Getting Started window that allows us to run various wizards for creating paginated reports with different types of content, such as tables, maps and charts. For our example, we will close this window and create a paginated report based on a dataset we already have in Power BI Service.

To connect to existing data, we will right click the **Datasets** folder in the side pane on the left-hand side of the screen and click **Add Dataset...** We will give our dataset a name and then create a new data source by clicking the **New...** button. Another window will open where we will add a data source name and select Power BI Dataset from the connection type drop-down menu.

After we do this, we need to build the connection string, so we will click the **Build...** button. We will be prompted to sign into the service, after which we will be able to browse the workspace in Power BI Service for the dataset, we wish to base our paginated report on. When we have selected the correct dataset, we can click **Select**. We can use the **Test Connection** button to make sure everything is fine and then click **OK**.

Next, we will use the **Query Designer...** button to open a window where we will define the data from the dataset that we need. First, let us switch the Query Designer to text mode by clicking the **Design Mode** button, which is the second to last button on the ribbon, to turn **Design Mode** off. Now, instead of writing a DAX query by ourselves, we can use the Performance Analyzer of Power BI Desktop as a cheat sheet. We will open the **.pbix** file that the dataset in Power

BI Service was made from and create a simple table visual. In this example, we are using a dataset based on the **AdventureWorksDW2019** data that comes along with this book.

Let us drag **DimProduct[EnglishProductName]**, **DimDate[CalendarYear]** and a simple **Total sales** measure with the following formula to the table visual:

```
Total sales =
SUMX (
    FactInternetSales,
    FactInternetSales[OrderQuantity] * FactInternetSales[UnitPrice]
)
```

Make sure the **CalendarYear** column is not summarized. We may also wish to turn off Totals. Once we have created the visual, we can turn on the performance analyzer, start recording, refresh the visuals, expand the information regarding our table visual and click the **Copy query** link. We can now go back to Query Designer in Power BI Report Builder and paste the query we copied into the upper-left pane, as seen in *Figure 7.16*. When we are done, we can click **OK** to close the Query Designer and **OK** again to close the Dataset Properties window:

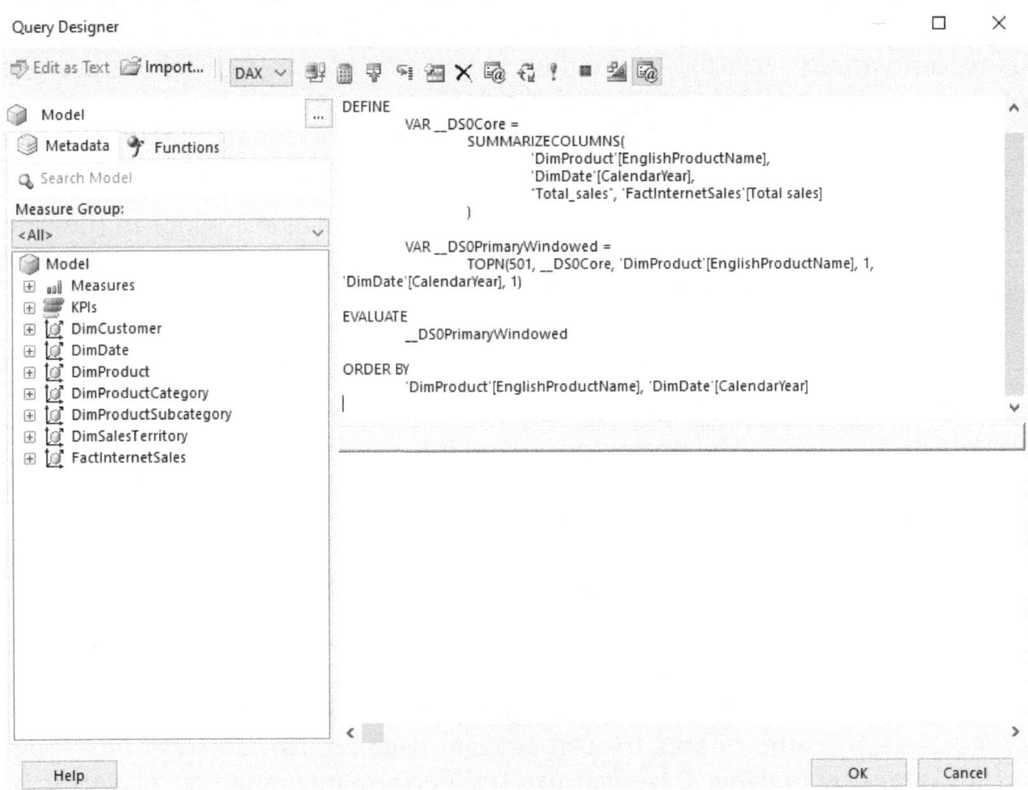

***Figure 7.16**: Entering a DAX query into Query Designer*

To create a paginated report that will contain a table with the imported data, we can click the **Insert** tab, click **Table** and use the **Insert Table** command to draw a table on the report. By default, the command draws three columns but if we need more, we can right-click the table and use the **Insert Column** command.

After we have the appropriate number of columns, we can drag the columns from the dataset in the left pane into the table in the order we wish to display them. For our example, we will insert them in the same order as in the table visual in Power BI Desktop – **EnglishProductName**, **CalendarYear** and **Total sales**. We can also use the text box at the top to enter a title for our paginated report, for example, ***Sales by product and year***. When we are done, we can go to the **Home** tab and click **Run** so that we will see the rendered report.

If we are satisfied with the results, we can click **File** and select **Publish**. This will open a window called **Publish to** – Power BI Service, where we can select the workspace, we wish to publish the report to and enter the name we wish to use for the report. When we are finished, we can click **Publish**.

The report will now be accessible in the Power BI Service, where it can be viewed, like in *Figure 7.17*. In the workspace we published it to, in the **Type** column, it will be defined as **Report**, but the icon will be different than standard Power BI Service reports:

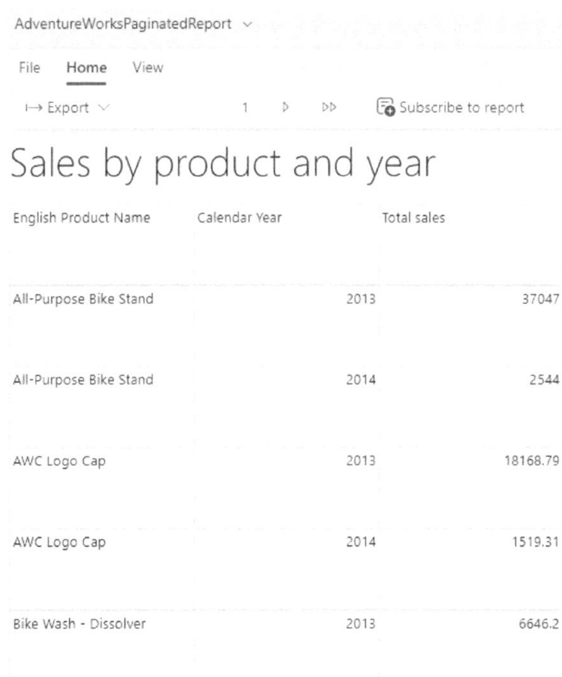

***Figure 7.17**: Paginated report published to Power BI Service*

On-prem reporting with Power BI Report Server

Certain industries and organizations may have concerns regarding publishing sensitive data into a public cloud. There may also be legislation in place that prohibits storing data outside the borders of a country. For these types of scenarios, an on-premises reporting solution called Power BI Report Server exists.

If we decide to use Power BI Report Server, we will of course be responsible for maintaining the report server itself and also any database servers that will hold the report server configuration databases. We will also be responsible for correctly configuring the server so users can securely browse the reports with as few interruptions as possible.

Like reports that we publish to Power BI Service, we also create reports that we wish to publish to the Power BI Report Server in Power BI Desktop. However, we need to use a special edition of Power BI Desktop that is purpose-built for the version of Power BI Report Server. The reason is that Power BI Report Server has a much longer update cycle than the Power BI Service. Compared to the Power BI Service, which is updated monthly, Power BI Report Server is updated three times per year. Therefore, functionalities that are available in the Power BI Service might only come to Power BI Report Server at a much later time or not at all. Power BI Desktop for Report Server must be in step with the functionalities available in Power BI Report Server.

If we have already implemented Power BI Report Server in our organization, we can download the appropriate edition of Power BI Desktop from the report server web portal by clicking the downward-facing arrow in the upper-right corner of the portal window and selecting Power BI Desktop. Alternatively, we can use a search engine to find the Microsoft page for downloading Power BI Desktop (Optimized for Power BI Report Server).

If we wish to create paginated reports for Power BI Report Server, we also need to download Report Builder. Again, we can use the report server web portal to download the appropriate edition (the downward-facing arrow in the upper-right corner of the web portal) or find Microsoft's download page. In the latter case, make sure you are not downloading Report Builder for the Power BI Service.

Like in Power BI Service, we also view reports hosted on Power BI Report Server in a web browser, but instead of the reports being hosted in the Microsoft cloud, they are hosted in our environment. When we open the report server web portal, an example of which is visible in *Figure 7.18*, we may notice that compared to the Power BI Service, it looks quite bare. Instead of the many colorful buttons and tiles, we are only presented with a simple window containing the tiles that represent the KPIs, reports, paginated reports, Excel workbooks and other items we have access to. We can also organize content into folders to make browsing content easier. Of course, clicking a tile, such as a report tile, will open the published report, just like we saw in the Power BI Service:

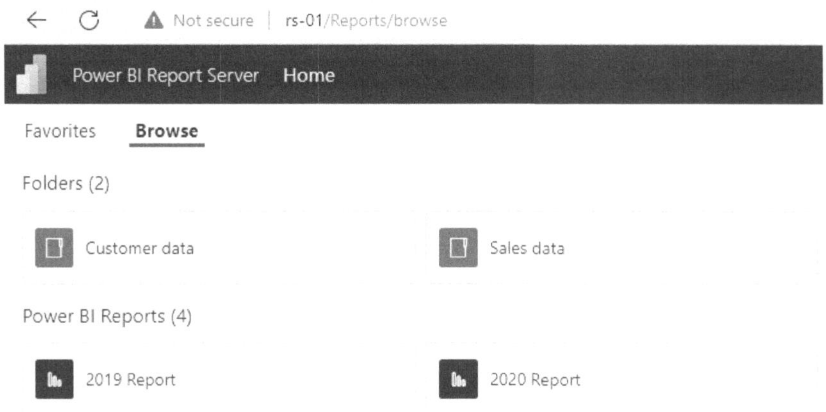

***Figure 7.18**: The Power BI Report Server web portal*

If we ever decide to migrate content to Power BI Service, we can click the **`Publish`** button on the Power BI Report Server ribbon, and either choose to upload all reports or only selected reports.

Conclusion

This chapter was an overview of the various components and functionalities of the Power BI Service. We described what workspaces are and made a brief overview of permissions, we saw how we can publish and manage reports, and how to create dashboards from existing reports. We also learned how we can package the content into apps and distribute them to different audiences. Then we made an introduction into creating paginated reports with Power BI Report Builder, and into dataflows and datamarts, two functionalities that allow to perform data transformations and data modelling without leaving the Power BI Service. We also saw that we are not limited to publishing our reports into the cloud, as there is a product called Power BI Report Server which allows us to keep our data and reports on-premises. In the next chapter, we will take a look at how to use Power BI as an advanced data science tool.

Key Terms

- **Power BI Service**: A software as a service offering from Microsoft used for creating, distributing, and viewing insights into data.
- **Workspace**: Workspaces serve as containers for other content in Power BI Service. They can also be used for defining general permissions on the content contained in the workspace.
- **Dataset**: Datasets are how Power BI Service presents the data we imported or connected to. Content such as reports and dashboards that we create sources its data from a dataset.
- **Report**: A report is composed of one or more pages that contain visuals which display data. Reports are most commonly created in Power BI Desktop, but they can also be created directly in Power BI Service.
- **Dashboard**: A dashboard is a single-page aggregation of the most important visualizations related to a specific topic. The visualizations can come from many different reports. Dashboards can only be created in Power BI Service.
- **App**: We can combine content, such as dashboards, reports and datasets, into an app. This makes it easy to distribute information about a subject in a single package. An app is created in a workspace but can have different permissions than the workspace.

Questions

1. What role does the Power BI Service fill in Microsoft's Power BI offering?
2. What are the basic components of Power BI Service?
3. What is the difference between a report and a dashboard?
4. What is an app?
5. What options do we have for creating Power BI Paginated Reports?

CHAPTER 8
Data Science in Power BI

Introduction

Besides report elements like tables, matrices and graphs, you can use Power BI as an advanced data science tool. This chapter introduces advanced analytics capabilities in the core Power BI and shows what you can do with the help of external languages, namely R and Python, or external services that include Azure Artificial Intelligence.

Structure

In this chapter, let us discuss the following topics:

- Analytics in base visualizations
- Advanced Power BI visuals
- Adding custom visualizations
- Using R and Python in Power BI
- Leveraging Azure AI
- Bypassing the R, Python and AI limitations

Analytics in base visualizations

In Power BI, even some very simple visualizations, like column and bar charts, include some basic statistical analysis. When setting up your visuals in a report, you can check the third, the **Analytics** tab, to see whether a visual includes some analytics. Remember, in the **Visualizations pane**, there are three tabs: the **Build visual** tab, where you can select the visualization and define the data used by the visual, the **Format visual** tab, where you can format the appearance of the visual, and the **Analytics** tab. For some visuals, for example, Pie and Donut chart, this tab is empty. *Figure* 8.1 shows this tab for a clustered column chart:

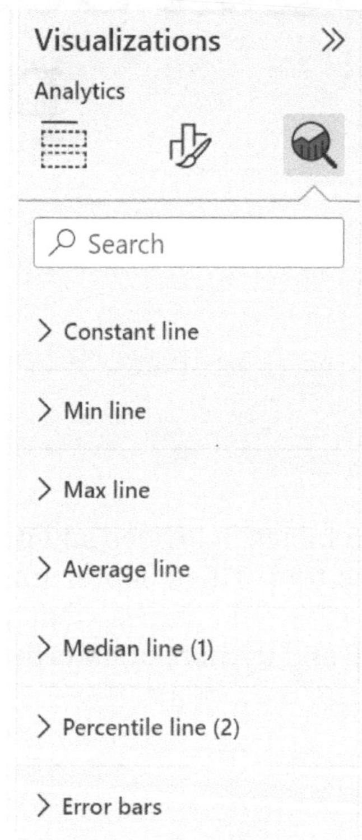

Figure 8.1: *The Analytics Tab for Clustered Column Chart*

From the picture, you can see that three lines are added – the Median line and two percentile lines. The result is shown in *Figure* 8.2:

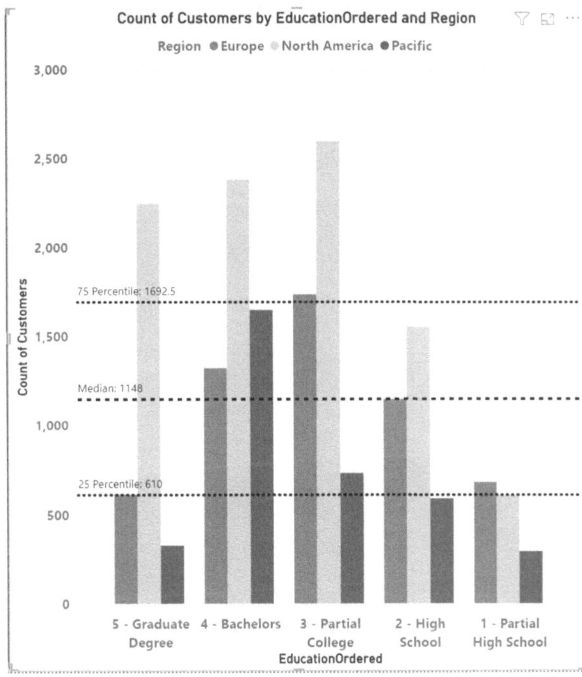

Figure 8.2: *Clustered Column Chart with the Three Lines from Analytics Tab*

The chart shows the distribution of the customers by education in three different regions. The data comes from the **AdventureWorksDW2019** demo database, the **dbo.vTargetMail** view. The percentile lines are showing the value (count of customers) on the 25th percent (610) and 75th percent (1,692.5) of the population, or on the first and the third quartile. The median is the middle value (1148), or the value on the second quartile. You can easily see which bars include quite a high number of customers, above the third quartile, and which bars include a low number of customers, below the first quartile. For example, the group of customers with partial college from North America is a big one, while the graduate degree group from the Pacific region is not that big.

Scatterplot and **Line chart** can include the Trend line, which is actually the Linear regression line. If the **Line chart** has time data on the X-axis, you can also make forecasts. You can select how many time points in the future you want to forecast, and whether you want to include the confidence interval. You can also define the seasonality period. In *Figure* 8.3, you can see a line chart with a regression line and forecast for six points in the future:

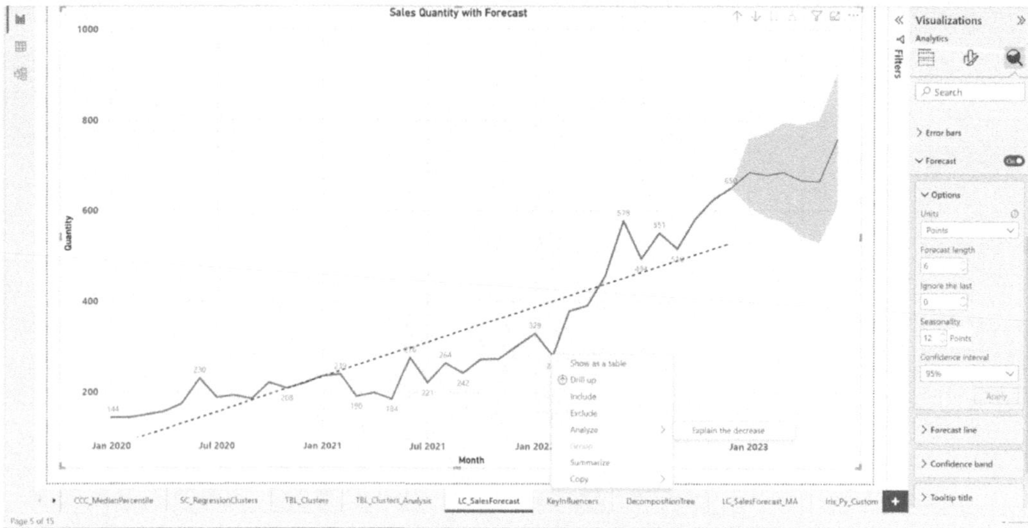

***Figure* 8.3**: *Line Chart with Trend and Forecast*

The data for this chart comes from the **dbo.vTimeSeries** view from the **AdventureWorksDW2019** demo database. The view aggregates the quantity, and the amount sold by months for three consecutive years from January 2020 to December 2022. Additional six time points are forecasted. You can see that we have defined the seasonality period to 12 points, or 12 months. If you are interested, the method used for forecasting is the Autoregressive integrated moving average or ARIMA method. The graph includes the Linear regression (or trend) line. You can also see a pop-up menu. In the line, you can see that the value for February 2022 is quite a lot smaller than the value for the previous month. If you right-click the line at that point, you get a pop-up menu with the Analyze option, which leads you to the **Explain the decrease** option. Many visualizations have the possibility to analyze a data point by using other data in your dataset. There is quite a lot of intelligence built into these explanations. You should check these explanations in different visualizations to find additional insights.

The Scatterplot visual has even more intelligence built in. You can find groups of data points based on the similarity of the values in the columns. This is the so-called clustering analysis. In a Scatterplot, clustering is based on two input variables, used in the X and Y axes. However, in the Table visualization, you can define clusters based on up to 15 input variables. You can get the clustering option by clicking the More options button, represented by the three small dots in the upper right corner of the visualization. *Figure* 8.4 shows a Scatterplot visual with a trend line and data points grouped in three clusters:

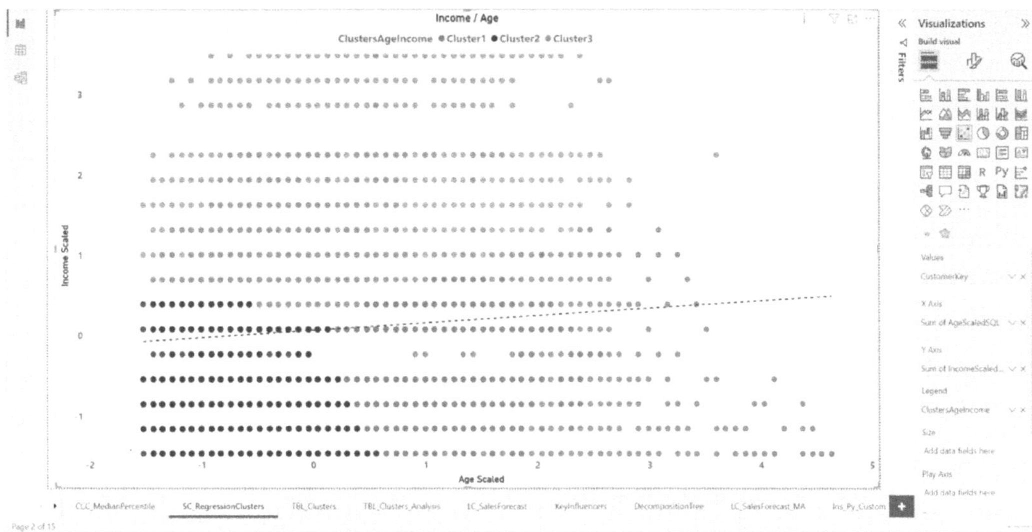

***Figure 8.4**: Scatterplot with Trend and Clusters*

Clustering is useful to find specific groups of cases, for example, groups of customers. In the scatterplot, which is based on the **Age** and **Income** continuous numerical columns from the **dbo.vTargetMail** view, you can notice three groups of customers: those with high income (**Cluster3**, represented by the orange color), young with low income (**Cluster2**, dark blue), and older with low income (**Cluster1**, light blue). The question is which is the proper number of clusters? You can leave the Power BI to determine the number automatically. However, the number selected automatically is typically quite high. The correct number is the one where you can easily interpret the clusters. You interpret them with the values of the variables in the clusters. With three clusters, it was quite simple to interpret the three groups of customers in the scatterplot. If you cannot interpret the clusters, the clusters are useless.

The algorithm used for clustering is the K-Means algorithm. Clustering creates a new calculated column. For the scatterplot from the previous figure, the name of the column is **ClustersAgeIncome**. You can click the **More options** button (three dots) near the column in the **Data pane** to access the Edit clusters in a pop-up menu and change the number of the clusters. We decided to spit the cases into three clusters again.

Figure 8.5 shows a few rows of the Table visualization with three clusters calculated based on seven input variables:

CustomerKey	BikeBuyer	RegionNumeric	EducationNumeric	CommDistNumeric	NumberCarsOwned	TotalChildren	AgeDiscretized	ClustersTable	Col...
11009	1	3	4	4	1	0	2	Cluster2	Yellow
11010	1	3	4	4	1	0	2	Cluster2	Yellow
11011	1	3	4	5	4	4	2	Cluster2	Yellow
11012	0	2	4	2	2	2	1	Cluster3	Pink
11013	0	2	4	1	3	2	1	Cluster3	Pink
11014	0	2	4	2	3	3	2	Cluster1	Lime
11015	1	2	3	4	1	0	1	Cluster2	Yellow

Figure 8.5: *Table with Clusters*

Because the cluster membership is marked in a calculated column, it is easy to analyze the clusters with other Power BI visualizations. *Figure* 8.6 shows a small analysis of the three clusters calculated in the Table visual:

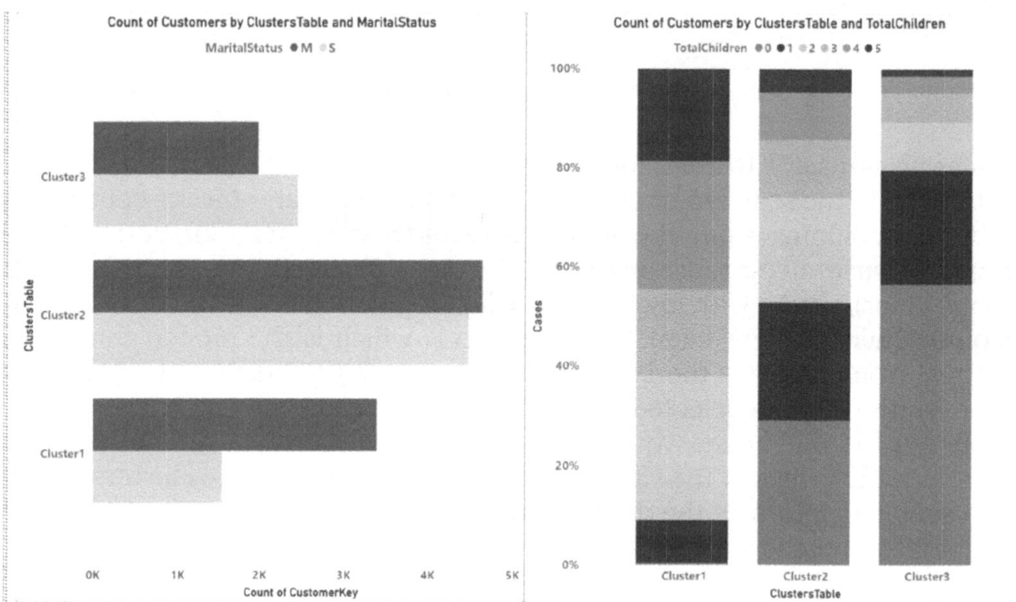

Figure 8.6: *Analyzing Table*

You can see that in **`Cluster1`**, we have many married customers, while there are more single customers in **`Cluster3`**. In addition, customers in **`Cluster3`** tend to have a small number of children. You can continue with the analysis until you completely understand the groups of customers you found.

Advanced Power BI visuals

Bar, column, line, pie, donut charts, and scatter plots are very common and without analytics are also quite basic visualizations. Power BI includes out-of-the-box advanced visualizations that allow us to observe associations between multiple variables or even use some advanced data science algorithm to analyze the data.

The first visualization we are introducing is the Treemap. *Figure* 8.7 shows an example of the Treemap. We are using the data from the **`dbo.vTargetMail`** view to analyze the **`BikeBuyer`** variable and explain it with two independent variables, namely **`Region`** and **`MaritalStatus`**. The **`BikeBuyer`** variable is a dichotomous one, or a flag, stored as an integer with values 0, denoting non-buyers, and 1, denoting buyers. If we calculate the average of this variable, we get the proportion of bike buyers. From the Treemap we can see that in the group of single persons from the Pacific region, we have 69% of bike buyers, while in the group of married people from North America, we only have 42% of buyers. The size of the rectangles for a specific region and marital status is aligned with the percentage of bike buyers in that specific group. We could add more independent variables, but the visualization would become cluttered and hard to read:

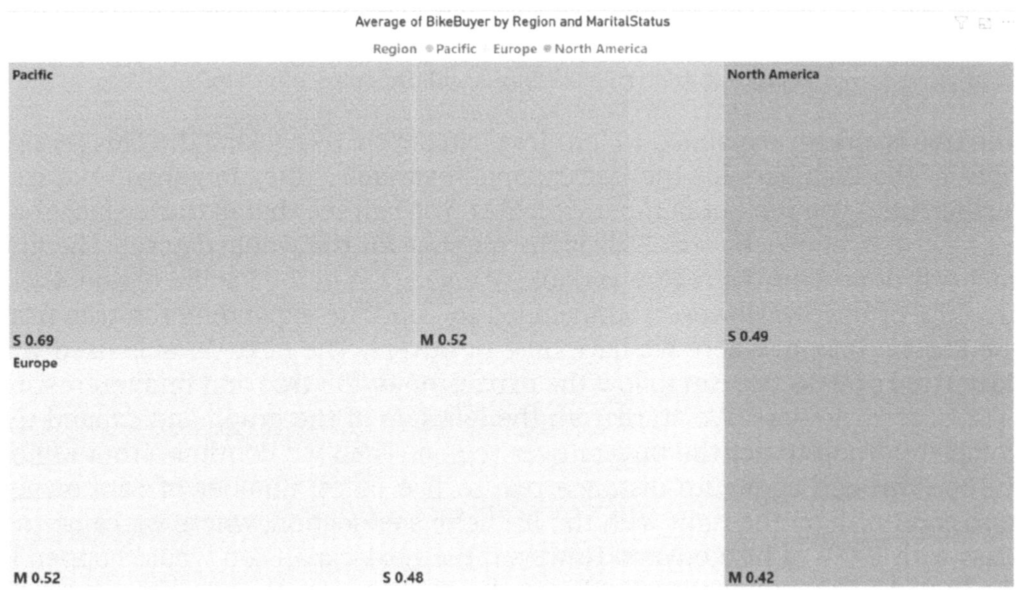

Figure 8.7: *Treemap with Three Variables*

Even better than Treemap is the Decomposition tree visualization. You can interactively analyze one target discrete variable using multiple input discrete variables. *Figure* 8.8 shows an example of the Decomposition tree, together with the fields chooser pane. Again, we are analyzing the **`BikeBuyer`** variable using five independent variables:

Figure 8.8: *Analyzing BikeBuyer with Decomposition Tree*

The tree is already expanded to four levels in depth. By clicking the plus (+) sign right of the data bars for the last expanded variable, you can expand the tree further, until you run out of input variables. You can see that in the leftmost bar, we have 49% of bike buyers. This is the number for the whole dataset. The first split was done over the region variable. We see that in the Pacific region, there are 60% of buyers. However, we decided to continue expanding the tree from the Europe region, where we have 50% of buyers. The next variable used was **`CommuteDistance`**. We can follow the expansion of the tree and find interesting classes of customers. We start from the left side of the graph and expand the complete group to get the buyers over region. Then we continue from region Europe through commute distance two to five miles, number of cars owned zero and finish on the right with the Bachelor's education, where we came to a class with 100% of bike buyers. However, the next expansion would happen at the Partial College education level, in order to find potentially useful subgroups in the group, we have only 42% of buyers. You can see that the expansion can be done on the high value of the target variable, which is one in this case, low value, which denotes non-buyers, or the last input variable left, in this case, Occupation. High value of the target variable means expanding to find classes with more bike buyers.

Probably the most advanced visualization available in core Power BI is the Key influencers visualization. Again, you can use it to explain the values of a single target variable with few input variables. However, you do not develop the visualization interactively as we did with the Decomposition tree. The

Key influencers visually perform the analysis automatically, using the Logistic regression algorithm. In *Figure* 8.9, you can see an example of the Key influencers visual. For this visualization, we used four independent variables: **`CommuteDistance`**, **`Education`**, **`Occupation`** and **`Region`**, and analyzed the three clusters we calculated with the Table visual:

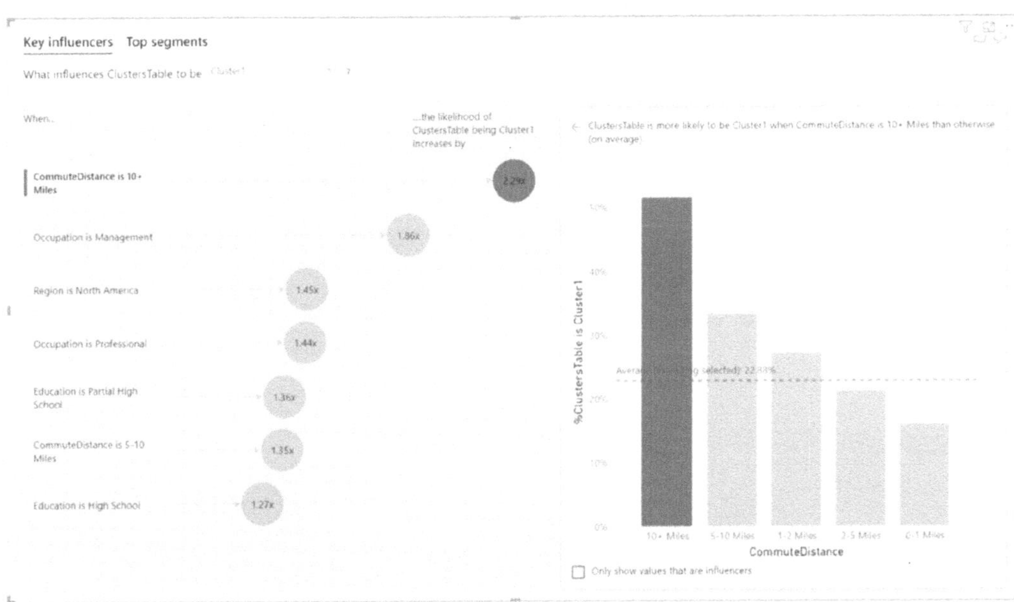

Figure 8.9: *Analyzing Table Cluster with Key Influencers*

You can see that the most important variable for **`Cluster1`** is the **`CommuteDistance`** with a value of 10+ Miles. If you include a few more input variables, you can now identify customers in **`Cluster1`**. These are managers and professionals who commute quite long distances, mostly from North America. You could change the cluster analyzed in the drop-down list in the top left corner of the visual. With the **`Top segments`** tab, you can get even more details about the customers in specific clusters.

Adding custom visualizations

Even with all the great visualizations that come out of the box with Power BI, there is always a need for more. In Power BI desktop, it is really simple to add a custom visualization. In the **`Visualizations`** tab, you can click the last option after the default visuals, marked with three dots. A pop-up menu shows, as you can see in *Figure 8.10*:

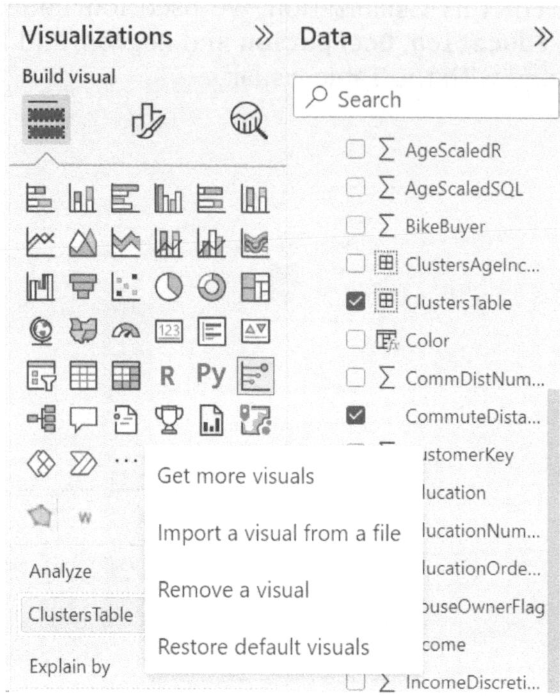

Figure 8.10: *Adding a Custom Visual*

You can use the **`Get more visuals`** option to automatically connect to the Power BI visuals marketplace, or you can import a visual from a previously downloaded file. You can also remove a custom visual, or remove all of them and restore the default visuals only.

In the Power BI visuals site, you can list all available custom visuals, select subgroups of visuals and list a subgroup only, or search for a specific visual. When you select a visual you want to download, you get to the main page for that visual, which is shown in *Figure 8.11*:

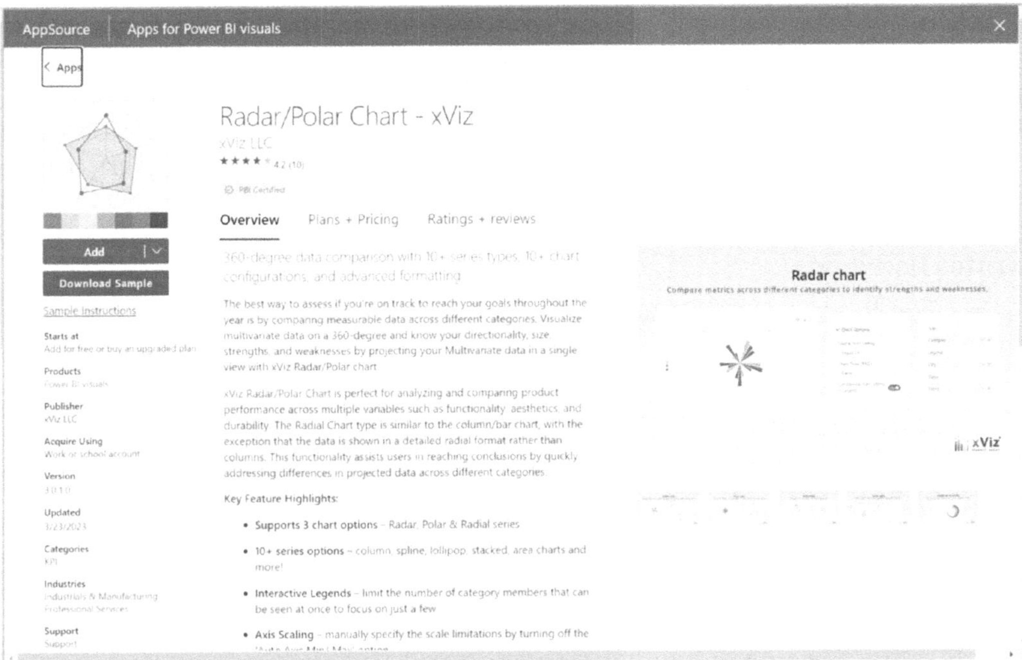

Figure 8.11: *The main Page for the Radar/Polar Chart Visual*

Here you can check whether the visual is free or payable. In our example, the basic version of the visual is free, but you can also buy an upgraded plan, as you can see on the left side of the page, where you can also see other basic information about the visual. In the main part of the page, right below the name of the visual, the producer of the visual, and the ratings, you can see whether the visual is Power BI certified. It is advisable to use certified visuals only. You should also read the overview of the visual and check the plans and pricing along with, ratings and reviews. By clicking the Add button on the left side, you add the visual to your Power BI Desktop file. Later in this chapter, we will use the free version of this Radar/Polar Chart visual by xViz and the Word Cloud visual from Microsoft Corporation, which is free as well.

Using R and Python in Power BI

The real data science power comes to Power BI with the support for R and Python languages. Both languages are very popular and both have really strong support for data science. Of course, you can use both languages without Power BI. However, besides Power BI, you can also run R and Python code inside SQL Server, by using SQL Server Machine Learning Services. In order to follow the examples in this chapter, you should have SQL Server Machine Learning Services, R and Python installed. To install all of these, please follow the *Install*

SQL Server 2022 Machine Learning Services (Python and R) on Windows article on MS Learn (**https://learn.microsoft.com/en-us/sql/machine-learning/install/sql-machine-learning-services-windows-install-sql-2022?view=sql-server-ver16**). For the demos in this chapter, you should also install the following packages (or libraries) in the same way as it is described in the MS Learn article for the RevoScaleR and revoscalepy packages (please note that both languages are case sensitive, so you have to type the package names exactly as they are written here):

- For R, we are going to use the RODBC, reshape2, dplyr and rpart.plot libraries.
- For Python, you need the numpy, pandas, matplotlib, seaborn and sk-learn libraries.

Finally, for code development in R, we used RStudio Desktop free version by Posit (**https://posit.co/download/rstudio-desktop/**), and for Python development, we used Visual Studio Code (**https://code.visualstudio.com/**). If you have issues with Python in VS code, please check this short video at **https://www.youtube.com/watch?v=zk5qOQBvuK4**.

In order to use R and Python with Power BI, you have to make a short setup. In Power BI Desktop, use the **`File`** menu, go to **`Options and Settings`**, and select **`Options`**. Then in the **`Global options`** pane, select R scripting or Python scripting option, as you can see in *Figure* 8.12 for R:

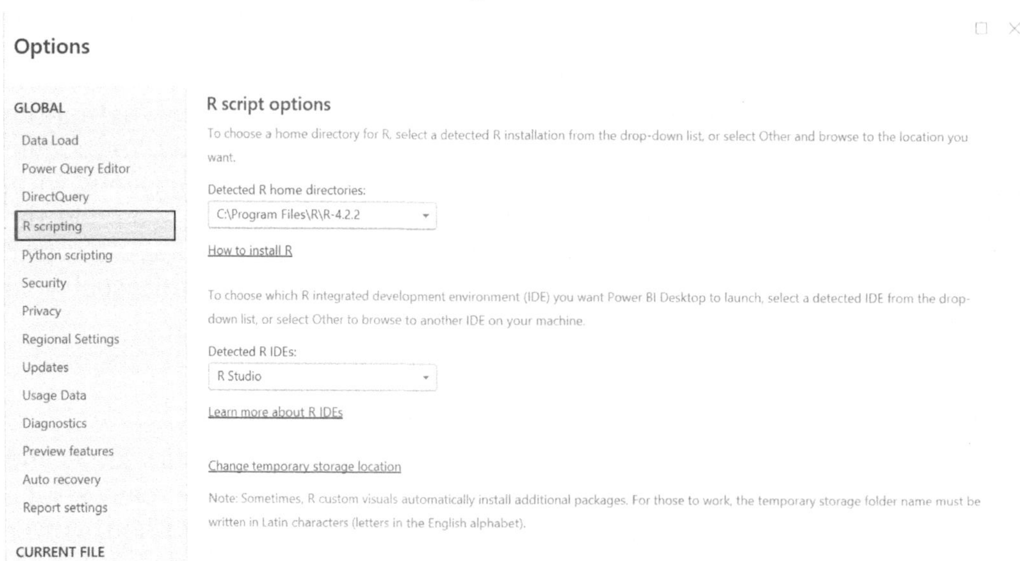

***Figure 8.12:** Setting up R in Power BI Desktop*

Note that besides the path to the R home folder, we have also set up the integrated development environment (IDE), for R namely RStudio. You can use this IDE when you edit the code for the R visual. Of course, there is a similar setting for the Python visual.

After the setup is done, you can start using both languages. You can use them to make a new source of data, inside Power Query for advanced transformations, or in visuals to leverage the great graphical capabilities of both languages. We are starting by using R as a data source.

Power BI works with tables similar to relational tables in the SQL Server. Although physical storage is columnar, logically we are using tables. Since a table represents a set, the order of rows and the order of columns is not important or is undetermined, as it stems from the set theory. Therefore, if you want to read a piece of data, you need to find it in a cell by using the key to find the row and the unique column name in the table to find the appropriate column.

R is a very statistics and data science focused language. Statistical algorithms initially analyzed data stored in two-dimensional matrices. In matrices, data is ordered, and you can refer to a value by position, for example, read the value from row 10, column 4. Matrices are limited to values of a single data type. On the top of matrices, R has built the data frame object. In a data frame, every column can have a different data type and must be given a unique name. You can also define a key to identify the rows. Although a data frame looks like a table, it is an object between a matrix and a table. From the matrix part it still preserves the physical order. You can still refer to values by their position.

In R, we get the data frame object in the core engine. Python does not include matrix operations in the core engine. You need to install the NumPy to get the matrix operations. On top of NumPy, the pandas package brings the data frame object. When you use R or Python as the source, your code must return at least one data frame. This data frame is then automatically converted inside Power BI to a Power BI table.

In R, probably the most popular demo dataset is the iris dataset. It has five columns, one character with three different species of flowers, and four numeric ones for sepal length, sepal width, petal length and petal width. Here is a small snippet of R code that shows the iris data and then unpivots it. The unpivoted version will be used as the source for Power Query:

```
# R as a data source
# Use the iris dataset
View(iris)

# Unpivot (melt) the data
```

```
# install.packages("reshape2")
library(reshape2)
mi  <- melt(iris, id.vars = "Species")
# irisMeltR is the data source
```

Figure 8.13 shows a few rows of this dataset:

Ch08_RCode.R × iris ×

Filter

	Sepal.Length	Sepal.Width	Petal.Length	Petal.Width	Species
1	5.1	3.5	1.4	0.2	setosa
2	4.9	3.0	1.4	0.2	setosa
3	4.7	3.2	1.3	0.2	setosa
4	4.6	3.1	1.5	0.2	setosa
5	5.0	3.6	1.4	0.2	setosa
6	5.4	3.9	1.7	0.4	setosa
7	4.6	3.4	1.4	0.3	setosa
8	5.0	3.4	1.5	0.2	setosa
9	4.4	2.9	1.4	0.2	setosa
10	4.9	3.1	1.5	0.1	setosa
11	5.4	3.7	1.5	0.2	setosa
12	4.8	3.4	1.6	0.2	setosa
13	4.8	3.0	1.4	0.1	setosa

Figure 8.13: *The Iris Dataset*

We are going to use this dataset in Power BI. In Power BI Desktop, we can select the **`Get Data`** symbol. In the interface window under **`Other category`**, we can select the R script and press the **`Connect`** button. We can copy the R code from RStudio, just without the View command, so the code should look like this:

```
# R as a data source
# Unpivot (melt) the data
library(reshape2)
irisMeltR <- melt(iris, id.vars = "Species")
# irisMeltR is the data source
```

After selecting the **`OK`** button in the interface window, we can select the irisMeltR dataset in a similar way as an Excel sheet. After **`irisMeltR`** dataset is selected, we can click the **`Transform Data`** button to enter Power Query Editor. We will add an index to the data by going to the **`Add Column`** tab, selecting the arrow next to the **Index Column** option and selecting the **From 1** option. Next, we can rename the variable column to **Measure** and the value column to **Value**. We can do this by double-clicking the column names. Also, by double-clicking, we can give the query a meaningful name, such as **IrisUnpivoted**. The query should look like *Figure* 8.14 here:

Figure 8.14: *The Iris Dataset in Power Query*

You can close the Power Query window and apply the changes. You have just imported your first dataset from R to Power BI. Now let us use this data with the help of the Python language.

In Power BI Desktop, create a new page for a new report. Add the Python visual and enable the script visuals. You can start editing the script. From the imported **IrisUnpivoted** dataset, select all columns. In *Figure* 8.15, you can see the Python script editor from the Python visual:

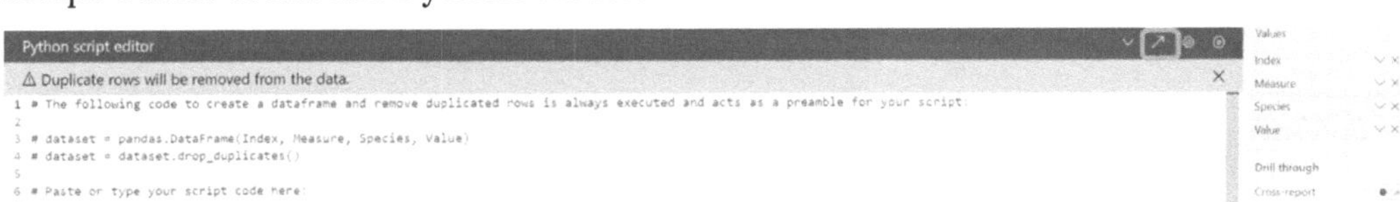

Figure 8.15: *The Python Script Editor of the Python Visual*

In the script editor, you can see that a data frame with a name dataset was created. Also, duplicate rows were removed. The two commented outlines of code show you what the visual has done:

```
# dataset = pandas.DataFrame(Index, Measure, Species, Value)
# dataset = dataset.drop_duplicates()
```

We used the data from Power BI, which is in tabular format. The visual automaticity created a data frame from the table. Looks a bit convoluted, right? We created a data frame in R, converted it to a table with Power Query, and then converted it back to a data frame in Python. Note the second line of the code. R and Python visuals automatically select distinct rows only. This is why we added an index in Power Query, we want to use all the rows in the visual.

In *Figure* 8.15, you can also note the arrow in the top right corner. The arrow opens the IDE selected when we set up R and Python scripting. Other buttons in this area are for minimizing and maximizing the script editor, a shortcut to the settings, and the Run button you use to run the code.

When you click the arrow, the selected IDE, in our case Visual Studio Code, opens with some auto-generated code. You can insert your code after the comment "# Paste or type your script code here:" and before the comment "# Epilog - Auto Generated #". The following code creates a Python graph called swarmplot from the seaborn library.

```
# Paste or type your script code here:


# The swarmplot
# Imports
import matplotlib as mpl
import matplotlib.pyplot as plt
import seaborn as sns
# Set the style
sns.set(style="whitegrid", palette="muted")
# Plot
sns.swarmplot(x="Value", y="Measure", hue="Species",
              data=dataset)
plt.show()

# Epilog - Auto Generated #
```

The swarmplot graph is very useful for showing the distribution of numerical variables in classes of categorical variables. After you create and test the code in the Visual Studio Code, you can copy it to the script editor of the Python visual and run it.

Before showing the results and the graphical presentation of the iris data, we are adding another visual to the same page. We are going to present the same iris data with the xViz Radar Chart visual. For this visual, we use the Measure column from the IrisUnpivoted dataset for the Axis, the Species column for the Legend, and the Average of Value for the Value settings. You can see the results in *Figure* 8.16.

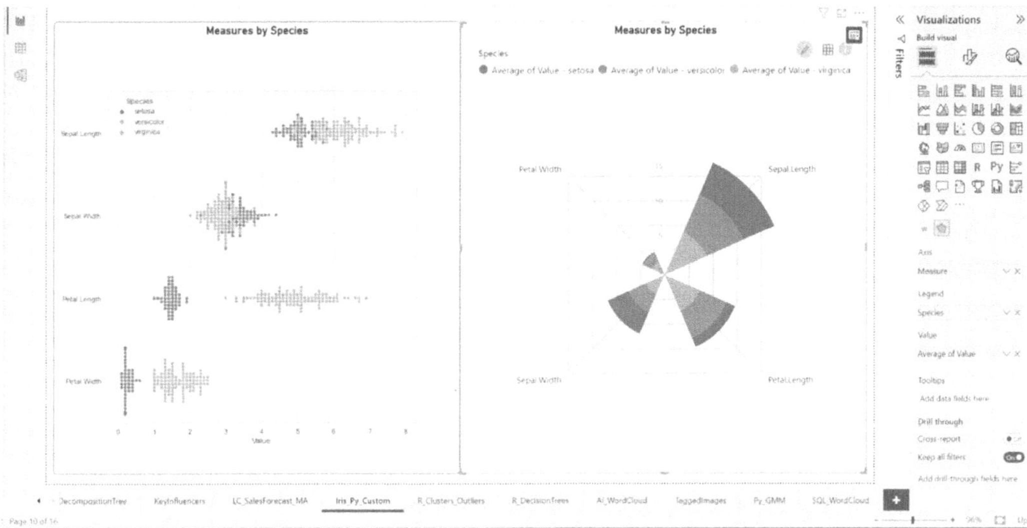

Figure 8.16: *The Python Visual and the Radar Chart*

When you run the Python script, you might notice in the top left corner of the Python visual dots moving in a small circle. They are moving until the script is finished. The processing of the data could take quite a long time. Because of that, R and Python visuals have some limitations, including the following most important two:

- Data is limited to 150,000 rows; if you try to process more rows, only the first 150,000 are used, and a warning is displayed.
- Processing time is limited to five minutes; if the processing exceeds five minutes, a time-out error occurs.

There are more limitations to deploying the Power BI reports with R and Python code. In order to refresh the reports, the portal where you are deploying them must have access to an R and/or Python engine. Power BI Report Server currently does not support R and Python code. Power BI Service allows usage of R and Python code but with some additional limitations. The R and Python engines do not belong to you, they are maintained by Microsoft. Microsoft verifies every single library before it is allowed in the service. You can find the list of supported libraries and other limitations on Microsoft Learn pages:

- For R, use the **Create visuals by using R packages in the Power BI service** page (**https://learn.microsoft.com/en-us/power-bi/connect-data/service-r-packages-support**)
- For Python, use the **Learn which Python packages are supported in Power BI** page (**https://learn.microsoft.com/en-us/power-bi/connect-data/service-python-packages-support**)

The problem with the limitations can arise with some more advanced algorithms, which might use many iterations for processing the data and scanning the data many times. For example, the K-Means clustering algorithm is computationally very intensive. But if we run it from R or Python, we can get additional possibilities. For example, we can find the coordinates of the centers of the clusters, and find the outliers. We define outliers as the points that are the farthest from the center or their cluster. Since they are far away from their own center and even farther away from other centers, they do not fit well in any of the clusters and are thus somehow different from other cases. You can inspect the outliers graphically or by using the values of their input variables.

Finding outliers is a very important data science task. Finding outliers for a single variable is quite simple, for example, for a discrete one, you check the states with very low probability, while for a continuous one, you check the cases that are far away from the mean value. Finding outliers defined by the values of multiple variables is much more complex. Every single piece of data might look correct; however, multiple pieces combined could be very suspicious. For example, imagine that you have a person with a PhD, has five children, but is 21 years old. Every single piece of this data looks logical, but all three together make a very unlikely combination.

Before proceeding with R, here is the source T-SQL query that retrieves the data from the **dbo.vTargetMail** view and adds few derived variables, including properly ordered education, discretized age and income, education, commute distance, region, and marital status expressed with integers, and age and income scaled using Z-score normalization with mean at zero and standard deviation at one:

```
SELECT CustomerKey,
 Age, YearlyIncome AS Income,
 BikeBuyer, MaritalStatus,
 TotalChildren, NumberChildrenAtHome,
 CASE EnglishEducation
  WHEN N'Partial High School' THEN N'1 - Partial High School'
  WHEN N'High School' THEN N'2 - High School'
  WHEN N'Partial College' THEN N'3 - Partial College'
  WHEN N'Bachelors' THEN N'4 - Bachelors'
  WHEN N'Graduate Degree' THEN N'5 - Graduate Degree'
  ELSE N'0 - Unknown'        -- Handling possible NULLs
 END AS EducationOrdered,
 EnglishEducation AS Education,
 EnglishOccupation AS Occupation,
 HouseOwnerFlag, NumberCarsOwned,
```

```
 CommuteDistance, Region,
 NTILE(3) OVER(ORDER BY Age) AS AgeDiscretized,
 NTILE(3) OVER(ORDER BY YearlyIncome) AS IncomeDiscretized,
 CASE EnglishEducation
  WHEN N'Partial High School' THEN 1
  WHEN N'High School' THEN 2
  WHEN N'Partial College' THEN 3
  WHEN N'Bachelors' THEN 4
  WHEN N'Graduate Degree' THEN 5
  ELSE 0         -- Handling possible NULLs
 END AS EducationNumeric,
 CASE CommuteDistance
  WHEN N'0-1 Miles' THEN 1
  WHEN N'1-2 Miles' THEN 2
  WHEN N'2-5 Miles' THEN 3
  WHEN N'5-10 Miles' THEN 4
  WHEN N'10+ Miles' THEN 5
 END AS CommDistNumeric,
 CASE Region
  WHEN N'Europe' THEN 1
  WHEN N'North America' THEN 2
  WHEN N'Pacific' THEN 3
 END AS RegionNumeric,
 CASE MaritalStatus
  WHEN N'S' THEN 0
  WHEN N'M' THEN 1
 END AS MarStaNumeric,
 ROUND(
 (1.0*Age - AVG(1.0*Age) OVER()) /
  STDEV(1.0*Age) OVER(), 2) AS AgeScaledSQL,
 ROUND(
 (1.0*YearlyIncome - AVG(1.0*YearlyIncome) OVER()) /
  STDEV(1.0*YearlyIncome) OVER(), 2) AS IncomeScaledSQL
FROM dbo.vTargetMail;
```

We are going to use the following code in R to find three clusters in the data from the T-SQL query, add the centers, and find the first five outliers:

```
# Select some numerical columns only
TM1 <- dataset[, c("NumberCarsOwned", "NumberChildrenAtHome",
               "BikeBuyer", "EducationNumeric",
               "AgeScaledSQL", "IncomeScaledSQL")]
# 20% sample
library(dplyr)
TM1 <- sample_frac(TM1, 0.2)

# Create the clustering model
cl3 <- kmeans(TM1, centers=3)

# Create a data frame with centers' coordinates for all cases
dfcenters <- cl3$centers[cl3$cluster, ]

# Difference between original data and centers for each case
TM1 - dfcenters
# Row sums of differences
rowSums(TM1 - dfcenters)
# Distances
distances <- sqrt(rowSums((TM1 - dfcenters)^2))

# Find top 5 outliers
outliers <- order(distances, decreasing=T)[1:5]

# Plot data and centers and outliers
# Add the scaled variables Age and Income
plot(TM1[,c("IncomeScaledSQL", "AgeScaledSQL")], pch=19,
col=cl3$cluster, cex=1)
points(cl3$centers[,c("IncomeScaledSQL", "AgeScaledSQL")], col=1:3,
pch=15, cex=3)
points(TM1[outliers, c("IncomeScaledSQL", "AgeScaledSQL")], pch="+",
col=4, cex=4)
```

Note that we used the **sample_frac()** function from the dplyr package to randomly select 20% of the rows only. Even with 18,484 cases, the processing could already take over five minutes, and we would get a time-out error. *Figure 8.17* shows the result of this R code:

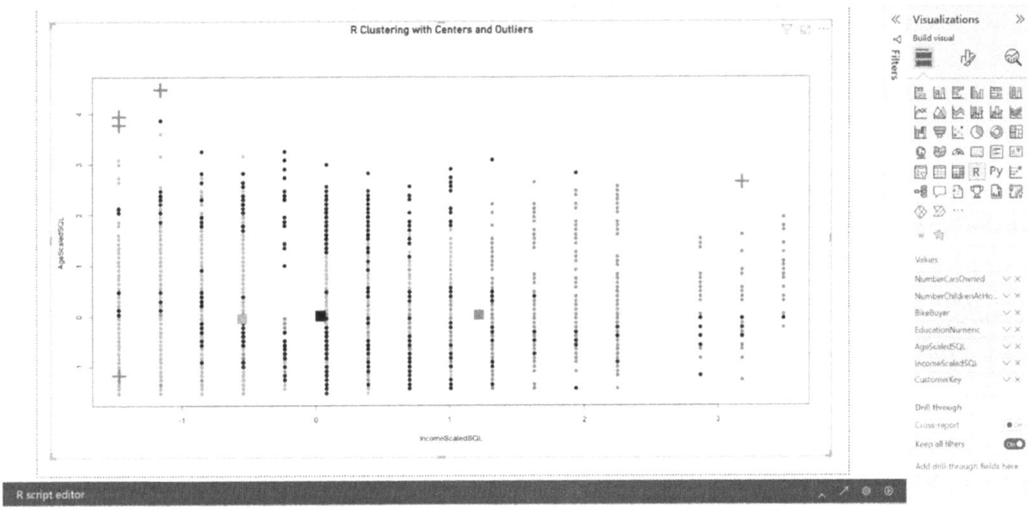

Figure 8.17: *R K-Means with Centers and Outliers*

The three centers of the clusters are marked with a square in the same color as the cluster points, and the five outliers are marked with the plus sign. The plot is limited to two input variables, in this case, Age and Income, although seven input variables were used to train the model. You can check the outliers in additional graphs by using other input variables for the axes.

Inside Power query, you can use the R and Python script transformations. You can get them through the last two icons in the Transform ribbon, the Run R script and Run Python script icons. *Figure* 8.18 shows the R script transformation used in the TM dataset:

Figure 8.18: *R Script Transformation in Power Query*

This R code creates a scaled version of the Age and Income variables. Scaled means that the mean value is subtracted from every value and then the result is divided by the standard deviation of the variable. After the scaling, the new variables have a mean at zero and a standard deviation at one. This way, the values of the variables that initially had different scales are easier to compare. For example, Age is measured in years and income in units of ten thousand dollars. We did the scaling in three ways. The first one was done in the source query with T-SQL:

```
ROUND(
 (1.0*Age - AVG(1.0*Age) OVER()) /
  STDEV(1.0*Age) OVER(), 2) AS AgeScaledSQL,
 ROUND(
 (1.0*YearlyIncome - AVG(1.0*YearlyIncome) OVER()) /
  STDEV(1.0*YearlyIncome) OVER(), 2) AS IncomeScaledSQL
```

The next one was done with a Python transformation:

```
# 'dataset' holds the input data for this script
from scipy.stats import zscore
import numpy as np
import pandas as pd
# Calculate the zscores and drop zscores into new column
dataset['AgeScaledPy'] = zscore(dataset['Age'])
dataset['IncomeScaledPy'] = zscore(dataset['Income'])
```

And finally, we also have the Python code for the same task:

```
# 'dataset' holds the input data for this script
dataset$AgeScaledR <- scale(dataset$Age)
dataset$IncomeSCaledR <- scale(dataset$Income)
output <- dataset
```

Which solution would you use? For now, use the one in the language that is the closest to you. In the next chapter, we are going to discuss different solutions from the performance perspective.

Before finishing this section, let us remember the decomposition tree advanced visual. We were searching for the factors that influence the decision whether to buy a bike or not. We developed the tree manually; we expanded it step by step. A very popular data science algorithm is the Decision Trees algorithm. A decision tree expands the branches automatically and thus helps us easily spot interesting groups. We are going to use the R visual again, using the **dbo.vTargetMail** data, this time with the following R script:

```
library(rpart)
TMRP <- rpart(BikeBuyer ~
                MaritalStatus + TotalChildren +
                NumberChildrenAtHome +
                Education + Occupation +
                HouseOwnerFlag + NumberCarsOwned +
                CommuteDistance + Region +
                AgeDiscretized + IncomeDiscretized,
              data = dataset, cp = 0.007)

# Plot the tree
library(rpart.plot)
rpart.plot(TMRP,
           box.palette = c("tomato", "plum1", "yellow", "greenyellow",
"green"),
           type = 4, branch = 0.4, tweak = 1.5)
```

Figure 8.19 shows the result of the script, the fully developed tree:

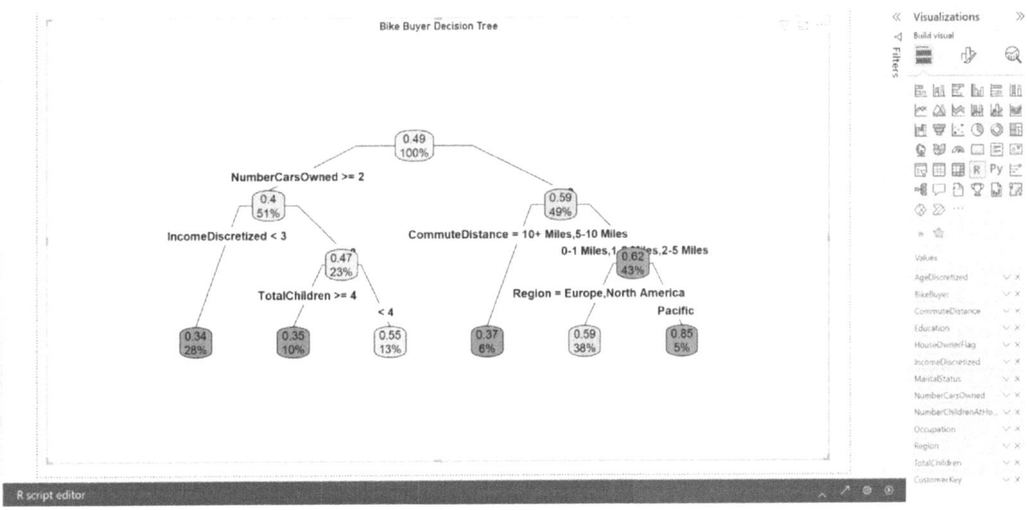

Figure 8.19: *A decision tree*

In this decision tree, you can easily find the path to bike buyers and the path to non-buyers as well.

Leveraging Azure AI

From Power Query Editor, you can use Artificial Intelligence (AI) to get more advanced insights into your data. You have access to AI and Azure Machine Learning (ML) models through three options in the Home and Add Column ribbons in Power Query, as *Figure* 8.20 shows:

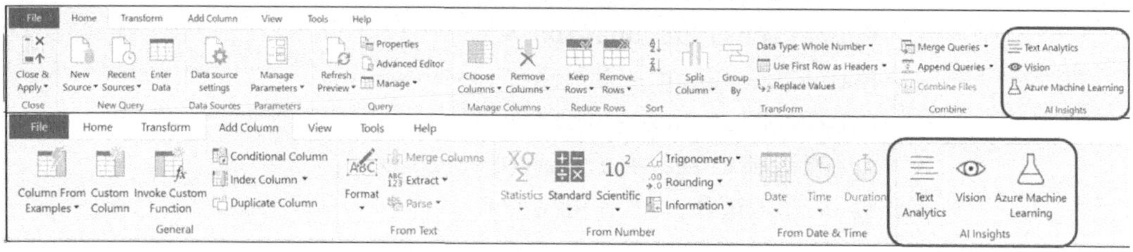

Figure 8.20: *Access to AI Insights*

Azure ML is a cloud service that helps you build machine learning models. It has a graphical builder with some predefined machine learning tasks and algorithms that help you create a model. There is also an option to use Automated ML or Auto ML. Auto ML can quickly build multiple models for a single task. For example, it can build multiple predictive models using different ML algorithms with different parameters on the same data, evaluate the models to select the best one and deploy the selected best model. Then you can use this model for predictions.

Using Azure ML looks quite tempting. However, there are a few drawbacks. For any more advanced machine learning problems, you run out of simple options, and you have to use Python to build, deploy and use the model. However, Azure ML is not for free, or at least is not going to be free anymore soon, based on the time of writing this book. The free Azure ML Studio is being discontinued. Although at the time of writing this book (May 2023) the ML Studio (Classic) still works, you immediately get a big warning: *Machine Learning Studio (classic) will retire on 31 August 2024 - transition to Azure Machine Learning*. But the new Azure ML is not free anymore. Therefore, since we already can use Python (and R) in Power BI for free, Azure ML is not that tempting anymore. We are not going to use it in this book; nevertheless, you, the reader, are welcome to test it.

Using text Analytics and Vision AI insights is also not cheap. You need a Power BI Premium license for it. For single user usage, the price is still quite low, so you might want to pay it for a month in order to check it. At the time of writing this book, the price for Power BI Premium for a single user is $20 per month. You might want to check the current price on the Power BI pricing Web page (**https://powerbi.microsoft.com/en-us/pricing/**).

For testing the Text Analytics, we are using the following query to extract the product information, including the description, from the **AdventureWorksDW2019** demo database:

```
SELECT TOP 10 p.ProductKey,
 p.EnglishProductName AS ProductName,
 p.EnglishDescription AS ProductDescription,
 s.EnglishProductSubcategoryName AS ProductSubcategory
FROM dbo.DimProduct AS p
 INNER JOIN dbo.DimProductSubcategory AS s
  ON p.ProductSubcategoryKey = s.ProductSubcategoryKey
WHERE EnglishDescription IS NOT NULL
ORDER BY NEWID();
```

The query returns the result ordered by the **NEWID()** function in order to get random ten rows. After you read the rows, you insert the Text Analytics step. When you use this feature (or the Vision) for the first time, Power BI asks you to log in with an account that has got premium capacity. Then you get three options:

- Detect language, which can help you detect one of more than 120 languages supported, and add the language ISO code as a new column.
- Extract key phrases, which is extracting words and multi-word phrases in one of the supported languages.
- Score sentiment, which scores the sentiment of the text column you are evaluating with a score between 0 and 1, where 0 means totally negative and 1 means totally positive score.

Sentiment analysis currently supports four languages only, namely English, German, Spanish, and French. *Figure* 8.21 shows the setting up extraction of key phrases for the **ProductDescription** column:

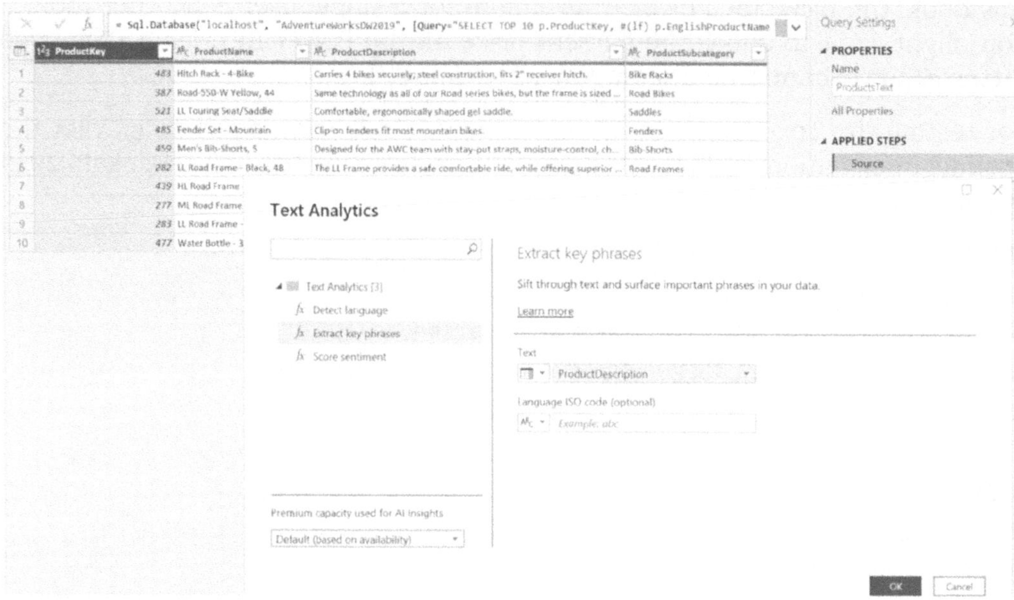

Figure 8.21: *Extracting Key Phrases*

In the result of the Extract key phrases AI insight, we can get multiple rows for a single original row, in our case multiple rows for a single product. We get two additional columns:

- Extract key phrases, which hold all key phrases extracted together in a delimited list and is the same for all the rows of a product.
- . **KeyPhrase** column, which holds a single key phrase per row and is the reason why we get many rows for a single input row.

Figure 8.22 shows the result of the extraction of key phrases:

Figure 8.22: *Extracted Key Phrases*

What you do with the extracted key phrases is up to you. You can count the terms to get the **term frequency (TF)** score. You can use a bit more advanced score called **term frequency / inverse document frequency (TF/IDF)** score. The formula for the TF/IDF score is term frequency multiplied by the logarithm of the number of documents divided by the number of documents with the term in them:

$$TFIDF = TF * Log(\frac{N\ docs}{N\ docs\ with\ term})$$

TF/IDF punishes the terms that appear in many documents and thus do not determine well any particular document and give a higher score for the terms that are frequent in a small number of documents. We did not calculate these scores, we have just used the WordCloud custom visualization, as you can see in *Figure* 8.23.

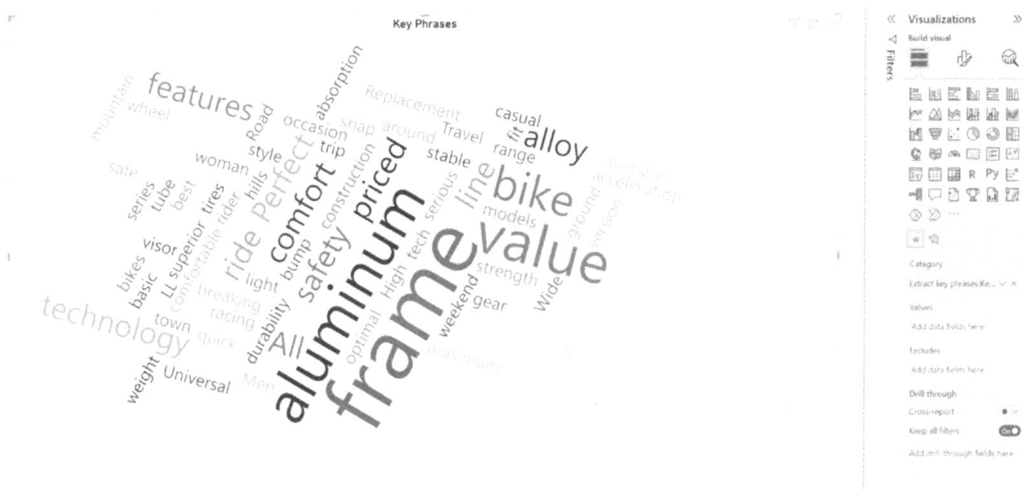

***Figure 8.23:** Extracted Key Phrases in a Word Cloud*

To test the Vision AI insights, we are going to start with the following query:

```
SELECT TOP 10 p.ProductKey,
 p.EnglishProductName AS ProductName,
 s.EnglishProductSubcategoryName AS ProductSubcategory,
 p.LargePhoto
FROM dbo.DimProduct AS p
 INNER JOIN dbo.DimProductSubcategory AS s
  ON p.ProductSubcategoryKey = s.ProductSubcategoryKey
WHERE EnglishDescription IS NOT NULL
ORDER BY NEWID();
```

With Vision AI insights, you can tag images. Behind the scenes, Azure AI holds more than 2,000 already known and recognizable images, including sceneries, living beings like people and animals, and general objects and actions, and the number is constantly increasing. In the previous query, we returned the **LargePhoto** binary column. We will try how the image tagging works with this column. In addition, the query returns also the product subcategory, which will together with the product name tell us how well the Vision AI insight tagged the images. *Figure* 8.24 shows the usage of image tagging:

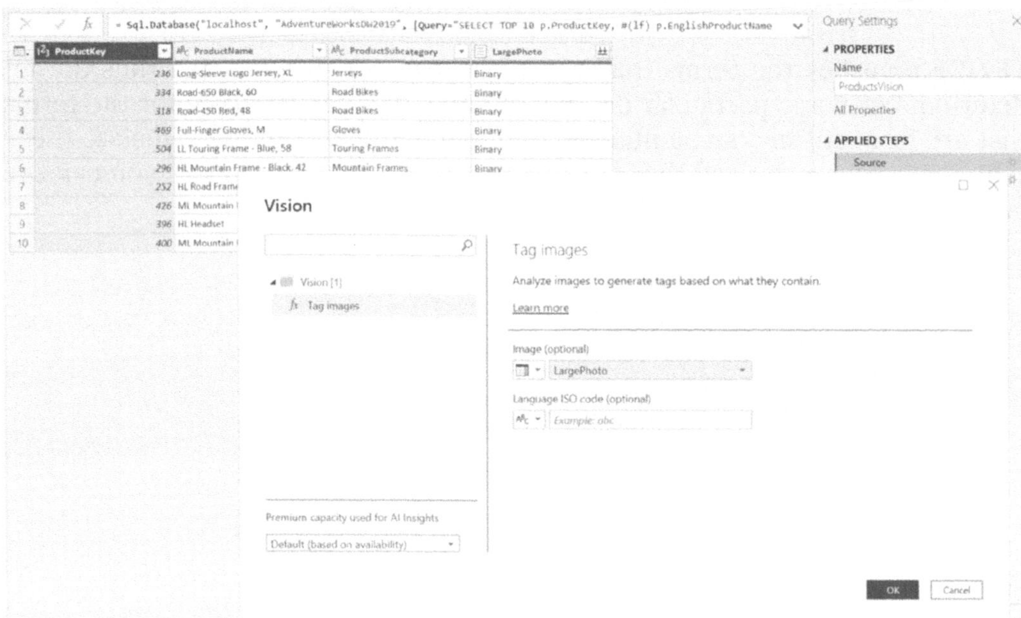

Figure 8.24: *Image Tagging*

Image tagging adds four columns to the dataset:

- **Tag images.Tags**, which holds all tags separated with a comma.
- **Tag images.Json**, which returns all information about the tags and the confidence level of the tags in JSON format.

- **`Tag images.Tag`**, which holds tags separately one in each row, and is the one that can cause to have multiple rows for a single one in the source.
- **`Tag images.ErrorMessage`**, which shows if an error occurred when tagging the images.

Here is an example of the JSON returned:


```
"{
  ""confidences"": [
    {
      ""name"": ""bicycle"",
      ""confidence"": 0.99978178739547729
    },
    {
      ""name"": ""outdoor"",
      ""confidence"": 0.88872230052948
    },
    {
      ""name"": ""transport"",
      ""confidence"": 0.80397087335586548
    },
    {
      ""name"": ""parked"",
      ""confidence"": 0.645069420337677
    }
  ]
}"
```

We are showing the tags of the images for 10 random products in *Figure* 8.25:

ProductKey	ProductName	ProductSubcategory	Tag images.Tag	Tag images.Confidence
221	Sport-100 Helmet, Blue	Helmets	tool	0.30
294	HL Mountain Frame - Silver, 46	Mountain Frames	transport	0.77
305	HL Mountain Frame - Black, 38	Mountain Frames		
307	HL Mountain Frame - Silver, 38	Mountain Frames	transport	0.77
368	Road-250 Red, 44	Road Bikes	bicycle	1.00
368	Road-250 Red, 44	Road Bikes	outdoor	0.88
368	Road-250 Red, 44	Road Bikes	transport	0.93
399	ML Mountain Handlebars	Handlebars	tool	0.30
401	HL Mountain Handlebars	Handlebars	tool	0.30
507	LL Touring Frame - Yellow, 50	Touring Frames	bicycle	0.97
507	LL Touring Frame - Yellow, 50	Touring Frames	transport	0.87
507	LL Touring Frame - Yellow, 50	Touring Frames	wheel	0.28
565	Touring-3000 Blue, 54	Touring Bikes	bicycle	1.00
565	Touring-3000 Blue, 54	Touring Bikes	outdoor	0.85
565	Touring-3000 Blue, 54	Touring Bikes	parked	0.62
565	Touring-3000 Blue, 54	Touring Bikes	transport	0.91
565	Touring-3000 Blue, 54	Touring Bikes	wheel	0.27
570	Touring-3000 Yellow, 54	Touring Bikes	bicycle	1.00
570	Touring-3000 Yellow, 54	Touring Bikes	parked	0.80
570	Touring-3000 Yellow, 54	Touring Bikes	transport	0.87

***Figure* 8.25:** *Tagged Images*

You can see that the tagging worked quite well. For example, for product 368 with the name Road-250 Red, 44 and subcategory Road Bikes, we got tags bicycle, outdoor and transport, with confidences 1.00, 0.88 and 0.93. However, you can also notice that image tagging is not perfect. For example, products 294 and 307, both in the subcategory Mountain frames, both got tag transport with confidence 0.77, while product 305, which is also a mountain frame, did not get a tag at all, and there was also no error message.

Bypassing the R, Python and AI limitations

Using Python, R, Azure ML and Azure AI in Power BI helps you create really powerful analyses. However, as we already mentioned in this chapter, there are many limitations. Let us repeat some of them:

- Azure AI requires Premium Power BI capacity
- Azure ML is not free
- Power BI Report Server for on-premises deployment does not support R and Python scripts

- There is a limited number of additional R and Python packages supported in the Power BI Service
- R and Python visuals can process only up to 150,000 rows, and the processing time cannot exceed five minutes

Nevertheless, there is a really nice workaround that helps you bypass all of these limitations. You can use SQL Server Machine Learning Services and run R and Python scripts from inside the SQL Server. You use SQL Server as the source for your data. Machine Learning Services are available on SQL Server on-premises, versions 2016 (this one supports R only, while all others support R and Python), 2017, 2019 and 2022 (and probably also future versions), but also on Azure SQL Server Managed Instance, and of course on Azure virtual machines with SQL Server installed. From version 2019, also running Java inside SQL Server is supported, but Java is not really interesting for data science. Please note that Machine Learning Services are not supported in Azure SQL Database.

In the SQL Server, you run R and Python code with the **sys.sp_execute_external_script** system procedure. Before that, you need to use the **sys.sp_configure** system procedure to allow external scripts, which is an advanced option. Here is the T-SQL code that allows external scripts:

```
-- Allow external scripts
USE master;
EXEC sys.sp_configure 'show advanced options', 1;
RECONFIGURE
EXEC sys.sp_configure 'external scripts enabled', 1;
RECONFIGURE;
GO
```

In the following code, we are going to execute a Python script to create a clustering model based on the **dbo.vTargetMail** view data. This time, we are going to use **Gaussian Mixture Models (GMM)** clustering. K-Means clustering measures the distance from each case to each center and then assigns the case to the closest center with probability one and to all other centers with probability zero. GMM clustering covers cases around the centers with Gaussian curves for all input variables. This way, each case belongs to each center with some probability. For example, case A belongs to center 1 with a probability of 0.3, to center 2 with a probability of 0.00005, and to center 3 with a probability of 0.00000001. Case B belongs to center 1 with a probability of 0.000002, to center 2 with a probability of 0.15, and to center 3 with a probability of 0.00007. We assign the case to the center for which the probability is the highest. GMM clustering is also called soft clustering, while K-Means is called hard clustering. GMM clustering is more suitable when clusters tend to overlap. Without further hesitation, here is the code:

```
-- Execute Python script
USE AdventureWorksDW2019;
EXECUTE sys.sp_execute_external_script
  @language = N'Python'
 ,@script = N'
# Imports
import numpy as np
import pandas as pd

# GMM clustering
from sklearn.mixture import GaussianMixture

# Define and train the model
X = TM[["BikeBuyer", "TotalChildren",
        "NumberChildrenAtHome","HouseOwnerFlag",
        "NumberCarsOwned", "AgeDiscretized",
        "IncomeDiscretized", "EducationNumeric",
        "RegionNumeric", "MarStaNumeric"]]
model = GaussianMixture(n_components = 3, covariance_type = "full")
model.fit(X)

# Get the clusters vector
y_gmm = model.predict(X)

# Adding cluster membership to the original
TM["Cluster"] = y_gmm
TMPy = TM[["CustomerKey", "Cluster", "Education", "CommuteDistance",
"Occupation", "NumberCarsOwned"]]
'
 ,@input_data_1 = N'
SET QUOTED_IDENTIFIER OFF;   -- Double quotes as string delimiters
SELECT CustomerKey,
 Age, CAST(YearlyIncome AS INT) AS Income,   -- money data type not
supported
 BikeBuyer, MaritalStatus,
 TotalChildren, NumberChildrenAtHome,
 EnglishEducation AS Education,
 EnglishOccupation AS Occupation,
```

```
 HouseOwnerFlag, NumberCarsOwned,
 CommuteDistance, Region,
 ROUND(
 (1.0*Age - AVG(Age) OVER()) /
  STDEV(Age) OVER(), 2) AS AgeScaled,
 ROUND(
 (1.0*YearlyIncome - AVG(YearlyIncome) OVER()) /
  STDEV(YearlyIncome) OVER(), 2) AS IncomeScaled,
 NTILE(3) OVER(ORDER BY Age) AS AgeDiscretized,
 NTILE(3) OVER(ORDER BY YearlyIncome) AS IncomeDiscretized,
 CASE EnglishEducation
  WHEN "Partial High School" THEN 1
  WHEN "High School" THEN 2
  WHEN "Partial College" THEN 3
  WHEN "Bachelors" THEN 4
  WHEN "Graduate Degree" THEN 5
  ELSE 0         -- Handling possible NULLs - not needed here, just an
example
 END AS EducationNumeric,
 CASE CommuteDistance
  WHEN "0-1 Miles" THEN 1
  WHEN "1-2 Miles" THEN 2
  WHEN "2-5 Miles" THEN 3
  WHEN "5-10 Miles" THEN 4
  WHEN "10+ Miles" THEN 5
 END AS CommDistNumeric,
 CASE Region
  WHEN "Europe" THEN 1
  WHEN "North America" THEN 2
  WHEN "Pacific" THEN 3
 END AS RegionNumeric,
 CASE MaritalStatus
  WHEN "S" THEN 0
  WHEN "M" THEN 1
 END AS MarStaNumeric
FROM dbo.vTargetMail;
'
 ,@input_data_1_name =  N'TM'
```

```
 ,@output_data_1_name = N'TMPy'
WITH RESULT SETS
(
 ([CustomerKey]    INT NOT NULL,
  [Cluster]      INT NOT NULL,
  [Education]  NVARCHAR(20) NOT NULL,
  [CommuteDistance] NVARCHAR(20) NOT NULL,
  [Occupation]    NVARCHAR(20) NOT NULL,
  [NumberCarsOwned] INT NOT NULL)
);
```

The **sys.sp_execute_external_script** procedure accepts the following parameters:

- @language determines the languages used, with options R, Python or Java; in our case, this is Python
- **@script** is the script in the language defined in the previous parameter, in our case Python.
- **@input_data_1** is the query in t-SQL language that defines the input data for the script in the **@script** parameter.
- **input_data_1_name** is the name of the data frame for the input data inside the R or Python script; the results of the T-SQL query are automatically converted to this data frame.
- **@output_data_1_name** is the name of the data frame that is created inside the R or Python script and is converted by the procedure back to tabular format and returned to the client.
- **WITH RESULT SET** option defines the structure of the tabular data returned.

Once the procedure works correctly, you can use it for the source in Power Query. You load the data and you can start analyzing the results, in our case the clusters found with the Python code.

You can also use R and Python to replace AI Text Analytics and Vision insights. For text analytics, you can also use T-SQL. With SQL Server Full-Text Search, you get the sys.dm_fts_parser() **rowset** function that can parse text in more than 50 languages and return key terms. The function is not as powerful as Azure AI text Analytics, because it extracts single-word terms only without extracting phrases. However, often this is enough. You can read more about Full-Text Search at MS Learn (**https://learn.microsoft.com/en-us/sql/relational-databases/search/**

full-text-search?view=sql-server-ver16). The following code checks whether Full-Text search is installed.

```
-- Check whether Full-Text and Semantic search is installed
SELECT SERVERPROPERTY('IsFullTextInstalled');
```

Now we can extract terms from product descriptions for 10 random products:

```
-- Extracting key terms
WITH TOP10Products AS
(
SELECT TOP 10
 ProductKey,
 EnglishProductName AS ProductName,
 EnglishDescription AS ProductDescription
FROM dbo.DimProduct
WHERE EnglishDescription IS NOT NULL
ORDER BY NEWID()
),
KeyPhrases AS
(
SELECT p.ProductKey,
 p.ProductName,
 p.ProductDescription,
 t.display_term
FROM TOP10Products AS p
 CROSS APPLY sys.dm_fts_parser('"' + REPLACE(p.
ProductDescription,'"','') + '"', 1033, 0, 0) AS t
WHERE t.special_term = N'Exact Match')
SELECT ProductKey,
 MIN(ProductName) AS ProductName,
 MIN(ProductDescription) AS ProductDescription,
 STRING_AGG (display_term, ', ') AS KeyTerms
FROM KeyPhrases
GROUP BY ProductKey;
```

This query is our data source. *Figure* 8.26 shows the terms extracted in a word cloud:

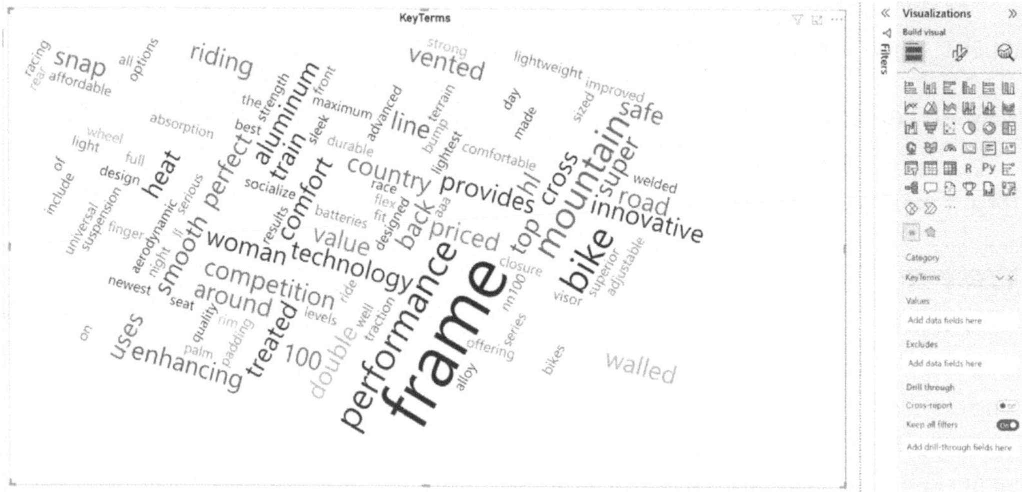

Figure 8.26: *Word Cloud for Terms Extracted with* T-SQL

You can notice that the word cloud looks very similar to the one in *Figure* 8.23, which was created on phrases extracted with Azure AI.

Conclusion

Power BI is definitely not just a reporting tool. You can use it for in-depth analyses as well. With the help of external languages, including R, Python, and even T-SQL, you can extend it to unprecedented levels. There is a lot of data science already built into some basic visualizations. There are also some advanced visualizations. You can leverage Azure ML and Azure AI inside Power BI. Finally, you can add custom visualizations and extend the capabilities of Power BI even further.

In the next chapter, we are going to discuss how to optimize Power BI data loads and reports. We will use a holistic view, including explaining the impact on the source SQL Server databases.

Key terms

- **Clustering**: The algorithm and the process of finding hidden groups of cases based on the similarity of their input attributes.
- **Decomposition tree**: The visualization that helps you manually build the tree that shows you the path to a decision.
- **Decision tree**: The algorithm that builds the tree that shows you the path to a decision automatically.
- **Term extraction**: The process of extracting key terms from texts.
- **ARIMA**: The algorithm used for forecasting in line charts, of course, in R or Python code.
- **Logistic regression**: The algorithm used in the Key influencers visual.
- **Linear regression**: The algorithm used in Scatterplot or Line chart for the trend line.

CHAPTER 9
Optimizing Power BI Models and Reports

Introduction

Power BI was created for the lightning speed of reports. Nevertheless, it is still good to know how to create efficient datasets. In addition, Power BI can operate in DirectQuery mode, where the data is stored in the source, and Power BI serves as the client tool only. For example, if the data remains in SQL server, then you also have to know how to optimize Transact-SQL queries. Efficient queries also help shortening data refresh times. This chapter provides many useful tips for creating efficient models and reports. We are introducing a holistic view on the optimization, covering all steps involved in creating a Power BI solution, from data source queries to final reports.

Structure

In this chapter, we cover the following topics:

- Optimizing the data model
- Query folding
- Performance of reports
- Aggregate and dual storage tables

Optimizing the data model

The first thing to remember is that Power BI datasets are always loaded in memory. Therefore, you have to take care to only import the data that is really needed for analyses. When you are preparing the data, you are tempted to include in the dataset as much data as possible just in case somebody needs this data in the future. This is quite a common mistake. It is relatively easy to add new tables to the model when they are needed. Many times, it is also better to have smaller data models, covering just a single reporting area each, than one big data model with all possible dimensions and fact tables.

For any long-term analytical solution, it is always recommendable to use a **data warehouse** (**DW**) as the source for Power BI datasets. With the **extract-transform-load** (**ETL**) process, you load the data from the line of business and external sources to your DW, which consists of multiple star schemas. As we discussed in *Chapter 1*, *Introducing the Theoretical Background for Democratizing Analytics*" you should always use the star schema logical model. A single star schema from a DW might be a good candidate for a single Power BI dataset.

Limiting the amount of data loading can mean many things:

- **Projection**: Select part of the columns from the source table
- **Filtering**: Filter the rows from the source table
- **Aggregating**: Aggregate the data from the source; for example, instead of using data on the day level, maybe the data on the month level could be sufficient for the analyses

Aggregating the data means lowering the granularity; after aggregation, the data is less granular and stored on a higher level, for example, in the date dimension on the level of the month instead of the level of the day. Measures are aggregated over some dimension attribute. Let us call this fact table granularity. We can define another kind of granularity, dimension granularity. Dimension granularity is defined by the number of dimensions in a star schema. A lower number of dimensions means higher granularity. For example, imagine a simple star schema covering sales with three dimensions for customers, products, and dates. The lowest level of granularity is sales of a specific product for a specific customer on a specific day. If you omit the dimension for products, then the lowest level of granularity is sales of all products for a specific customer on a specific day.

Power BI was designed to help democratize analytical processing. This means that it should be simple to use. You cannot expect that users that are specialists in their own business area, for example, accounting, also become Power BI specialists. The simplicity starts with the data model. We already know that we should always use star schema. Too many tables in the dataset clutter the Data pane when you create reports in Power BI Desktop or Service, and even a star schema model, becomes complex to use. Therefore, besides improving performance, smaller datasets also simplify reporting.

A good data model includes explicitly defined measures and hierarchies. You might remember from *Chapter 1, Introducing the Theoretical Background for Democratizing Analytics*, that with explicitly defined measures and hierarchies, you prevent users from creating meaningless reports. Hierarchies define drill-down paths. Most of the time, you should use natural hierarchies, hierarchies that stem from real life and from the source systems, for example, year – quarter – month - day. Natural hierarchies can be easily spotted in a snowflake schema. In a star schema, they are flattened in a single table and thus, harder to notice. Therefore, you should recreate them in your data model.

Hierarchies can also help with the performance of reports. When you create a hierarchy, you should consider that after the drill-down action, only a limited number of rows should be included in the expanded level, especially when the details are shown in the visual. Table and Matrix visuals can drill down to the lowest level of granularity. Imagine a table where initially you show three rows only, let us say, for three categories of products. Then you drill down from category to product level for a single category. However, this category might include 100,000 products, which is not extraordinary for retail shops. A user of the report requests 100,000 rows with a single click in the visual. Expanding a level to 100,000 rows is always slow in Power BI Desktop, Power BI Service and especially in Excel. You should create an intermediate level of hierarchy; let us call it subcategories.

When you do not have natural hierarchies and deal with many detail rows, you might consider even creating artificial hierarchies if you expect that your users would use visuals that can show the most detailed level. For example, you might include the order id and line-item id from the source order in your data model. This way, you enable end users to track down the source of the data for every single row and check whether the data in your Power BI dataset is correct and is the same as in the source. There is no natural hierarchy for the id numbers. But you can create your own one. For example, you can use dates to create a hierarchy year – month – day, and end users can use this hierarchy to drill down gradually to a single order line. The following code shows the source query for this example:

```
SELECT CAST(RIGHT(SalesOrderNumber, 5) +
 CAST(SalesOrderLineNumber AS CHAR(1)) AS INT) AS Id,
 YEAR(OrderDate) AS CYear,
 MONTH(OrderDate) AS CMonth,
```

```
 DAY(OrderDate) AS CDay,
 OrderQuantity, SalesAmount
FROM dbo.FactInternetSales;
```

This query was used for the source of the data model in Power BI. In the data model, we created a hierarchy named **Calendar**, with levels **CYear**, **CMonth**, **Cday** and **Id**. *Figure* 9.1 shows the report we created:

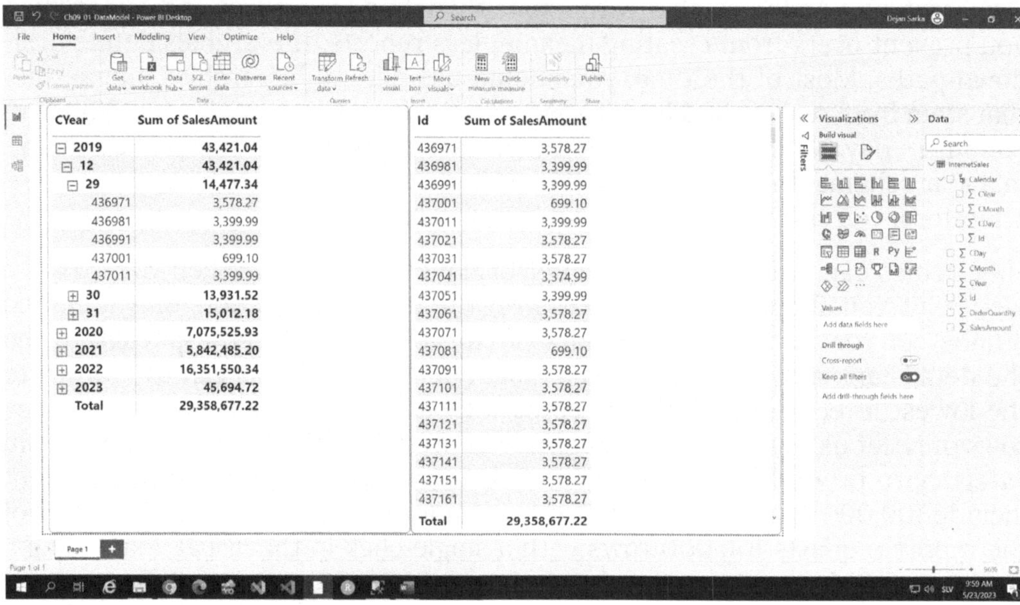

Figure 9.1: *Report with an Artificial Hierarchy*

In the report, you can see two matrix visualizations. In the first one, we used the Calendar hierarchy on rows; in the one on the right side of the report, we used the ID column for rows. You can immediately notice how much simpler it is to locate a specific order id on the left side because only a few are available on the lowest level of the hierarchy. It is also faster to use the left matrix than the right matrix, which takes more time to refresh.

You can probably remember from the previous chapter the limitation for R and Python visuals. You can process only up to 150,000 rows when using R and Python visuals, and the maximum processing time before you get an error is five minutes. You might think that this is a very strict limitation since fact tables are many times old, with millions, if not billions of rows. However, with advanced data science algorithms, you usually work with samples. These advanced algorithms, for example, the clustering algorithm that we used in the previous chapter, process the data in many loops, so they scan the data many times. The number of passes through data can be really high; a couple of hundred times is not completely unusual.

For data science, you prepare the data in a separate table, either inside a data warehouse or in your Power BI dataset. You collect all the knowledge you have about the cases you are analyzing and store this knowledge in columns. The rows in the table represent cases. In the previous chapter, we used a couple of times the **`dbo.vTargetMail`** view from the **`AdventureWorksDW2019`** sample database. In this view, all the information available about customers is collected, including demographics and the flag showing whether the customer purchased a bike in the past or not. This view is an example of how you prepare data for advanced analyses.

The question is, how many cases do you need in your sample? Statistical sampling is a well-known topic, and you can easily find many articles on it. We are not going into details about statistical sampling and how to calculate the sample size in this book. We are just defining the basics and showing appropriate sample sizes in a table.

First, we have to define two terms: confidence interval and confidence level. These two measures define how precise and how certain the estimate for a value of a target variable is. The confidence level tells you how many times the true value of the target variable would be inside the confidence interval when you create different samples. For example, a confidence level of 0.95 with a confidence interval of 0.05 means that the true value would be inside the interval between the estimated value minus 2.5% and the estimated value plus 2.5% in 95% of cases, or 19 out of 20 times, in 19 out of 20 random samples. Table 9.1 shows how many cases, assuming that you have a big dataset, you need minimally in your sample for confidence levels of 0.95 and 0.99 for different confidence intervals between 0.10 and 0.01:

Confidence Interval	Confidence Level 0.95	Confidence Level 0.99
0.10	96	166
0.09	119	205
0.08	150	260
0.07	196	340
0.06	267	462
0.05	384	666
0.04	600	1,040
0.03	1,067	1,849
0.02	2,401	4,160
0.01	9,604	16,641

***Table 9.1**: Sample Sizes*

Two numbers are bolded – 384 for the confidence interval of 0.05 and confidence level of 0.95 and 16,641 for the confidence interval of 0.01 and confidence level of 0.99. These are the typical confidence intervals and confidence levels used by statisticians. You can see that for advanced analytics, you do not need really huge datasets. You do not want to scan a huge dataset again and again in a long loop. The only question is how to select sample rows randomly. Of course, you can do it in many ways. Here, we are introducing three possibilities: selecting random rows with T-SQL, R and Power Query.

With T-SQL, you can use the TOP operator together with the **CRYPT_GEN_RANDOM()** function. With the function mentioned, you generate random numbers. You can order the data by these numbers and then select the top number of rows or the top percentage of rows with the TOP operator. The following code selects 30 percent random rows from the **dbo.vTargetMail** view. This query is the source for a Power BI table:

```
-- Sampling with T-SQL
SELECT TOP 30 PERCENT
 CustomerKey,
 YearlyIncome AS Income,
 BikeBuyer, Region,
 CASE EnglishEducation
  WHEN N'Partial High School' THEN N'1 - Partial High School'
  WHEN N'High School' THEN N'2 - High School'
  WHEN N'Partial College' THEN N'3 - Partial College'
  WHEN N'Bachelors' THEN N'4 - Bachelors'
  WHEN N'Graduate Degree' THEN N'5 - Graduate Degree'
  ELSE N'0 - Unknown'         -- Handling possible NULLs
 END AS Education
FROM dbo.vTargetMail
ORDER BY CAST(CRYPT_GEN_RANDOM(4) AS INT);
```

With R, you can read the whole data and then use the **sample_frac()** function from the **dplyr** package to select the desired proportion (or percentage) of the data. Here is the complete R code you can use for the data source for a Power BI table:

```
# Sampling with R
# install.packages("RODBC")
library(RODBC)
# Read SQL Server data
con <- odbcConnect("AWDW", uid = "RUser", pwd = "Pa$$w0rd")
```

```
TMRandR <- sqlQuery(con,
"
SELECT
 CustomerKey,
 YearlyIncome AS Income,
 BikeBuyer, Region,
 CASE EnglishEducation
  WHEN N'Partial High School' THEN N'1 - Partial High School'
  WHEN N'High School' THEN N'2 - High School'
  WHEN N'Partial College' THEN N'3 - Partial College'
  WHEN N'Bachelors' THEN N'4 - Bachelors'
  WHEN N'Graduate Degree' THEN N'5 - Graduate Degree'
  ELSE N'0 - Unknown'         -- Handling possible NULLs
 END AS Education
FROM dbo.vTargetMail;
")
close(con)
# View(TMRandR)
# 30% sample
# install.packages("dplyr")
library(dplyr)
TMRandR <- sample_frac(TMRandR, 0.3)
# View(TMRandR)
```

With Power Query, you select all rows from the source, the **dbo.vTargetMail** view. Then you can add random numbers to each row by creating a custom column using the **List.Random(1)** function. Since you get a list of one element, you have to expand the list. Then you can sort by this new column and select the top number of rows. Note that we used a fixed number of rows since the **Table.FirstN()** function does not support percentage as a parameter. Here is the complete M code:

```
let
    Source = Sql.Database("localhost", "AdventureWorksDW2019",
[Query="SELECT …"]),
    #"Added Custom" = Table.AddColumn(Source, "RandomNumber",
each List.Random(1)),
    #"Expanded RandomNumber" = Table.ExpandListColumn(#"Added Custom",
"RandomNumber"),
    #"Sorted Rows" = Table.Sort(#"Expanded RandomNumber",{
```

```
{"RandomNumber", Order.Ascending}}),
    #"Kept First Rows" = Table.FirstN(#"Sorted Rows",5545)
in
    #"Kept First Rows"
```

We tested the samples created with all three methods. We created a report with three pairs of two visuals, each pair for one sample table. If the samples are really random, there should not be a lot of difference in the values of the variables from different samples. *Figure* 9.2 shows the report that compares the data from the samples created with different languages:

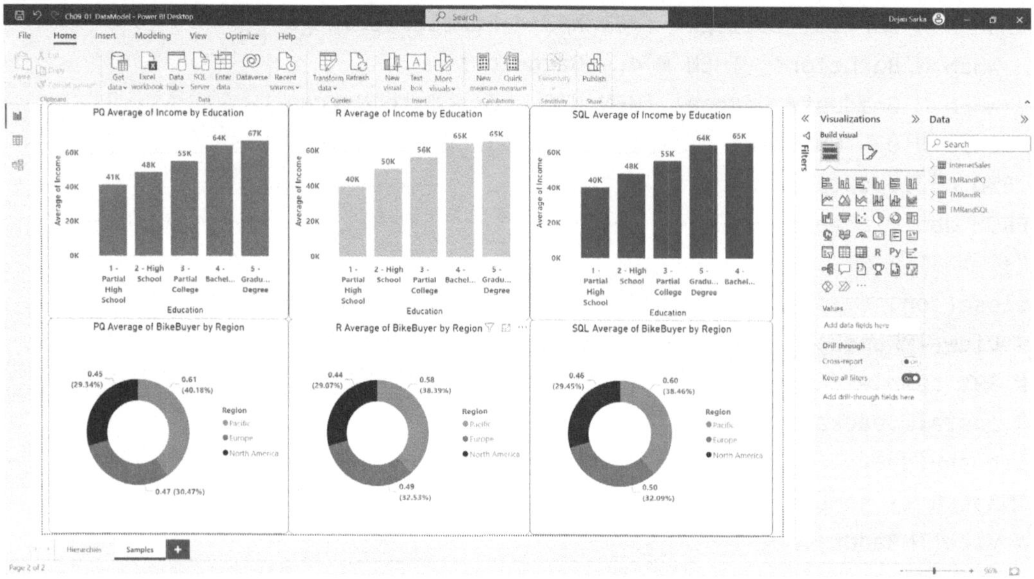

Figure 9.2: *Checking the samples*

We compared the average income in the classes of education and the proportion of bike buyers in different regions. You can see that in the visuals, the bars, and the donut proportions, and also the data labels do not differ a lot. You can also refresh data multiple times to get different samples. After a few refreshes, if you do not notice some important difference in visuals from different samples, you can trust that the sampling was random.

We have again seen that we can achieve the same result in different ways. We could also use even more options, including Python and DAX, for the same sampling task. Which language should you use? You start with the language you are familiar with. However, if you reach performance problems, you might need to implement a different solution. From a performance perspective, you should do as much processing as possible and as close to the data source as possible. In our sampling case, the T-SQL solution would be preferred. Power Query understands this logic and tries to push the processing down the pipeline as much as possible through a feature known as query folding.

Query folding

Power Query pushes the processing down the pipeline by creating a source query for a series of transformations. You read source data directly from a table or a view. This is like using **`SELECT * FROM schema.table`**, except that Power Query immediately expands all columns and uses explicit column names. Then you create multiple transformations. Power Query, instead of using M functions, tries to add these transformations to the source query. It develops the source query step by step. When the query is executed, the processing is pushed to the source.

Of course, the source has to be able to process the query. It means that there must be some kind of database management system in the source; otherwise, query folding makes no sense and is not available. Some of the sources that can support query folding are:

- Relational database management systems, like SQL Server, Azure SQL Database, Azure Synapse Analytics, PostgreSQL, Oracle and more
- OData feeds, like SharePoint lists, or SQL Server Reporting Services reports
- Exchange Server
- Active Directory

Data sources that do not support query folding include:

- Flat files, like CSV and XML files
- Blobs, including Azure Blobs
- Web pages

Not every single transformation can benefit from query folding. If we think from a T-SQL perspective, query folding can create the following **`SELECT`** statement parts:

- SELECT expanding column list
- SELECT adding simple custom columns
- SELECT renaming columns
- SELECT removing columns
- FROM with JOINs

- WHERE for filtering, including mimicking the HAVING clause with WHERE
- ORDER BY
- TOP N filtering
- Subqueries in parentheses
- PIVOT and UNPIVOT

You can notice if query folding can manage your transformations in the Power Query editor. Right-click the transformation you just created and check whether the **`View Native Query`** option is enabled in the pop-up menu, as *Figure* 9.3 shows:

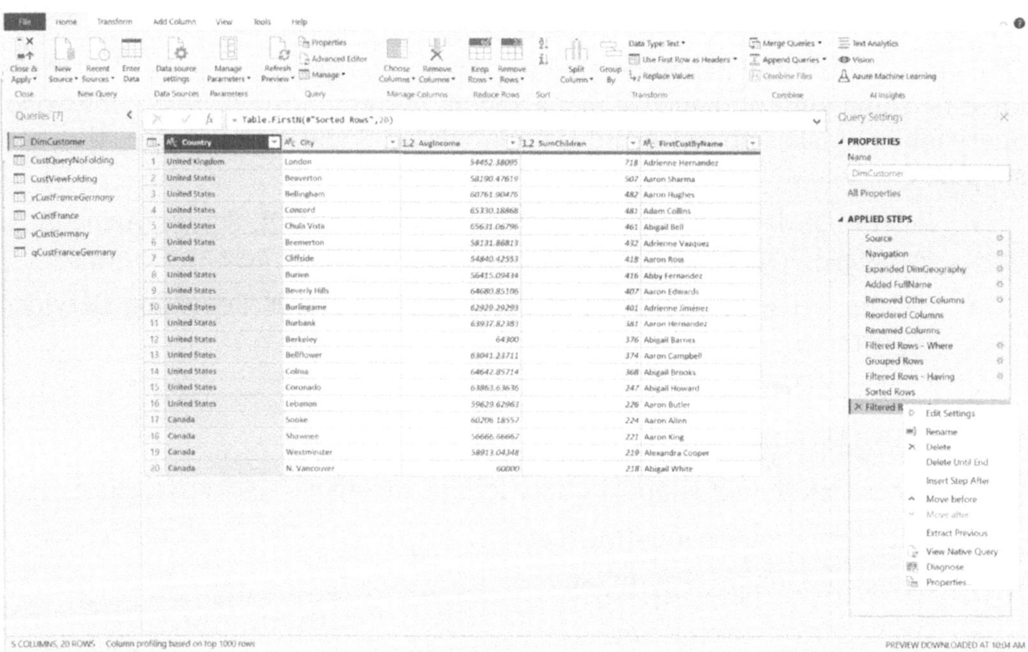

***Figure* 9.3:** *Checking for Query Folding*

In the figure, you can see that we created all together 12 steps, and query folding is still enabled. We selected the **`dbo.DimCustomer`** table from the **`AdventureWorksDW2019`** demo database. Then we expanded the related **`dbo.DimGeography`** table to include the **`County`** and **`City`** columns. Then we created a calculated column **`FulllName`** by concatenating FirstName and **`LastName`** columns. Then we removed all columns we did not need. Then we reordered the columns. Then we implemented the first filter on the source data by selecting countries Australia, Canada, the United Kingdom, and the United States only. Then we aggregated the data over countries and cities. We calculated the average income, the sum of the number of children, and the minimal full name. Then we implemented the second filter to select rows where the sum of children is greater than eight. Then we sorted the rows by the sum of children descending. Finally, we filtered the dataset the third time to only include the first twenty rows in the result. For all of these actions, Power Query could still use query folding. *Figure* 9.3 shows part (approximate half) of the native query:

Native Query

```
select top 20
    [_].[EnglishCountryRegionName] as [Country],
    [_].[City] as [City],
    [_].[AvgIncome] as [AvgIncome],
    [_].[SumChildren] as [SumChildren],
    [_].[FirstCustByName] as [FirstCustByName]
from
(
    select [_].[EnglishCountryRegionName],
        [_].[City],
        [_].[AvgIncome],
        [_].[SumChildren],
        [_].[FirstCustByName]
    from
    (
        select [_].[EnglishCountryRegionName],
            [_].[City],
            [_].[AvgIncome],
            [_].[SumChildren],
            [_].[FirstCustByName]
        from
        (
            select [rows].[EnglishCountryRegionName] as [EnglishCountryRegionName],
                [rows].[City] as [City],
                avg(convert(float, [rows].[YearlyIncome])) as [AvgIncome],
                sum([rows].[TotalChildren]) as [SumChildren],
                min([rows].[FullName]) as [FirstCustByName]
            from
            (
                select [_].[CustomerKey] as [CustomerKey],
                    [_].[YearlyIncome] as [YearlyIncome],
                    [_].[TotalChildren] as [TotalChildren],
                    [_].[EnglishEducation] as [EnglishEducation],
                    [_].[EnglishOccupation] as [EnglishOccupation],
                    [_].[City] as [City],
                    [_].[EnglishCountryRegionName] as [EnglishCountryRegionName],
                    ([_].[FirstName] + ' ') + [_].[LastName] as [FullName]
                from
                (
                    select [_].[CustomerKey],
                        [_].[FirstName],
                        [_].[LastName],
                        [_].[YearlyIncome],
                        [_].[TotalChildren],
                        [_].[EnglishEducation],
                        [_].[EnglishOccupation],
                        [_].[City],
                        [_].[EnglishCountryRegionName]
                    from
                    (
                        select [$Outer].[CustomerKey],
                            [$Outer].[FirstName],
```

OK

***Figure 9.4**: Query created by Query Folding*

You can see that the query looks quite complex. For the sake of brevity, we are not showing the full code here. Query folding does not use all possible T-SQL **`SELECT`** clauses. It did not use the **`HAVING`** clause, for example; it rather calculated the aggregates over groups (the **`GROUP BY`** clause) in a subquery and then used the **`WHERE`** clause in the outer query instead.

We added just one more transformation. We changed the data type of the **SumChildren** column from decimal, which was defined by default, to integer. With this step, query folding is not available anymore. If we had added this step earlier in the pipeline, query folding would become unavailable earlier. Therefore, it is important that you check after each step you add whether query folding is still available or not.

As we mentioned, query folding tends to create quite complex queries. Complex queries are harder to optimize than simple ones. It is still possible to improve the performance by manually writing source queries. Here is the rewritten query that is logically equivalent to the one we introduced with query folding:

```
SELECT TOP 20
 g.EnglishCountryRegionName AS Country,
 g.City,
 AVG(YearlyIncome) AS AvgIncome,
 CAST(SUM(c.TotalChildren) AS INT) AS SumChildren,
 MIN(c.FirstName + ' ' + c.LastName) AS FirstCustByName
FROM dbo.DimCustomer AS c
 INNER JOIN dbo.DimGeography AS g
  ON c.GeographyKey = g.GeographyKey
WHERE g.EnglishCountryRegionName IN
       (N'Australia', N'Canada',
           N'United Kingdom', N'United States')
GROUP BY g.EnglishCountryRegionName, g.City
HAVING SUM(c.TotalChildren) > 8
ORDER BY SumChildren DESC;
```

We executed both queries in a single batch and measured CPU and elapsed times. Turns out that the manual query is about two times faster than the complex query created by query folding. We executed both queries multiple times, and the results were quite consistent. Here is an example of the results measured with the **SET STATISTICS TIME ON** T-SQL command.

```
(20 rows affected)

 SQL Server Execution Times:
   CPU time = 32 ms,  elapsed time = 38 ms.

(20 rows affected)

 SQL Server Execution Times:
   CPU time = 15 ms,  elapsed time = 19 ms.
```

The first result is for the query created by Power Query, and the second result is for the manual query. In *Figure* 9.5, you can notice that also the execution plans are slightly different, and that SQL Server estimates the first query (the query folding query) would cost 54% of the batch and the second query 46%. Note that we are not drilling into details of the execution plan; all we wanted to show is that we get two different plans:

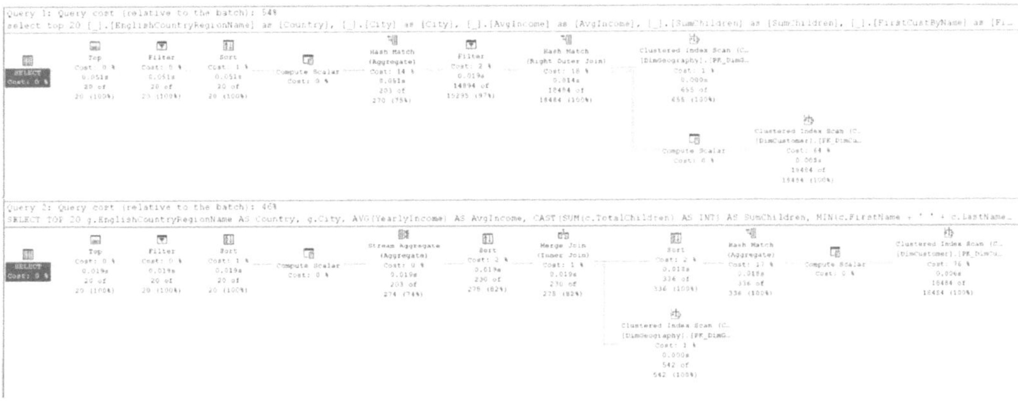

***Figure* 9.5**: *Execution Plans for Query Folding and Manual Queries*

Unfortunately, if you write the source query manually, query folding is not available for any additional transformation. However, you can bypass this limitation by creating a view from the source query. If you want to parameterize the query, then you can use an inline table-valued function instead of a view in SQL Server. For example, we used the following query as the source:

```
SELECT CustomerKey,
 FirstName + ' ' + LastName AS FullName,
 YearlyIncome, TotalChildren,
 EnglishEducation,  -- Renaming the column in PQ
 EnglishOccupation  -- Renaming the column in PQ
FROM dbo.DimCustomer;
```

Then we renamed the **`EnglishEducation`** column to **`Education`** and **`EnglishOccupation`** to **`Occupation`**. Unfortunately, query folding was unavailable for this action. However, we created a view from the query, as you can see in the following code:

```
CREATE VIEW dbo.vDimCustomer
AS
SELECT CustomerKey,
 FirstName + ' ' + LastName AS FullName,
```

```
 YearlyIncome, TotalChildren,
 EnglishEducation,  -- Renaming the column in PQ
 EnglishOccupation  -- Renaming the column in PQ
FROM dbo.DimCustomer;
GO
```

Then we used this view for the source and renamed the columns in Power Query. Query folding worked this time and created the following query:

```
select [_].[CustomerKey] as [CustomerKey],
    [_].[FullName] as [FullName],
    [_].[YearlyIncome] as [YearlyIncome],
    [_].[TotalChildren] as [TotalChildren],
    [_].[EnglishEducation] as [Education],
    [_].[EnglishOccupation] as [Occupation]
from [dbo].[vDimCustomer] as [_]
```

It is recommendable to use query folding as much as possible. In rare cases, like with quite complex queries we have shown, you can get better performance if you write your own query. However, you really have to know how the source system works and how to optimize the query for the specific source. In our case, we wrote an optimized query for SQL Server. Query folding is not limited to SQL Server only; it can create very decent queries for multiple sources.

We are showing here another example of when you can achieve better performance on the source with manual queries. This quite simple example shows something very important: you must always use a holistic approach to optimization in order to look at the greater picture. First, we created a view that selects customers from France and Germany with the following code:

```
CREATE VIEW dbo.vCustFranceGermany
AS
SELECT c.CustomerKey,
 g.EnglishCountryRegionName AS Country,
 g.City,
 c.YearlyIncome AS Income,
 c.TotalChildren
FROM dbo.DimCustomer AS c
 INNER JOIN dbo.DimGeography AS g
  ON c.GeographyKey = g.GeographyKey
WHERE g.EnglishCountryRegionName IN
       (N'France', N'Germany');
GO
```

Then we used this view as the source for a query named **vCustFranceGermany**. Next, we copied this query twice and renamed the copied queries **vCustFrance** and **vCustGermany**. Then we disabled the load for the original **vCustFranceGermany** query as you can see in *Figure 9.6*:

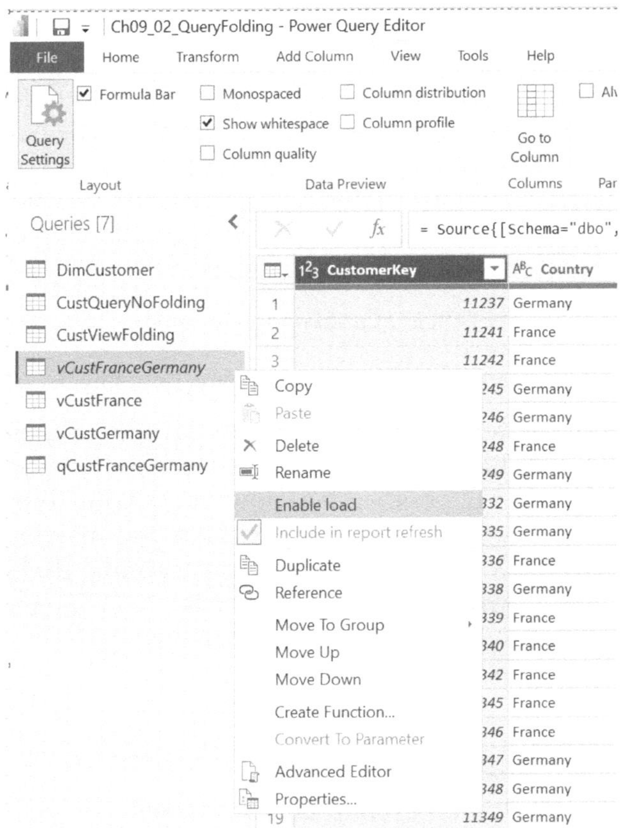

Figure 9.6: *Load disabled for a Query*

In the two copied queries, we added a step to filter the customers to France only in the first query and to Germany only in the second query. Query folding works; here is an example of the source query for France customers created by Power Query:

```
select [_].[CustomerKey],
    [_].[Country],
    [_].[City],
    [_].[Income],
    [_].[TotalChildren]
from [dbo].[vCustFranceGermany] as [_]
where [_].[Country] = 'France' and [_].[Country] is not null
```

What is the catch here? On the first glimpse, everything looks great. Nevertheless, there is room for optimization on the source. The `WHERE` predicate is not very selective, neither for France nor for Germany. SQL Server needs to scan all of the data twice, once for each country. If we would read data for both countries at the same time, then would SQL Server scan the data only once?

Power Query creates queries. Data is materialized from queries to tables (Power Pivot tables) in the dataset when the queries are executed. In order to create two tables, one for each country, and to prevent reading the data twice, we must materialize the query that retrieves the customers for both countries. Once the query is materialized in a dataset table, we can use the **`CALCULATETABLE()`** DAX function to extract data for a single country. The following code extracts the data for Germany and creates a calculated table:

```
qCustGermany = CALCULATETABLE(qCustFranceGermany,

FILTER(qCustFranceGermany,qCustFranceGermany[Country]="Germany"))
```

Calculated tables are materialized. We scanned the source tables only once, but the price is that now we have all of the data twice in the model. This does not look good from the Power BI perspective. However, if your source is quite a busy system, optimizing the source queries could help you make a viable analytical solution. If the source is a data warehouse, then scanning the data twice should not be a problem since a data warehouse is occasionally updated only and then used mostly for reading. We can see again that having a data warehouse in a larger system is very recommendable, this time from the performance perspective.

Performance of reports

If the data model is good, then usually, the performance of your reports is good as well. Nevertheless, you can always check a few things in order to improve it. We have already explained in this chapter that you should use hierarchies as natural drill-down paths. You should also create your own hierarchies in the date dimension. You probably noticed that Power BI creates calendar hierarchies for all date data type columns in your model automatically. These hierarchies are actually calculated tables and are slower than your own hierarchies that you create based on physical columns. You should disable these auto-created date hierarchies. We already discussed them in *Chapter* 5, *Enhancing the Model and Business Analysis with* DAX. Let us quickly repeat how you can get rid of them. Go to **`File`** > **`Options and settings`** > ***`Options`***. There are two settings you can change here. In the Global part, check **`Data Load`** and disable the **`Auto date/time`** for new files option in order to prevent these hierarchies for new Power BI files. To prevent the generation of these hierarchies in the current file, go to the **`CURRENT FILE`** section, **`Data Load`**, and disable the **`Auto date/time`** option, as *Figure* 9.7 shows:

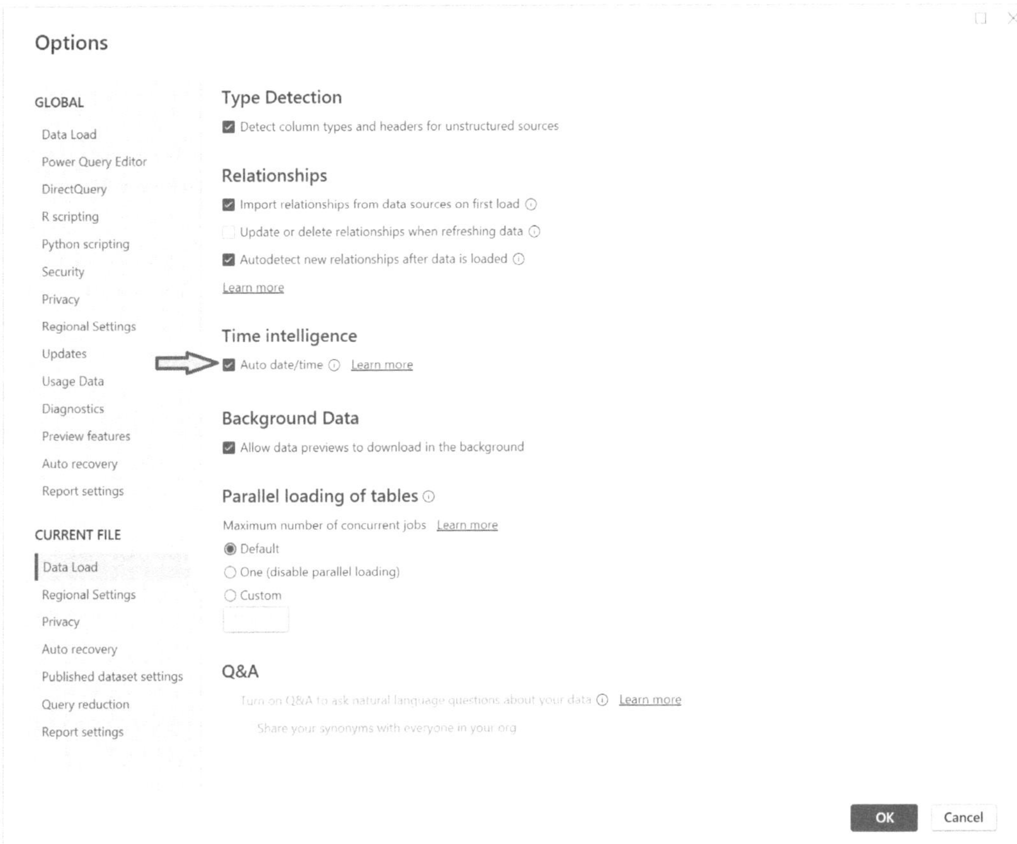

Figure 9.7: *Disabling Auto Data/Time Hierarchies*

By default, whatever you change in the report, the change is reflected immediately. This can be quite annoying when you need to create a report with multiple visuals, including slicers and other filtering elements, especially if you use the DirectQuery mode. For every change, Power BI sends a query to the data source. You can temporarily pause visuals. You can find this option in the Optimize ribbon in Power BI Desktop. Just select this ribbon and click the **`Pause Visuals`** button, as you can see in *Figure 9.8*:

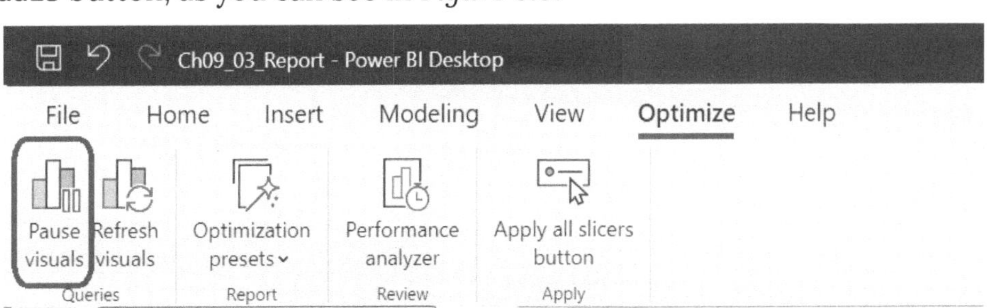

Figure 9.8: *Pausing Visuals*

You can refresh your visuals manually by using the Refresh visuals button at any convenient time.

There are other interesting options in this ribbon. The Optimization presets drill-down list is the shortcut for the Query reduction page, which you can find in the **File** > **Options and settings** > **Options** > **CURRENT FILE** section. If you select the **Customize** option in the Optimization presets drill-down list, you come to this page directly. The other two options are shortcuts for setting the options on this page. By default, the Interactivity option is selected. This means that all of the cross-filtering, cross-highlighting and slicer option selections cause a refresh of visuals immediately. This setting is probably the best for the Import mode of your data. The third option in the Optimization presets list is the Query reduction option. This option turns off cross-filtering and cross-highlighting and adds Apply button to the Filter pane if you use it. Query reduction setting is recommended for the DirectQuery mode.

As we mentioned, by clicking the Customize option in the Optimization presets list, you get to the Query reduction settings page. On this page, you can notice an information message telling you that instead of adding an **Apply** button to each slicer, it is recommended to add an **Apply all slicers** button to your report. You can implement this recommendation by clicking the last button, the **Apply all slicers** button, in the Optimize ribbon. You can also add this button from the Insert ribbon, Buttons drill-down list, where you can also add the **Clear all slicers** buttons. Then you must configure the added buttons like you configure other buttons in your reports. A little bit less work with designing the report is if you use a separate **Apply** button for each slicer. In the Query reduction options page, you select the **Add an Apply button to each individual slicer (not recommended)** check box. Although this is not recommended, it is a very quick and simple option. If you do not use too many slicers, you might prefer this option. After you select it, there is nothing more to do; the **Apply** button in each slicer just appears and works. *Figure* 9.9 shows a report with two slicers with separate **Apply** buttons:

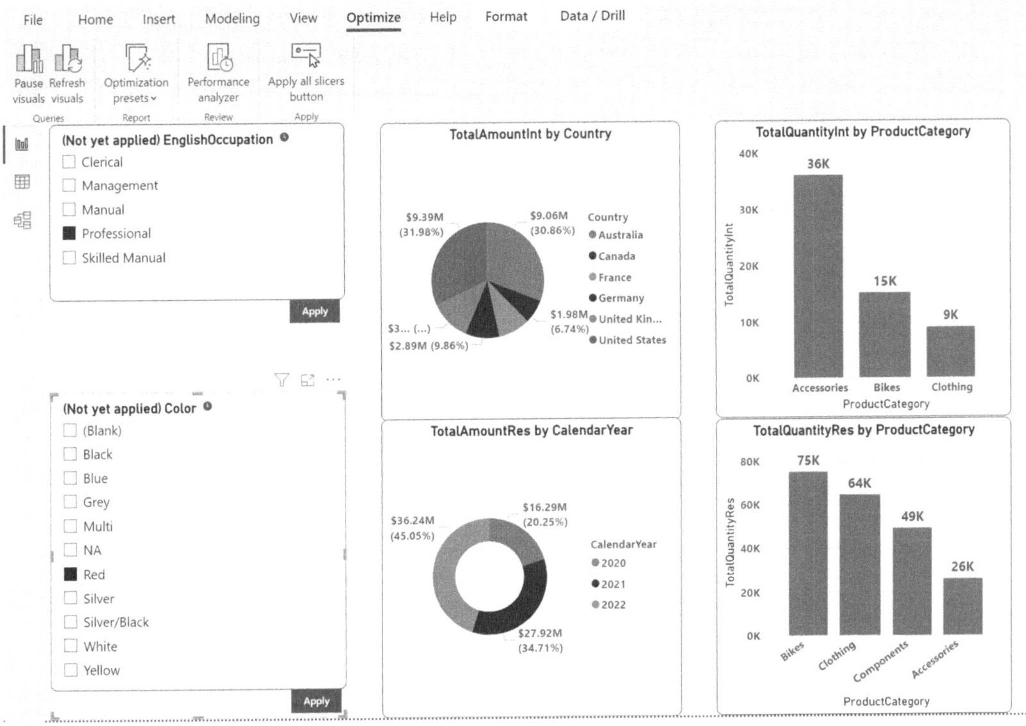

***Figure 9.9**: Using the Apply Button in Slicers*

As you can see, there were some selections made in the two slicers; however, none of the selections was applied yet. The **`Apply`** buttons are colored green, and in the header of the slicers, you can see the text (Not yet applied) added before the header and a clock icon after the header. Of course, you need to click the buttons in order to apply the filters, and the queries will be executed twice. If you implemented the **`Apply all slicers`** button, the queries would be executed once only. Therefore, let us use this option.

First, we need to clear the **Add an Apply** button to each individual slicer (not recommended) option. Then we can add the **Apply all slicers** from the Optimize or from the Insert ribbon and the **Clear all slicers** button from the Insert ribbon. Now you have to format these two buttons. Seems like a good trade, not that much work compared to adding the Apply button to each slicer individually option for an important performance gain. Initially, the Apply all slicers is disabled. It becomes enabled as soon as you select any slice in any of the slicers. The slicer with the selection gets the text (Not yet applied) added before the header and a clock icon after the header. *Figure* 9.10 shows a report on the **Apply all slicers** and **Clear all slicers** buttons, with selections in both slicers that were not implemented yet. Note that in Power BI Desktop, you have to use *Ctrl* and click for the button actions instead of just simple clicking:

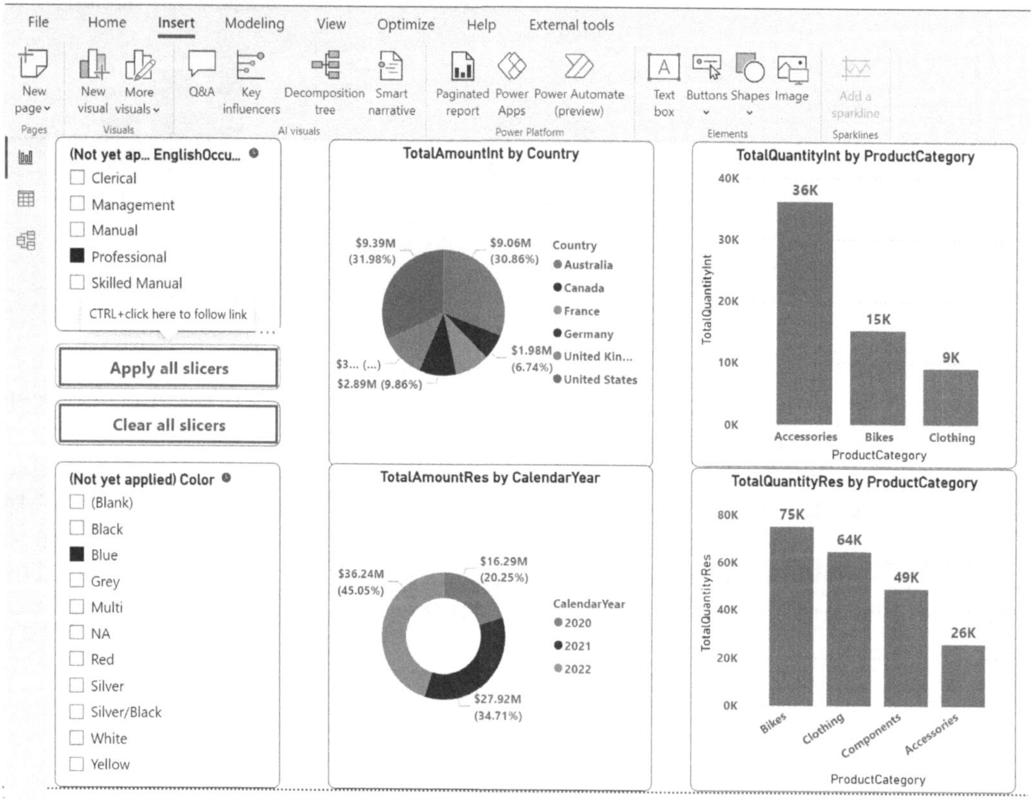

Figure 9.10: *Using the Apply All and Clear All Slicers Buttons*

There is one more button left in the Optimize ribbon, the Performance Analyzer button. This is a very powerful button. When you click it, the Performance Analyzer pane opens on the right side of the report, between the Filters and Visualizations panes. In this pane, you have three options. With the **Start Recording** button, you can start the recording of the performance of your visuals.

Then you can manually refresh them by selecting different slicers or cross-highlighting and cross-filtering options. You can use the **`Stop`** button to stop the recording. Once the recording starts, you can also use the Refresh visuals button to refresh all visuals in the report automatically, and the duration of the actions needed to refresh the visuals is recorded. In *Figure* 9.11, you can see the result of refreshing all of the visuals in the report. The worst performance was for the **`TotalQuantityRes`** by **`ProductCategory`** visual, with the longest duration in milliseconds:

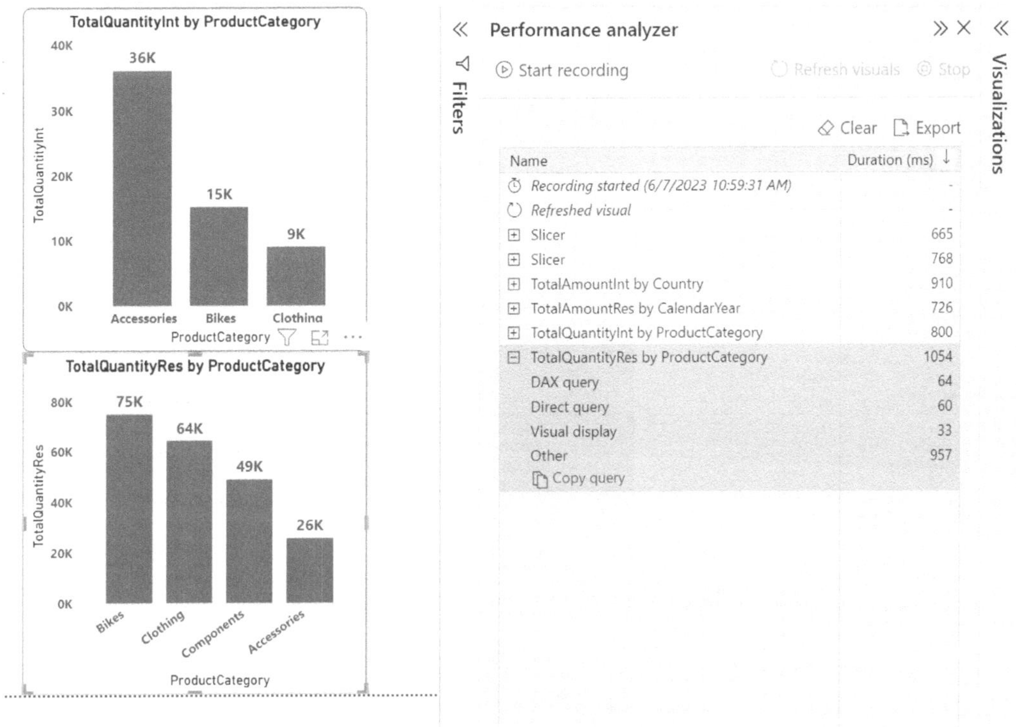

***Figure* 9.11**: *Performance Analyzer*

The recording for the mentioned visual is expanded. You can see that the visual used two queries – a DAX query and a Direct query to the source. Apparently, at least some tables in the dataset use the DirectQuery mode. You can copy the queries immediately by using the Copy query button under the expanded result for the visual. In our case, the source is SQL Server. Both DAX and T-SQL queries are copied to the clipboard. You can paste them into any text editor and inspect them. You can also use SQL Server Management Studio or Azure Data Studio, two free tools for SQL Server provided by Microsoft, to analyze in detail the T-SQL query. Both tools can generate a graphical execution plan. You can analyze the DAX query with the free community tool DAX Studio, which you can download from **https://daxstudio.org/**. *Figure* 9.12 shows the DAX Studio with the DAX query copied from the Performance analyzer results with the Query Plan window opened:

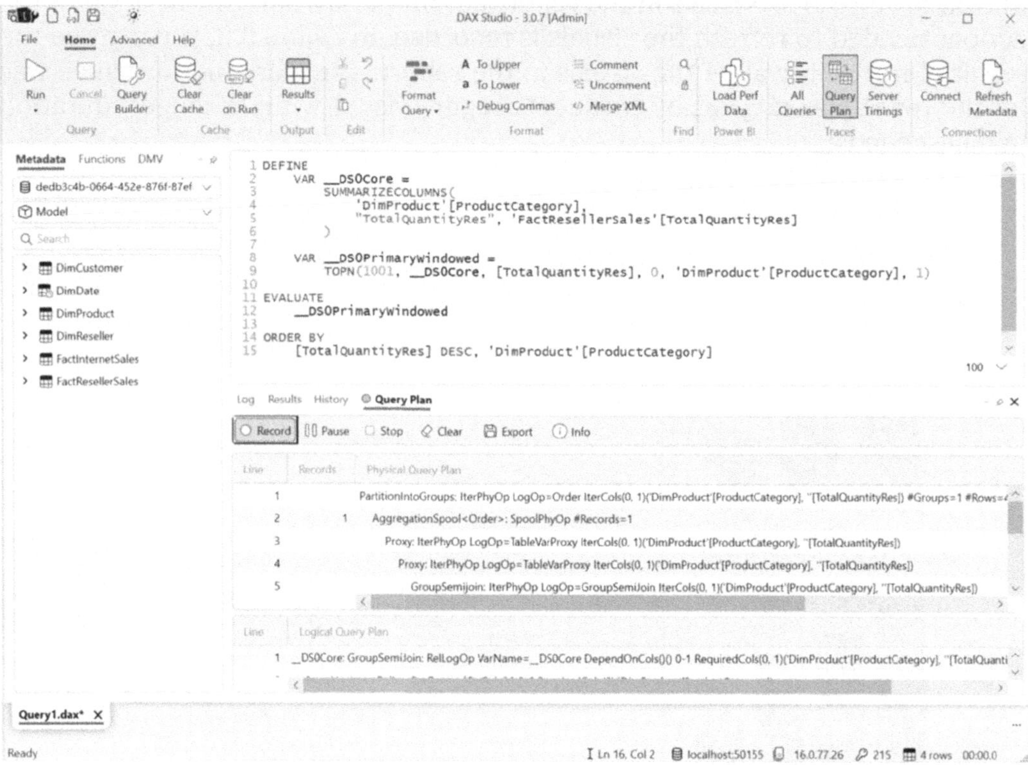

Figure 9.12: *Using Dax Studio to Analyze a Query Plan*

You can also export the results of the Performance analyzer in a JSON file. Then you can open this file with a text editor or even with Power Query in order to inspect all recorded queries.

Note that Power BI Desktop caches the result of the DirectQuery query. If you want to repeat performance measuring in completely the same conditions, you might want to close and reopen Power BI Desktop. You can also clear the cache with DAX Studio.

Going into details of query plans for T-SQL and DAX queries is well beyond the scope of this book. However, before finishing this section, we want to mention another small thing. When you create complicated measures in DAX, you can use variables for storing partial results in them. The following DAX code creates two measures, both showing year-to-year growth of sales:

```
NoVarISalesYoYGrowth = DIVIDE (
        (FactInternetSales[TotalAmountInt] -
        CALCULATE ( FactInternetSales[TotalAmountInt],
         PARALLELPERIOD ( DimDate[FullDateAlternateKey], -12, MONTH ) )
) ,
        CALCULATE ( FactInternetSales[TotalAmountInt],
          PARALLELPERIOD ( DimDate[FullDateAlternateKey], -12, MONTH ) )
 )

VarISalesYoYGrowth =
VAR SalesPriorYear =
        CALCULATE ( FactInternetSales[TotalAmountInt],
            PARALLELPERIOD ( DimDate[FullDateAlternateKey], -12, MONTH )
)
VAR SalesVariance =
        DIVIDE ( ( FactInternetSales[TotalAmountInt] - SalesPriorYear ),
                    SalesPriorYear )
RETURN
        SalesVariance
```

The first measure (**NoVarISalesYoYGrowth**) does not use variables; everything is calculated in a single, complex expression. The second measure (**VarISalesYoYGrowth**) uses variables to store partial results. Not only the second code is more readable and simpler to maintain, but it is also worth mentioning that the second code is even faster. Therefore, it is recommended to use DAX variables for complex calculations.

Let us add a final, small note on the performance of the reports. Having too many visuals in a report not only makes the report cluttered but also makes the report slower because all of them need to be processed when you open the report. For example, instead of multiple individual card visuals, you could use a single Table visual.

Aggregate and dual storage tables

From the Performance analyzer result, you could conclude that in the report we are optimizing, at least some tables were in DirectQuery mode. If we check the Model view, we can see that the **DimProduct** and **FactResellerSales** tables are in the DirectQuery mode. You can notice this is the diagram view, where the tables are marked with a quite thick blue line at the top of the rectangle for the table and in the Advanced part in the **`Properties`** pane for the table. You can click the **`Storage mode`** drop-down list to see the available options for the table, as you can see in *Figure* 9.13:

Figure 9.13: *Storage Modes for the FactInternetSales Table*

Of course, the most efficient option would be to change the storage mode to Import for all tables. However, you might get stuck in the DirectQuery mode for some really big, usually fact tables. In our example, we have used the DirectQuery mode for one fact and one dimension table.

From the Performance analyzer results, we could see that some visuals use DAX queries only, while some use both DAX and T-SQL queries. Of course, as soon as a table in the DirectQuery mode is used in a visual, you get, besides a DAX query, also a T-SQL query in the Performance analyzer recording for the visual. For example, the recording for refreshing the **`TotalQuantityInt`** by **`ProductCategory`** visual shows both, Direct query and DAX query. In this case, the bigger table, the fact table, is in the Power Pivot cache (imported), while the smaller table uses the DirectQuery mode and is queried from the SQL Server source with a T-SQL query. The question is whether we could improve the performance for this visual to query the cache only. But we do not want to import the **`DimProduct`** table because it is also used for the **`TotalQuantityRes`** by **`ProductCategory`** visual, which uses **`DimProduct`** and **`FactResellerSales`** tables. We do not want to import the fact table. Therefore, we want to have the **`DimProduct`** table in the DirectQuery mode in order to propagate the join between two tables to the source SQL Server.

How can we make a compromise between two different requests for two different visuals? We can set the dimension table to the Dual storage mode. This means that the table will be both cached and queried directly, depending on the needs of the visuals. In the model view, Properties pane, Advanced part, change the storage mode to Dual. In the pop-up window, you get a warning that this action might take some time. Just click **OK**. The importing of the data starts immediately. In the Model view, in the diagram, the blue line at the top of the **DimProduct** table becomes dashed, denoting that this is now a dual storage mode table.

We can go back to the Report view. In the Performance analyzer, we can clear the results from the previous refresh, start recording again and refresh the visuals. If we check the recording for the **TotalQuantityInt** by **ProductCategory** visual, we can notice that the DirectQuery part has gone. This visual is now fully refreshed from the cache.

The Dual mode looks very good. Actually, it seems even a bit too good initially. There is an important catch with the Dual mode. Imagine a situation when the table, in our case, the **dbo.DimProduct** table was already updated in the source SQL Server database, while the Power Pivot cache was not updated yet. Now we have two versions of the table in the same report. One visual could already show the new state, while the other visual could still use the old state. This problem is solvable in a very simple way if you use a data warehouse. Once you refresh the data in the data warehouse, you also refresh the Power BI cache, and the data is synchronized between both versions, cached, and queried, of the same table. Using the Dual mode for a data source that is updated frequently is not recommended. This is another good reason to implement a data warehouse for practically any long-term analytical solution.

Let us now focus on the **TotalAmountRes** by **CalendarYear** visual. This visual was also refreshed partially from the cache and partially with a query to the source database. The visual uses the imported dimension **DimDate**, and the fact table **FactResellerSales**, which is left in the DirectQuery storage mode. Of course, we still do not want to change the fact table storage mode. Imagine that this table is simply too big to import it. The visual aggregates data over calendar years. When you aggregate data over some groups, the number of rows lowers, and the size of the aggregated table becomes smaller. In Power BI, we can create aggregate tables.

We need to switch to the Power Query window. Then we copy the **FactResellerSales** query and rename it to copied query to **FactResellerSalesAgg**. Then we have to implement the Group By transformation, which can be found in the Transform menu. Name the new column **TotalAmountRes** and sum the **SalesAmount** over the **OrderDateKey**, as you can see in *Figure 9.14*:

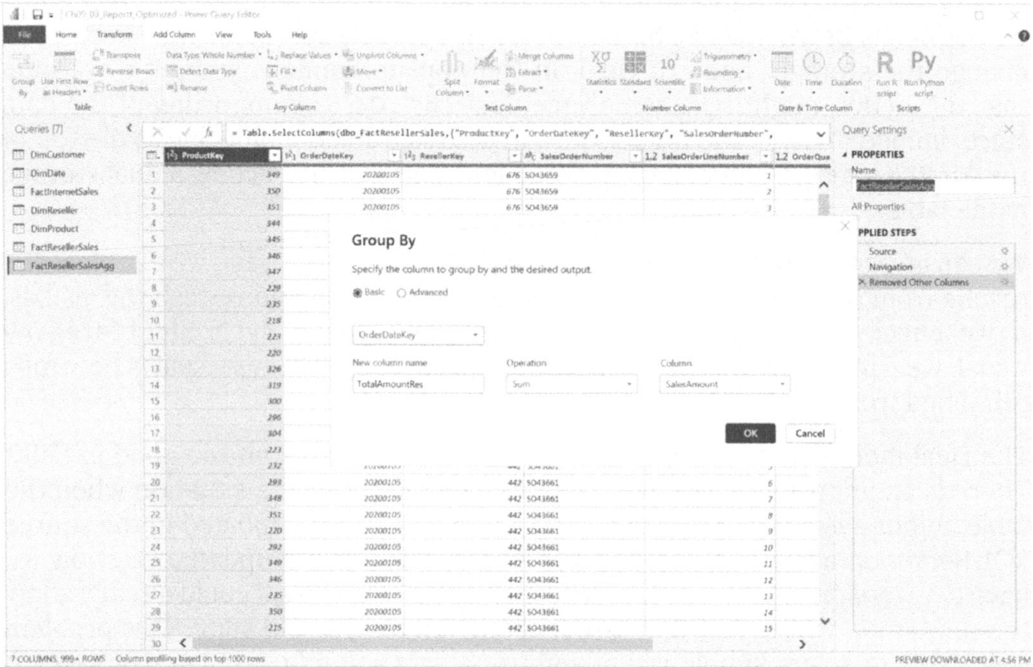

***Figure 9.14**: Aggregating Reseller Sales in Power Query*

Before finishing with the Power query, make sure that you have exactly the same data types for the source columns in the **FactResellerSales** query and the aggregated **FactResellerSalesAgg** query. If the data types do not match, you will not be able to manage the aggregations properly. In our case, the source, and the destination **OrderDateKey** columns are both of the **Whole Number** data types. However, the source **SalesAmount** column in the **FactResellerSales** table uses the Fixed decimal number data type, while the **TotalAmountRes** column in the aggregated table uses the **Decimal Number** data type. You have to change this data type to a Fixed decimal number, as you can see in *Figure 9.15*:

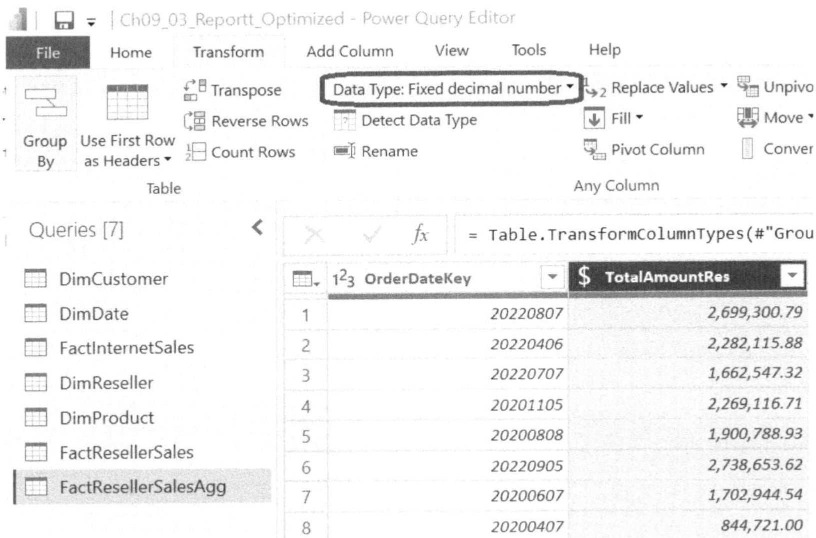

***Figure 9.15**: Correcting the Data type of the Aggregated Column*

Close the Power Query window and apply changes. Then in Power BI Desktop, in the Model view, change the storage mode for this new table to Import. Create a relationship from the **OrderDateKey** in this table to the **DateKey** in the **DimDate** table. The new aggregated fact table must be on the many sides of the relationship, and the Cross-filter direction must be **Single**, as *Figure 9.16* shows:

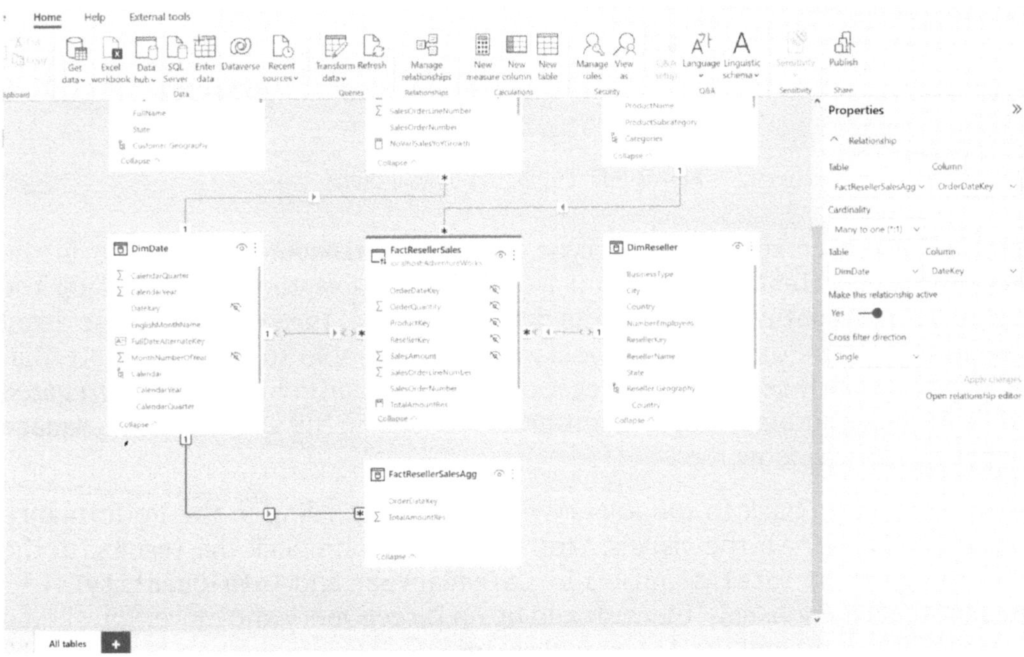

***Figure 9.16**: Aggregating Reseller Sales in Power Query*

After the relationship is properly established, in the Model view, right-click the **FactResellerSalesAgg** table and select the **Manage aggregations** option. In the pop-up window, set up the aggregations, as you can see in *Figure 9.17*:

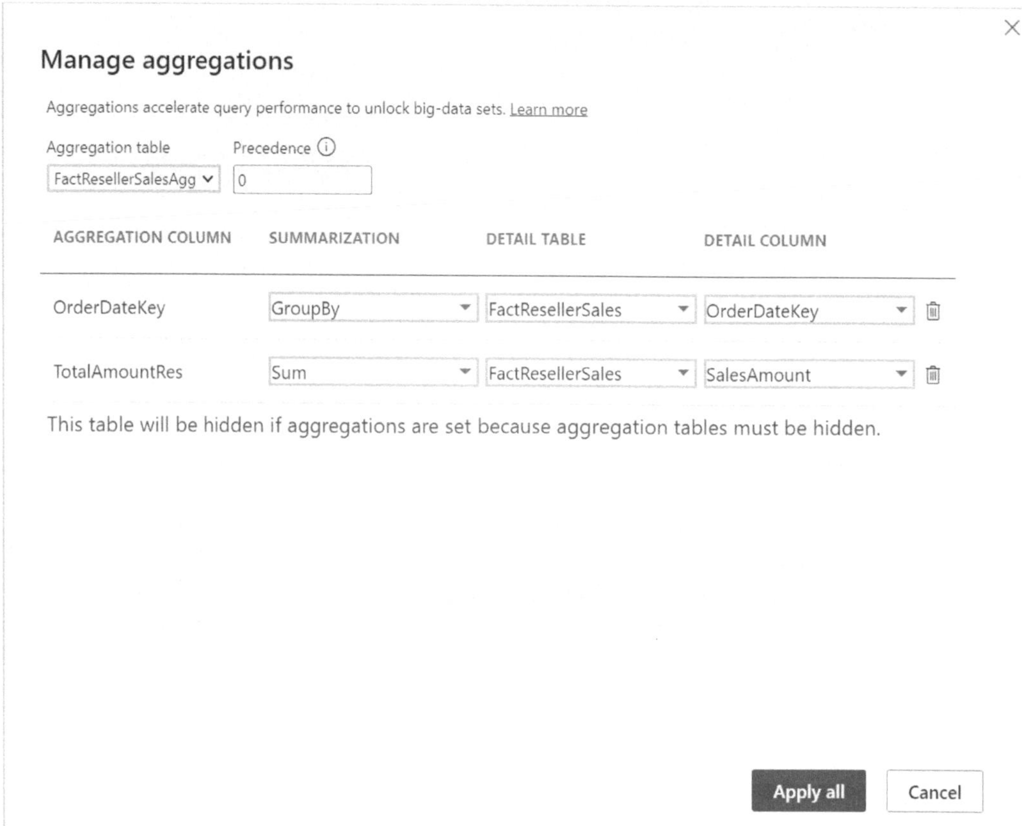

Figure 9.17: *Managing Aggregations*

If you did not correct the data type for the **TotalAmountRes** column in the **FactResellerSalesAgg** query, you would not be able to properly set up the detail **SalesAmount** column from the detail **FactResellerSales** table. The detail column would be dimmed, and you would not be able to select it. Note that after you properly set up the aggregation and the detail columns, the aggregated table becomes automatically hidden, as it is written in the warning in the **Manage aggregations** window.

Now you can go back to the Report view. Start recording in the Performance analyzer and refresh the visuals. Stop recording and check the results. In the recording for the **TotalAmountRes** by **CalendarYear** and **TotalQuantityInt** by **ProductCategory** visuals, there should be no DirectQuery and more; you should see the DAX query only, as *Figure 9.18* shows:

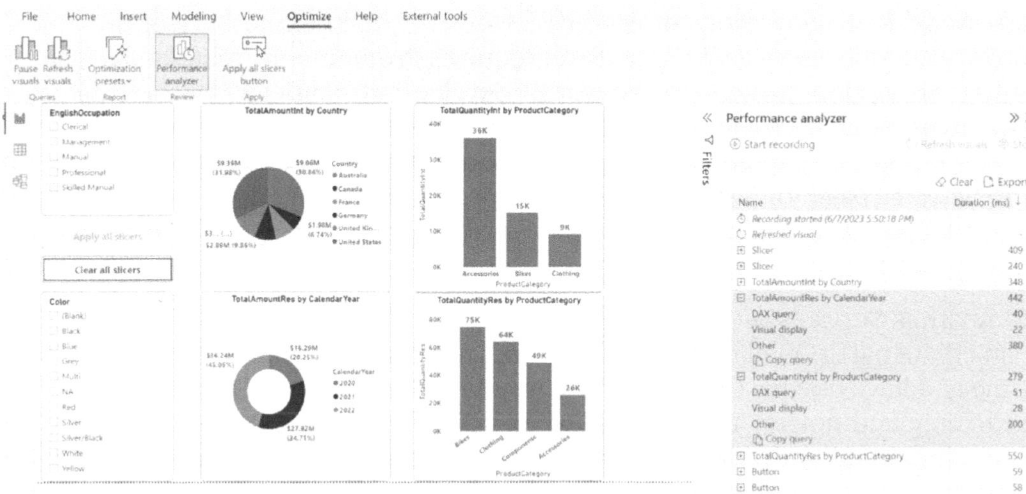

Figure 9.18: *No Direct Queries after Optimization*

There are many more options for optimization. There is no place for everything in a single book. We are giving just short descriptions of some features and links to the sources where you can learn more about a specific optimization option.

In Power BI Service, you can create automatic aggregations for DirectQuery datasets and also work in composite models that use both Import and DirectQuery tables. Automatic aggregations are simple to use; however, there is a lot of knowledge behind them. They use machine learning to find the best possible aggregations. Not every aggregation is a good one. If aggregation consists of one million source rows, then reading a single row of aggregation is a million times faster than reading the original row. If an aggregation consists of a single row, then this aggregation even can slow down the reports only because they occupy additional space. Automatic aggregations are available for the following sources:

- On-premises SQL Server 2019 or later
- Azure SQL Database
- Azure Synapse Dedicated SQL pool
- Snowflake
- Databricks
- Amazon Redshift
- Google BigQuery

You can learn more about automatic aggregations at **https://learn.microsoft.com/en-us/power-bi/enterprise/aggregations-auto**. Automatic aggregations are available in all versions of Power BI. However, the next feature of the Power BI Service, the Query caching feature, requires Premium or Embedded capacity. With this option turned on, Power BI Service automatically cached data for DirectQuery tables the first time when a user opens a report. Caching is user and dataset-specific. Like automatic aggregations, you also turn on query caching on the Settings page for a specific dataset. You can learn more about query caching at **https://learn.microsoft.com/en-us/power-bi/connect-data/power-bi-query-caching**.

In Analysis Services on-premises or in the cloud and in Power BI Premium, you can create partitioned tables. For example, you can partition a big fact table over time and have one partition per year. The data probably changes for the current year only and not for the previous years. When you refresh the data, you can refresh the current partition only, and thus speed up the refresh substantially. You can learn more about tabular model partitioning at **https://learn.microsoft.com/en-us/analysis-services/tabular-models/create-and-manage-tabular-model-partitions?view=asallproducts-allversions**.

If you use SQL Server version 2016 and later, Azure SQL Database, or Azure SQL Managed Instance for your data warehouse, you can also use table partitioning in every version of your database management system. It makes sense to use the same partitioning logic in your data warehouse as in your tabular model. You can learn more about SQL Server partitioning at **https://learn.microsoft.com/en-us/sql/relational-databases/partitions/partitioned-tables-and-indexes?view=sql-server-ver16**.

If you have Power BI Premium capacity, you can also use hybrid tables. A hybrid table uses one partition in the DirectQuery storage mode and one or more partitions in the Import mode. If you partitioned over time, then the DirectQuery mode partition is probably the last one with the current data. Because this partition uses DirectQuery mode, you can see the latest changes in the source data immediately when you refresh a visual. You can learn more about hybrid tables and dataset storage modes at **https://learn.microsoft.com/en-us/power-bi/connect-data/service-dataset-modes-understand**.

For DirectQuery tables and partitions, it is important to understand how to optimize the source as well. First of all, you must have some database management system at the source. There is no optimization for CSV, XML, JSON or other flat files. This optimization is source-specific. If your source database management system is SQL Server, you have to know how to optimize SQL Server databases. For example, here are a few options to consider for SQL Server optimization:

- If you use a data warehouse that is refreshed occasionally and then used for read-only purposes, then you should definitely consider using columnstore indexes. Columnar storage in SQL Server is the same storage as the power BI datasets and Analysis Service Tabular databases use. However, in SQL Server, the data is on disk. You are not limited to memory. You can handle any size of data.

- You can mimic aggregated tables in Power BI with indexed views in SQL Server. The view is a stored query. By creating a clustered index on a view, you materialize the view. Unfortunately, indexed views have many limitations. A very important limitation is that SQL Server uses an indexed view instead of a query it gets from a client, in our case Power BI, only if the query in the view definition completely matches the query that it gets. Because the queries created with query folding are extremely complicated, the view definition becomes complex as well. Therefore, we suggest that you use manual source queries in Power Query. Of course, these queries should aggregate the data; using an indexed view based on detailed data would make no sense, as it would not speed up the query.
- If your data source is also frequently updated, then optimization becomes very complex. In SQL Server, you might decide to use memory-optimized tables to get the best possible performance. If you use regular SQL Server tables, then we suggest you consider using read Committed Snapshot or Snapshot transaction isolation levels in order to lower the locking contention with the transactions that update the data.
- For queries that select small portions of source data and queries that include a quite selective `WHERE` clause, consider creating non-clustered indexes in SQL Server to support them.

Even this bulleted list is still a very brief overview of optimization options in SQL Server. As you can see, performance tuning is not simple. However, we have many tools and options in Power BI and in SQL Server that help us create a fast analytical solution.

Conclusion

Optimizing Power BI is not a simple task. The most important part starts by optimizing the data model. Use star schema. Limit the amount of data you are loading in your dataset. Push the calculations as down the data pipeline as possible. If possible, do the calculations in source queries; if not, use Power Query Formula Language (M); only if this is not possible, use DAX for calculations. Create natural hierarchies and measures. Disable automatic creation of date hierarchies. For advanced data science analyses, prepare an appropriate sample of data. You should use query folding as much as possible. However, on some occasions, manual source queries can still perform better.

There are many options to improve the performance of reports as well. The Performance analyzer tool in Power BI Desktop can become very handy when you need to find out why some visuals are slow. Use dual and aggregate tables when appropriate. Power BI Service has some additional options and tools for performance tuning.

In the next chapter, which is also the last chapter of this book, we will introduce how you manage your Power BI datasets and reports after you deploy them.

Key terms

- **Query folding**: The feature of Power Query that helps you to push the processing of the query down the pipeline as much as possible.
- **Natural hierarchies**: The hierarchies that stem from real life and source systems.
- **Query reduction**: An option to send fewer queries to the source when you develop your reports with multiple visuals.
- **Performance analyzer**: A tool in Power BI Desktop to record the performance of your visuals.
- **Dual storage**: A storage mode when a table uses the DirectQuery mode for some queries and Import mode for others, and the table is thus logically duplicated.
- **Aggregate table**: A table with aggregated data that can be used with some visuals instead of the source table with the data on the lowest level of granularity.

CHAPTER 10
Deploying, Maintaining and Securing Power BI Assets

Introduction

This is the last chapter of the book. We would like to congratulate the readers for having come so far. Rather than worrying about remembering every single detail written in this book, the reader should try to remember general principles for creating data systems of good quality. Some of the principles that were listed in this book are as follows:

- Building the logical star schema
- Keeping a good naming convention throughout the data system
- Ensuring automated connectivity from data sources to end reports
- Keeping things well-organized and simple for as long as possible

After understanding the general principles of creating a good data system, again rather than focusing on the detailed implementation of every technology and capability we have discussed in this book, the reader should focus on remembering what is possible with the tools we have described. After understanding things on those two levels, the reader can focus on implementing technologies that were clearly described through guided exercises that were included in this book. This should help the reader get some practice and make him more proficient when facing challenges in real-life scenarios. The reader should then try to implement techniques that were mentioned in lesser detail, as well as find the concrete requirements and focus on solving those.

Because of the ever-changing interface, some of the instructions or figures in this book may become outdated. Excel is more stable than Power BI. Power BI Service and Power BI Desktop are rapidly changing. Nevertheless, we believe that users can overcome the possible differences, perhaps with the use of internet searching when the challenge arises. Changing interfaces bring frustration to both students and professional developers. Microsoft might be prone to changes in order to keep the internet community and influencers interested in constant novelty, but there is a case to be made for the importance of stability. When you invest in BI system, you would first and foremost expect stability. All the novelty comes long after stability is achieved, because if the system is not working as expected, the new features don't work - none of the features work. We should, therefore, as professional developers of BI systems, always strive for stability first. With a stable environment, everything else becomes possible. When an organization reaches a certain level of maturity, it can invest in advanced features and data science to get the most valuable BI insights. But again, that comes after a stable environment is achieved.

Stability should, therefore, be our first goal, and to achieve stability, we have to build the data system so that it is easily maintainable. All of those principles we have pointed out will come in handy. In this chapter, we are going to introduce some discussions on how to keep our BI systems maintainable, as well as introduce some other technical instructions on deploying Power BI systems.

There is also a point to be made about data privacy and security. These topics should be important to any organization. There are now many rules and regulations in place in different countries that organizations have to follow to avoid running into problems with regulatory agencies. But that is not the only issue. Organizations have to keep their data hidden from their competition, as well as from cybercrime. Data breaches are increasingly a threat in the modern world and can financially ruin a company. We should take a careful approach regarding data privacy and security in an organization, and we are going to provide some tips.

Structure

In this chapter, we will discuss the following topics:

- Well-maintained BI system
    - Organizing fields into display folders
    - Forming the naming conventions
    - Keeping the Selection pane organized

- Gateways for on-premises data sources and scheduled refresh
- Power BI Service security
    - Tenant-level security settings
- Row-level security
    - Defining the roles in Power BI Desktop
    - Assigning users to roles in Power BI Service
- Power BI Service Apps for end-user experience

Well-maintained BI system

Every part of the BI system, that is the whole data system for reporting, should be well-maintained. If our development is sloppy, we can expect increasing problems as we add complexity to the system. Complexity is added as the system is scaled, as new requirements are introduced, and as business rules change. Therefore, building the data system should always come with maintainability as a goal while expecting and considering the expansion of the system.

We can probably already see how a multitude of end users connecting to all the data sources in an uncontrollable manner, while developing their own reports, each following their own development principles, can be chaotic. It is impossible to assume that such an approach will bring high-quality data solutions, even though this approach is being strongly advertised. Such a development can be described as a stage within an organization before the adoption of an organized BI environment. As an organization, we should move away from a free-for-all approach as soon as a suitable budget for BI projects is introduced. That is, once the management reaches a decision to support and finance the BI system development.

The next stage is the one where the company is adopting the BI in an organized manner, where the company is introducing the rules that will help with the maintainability of data system. These rules should be constructed and maintained by quality assurance engineers that overview the work of developers to ensure compliance with the highest standards. Such an approach requires larger investments and can be slower, but the benefits in the long run are excellent. We will take a look into some of the tips for keeping a well-maintained system with focus on the BI visualization tools.

Organizing fields into display folders

All the fields in our data model can be organized into display folders in Power BI's Model view. This can help in the long-term organization of our data model. We can create a folder by going to the Model view and selecting any field in the **Data** pane. Under the Properties pane, we can notice the Display folder property. We can write any name for the display folder for it to appear in the Data pane. It is encouraged that readers define their own naming convention, or they can follow our suggestion and use these display folders as follows:

- 0_Measures
- 1_Hiearchies
- 2_Columns
- 3_CalculatedColumns

Readers can add more complexity if they find it necessary, perhaps by creating a distinct display folder for columns of different data types, or by further dividing measures into basic and advanced measures, or into supporting measures. However, we find the ones we listed enough for providing organization. To add a column to a display folder, or to add a display folder's property to a column, we can go to the Model view. We can select a column in a table and write **2_Columns** under the Display folder in the **Properties** pane. You will immediately notice that the new display folder is added to the Data pane. Additional columns can be added to this display folder by simply dragging-and-dropping. Alternatively, we can select several fields by using Ctrl + left-click or Shift + left-click. Even when multiple fields are selected, we can still edit the Display folder property. If the need arises, we could also nest the display folders. To do that, find the Display folder property and write the first folder's name, followed by the backslash, and then enter the second folder's name. It should be written like this: First folder\Second folder. We can see the usage of display folders in the Power BI's Data pane on the right side, as shown in *Figure 10.1*:

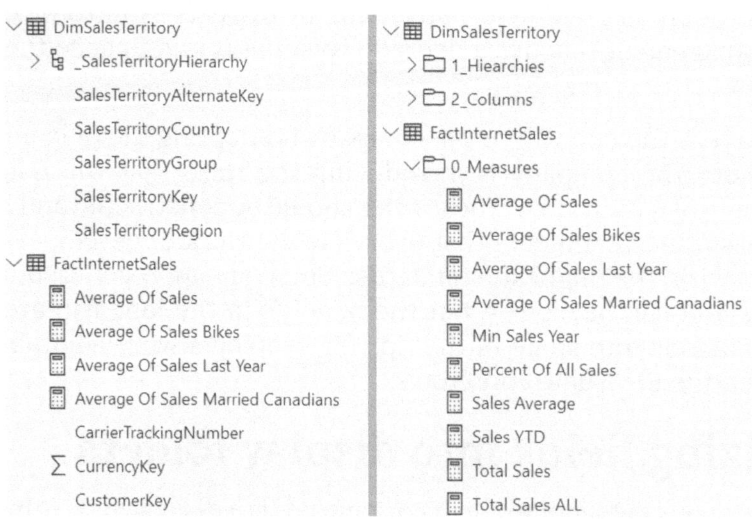

***Figure 10.1**: Using display folders to organize fields*

We can see that the organization is much better when using display folders. Now imagine the effect of keeping things neatly organized throughout the whole data system for reporting. The effect is huge, and it is especially important when development moves from one person to another. When we inherit a neatly organized data system for reporting, our learning curve is exponentially shorter. We can use display folders when designing tabular models in Visual Studio as well. Selecting any field, we can modify the Display Folder property in Properties Window. If the Properties Window is not visible, we can display the window by going to the View tab in Visual Studio's upper ribbon and selecting Properties Window in the drop-down list. We can also edit the display folders for multiple selected fields.

Forming the naming conventions

We have already stressed the importance of naming conventions and we would like to stress it again. Naming conventions not only add organization to the data warehouse but also allow for better traceability of data. Imagine a scenario that we might be facing as developers. We have several large data sources, similar to the ones described in *Figure 2.6 in Chapter 2, Acquiring and Transforming Data from Multiple Sources*. In addition, we have a data warehouse with 15 fact tables and 12-dimension tables. We might be taking care of 12 Power BI reports deployed on Power BI Service, each of which consists of 10-25 report pages.

An end user reports a problem by sending a screenshot of the visualization that is not working properly and by loosely describing what is wrong, along with the name of the report. It is our job as developers to trace the data back from the measure displayed in the visualization to the data source and all the areas in between. Those can be semantic models, any table in a data warehouse, or in a staging area. It is possible for a mistake to reside anywhere, even in procedures that may be forming these areas. The complications are increasingly significant if we were not present during their development, and we inherited the data system. Good naming conventions are a must-have. Good naming conventions, along with properly kept documentation, can help the developer quickly make sense of what is going on. They should help end users in understanding what they are viewing, removing the need to rename any fields in BI tools. Perhaps, even removing the need to use Titles and Subtitles in visualizations to convey additional information. Ideally, we should not be changing field names at all in BI tools. The names should be properly defined when we design the data warehouse, solutions in Power Query, or semantic models.

Naming conventions for data warehouses are past the topics covered in this book. For ideas, one can take a look into the naming convention of **AdventureWorksDW2019** and adapt it to suit their own environment. We are going to focus on naming conventions for measures. We have already seen some recommendations in this book, some measures contained spaces and others did not. The advantage of using spaces is the end users' experience, as the measures with spaces have better readability for end users. Also, words with spaces wrap better in Power BI when the Text wrap option is turned on during the formatting of the visualization. There is a decision to be made when naming measures, that is, whether we are going to use technical names or descriptive names. Let us take a look at a very simple example, with the part of a data model, as shown in *Figure 10.2:*

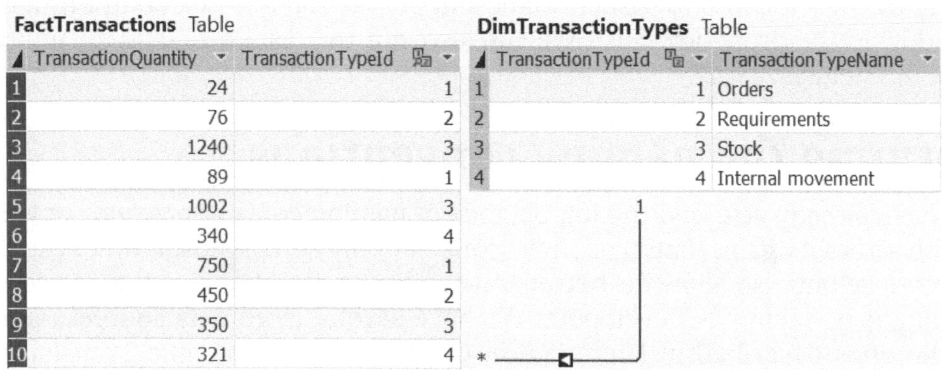

FactTransactions Table

	TransactionQuantity	TransactionTypeId
1	24	1
2	76	2
3	1240	3
4	89	1
5	1002	3
6	340	4
7	750	1
8	450	2
9	350	3
10	321	4

DimTransactionTypes Table

	TransactionTypeId	TransactionTypeName
1	1	Orders
2	2	Requirements
3	3	Stock
4	4	Internal movement

Figure 10.2*: Example of the part of a data model*

The environment we are seeing is a tabular model in Visual Studio. We can see the two tables, the first one is a fact table with data on item transactions. Imagine that this table is much larger, possibly containing millions of rows of data, showing the daily status for each of the items in the company's portfolio. We can see that it contains transactions of different types. We can also see the dimension table that describes the transaction type's names. Furthermore, we can see the relationship between tables; it is a one-to-many relationship filtering from dimension to the fact table, as we would expect in a logical star schema.

The sum of transaction quantity by itself would not produce very meaningful results, as adding together orders, which is the quantity of items coming into the company, and requirements, which is the quantity of items leaving the company, will not tell us much. However, we can still create a base measure that summarizes the **`TransactionQuantity`** column. The base measure will be filtered by **`CALCULATE`** function in sequent measures. We have a decision to make here on how we are going to name this base measure. We can go with "SUM Transaction Quantity", or we can go with "Transaction quantity SUM". The first option is closer to natural language, but the second option might be better for searching and sorting. The second option ensures that all the measures starting with the transaction will be sorted together, whether they calculate "Transaction quantity AVG", "Transaction quantity STDEV", or even "Transaction value SUM", which is very likely to be another column in the fact table. We must also decide what, if anything, are we going to abbreviate and in what cases will we use upper-case letters.

We may have another decision to make. SUM function is so common that we may choose to skip the word altogether. So, let us say we will create a measure with the following name and formula: **`Transaction quantity := SUM ( FactTransactions[TransactionQuantity] )`**. Remember, in the Visual Studio environment, we have to use := instead of = to define measures. Also, if this was a real-world case, we would be hiding the base measure, as per suggestion, that every field not immediately necessary for the end user should be hidden. After the base measure is created, we have got another decision to make, that is, if we are going to name the rest of the measures using technical or descriptive names. Technical names are much better for the developer's ability to trace data throughout the data system, while descriptive names will be much more pleasant for end users. Examples for technical names are placed on the left side, while descriptive names are on the right side, as shown in *Figure 10.3*:

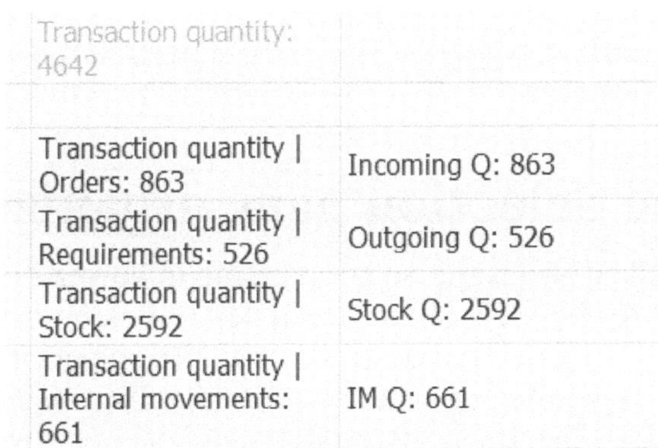

Figure 10.3: *Measures with technical and descriptive names*

These are examples of formulas, either of which could be used to calculate the first measure. By following the same logic, we could calculate the rest of them:

```
Transaction quantity > Orders :=
CALCULATE ( [Transaction quantity], FactTransactions[TransactionTypeId]
= 1 )
Transaction quantity > Orders :=
CALCULATE (
    [Transaction quantity],
    DimTransactionTypes[TransactionTypeName] = "Orders"
```

The technical names on the right describe clearly how the measure is calculated. Let us say we have established that SUM can be omitted. It is very clear which column the measure is calculated from. By the usage of spaces, we can immediately notice if a field is a measure or a column. The ">" symbol is used to indicate filtering, let us say we have established the meaning for that symbol in the naming convention. However, end users might not be happy with technical names. On the right side, we have very descriptive names, such as quantity incoming to our company, outgoing from the company, and stock. In addition, we have abbreviated "IM" for internal movements and "Q" for quantity. Let us assume these abbreviations were established in agreement with the end users and are understood in our company.

We will probably going to have to balance between technical and descriptive names. Luckily, we can add Description to fields, in Visual Studio under the Properties Window, and in Power BI's Model view under the Properties pane. End users and developers can see the descriptions in the Report view's Data pane, once they hover over the field, as shown in *Figure 10.4*:

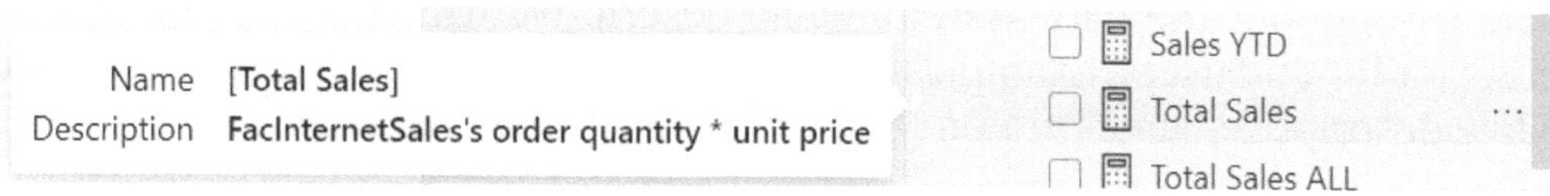

Figure 10.4: *Description can be used to provide additional information or an alternative name to the measure*

Keeping the Selection pane organized

We have already talked about the Selection pane in Power BI Desktop. It can be displayed by going to the View tab in the upper ribbon and selecting Selection. This will display the Selection pane and show all the objects in a report page in a hierarchical order depending on which one will be displayed above the other in a canvas. Usually, the objects on the report page will not cover each other, and if they do, several of them will usually be hidden with the help of bookmarks. As we have stated, bookmarks can be used to switch between two visualizations occupying the same space in the canvas.

But even if the objects do not cover each other, the order in the **`Selection`** pane can still matter. This can happen because of visual headers or header icons. If we can remember, these will be displayed above the visualization when the visualization's title is turned off. If the first visualization is below the second in the canvas and, at the same time, it is listed below the second in the Selection pane, whenever we hover over the first visualization, we will not see header icons. The icons will appear, but the second visualization will cover them. This problem is non-existent when titles are turned on. However, we probably will not be using titles for all of the visualizations, but rather mostly for charts of different types.

In a standard 16:9 canvas size, we are likely not going to use more than three rows of visualizations. The first row will often have some type of heading, which may contain slicers, cards with important information, and text boxes. The second row usually contains KPIs and a couple of charts. The third row may contain charts and matrices or tables. The KPIs in the second row could be three small objects like cards one below the other.

Hence, we should remember this order as a good practice: The bottom visualizations in the canvas should be listed at the top of the **Selection** pane, the middle should be placed in the middle, and the top visualizations in the canvas should be listed at the bottom of the **Selection** pane. The order from left-to-right does not seem to matter; even when using on-object interaction, the buttons on the right of the object ignore the order in the **Selection** pane. We suggest, for simplicity, putting the leftmost visualization in a row of visualizations at the top. By this logic, the bottom-left visualization in the canvas will be listed as the first in the **Selection** pane, while the top-right visualization will be listed last.

Sometimes we can group visualizations together when we want them to act as a single object. Maybe we want to add a couple of cards or KPIs next to the chart and provide the group with a common background. We may also use groups for organizational purposes; however, we have to remember that when we select the grouped visualizations on the canvas, we select the whole group with the first left-click and the single visualization only with the second left-click. With this in mind, we do suggest using groups only after the majority of report development is finished; otherwise, the necessity of double-clicking may bring frustration. We can use descriptive names of groups, such as **KPIs** or **Heading** pane to name groups of visualizations. However, when we run out of ideas for descriptive names, we may simply use their locations on the canvas. Group names such as **Bottom row** and **Middle-left row** serve the purpose of organization well enough.

The last thing we should mention is naming each individual visualization. If the visualization's title is turned on, the visualization's name in the Selection pane will be the same as the name written in the title. But many of the visualization types, such as tables, matrices, and slicers will often be placed without a title. We should use descriptive names for those. For example, every slicer that is added to the canvas is automatically named Slicer, regardless of what field we add to it. **Slicers** rarely use titles, as the attribute or hierarchy they are containing is already displayed by turning on the Slicer header option, which is a distinct formatting option from Title. We can then freely add the attribute to their name in the Selection pane by double-clicking the object name. We can use names such as Slicer **CalendarYear** or **Slicer SalesTrtHrh**.

Matrices and tables are also often used without titles. If a single matrix or table exists on a report page, the most descriptive name will simply be **Matrix** or **Table**. However, if there are multiple objects of the same visualization type, we can name them in a similar descriptive sense as with slicers. We can also use groups within groups, so even if all the slicers are in the Heading pane group, along with other objects, they can be in the Slicers group as well. Organizing objects in a neat manner after we finish the report page will help a lot if we have to return to the report page much later to add additional features or to fix an issue end users are having.

Gateways for on-premises data sources and scheduled refresh

Often, we are going to use on-premises data sources in our BI tools, whether we are building composite models and have a flat file in a remote folder location on the company's network, or when we have a connection to the on-premises data warehouse. Once we deploy a Power BI Desktop report that is based on on-premises data sources to Power BI Service, we will only be able to see the data that was available the last time we refreshed the data model inside Power BI Desktop. We cannot schedule a refresh because we have not set up the gateway. Gateways allow for the communication between the on-premises system and Power BI Service environment. If we have connected Power Desktop to tabular model deployed to SQL Server Analysis Services, we will only see a grey screen on a published report without a gateway.

To create a gateway, we must first install the **`On-premises data gateway`** application. The preferred method to download the gateway application is from Power BI Service, although we can also find it by internet searching and by links provided in the official documentation. On the upper-right side of Power BI Service, there are a couple of options. We can select the Download option with the downward arrow symbol. This brings up the drop-down window where we can select **`Data Gateway`**. We are directed to a website that offers the selection of the gateway mode. Another possibility is to download the gateway from the following link: **https://go.microsoft.com/fwlink/?LinkId=820925&clcid=0x409**.

There are two modes to choose from: Standard mode and personal mode. The Standard mode offers more functionalities, including support for DirectQuery and live connections to Analysis Services. It works with more cloud services and allows access for multiple users per data source. On the other hand, the personal mode works for Power BI and can be run by users who are not administrators, using their credentials.

We may choose the standard mode, which downloads the **`GatewayInstall`** application. If we have already downloaded the gateway application from the link provided, we can choose the mode during the installation process in the second interface window after the general overview. The recommended mode is the standard mode. However, if we have chosen the mode from the website, we are only given one option, which is to select the installation path. The default path is **C:\Program Files\On-premises data gateway**. After selecting **I accept the terms of use and privacy statement**, we have to click Install. In the next step, after installation, we can provide the email address to use with the gateway. We can use the one that we are using with Power BI Service. After signing in, we can select **Register a new gateway on this computer**.

In the next step, we have several inputs. We can define **New on-premises data gateway name and recovery key**. The first option is the name of the gateway instance. This will usually contain the server's or computer's name and can be used to differentiate if we are hosting reports from multiple on-premises systems. Whatever we write here will appear under the name of the gateway cluster in Power BI Service. The recovery key is used if we want to modify the existing gateway - that is, if we would have selected the option **Migrate, restore, or takeover an existing gateway** in the previous installation's interface window. We can add the recovery key, which we will surely remember, and then select **Configure**. A message will be displayed indicating that our gateway is up and running, as shown in *Figure 10.5*:

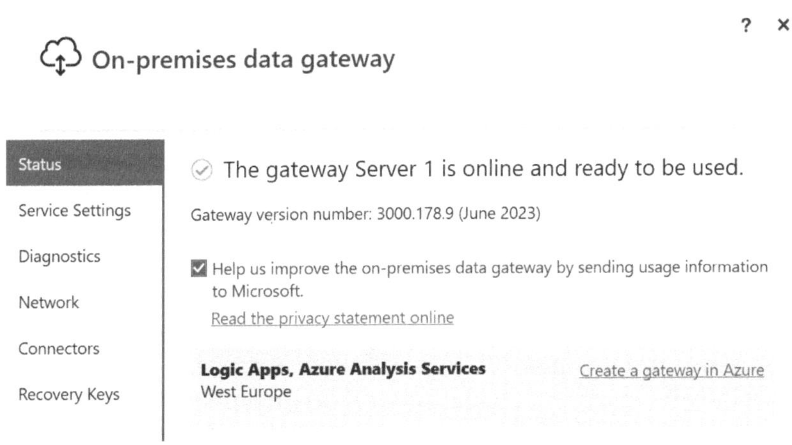

Figure 10.5: *Gateway successfully installed*

After the gateway has been successfully installed, we need to set it up by going to Power BI Service. We can check both the gateway settings and the schedule refresh for each individual dataset that was published along with the Power BI report. We can do this by selecting the workspace we have published the report to on the left ribbon of Power BI Service, and then by finding the dataset, hovering over it, and selecting More options with the icon representing three dots, as shown in *Figure 10.6*. Please note that we should not be selecting the report itself, but rather the dataset. Selecting the icon offers a drop-down list with several options, where we can select **Settings**. Alternatively, we can select the middle icon labeled Schedule refresh to open **Settings**. The leftmost icon will refresh the data once the gateway is properly set up:

Figure 10.6: *More options on the Power BI dataset*

Under **Settings**, we can see two sections that we can enlarge: **Gateway connections** and **Refresh**. Under the **Gateway connection** section, we will notice the status **Not configured correctly** and an error **You have no personal gateways installed**. The **Refresh** section will either be greyed-out and unselectable, or it will have all the options greyed-out.

To set up the gateway on Power BI Service, we need to go to **Manage connection and gateways**. This can be done by selecting the gear icon in the upper-right corner of Power BI Service, which is labeled **Settings**, and then selecting **Manage connection and gateways**. Once we select this option, the page is called **Data (preview)**, and within this settings page, we can see three tabs. Alternatively, we can also get to the **Data (preview)** settings page from the **Gateway connections** section under **Settings** by selecting the gear icon next to **Status**.

We can select the **Connections** tab, and then at the top left of the page, we can select the **New option** next to the plus symbol. This will open a side pane on the right side of the screen. Under **New connection** in the side pane, we can keep **On-premises** selected. Under the **Gateway cluster name**, we can select the gateway name we defined during the installation. We need to enter the connection name, and it is a good idea to follow some naming conventions here as well, especially if we expect to use several on-premises data sources. We have named our connection **_0 SQL Server1 AdventureWorks2019**, since our data source is an on-premises SQL Server. We have also selected the **Connection type** as **SQL Server**. After selecting the **Connection type**, we are given new and specific options for the selected type.

We can define the server's name under **Server**, the database's name under **Database**, and set up the **Authentication method**. Under the **Server**, we can enter the exact same name as we would when connecting to Database Engine with SQL Server Management Studio, an application for governing our SQL Server. Under database, we may simply copy and paste the database name, such as, **AdventureWorksDW2019**. Under authentication, it is probably best security practice to create SQL Server Authentication and give it precisely enough access as it needs. How to do this is beyond the scope of this book. We can also choose the Windows Authentication method and then type the username and password.

After we have typed the same authentication, we are using when we log in to our computer, which is the whole username in the form of **`*DomainName*\*UserName*`**, we can select **`Save`**. Selecting Save will try to establish the connection and will close the window if it is successful. If there are any errors, we should first check the credentials. Once the gateway setting has been successfully established on Power BI Service, we can return to the Gateway connections section in the dataset's Settings of the on-premises dataset. Here, we will see the changed status now highlighted in green, saying **`Running on *DomainName*, select all datasources to use`**. The only thing left to do is to set up the **`Maps to`** option to the newly created gateway setting, as shown in *Figure 10.7*:

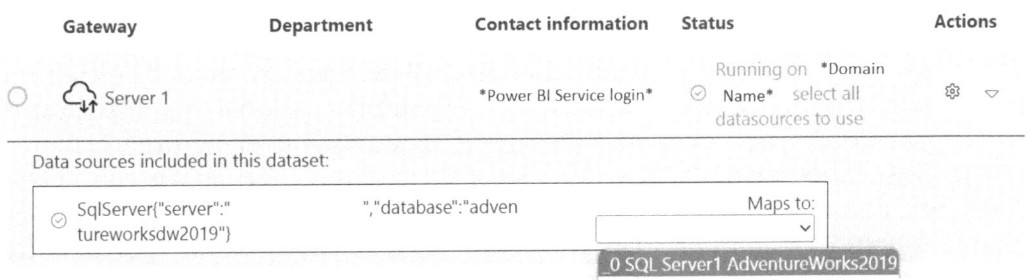

***Figure 10.7**: Finalization of the gateway settings*

After Maps has been selected, we can select **`Apply`** at the bottom left of the **`Gateway connections`** settings. The Data source credential section should then inform us whether access was granted. We may also set the scheduled refresh under the Refresh section, by first setting it to **`On`**, defining the **`Refresh frequency`** to **`Daily`**, and adding the exact times of refresh by clicking **`Add another time`** option. There is also an ability to send refresh failure notifications to either the Dataset owner or to defined contacts. We must apply settings by selecting Apply on the bottom-left of the **`Refresh`** section. The scheduled refresh is paused if the related report has not been opened for two months, or after four consecutive failures. With the Power BI Pro license, we can currently schedule refresh up to eight times daily. If any more is required, we will need to upgrade the license.

Power BI Service security

Since content published on the Power BI Service can be made available to anyone with an internet connection, properly managing access to the content becomes an important topic. In the Power BI Service, workspace administrators can manage who can do what with the content the workspace contains. On a higher level, the Power BI administrator can set more general organizational policies, such as features that are available for use and defining users who have permission to use those features.

We have already made a brief overview of the various workspace roles (**Admin**, **Member**, **Contributor**, and **Viewer**) in *Chapter 7, Using the Power BI Service*. In this section, we will focus on tenant-level settings. We should also be aware that Power BI Service relies on Azure AD (Azure Active Directory) for user authentication. Therefore, certain Azure AD settings have a direct effect on what we can and cannot do in Power BI Service. For example, if our organization's global administrator has blocked adding guest users from specific domains, we will not be able to share content with users from that domain, even though the proper settings are configured in Power BI Service.

Tenant-level security settings

To make changes to the organizational Power BI settings, we must be either the Fabric administrator, Power Platform administrator, or Global administrator of our organization. Each of these roles gives us control over all organizational Power BI settings through the so-called Fabric admin portal. We can access the Fabric admin portal by signing-in to the Power BI Service, clicking the gear icon in the upper-right corner of the screen, and selecting Admin portal in the Governance and Insights section of the drop-down menu.

Let us browse the **Tenant settings** section and describe some of the available settings. In the central pane, let us scroll down until we get to the Information protection section. In this section, we can turn on various settings regarding sensitivity labels. Sensitivity labels are a security and compliance feature of Microsoft Purview. When a user opens a **file marked with a sensitivity label, the file will contain a tag, notifying the user of the** sensitive nature of the file's content. We can also apply additional protection through sensitivity labels, such as watermarks and file encryption.

Creating sensitivity labels and label policies probably will not be the job of someone who is also a Power BI administrator. This is normally taken care of by the organization's compliance officers. However, even if sensitivity labels have been set up, users will not be able to use them in Power BI Desktop or Service until we enable the first setting under the Information protection section called **Allow users to apply sensitivity labels for content**. Besides enabling this functionality, we can also set who can apply sensitivity labels. We can choose the Entire organization, or we can choose **Specific security groups** and explicitly define the security groups we wish to give permissions to apply sensitivity labels. When we are done with the configuration of this setting, we can click **Apply**. After we have enabled the setting, users with permission to apply labels will be able to do so to content in Power BI Service as well as to `.pbix` files in Power BI Desktop.

In Power BI Service, we can apply sensitivity labels to reports, dashboards, datasets, and dataflows. To apply a sensitivity label, we need to go to a workspace, hover over an item of the workspace (a report, a dataset...), click **`More options`** button, represented by three dots, and click **`Settings`**. The settings page will be different for various types of workspace items, but no matter the layout, we will need to find the Sensitivity label section, as shown in *Figure 10.8*, and pick the label we wish to apply from a drop-down menu and then save our changes:

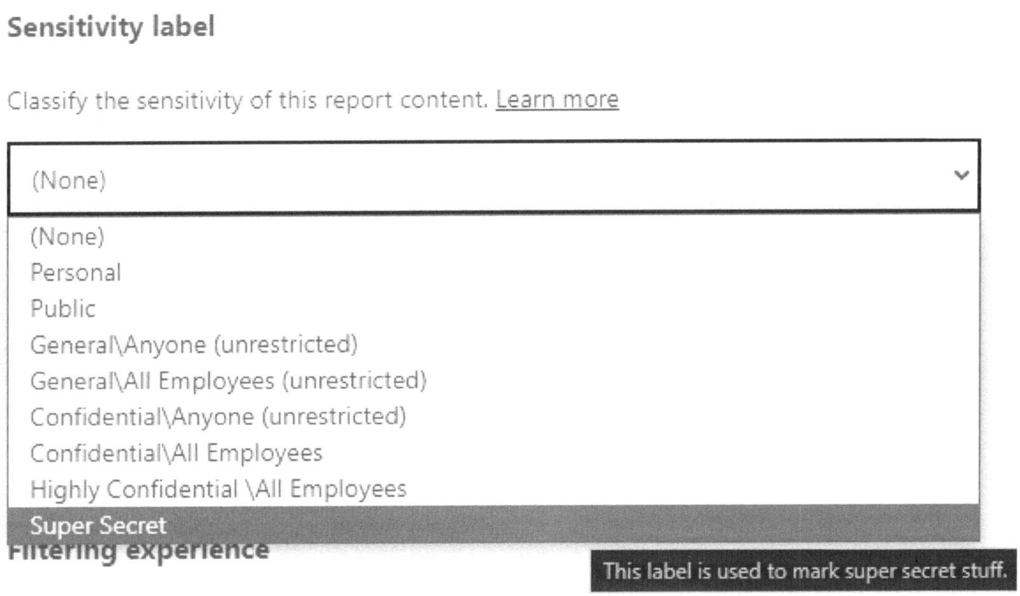

Figure 10.8: *Marking content with a custom sensitivity label*

After we come back to the workspace, the applied sensitivity label will be visible in the **`Sensitivity`** column, as shown in *Figure 10.9*:

Figure 10.9: *The Sensitivity column*

In Power BI Desktop, we can apply a sensitivity label with the **Sensitivity** command on the **Home** tab. Clicking the command will open a drop-down menu, listing the sensitivity labels available to us. By clicking a sensitivity label, it will be applied to the **.pbix** file and it will also be shown in the bottom-left corner of the Power BI Desktop window. It is important to note that the sensitivity label is applied to the **.pbix** file, but when we publish the file, the sensitivity label is also applied to the report and dataset in Power BI Service.

Note

We can also add sensitivity labels in SQL Server, in versions 2019 and later. Those sensitivity labels, however, are in no way connected to Power BI sensitivity labels. If you want to use sensitivity labels on both ends, you have to do the work manually twice.

Let us look at some other interesting settings in the **Tenant settings** section of the **Fabric admin portal**. Specifically, the **Export and sharing settings** section, as shown in *Figure 10.10*, is filled with useful settings related to guest user access as follows:

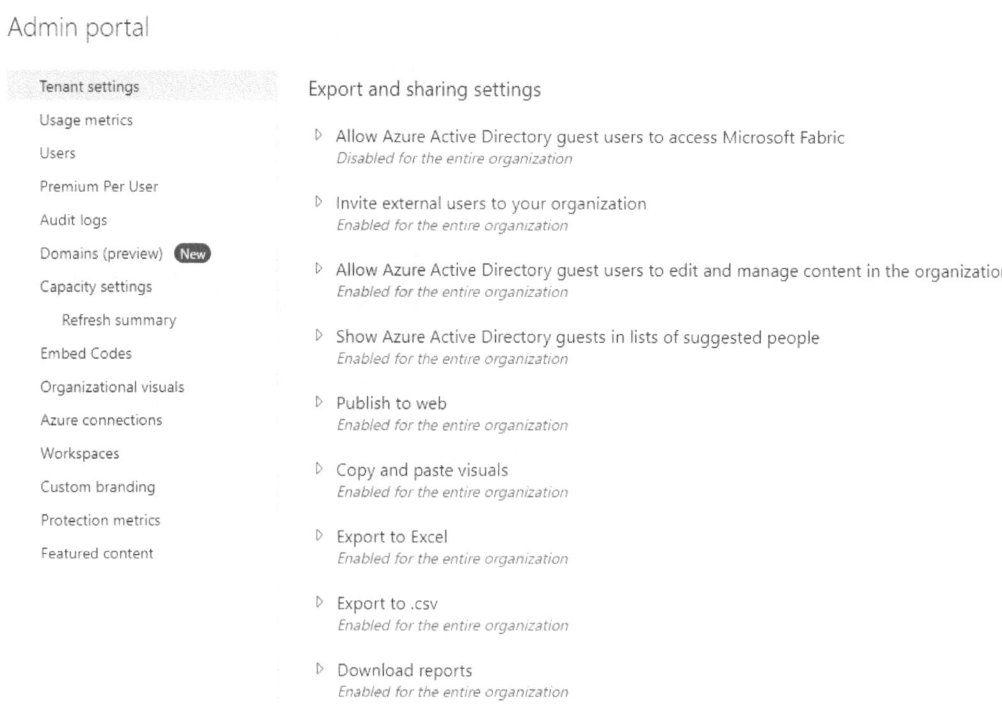

Figure 10.10*: The Fabric admin portal contains many settings*

- **Allow Azure Active Directory guest users to access Microsoft Fabric**: This setting must be enabled if we wish to allow guest users to access the content, they have access to in our Power BI tenant.
- **Invite external users to your organization**: If this setting is enabled, users who have the Azure Active Directory Guest Inviter role can share Power BI content with external users who are not yet part of our Azure Active Directory. In the background, the external user gets an email invitation to join our organization. When the invitation is accepted, the external user is added as a guest user created in Azure Active Directory.
- **Allow Azure Active Directory guest users to edit and manage content in the organization**: If this setting is enabled, guest users will be able to browse the content of our Power BI tenant through the navigation pane on the left-hand side of the Power BI Service window. They will also be able to request access to the content they find by browsing.

Additionally, the **Export and sharing settings section** also contains settings related to how users, in general, can interact with the content in Power BI Service, for example:

- **Publish to web**: When this setting is enabled, users with edit permissions to a report can publish such a report publicly. This means that a report will be accessible to anyone with an internet connection without the need to authenticate. Organizations often disable this setting because of obvious data leakage concerns. We can view existing embed codes in the Embed Codes section on the left-hand side of the Fabric admin portal.
- **Download reports**: If this setting is enabled, users who have at least Contributor permissions to a workspace can open a dataset in the workspace, click the **File** button on the left side of the ribbon and use the **Download this file** command to get a copy of the **.pbix** file that was published to Power BI Service to create this dataset.
- **Certification**: If we enable this setting, we can allow all users or specific security groups to certify content, such as reports, to give it more credibility. Content certification can be done under the Endorsement section of the settings page of a specific type of content. It is a good idea not to give a lot of people permission to certify content.

Row-level security

Even though we normally create reports for a wide audience of users, we may not want all users to see all the data contained in a dataset a report is built from. Power BI row-level security allows us to define roles with permissions on a subset of data in a dataset. We apply these permissions with DAX expressions that filter out data with one or more specific properties. For example, we might want to give our country sales managers access only to data for their specific country. The sales manager for Germany would only have access to sales data for Germany, while the sales manager for France would have access to sales data for France.

Note

SQL Server introduced row-level security in version 2016. Like with sensitivity labels, there is no connection between the SQL Server row-level security and Power BI row-level security.

Defining row-level security is a two-step process. We must first create the security roles and the DAX filter expressions that define the data users assigned to these roles will have access to. In most cases, such as for data models using **`Import mode`** or **`DirectQuery mode`**, we perform this first step in Power BI Desktop. After we publish the **`.pbix`** file to Power BI Service, we can perform the second step, which is assigning users to the roles we defined in Power BI Desktop, thus restricting the access to data underlying a report.

For the exercises described in the next section, we can use the same model we developed in *Chapter 5*, *Enhancing the Model and Business Analysis with* DAX.

Defining the roles in Power BI Desktop

We can access the command for managing row-level security roles, called **`Manage roles`**, through all three different views of Power BI Desktop. In the report view, it is located on the **`Modeling`** tab, while on the data and model views, it is located on the **`Home`** tab. clicking it will open the **`Manage roles`** window. The window is separated into three sections. From left to right, they are **`Roles`**, **`Tables`**, and **`Table filter DAX expression`**.

In the **`Roles`** section, we can create new roles and edit or delete roles that already exist. In the **`Tables`** section, the tables of our data model are listed. As we will see, we use this section to select the table on which we will apply a DAX filter expression. In the final section, **Table filter DAX expression**, we enter the DAX statement that defines the data that will be visible to users assigned to a certain role. Let us create a few row-level security roles, starting with a role that will only be able to see data for Germany.

We create a new row-level security role by clicking the **Create** button in the **Roles** section. Doing so creates a new entry under the **Roles** section, which we can immediately give a name, for example, **Germany data**. Next, we must select the table on which we will define the DAX filter expression. Since descriptive metadata is usually contained in dimension tables, we will most often define DAX expressions on dimension tables. For our first example, let us select **DimSalesTerritory**.

With the table selected, we use the text box in the last section to enter the DAX expression. The DAX expression must be written as a Boolean expression, so the result can be either **true** or **false**. If we are not familiar with the columns of the selected table and the structure of DAX that we need to type, we can click the three dots to the right of the table name in the **Tables** section. This will open a drop-down menu with an **Add filter...** button. Clicking it will display a list of the columns of the table, from which we can select the column we wish to apply a filter on with DAX. In our example, we will select **[SalesTerritoryCountry]** of the **DimSalesTerritory** table.

Selecting the column will enter the following DAX expression into the window in the last section:

```
[SalesTerritoryCountry] = "Value"
```

We will now replace the text in quotation marks with the country tied to the data we wish to give users assigned to this role access to, in our case **Germany**:

```
[SalesTerritoryCountry] = "Germany"
```

When we are done with the DAX, we can click the checkmark in the upper-right corner of the Manage roles window, as shown in *Figure 10.11*, to verify the DAX expression is syntactically correct. If no message is displayed, we can either add another filter to this role on some other table, create another role from scratch, or click the **Save** button in the bottom-right corner of the window, which will bring us back to the main Power BI Desktop window. Let us press the **Save** button:

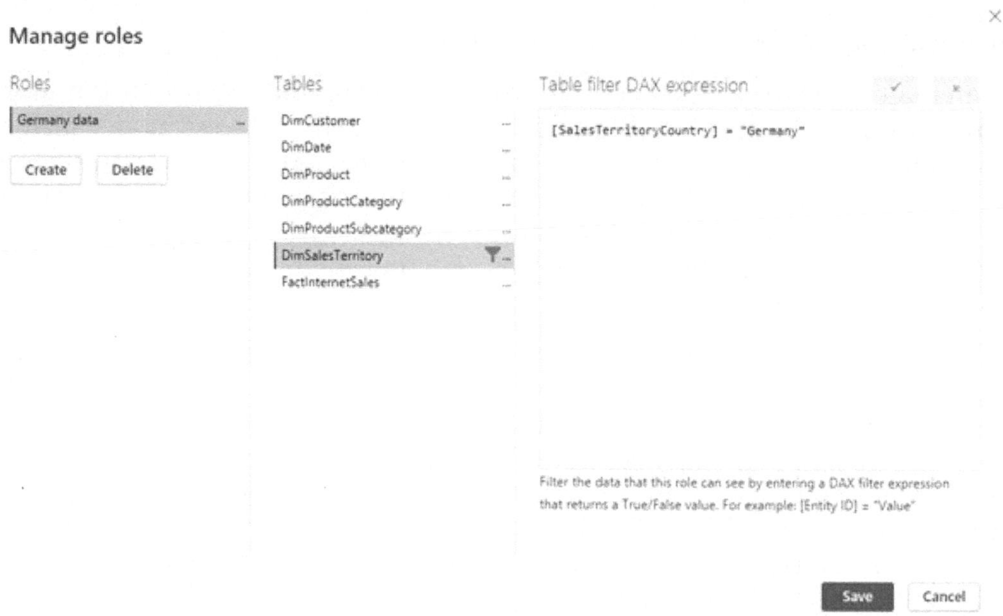

Figure 10.11: *Creating a new row-level security role*

When we create a row-level security role, it is a good idea to test it. We can do this with the **View as** command, located next to the **Manage roles** command. Clicking the **View as button** will display the roles currently defined in the file. We can select the checkbox next to a role we would like to test (for example, **Germany** data in our example) and click **OK**. Doing so will apply the filter we previously defined with DAX on the entire file. If the file contains some report visuals with sales data, only sales for **Germany** will be shown. If we switch to the Data view and display the **DimSalesTerritory** table, only the row containing **Germany** will be shown. Similarly, if we display the **FactInternetSales** table, only rows where the **[SalesTerritoryKey]** equals eight, which is the key for **Germany**, will be displayed.

Note

At the time of writing, July 2023, there is a preview feature available called Enhanced row-level security editor. If enabled, the Manage roles command will open a window with the option of creating security roles with either DAX code or through a simpler editor, where we can use drop-down menus to build conditions without writing any code.

Let us define another role for data related to France. Let us click the **Manage roles** button and click **Create** in the **Roles** section. We will name the role France data and add a filter to the **[SalesTerritoryCountry]** column with the following formula:

```
[SalesTerritoryCountry] = "France"
```

Note that we can add the column we wish to use in the DAX expression by clicking the three dots icon as explained before or, if we are familiar with the model, by simply typing the column name in square brackets directly into the DAX expression window. When we are finished with the DAX expression, it is always a good idea to click the checkmark in the upper-right corner of the **Manage roles** window to validate it. After we are done, let us click **Save**.

Let us perform another test, this time by assigning two roles to ourselves. Let us click **View as** and check the **Germany data** and **France data** checkboxes. If we look at the **DimSalesTerritory** table in the **Data** view, we will be able to see the rows for **Germany** and **France**. We can see that assigning multiple roles to users gives them access to a union of the rows that each individual role can access. It is important to keep this in mind, so we do not intentionally give users access to too much data. What we are simulating here is how role assignment also works in Power BI Service. We will demonstrate this behavior with a very straightforward example.

Let us use the **Manage roles** command to define a new role named All data except **Germany**, with the following DAX expression:

```
[SalesTerritoryCountry] <> "Germany"
```

After saving it, let us use the View as command to assign ourselves the Germany data and the All data except Germany roles. By looking at the **DimSalesTerritory** table, we can see that we have permissions on rows for all the countries, even though one of the roles negates access to rows with **Germany** as the country.

Let us play around with the expressions a bit more. Let us create a role called Bachelors or graduate degree data. We will define the DAX expression on the **[EnglishEducation]** column of the **DimCustomer** table. We must define two conditions on the same column with an or logic between them. We write the logical operator **OR** in DAX with a double pipe operator (||), as seen in the following expression:

```
[EnglishEducation] = "Bachelors" || [EnglishEducation] = "Graduate
Degree"
```

Do not forget to validate the DAX expression and then save it. We can immediately check the results again with the View as command. We must make sure to uncheck all previous roles and only select the one we currently wish to test, Bachelors or graduate degree data. With this role selected, we can click **OK**.

In the Data view, we can see in the **DimCustomer** table that only customers with either Bachelors or Graduate Degree listed under the **[EnglishEducation]** column are still visible. Also, in the **FactInternetSales** table, only sales to those customers are listed. Of course, users who have row-level security roles assigned will not browse the table of the data model like we are doing now. We are just demonstrating the subset of the data that will be available to them and based on which visualizations on the report will be rendered.

Let us switch to the report view and create a line chart that will display the Total sales measure sliced by **DimDate[CalendarYear]** on the X-axis. The chart will only display the sales data based on the security role we are currently viewing, as shown in *Figure 10.12*. We will quickly see the difference in the total sales amounts if we use the View as command and select **None** as the current role. After clicking **OK**, we will see that the sales numbers will be much bigger:

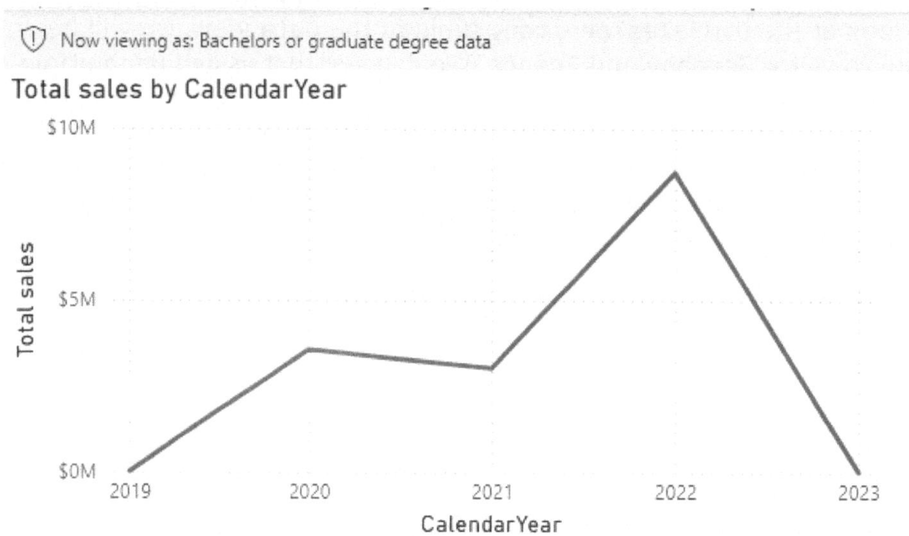

***Figure 10.12**: Viewing as a certain role in Power BI Desktop*

We can also define row-level security DAX expressions that filter based on multiple columns. For example, let us create a new role called **Married clerical data** and define the following expression on the **DimCustomer** table:

```
[MaritalStatus] = "M" && [EnglishOccupation] = "Clerical"
```

In the previous example, we used the double pipe operator, which stands for a logical or, while the double ampersand used in this example stands for a logical and, meaning both statements must be true at the same time.

What if we wanted to define a security filter for a specific subset of product colors, let us say red, black, and silver? We could do this by defining multiple or statements, but the more direct way is by using the IN operator to check if a column contains a value from a predefined array of values. For example, we could create a role called red, black and silver products data with the following expression on the **DimProduct** table:

```
[Color] IN {"Red", "Black", "Silver"}
```

We can also negate such conditions, giving users access to all colors except the ones we defined, by wrapping our condition in a **NOT** statement. For example, we could define a role called Not red black silver product data with the following DAX expression on the **DimProduct** table:

```
NOT ( [Color] IN {"Red", "Black", "Silver"} )
```

It is also possible to define DAX expressions on custom combinations of metadata, so that we do not, for example, get all red products and all black products, but only red products from a certain subcategory, let us say road bikes, and only black products from a different subcategory, for example mountain bikes. Let us create a role called Red road bikes and black mountain bikes data with the following DAX expression on the **DimProduct** table. Remember that we used the **RELATED** function to create the **[ProductSubcategory]** column in *Chapter 5, Enhancing the Model and Business Analysis with* DAX:

```
([Color], [ProductSubcategory]) IN {("Red", "Road Bikes"), ("Black",
"Mountain Bikes")}
```

Notice how we first defined the combination of columns we wish to check, **[Color]** and **[Subcategory]**, and then defined the specific combinations of values in those two columns that we wish to include in the row-level security role.

Up to this point, we have been defining roles with what is known as static row-level security. This is because the roles are defined by a DAX expression that has a static condition, such as **[SalesTerritoryCountry] = "France"**. But we can also define dynamic row-level security expressions by using specific functions, most commonly **USERPRINCIPALNAME()**.

The **USERPRINCIPALNAME()** function, as the name suggests, returns the principal name of the currently signed-in user, for example, user1@domain.com. It can be very handy when a table contains a column that specifies users who should have access to a particular row of that table. To demonstrate this, we will add a calculated column with user data to the **DimSalesTerritory** table, to simulate that a particular user is responsible for a certain sales territory. In the following code, replace **yourUser@yourDomain.com** with your actual username and `anotherUser@yourDomain.com` with some other user principal name from your organization:

```
User =
IF(
    DimSalesTerritory[SalesTerritoryKey] <= 6,
    "yourUser@yourDomain.com",
    "anotherUser@yourDomain"
)
```

After we have added the calculated column, let us use the **Manage roles** command to add another row-level security role. Let us name it User sales territory data and add the following DAX expression to the **DimSalesTerritory** table:

```
[User] = USERPRINCIPALNAME()
```

After we save the role, we can use the View as command to check the results of the User sales territory data role. When we apply it, we should only be able to see the data for the rows of the **DimSalesTerritory** table that were assigned to us in our simulation. This type of row-level security definition is called dynamic because the role compares the static values in the **[User]** column with the user principal name that is dynamically returned by the **USERPRINCIPALNAME()** function, based on the currently signed-in user.

Assigning users to roles in Power BI Service

Once we are done defining the security roles, we can publish the model to Power BI Service. When it is published, the roles are not assigned to anybody yet, they just exist as definitions in the dataset. To assign users or groups to a role, we need to log-in to Power BI Service, open the workspace that contains the dataset we published, hover over the dataset and click the **More options** button, represented by three dots, and select Security from the drop-down menu.

A new window, as shown in *Figure 10.13*, will open, containing the roles we defined in the side pane on the left-hand side. When we select a role, we can assign users or groups to it by entering their email addresses into the search box under the People or groups who belong to this role label. Note that you can use distribution groups, mail-enabled groups and security groups from Azure Active Directory as well as those synced from Windows Server Active Directory for role assignments. Once we have entered all the users and groups we wish to assign to the role into the search box, we can click the Add button and then the Save button at the bottom of the screen. If needed, we can also remove users and groups from a role in this window by clicking the x button next to their name in the central pane and clicking **Save**:

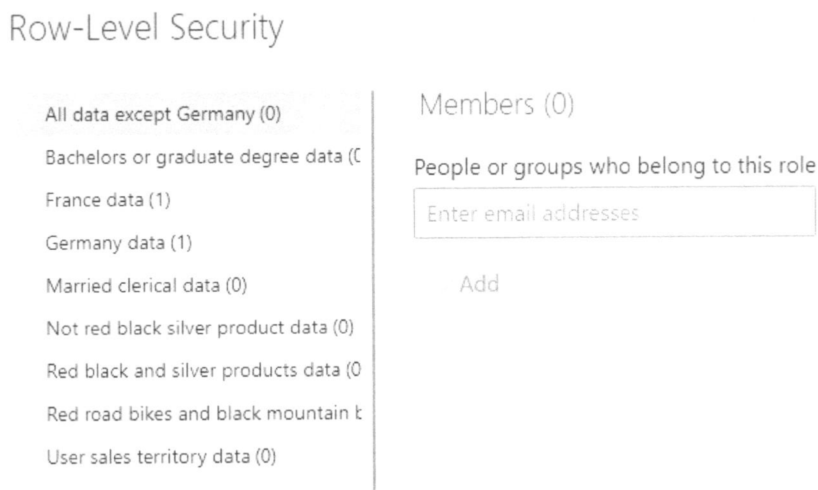

Figure 10.13: *Configuring row-level security in Power BI Service*

As we saw in Power BI Desktop, it is possible to assign a user or group to multiple roles in Power BI Service. The same logic we observed in Power BI Desktop applies here, that is, a user or group will obtain permissions based on the combination of all the data that each individual role has access to. Once we have assigned users or groups to one role and saved our settings, we can select another row-level security role in the side pane on the left-hand side and use the same process we described above to add the same users or groups to another role.

You may notice that the search box will give the option to assign roles to users and groups, even if they do not have permissions to the workspace. Assigning such users and groups to a role does not share anything with them. It is a way to define their permissions on the data before they even get access to it. If we share a workspace or a report before we assign users to roles, users will not be able to view anything on the report. They will only be shown a red ribbon on top of the window, notifying them that the report cannot be viewed because the underlying dataset uses row-level security, leading to a bad user experience.

To effectively apply row-level security, we must also be aware of how row-level security roles work with other permissions that users might have. If users have permissions in a workspace, row-level security roles only affect users who are assigned the Viewer workspace role. Users with higher privileges, such as `Contributor`, will still see all the data, no matter the restrictiveness of the row-level security role we assign to them on a dataset contained in the workspace. On the other hand, if a user was only given access to a report via the Share functionality, row-level security will apply, even if the user was also given reshare and build permissions.

Power BI Service Apps for end-user experience

We have already discussed creating Apps along with other elements in Power BI Service in *Chapter 7, Using the Power BI Service*, but let us expand that topic a little further. Microsoft labels Apps in Power BI Service as the experience that we as developers should be providing to most of our end users. According to their theory, access to workspaces should be provided to advanced users, moderators, and administrators, while a majority of end users should only interact with the application. Power BI App is a collection of content from the workspace provided in a single experience.

If we decide to adopt this approach, we will need at least a Power BI Pro license to create an App. We will usually create the App in our production workspace. There are a couple of options available at the top of our workspace such as New, Upload, Create app, Manage access, and Workspace settings. We can select the Create app option to start creating our application. In addition to the production workspace, in a large organization, we might also have a testing workspace where we deploy solutions before introducing them to the general public. Using Apps also provides a gap between what is deployed to the workspace and what is introduced to end users, as Apps have to be updated separately.

The first page when creating Apps is **`Setup`**. We can define the basic settings, which are **`App name`**, **`Description`**, **`App logo`**, and **`App theme color`**. There are also some advanced settings, such as **`Contact Information`**, **`Global App Settings`**, and Support site. The **`Allow users to make a copy of the reports in this app`** option allows users to create a copy of the reports in the application and customize them. The **`Install app automatically`** allows users to push the app to end users and have it appear under Apps automatically; however, you cannot push the app to the entire organization. Most of these settings can be modified later.

Next page is called **`Content`**. By selecting **`Add content`**, we can select any workspace object, such as dashboards, reports, or Excel workbooks. We can select the content by clicking the area to the left of the icon presenting each individual content. All the content we have added can be visible on the right side of the page. We can drag-and-drop objects we have added as content and also place them in the order that they will be appearing to end users in an application. We may place the dashboards first, then the reports and the Excel files at last. By selecting an object, we can view how it will appear to our audience. We can view the dashboards and Excel file with all the worksheets, while reports can be expanded to view every visible page.

The next page is called **Audience** and we can immediately notice a couple of neat features. We can see there are tabs available at the top of the **Audience** page. This tab can be used to create a variation of what is visible to different groups. In our example, we have created three audience types: **Executive view**, **Sales view**, and **Associate view**. In the **Executive view**, all the objects are visible. In the **Sales view**, we have hidden the Executive dashboard. In the **Associate view**, we have hidden the **Plans and goals** Excel document as well. This is often how the information is presented in larger companies, where the type of information available depends on the hierarchical position or department. We can see the **Audience** page in *Figure 10.14*. Please note that for a dashboard to work correctly, users have to be able to enter the underlying report as well:

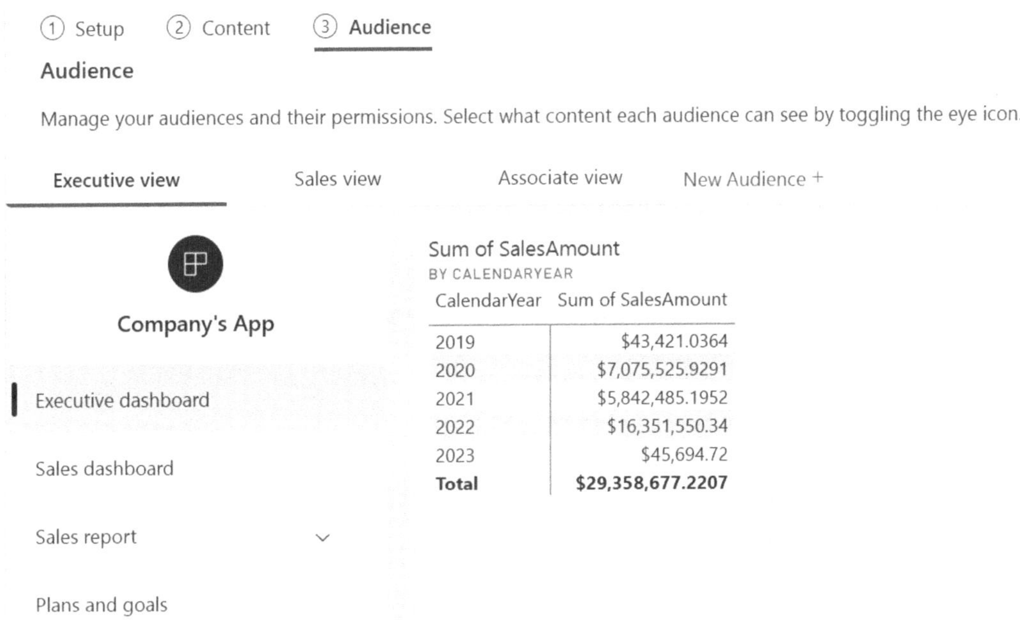

***Figure 10.14**: Different views for different audiences within the application*

On the right side of the **Audience** screen, we can see the **Edit Audience** pane, where we can grant access either to the **Entire organization** or **Specific users or groups**. If **Specific users or groups are selected**, we are given an option to enter a name or email address. Under **Advanced**, two additional options are presented. **Allow people to share the dataset in this app audience** relates to sharing underlying datasets behind reports, while **Allow users to build content with the datasets in this app** allows them to create their own reports and dashboards.

Publishing of the App is usually done in an instant, even though the message says that it can take up to ten minutes. An interface window informs us of success and offers the link to the application that we may share to end users. We can access the application through the link provided or by selecting Apps on the left ribbon and then selecting the app we have created in the list.

Whenever we re-publish the report, we can immediately see the change if we access the report from the workspace. However, the report that can be accessed from the App is still the old one, the one from before we re-published it. This means that App adds another layer to our production environment, perhaps allowing the team of advanced analytics with access to the workspace to first test the newly published report. After testing has been successful, we can update the application by selecting **Update app** in the workspace from which we published our application. The **Create app** option now becomes the **Update app** option. After we click **Update app**, we can again change settings that were available throughout the creation of the app. Then we can simply press the **Update app** button on the bottom-left of the screen. We are again offered the Successfully published window from which we can copy the link and send it to end users or go to app. If we choose the latter option, we can see our application, with an interface that is similar to the one shown in *Figure 10.15*:

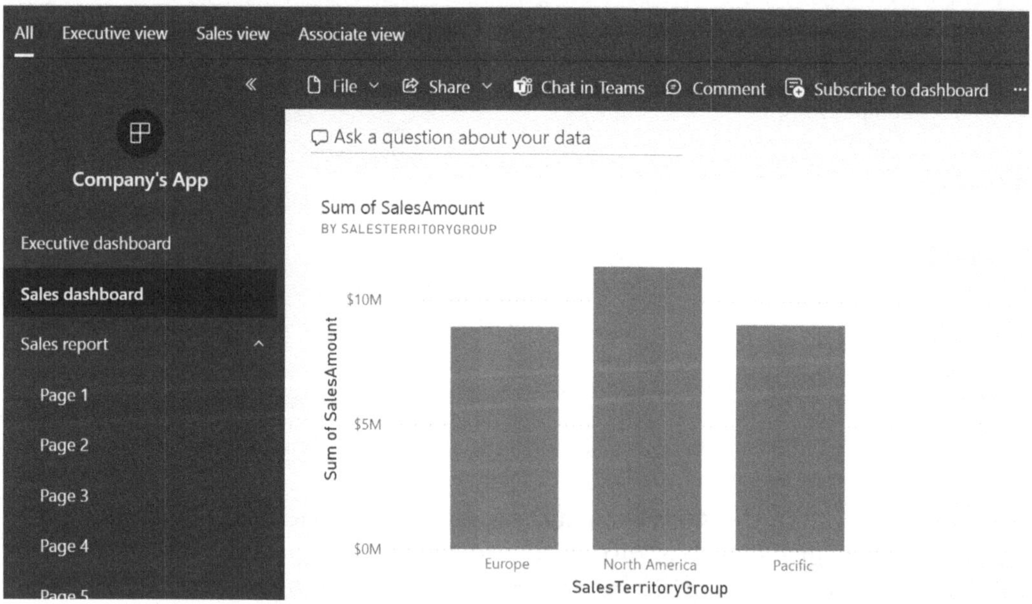

Figure 10.15: *App published in Power BI Service*

Conclusion

This chapter taught us some points regarding the maintainability of Power BI assets, some of which can be useful even when keeping the entire data system well-maintained. We have also looked into the aspects of security and data privacy, as well as some tips for deploying assets. Power BI can play a very important role within the entire data system, and so can Excel's Power Pivot. We, as developers, can pre-create Power BI reports to serve our end users in providing data-driven decisions. In reality, we cannot expect that every user will be their own report creator, despite perhaps some commercial learning material pushing this idea. Of course, there will be advanced users that can develop using BI tools and while the company's BI system is not well developed, these users may drive the development of the company's BI. They may connect directly to transactional systems and other data sources, to create composite data models.

This free-for-all approach should be allowed, but only up to the point of the company's maturity in aspects of BI. At one point, when the willpower and finances are gathered, we should be creating a centralized data warehouse. A place that can pre-transform data from all the data sources into a unified, centralized, well-organized, and maintainable system. As was described in *Chapter 1, Introducing the Theoretical Background for Democratizing Analytics*: A database with multiple star schemas, an explicit date dimension, a good naming convention, and cleansed data in the tables.

And this is also a tip for our readers on where to focus their attention next. After you believe that you have mastered the topics in this book, there are two possible journeys we would like to suggest. We can go towards *the front end of data analysis*, which is improving on data visualizations, getting into data science, artificial intelligence, machine learning, and other approaches to improve gathering insights from data. Prescriptive, predictive, and diagnostic analytics are all very important, this is where the highest value of data lies.

But before any of that is possible, data needs to be available, formatted, well-maintained, and traceable. In order to achieve that, we should create a data warehouse with all of the supporting systems, such as staging area and information area, in *the backend of data analysis*. Learning to develop with relational database management system like SQL Server is very important. A lot of value can be gained from a well-developed centralized data repository. It can present a single source of truth to an organization, as well as more closely manage the issue of data privacy and security. After a data warehouse is introduced to an organization, business analysts should only use this single data source from then on. If new requirements arise, instead of creating composite models by connecting to various new data sources, these data sources should be brought into the data warehouse in a structured manner, following the naming conventions and other quality assurance rules. Only then should data models be created by connecting to the data warehouse. Data models can be created inside Power BI, Power Pivot, or in Visual Studio for deployment to SQL Server Analysis Services.

These are the two possible paths for increasing knowledge and understanding of data analysis and the connected fields. Readers may choose whatever path they find more interesting, and we wish them good luck in their journey.

Key Terms

- **Gateway:** A component used for establishing communication between two networks, one of on-premises data sources and the other of Power BI Service. It is necessary whenever we use on-premises data sources.
- **Naming convention:** A set of rules that developers have to follow to establish consistent and meaningful names throughout the data system for reporting, which can ensure easier maintainability of the system and traceability of data.
- **Row-level security**: A Power BI feature that allows us to define roles that have access to only a subset of data in the data model. The level of access is determined with DAX code that filters rows based on values in columns used in the DAX filter expression.

Questions

1. Why should we keep a well-maintained data system for reporting?
2. Why are the issues of security and data privacy important?
3. What are some ideas for keeping the data system for reporting organized?
4. What is the point of the Power BI Service application?
5. Describe some of the Power BI Service security settings.
6. Why is using row-level security considered beneficial?

Index

A

advanced Power BI visuals 230-233

aggregate table 285-293

Application Programming Interface (API) 43

apps content

  organizing 212-214

artificial intelligence (AI) 57

automatic aggregations

  reference link 291

averages

  calculating 108-110

Azure AI

  using 248-260

Azure Data Studio (ADS) 33

B

base visualizations

  analytics 226-230

BI system

  fields, organizing into display folders 297-299

  maintaining 297

  naming conventions, forming 299-302

  Selection pane, organizing 302-304

Bookmarks pane 185, 186

C

calculated columns 96, 97

CALCULATE function 145-148

Classic Excel functionality 38-40

columnar storage 14-23

confidence interval 267

confidence level 267

CSV file transformation 64-69

Customer Relationship Management (CRM) 44
custom visualizations
  adding 233-235

D

dashboards
  creating 206-210
  managing 210, 211
data
  connecting, with Power Query 92-94
  managing, with dataflows 214-216
  modeling, with datamarts 217, 218
Data Analysis Expressions (DAX) 7, 24, 45, 96
data connection 125, 126, 127
Data Explorer 26
dataflows
  used, for managing data 214-216
datamarts
  used, for modeling data 217, 218
data model
  optimizing 264-270
  used, for creating pivot table 105-107
Data pane 164, 165
data source connectivity
  about 41-43
  versus data source copy 38
data source copy
  versus data source connectivity 38
data sources
  connecting 47, 48
  in Excel 52-54
  in Microsoft resources 54, 55
  in Power BI Desktop 49-52
data transformation exercise
  about 64
  CSV file transformation 64-69
Data view
  using 130-132
data warehouse (DW) 264
date table
  marking 132-139
DAX evaluation contexts
  about 139
  filter context 142
  query context 141
  row context 140, 141
DAX Studio
  reference link 283
diagram view 100, 101
dimensions tables 5-14
dimension table 101, 102
drillthrough page 166-170
dual storage table 285-293

E

endorsing content 211, 212
enterprise data warehouses (EDW) 23
enterprise resource planning (ERP) 2
evaluation context
  in calculated columns 142-144
  in measures 142-145
Excel
  data sources 52-54
existing data models
  importing 124, 125
existing measures
  editing 111, 112
extract-transform-load (ETL) 264

F

Fabric admin portal 308
fact table 101
fact tables 5-14

filter context 100, 142
filter flow 114-116
filters
  using 160
filters, option
  excessive options, hiding from end users 162
  filters' hierarchy 163, 164
  filters on this page 162, 163
  filters on this visual 160, 161
finished reports
  using 202-206
foreign keys 104
Full-Text Search
  reference link 258
functions for counting
  exploring 110, 111

G

Gaussian Mixture Models (GMM) 255
globally unique identifiers (GUIDs) 15
graphical user interface (GUI) 4, 26

H

header icons 176-178
hierarchies
  creating 150-152
hybrid tables and dataset storage modes
  reference link 292

I

integrated data systems 43-46
integrated development environment (IDE) 45
inverse document frequency (IDF) 251

K

key performance indicators (KPIs) 118-121

L

line of business (LOB) 2
logical design 2-5

M

measures 97-100
Microsoft resources
  data sources 54, 55
Model view
  about 187-189
  defining 127-130
multidimensional cube technology 44
Multidimensional Data Expressions (MDX) 45

O

online analytical processing (OLAP) 1, 44
online transactional system (OLTP) 2
on-object interaction 190, 191
on-premises data sources
  using 304-307
On-prem reporting
  with Power BI Report Server 222, 223

P

paginated reports
  creating 218-221
  option 180
Pane switcher 191
pivot table
  creating, with data model 105-107
Power BI
  history 23-35
  Python language, using 235-247
  R language, using 235-247
Power BI Designer 28

Power BI Desktop
data sources 49-52
reference link 157
roles, defining 312-318
used, for publishing reports 199, 200
Power BI Desktop views
exploring 127
Power BI environment
overview 156-158
Power BI Report Server
used, for On-prem reporting 222, 223
Power BI Report Server (PBIRS) 29
Power BI Service
need for 194
reports, creating 200, 201
users, defining 318, 319
Power BI Service apps
for end-user experience 320-322
Power BI Service components
about 194
dashboards 195
datasets 195, 196
reports 195
workspaces 194
Power BI Service security
about 307, 308
tenant-level security settings 308-311
Power BI user interface 124
Power Pivot add-in
enabling 94
Power Pivot data view 94-96
Power Query
about 46
used, for connecting data 92-94
using, in Excel 46, 47
using, in Power BI 46, 47
Power Query Editor
about 55
current view 55-57
home tab 55-57
queries pane 55-57
Power Query Formula Language (M)
about 26
conditions 78-81
custom functions 78-81
elements and data structures 71-75
functions and data types 75-78
operators 78-81
overview 69-71
Power Query Formula Language (M) code
additional transformation, performing 85-88
improvement 81-84
Premium Per User (PPU) 217
primary keys 104
Python language
using, in Power BI 235-247

Q

query caching
reference link 292
query context 141
query folding 271-278
Query Settings 57-61

R

Random Access Memory (RAM) 14, 100
ratios with DIVIDE
calculating 112-114
relational database management system (RDBMS) 11

Report Builder 28
reports
  creating, in Power BI Service 200, 201
  finished reports, using 202-206
  performance 278-285
  publishing, from Power BI Desktop 199, 200
  working with 199
Report view
  upper ribbon tabs 178-184
R language
  using, in Power BI 235-247
roles
  defining, in Power BI Desktop 312-318
row context 140, 141
row-level security
  about 311, 312
  roles, defining in Power BI Desktop 312-318
  users, defining to Power BI Service 318, 319
row-level security (RLS) 183

S

screen elements 158-160
Selection pane 185
semi-additive measures 148-150
SharePoint Server (SPS) 26
slicers
  using 161
solid-state drives (SSDs) 23
SQL Server Analysis Services Multidimensional (SSAS MD) 24
SQL Server Data Tools (SSDT) 45
SQL Server Integration Services (SSIS) 81
SQL Server Management Studio (SSMS) 2, 33
SQL Server partitioning
  reference link 292
star schema 5
Status bar 57-61
Sync slicers pane 186, 187
sys.sp_execute_external_script
  parameters 258

T

tables relationship
  establishing 102, 103
Table view 187
tabular model partitioning
  reference link 292
term frequency (TF) 251
tooltips 166, 167
Transact-SQL (T-SQL) 3

U

upper ribbon tabs
  in Report view 178-184
users
  defining, to Power BI Service 318, 319

V

visual headers 176-178
visualizations
  creating 170-176
Visualizations pane 164-170
Visual Studio (VS) 33

W

workspaces
  managing 196-199

X

X functions 116, 117